Atlas of the
CHRISTIAN CHURCH

Editor Graham Speake
Art Editor Andrew Lawson
Map Editors Nicholas Harris,
Zoë Goodwin, Olive Pearson
Picture Editor Linda Proud
Design Adrian Hodgkins
Index Sandra Raphael
Production Clive Sparling

AN EQUINOX BOOK

Planned and produced by
Andromeda Oxford Limited,
11-15 The Vineyard, Abingdon,
Oxfordshire, England OX14 3PX

Published by Time-Life Books, Amsterdam
Reprinted 1988, 1989, 1991, 1994

ISBN 0 7054 0866 3

Origination by Scantrans,
Singapore
Maps drawn and originated by
Lovell Johns Ltd, Oxford, and
Alan Mais, Hornchurch, Essex

Filmset by Hourds Typographica,
Stafford, England

Printed in Spain
by Fournier A. Gráficas SA, Vitoria

Frontispiece Details from the
Communion of the Apostles,
15th-century frescoes in the
Church of the Holy Cross at
Platanistasa, Cyprus.

30 29 28 27 26 25 24 23 22 21 20 19 18 17 16 15 14 13 12 11 10 9

Atlas of the CHRISTIAN CHURCH

edited by Henry Chadwick and G.R.Evans

TIME LIFE BOOKS

CONTENTS

Special Features

List of Maps

CHRONOLOGICAL TABLE

	0 · 200 · 400 · 600 · 800
MISSIONS AND COLONIZATION	46–62 Paul's missionary journeys Conversion of Ireland by Palladius and Patrick 596 Mission of Gregory the Great, who sends Augustine to convert the Anglo-Saxons Conversion of Germany by Wilfred of York and Willibrord and Boniface

Christian symbols from a Roman catacomb, c.200.

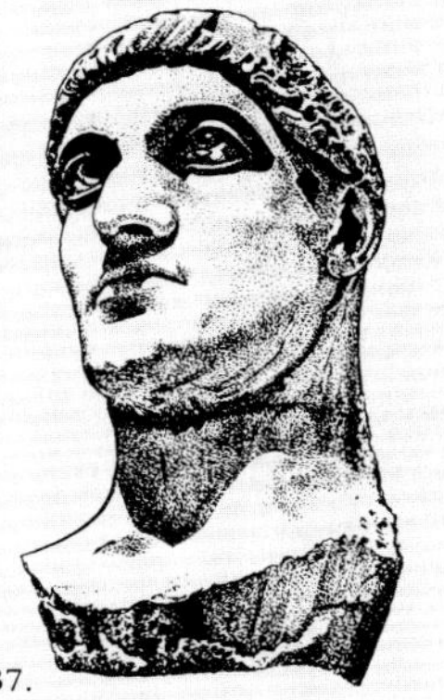

Constantine the Great, d.337.

St Sophia, Constantinople, 523–37.

Odo, bishop of Bayeux, c.1030–97.

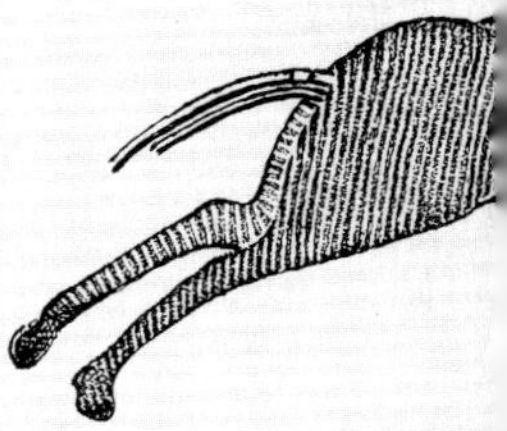

	0 · 200 · 400 · 600 · 800
COUNCILS	325 Council of Nicaea, condemns Arianism (Nicene Creed); first ecumenical council 381 Council of Constantinople; second ecumenical council 431 Council of Ephesus; third ecumenical council 451 Council of Chalcedon; fourth ecumenical council 553 Council of Constantinople fifth ecumenical council 680/1 Council of Constantinople; sixth ecumenical council 692 Council in Trullo 787 Council of Nicaea, restores icons; seventh ecumenical council
DIVISIONS AND MOVES TOWARDS UNITY	Donatism in North Africa 484–518 Acacian schism between Rome and the east Iconoclastic controversy
CHURCH AND STATE	312 Constantine wins battle of the Milvian Bridge 361–63 Julian the Apostate emperor 378–95 Theodosius emperor 410 Rome taken by Alaric 527–65 Justinian and Theodora; her death (548) means the end of Monophysite hopes in the empire Arab conquest of Syria, Palestine and Egypt 800 Coronation of Charlemagne
CHRISTIAN AUTHORS	New Testament Ignatius of Antioch d. early 2nd century Justin d.160s Tatian fl. c.170 Irenaeus fl. c.190 Origen 185–254 Tertullian c.190–215 Clement of Alexandria d. before 215 Hippolytus d.c.235 Cyprian, bishop of Carthage 249–58 Hilary of Poitiers c.315–67 Ambrose of Milan d.397 Jerome 347–419 Augustine of Hippo 354–430 Theodore of Mopsuestia d.427 Gregory the Great c.540–604 Bede, c.672–735 Alcuin c.735–804 Photius c.810–95
RELIGIOUS ORDERS	Desert saints Pachomius d.346 Antony d.357 Benedict of Nursia 911 Foundation of Cluny 962 First foundation on Mt Athos

1000 | 1200 | 1400 | 1600 | 1800 | 2000

Cistercian missionary preaching to convert heretics in southern France

Dominican missionary preaching in southern France and Spain

Jesuit missionaries in India and Japan (Francis Xavier)
Conversion of the New World – task ceded by pope to the Spanish and Portuguese crowns in a series of bulls 1456–1514
Conversion of China from 1583 (Matteo Ricci)

Protestant colonization of North America (1607 settlement at Jamestown, Virginia; 1682 Quakers found Philadelphia)

Calvinist-oriented Dutch Great Awakening in Middle Colonies of America

Missions to Africa
1840s Revival of Roman Catholic missions

By 1910 only Afghanistan, Nepal and Tibet closed to Christians

Baptist missionaries in India from 1790s

Martin Luther, 1483–1546.

St Peter's, Rome, completed in 1614.

Notre-Dame-du-Haut, Rondchamp, 1950–55.

1215 Fourth Lateran Council

1414 Council of Constance opens

1545 Council of Trent opens

1869–70 First Vatican Council

1962–65 Second Vatican Council

1054 Schism between Latin and Greek Christians

Cathars and Albigensians

1309–77 Papacy at Avignon

1378–1417 Great Schism

Reformation

1452 Greek Orthodox-Latin Union Decree read out in St Sophia, Constantinople

1910 Ecumenical movement begins at Edinburgh

1964 Second Vatican Council decree on Ecumenism, *Unitatis Redintegratio*

1000–03 Otto III emperor and Sylvester II pope
1096 First Crusade
1122 Concordat of Worms brings temporary peace in Investiture Contest

1204 Fourth Crusade

1453 Turks take Constantinople
1479 Spanish Inquisition
Cuius regio eius religio, Erastianism
1555 Peace of Augsburg
1572 Massacre of St Bartholomew's Day
1598 Edict of Nantes (revoked in 1685)

Reform of the Church in Russia

Anti-Erastianism
1828–29 British government removes most of the civil and political restrictions on Protestant dissenters and Roman Catholics

Anselm of Canterbury 1033–1109

Thomas Aquinas d.1274
John Wyclif d.1384
Thomas à Kempis 1380–1471

Erasmus 1466–1536
Luther 1483–1546
Zwingli 1484–1531
Ignatius Loyola 1491–1556
Calvin 1509–64

William Wilberforce 1759–1833
John Henry Newman 1801–90
Karl Barth 1886–1968

Cistercians
Carmelites

Franciscans
Dominicans

Jesuits
Ursulines

Sisters of Charity
Trappists

Marianists
Marists
Salesians

160°
140°
120°
100°
80°
60°
40°
20°
0°
20°
GREENLAND
Alaska
ICELAND
NORWAY
SWEDEN
CANADA
UNITED KINGDOM
DENMARK
IRELAND
NETH
E GER
POL
BELGIUM
W GER
CZECH
LUX
FRANCE
AUSTRIA
HUNG
SWITZ
YUGOSL
ITALY
L Superior
UNITED STATES OF AMERICA
PORTUGAL
SPAIN
ALB
GR
Azores
MALTA
TUNISIA
Mississippi
Madeira
MOROCCO
Canary Is
ALGERIA
LIB
MEXICO
BAHAMAS
WESTERN SAHARA
CUBA
JAMAICA
HAITI
DOMINICAN REP
MAURITANIA
BELIZE
PUERTO RICO
MALI
NIGER
GUATEMALA
HONDURAS
LESSER ANTILLES
CAPE VERDE
SENEGAL
EL SALVADOR
NICARAGUA
GAMBIA
Niger
GUINEA BISSAU
BURKINA
TRINIDAD AND TOBAGO
GUINEA
NIGERIA
COSTA RICA
PANAMA
Orinoco
ATLANTIC OCEAN
SIERRA LEONE
IVORY COAST
GHANA
TOGO
BENIN
VENEZUELA
GUYANA
FRENCH GUIANA
LIBERIA
COLOMBIA
SURINAM
CAMEROON
PACIFIC OCEAN
EQ GUINEA
SÃO TOMÉ & PRINCIPE
ECUADOR
GABON
Amazon
CONGO
ZA
PERU
BRAZIL
ANG
BOLIVIA
NAMI
PARAGUAY
Christians as % of total population
over 80
60-79
40-59
20-39
5-19
less than 5
URUGUAY
CHILE
ARGENTINA
Equatorial scale 1:60 000 000
Falkland Is (Br)

40°
60°
80°
100°
120°
140°
160°
180°
UNION OF SOVIET SOCIALIST REPUBLICS
Ob
Amur
Volga
MONGOLIA
BLACK SEA
CASPIAN SEA
N KOREA
S KOREA
JAPAN
TURKEY
SYRIA
CYPRUS
LEBANON
IRAQ
IRAN
AFGHANISTAN
CHINA
Yangzi
ISRAEL
JORDAN
KUWAIT
PAKISTAN
NEPAL
BHUTAN
PACIFIC OCEAN
Tropic of Can
EGYPT
Nile
BAHRAIN
QATAR
SAUDI ARABIA
UAE
Ganges
BANGLA-DESH
TAIWAN
HONG KONG (Br)
OMAN
INDIA
BURMA
LAOS
Hainan
ARABIAN SEA
VIETNAM
SOUTH CHINA SEA
THAILAND
YEMEN
S YEMEN
PHILIPPINES
SUDAN
CAMBODIA
DJIBOUTI
ETHIOPIA
SRI LANKA
SOMALIA
BRUNEI
MALAYSIA
SINGAPORE
MALDIVES
UGANDA
KENYA
L Victoria
Equa
RWANDA
BURUNDI
INDIAN OCEAN
INDONESIA
SOLOMON ISLANDS
TANZANIA
SEYCHELLES
PAPUA NEW GUINEA
COMOROS
MALAWI
MOZAMBIQUE
ZIMBABWE
MADAGASCAR
MAURITIUS
Réunion
SWAZILAND
Tropic of Capric
AUSTRALIA
LESOTHO
NEW ZEALAND
Tasmania

PREFACE

To understand themselves and their society human beings need to look back on their own past, not necessarily always the immediate past. History is a major element in a society's self-understanding, even though the retrospect may vividly show up how far apart ideal and reality are. So too church history is a study in which there is a powerful element of self-discovery, not only for the believer, but in some degree also for the unbeliever whose personal culture is rooted in western tradition. To know themselves Christians need to understand something about the long zigzag of their community, with its fierce family squabbles and counterbalancing diversity of rich experience. Because the Christian tradition has profoundly influenced western society and its values, the story told in this volume is also important to anyone wanting to comprehend something of that influence.

At the present time approximately a third of the world's total population professes the Christian faith, roughly 1430 million people. The number has markedly increased in the 20th century, though recently in some regions there has been decline, with powerful opposition from Communism and materialist secularism. A religion at the heart of which lies the redemptive example of Jesus of Nazareth can never be congenial to any society dominated by political power, economic prosperity and physical ambition or appetite. Moreover, Christianity in its classical forms has a long history of uneasy relations with political forces and government, to which its otherworldliness of principle and its relativizing of all earthly sovereignty have appeared as a thorn in the flesh. Today Christian churches remain as liable as at any time to subtle or violent persecution intended to eradicate them, and the historian cannot blandly report that suppression is sure to be unsuccessful. Secularist governments have admittedly found it easier to bend the Church to their own purposes than to crush religious belief out of existence.

In this Atlas we have sought to give in the text an accurate outline portrait at least of the main or majority Christian traditions, and through the maps and illustrations to represent to the eye some of the more telling visible manifestations. In focusing upon the main traditions, we have not thereby intended to exclude or to marginalize the rich multiplicity of other forms and expressions of Christianity, and some of the illustrations deliberately seek to take account of the variety. At the same time, in a historian's eyes, it is the main traditions of the visible community on which the less historical forms are in fact dependent, often to a larger degree than their adherents may realize.

Christianity is a community way of worship, informed by a doctrinal pattern usually expressed in the form of a story, and by an ethic determined by the central character in that story. The officers of the community are of far less importance than the offices and functions assigned to them, but they must be judged to have played a crucial role in the coherence of the community in face both of internal controversy and of external threat. The historic forms of the faith attach profound importance to continual renewal by contact with the community's roots, in particular through the Bible, and through the sacraments appointed by Jesus. Even though the legacy is in detail of the greatest intricacy, these main lines of Christian self-understanding and practice are clear and simple.

Christianity offers a paradox; it is a religion formed in the context of the Near East, with Hebrew prophecy as its matrix; but it underwent massive expansion in the Greek and Roman worlds of the Mediterranean and northwest Europe, suffering defeat at the hands of the Arabs (who had been shamefully neglected by the missionaries of the ancient Church) with their conversion in the 7th century to the militant religion of Islam, yet making common cause with Greek philosophy and with Roman law and government. In the Greco-Roman world language and culture, together with internal conflicts about power and authority concentrated for the west in Rome, led to a parting of the ways between the Greek east and the Latin west. Most of the bodies which separated from Rome at the Reformation of the 16th century, whether for political or religious reasons or both, have retained a sense of being defined by their rejection of pre-Reformation structures and patterns; yet they have also derived some of their raison d'être from the vigorous survival of that which they then rejected, in particular disliking what they have felt to be authoritarianism.

Naturally there have been and are even more authoritarian forms of Protestantism, whose various groups are particularly prone to self-definition in terms of very precise doctrines, mainly in reaction against the imprecision of vague elements in the broad Protestant tradition rather than against western Catholicism or eastern Orthodoxy. The late 20th century has felt the impact of a radically questioning Protestantism, for which none of the traditional structures of authority (biblical canon, creeds and confessions of faith, ministry) has sacredness but is rather a source of outmoded convention and cultural obsolescence. The continuity of the historic community, however, certainly provides a safeguard against mere individualism and pragmatic ad hoc reactions. This book accordingly seeks to illustrate both something of the diversity and something of this central continuity with Christianity's roots.

PART ONE
THE EARLY CHURCH

THE BEGINNING

The first Christians and the Jews

Judaea under Roman rule was a turbulent province to which governors of poor quality were sent. In the reign of the emperor Tiberius, during the prefecture of Pontius Pilate, perhaps about the year 30 of our era, at Passover, a young man called Jesus was executed by the cruel method of crucifixion. He was probably aged about 33, which would mean that he was born at the end of the reign of Herod the Great, the puppet king installed by the Romans to rule the Jews whose dislike of him compelled him to construct impregnable palaces like Masada and Herodion.

That Jesus was executed by order of the prefect shows that he was somehow thought a potential political threat. But to the people closest to him he was exclusively a religious figure, and the cause of his death was not really the charge of sedition on which he was "framed" but an incompatibility, less with the occupying Romans than with the religious leaders of his own people, above all the high-priestly Sadducees and some of the Pharisees. The Pharisees were the most militantly observant not only of the Mosaic Law but of the "scribal" school tradition which greatly refined upon the Law's precepts; and in their passionate concern to see God's will done, the Pharisees and Jesus stood close. Some Pharisees joined his followers. It was one thing to say the love of God has its substance in meticulous keeping of ceremonial and moral laws, another to proclaim that if ceremony is given priority it can obstruct morality.

Jesus came to Judaea from the rural north of Nazareth in Galilee, a land ringed by non-Jewish cities like Caesarea Philippi or Gadara, where Greeks might keep such un-Jewish animals as pigs, and citizens of high culture wrote poetry and philosophy. He gathered around him a community of disciples, an inner circle having a special commission (apostles = "sent men") to proclaim the arrival of God's rule on earth, manifest in his own presence and teaching.

If one asks what he taught which created so great a storm, the answer is surprising. He called people to repent, to live each day as their last, to love even outsiders and enemies, to set aside not merely adultery, murder and theft, but lust, hatred and covetous desires. Indeed, in the Kingdom of God, now being inaugurated, there would be no room for violence of any kind, for hurtful censoriousness, for the least anxiety about wealth and social status, for the values and priorities of ordinary society engaged in the cycle of birth, marriage, death, getting and spending. Those Jesus pronounced "blessed" are, by a sharp paradox, listed not as the successful but as the poor and humble, the pure in heart, those persecuted for righteousness.

Could death bring an end to a God-sent teacher and so good a man? The tomb was found empty.

The first disciples were all devout Jews. Like the Essenes, the ascetic sect by the Dead Sea from whose library the Qumran scrolls come, they studied Old Testament images, especially of suffering followed by divine vindication (the Servant of Isaiah 53; the Son of Man of Daniel 7). Their master was the Messiah, God's "Anointed," in Greek *Christos*. There was at first no move to break with Judaism, within which there were already numerous sects. In the dispersed Greek-speaking Jewish communities scattered throughout the Mediterranean world, there were some who became emancipated from Jewish particularism, though remaining negative towards pagan cult. At Jerusalem a colony of Greek Jews of the Dispersion joined the Christians; their leader Stephen interpreted the Old Testament as hostile to animal sacrifice and temple rites (not difficult to do), and he was stoned for blasphemy, as the little Christian society found itself harassed by strict Pharisees and expelled. Thereby the persecutors unknowingly sowed the seed of the universal mission of the Church to the Gentiles, for the expelled disciples took their word outside Judaea to Gentile ears.

St Paul

One of the persecuting Pharisees was indeed converted; he was also of the Dispersion, from Tarsus in Cilicia, possessing Roman citizenship and fluent, if angular, Greek. Paul became the major architect of Gentile Christianity. Through the passionate and extraordinary letters he addressed to a group of Gentile missionary churches, in personality and achievement this man appears as no other Christian of the apostolic age: energetic, dominating, abrasive, yet totally dedicated to the cause he knew to have been entrusted to him.

Two factors above all others made Paul's achievement momentous. He denied the assumption, self-evident to the Jerusalem Christians, that on becoming a baptized believer a Gentile was obliged to be circumcised, to observe the Sabbath and the ceremonial Law of Leviticus. Above all, the position was a deduction from a broad picture of God's redemptive purpose. At the heart of the picture lay Paul's conviction that monotheism cannot be compatible with permanently restricting a knowledge of the one God to one race. God chose the Jews and gave them the Old Testament, the aspirations of which have reached their realization in Jesus the Messiah, whose significance is universal. In him the heavenly wisdom of God has taken human nature, the form of a servant. The death of this innocent and obedient man is a high-priestly offering on behalf of the human race that he presents before God, and an expiation of the sins of the world. His death and Resurrection are the cardinal point in world history, the hinge on which all things turn in the purpose of God. Believers are made one with him by faith, incorporated by baptism in him and his Church. Before Moses the Jews

The Acts of the Apostles tells how St Paul (*below*), the apostle of the Gentiles, contrary to every human intention and hindered by storm and shipwreck, succeeded in making his way to Rome, the capital of the Gentile world.
Right Malta, where a statue of Paul stands to recall his presence on the island "where two seas met." Thence he went to Puteoli by Naples where there were Christians to welcome him.

The Gentile churches often recalled in art their debt to Paul. The picture (*bottom*) of a sheep with baskets of bread (evidently eucharistic symbols) is from the cemetery of Commodilla at Rome in the Via delle Sette Chiese, where the matron Commodilla owned the property. *Bottom right* Christ teaching the Apostles, a 4th-century fresco.

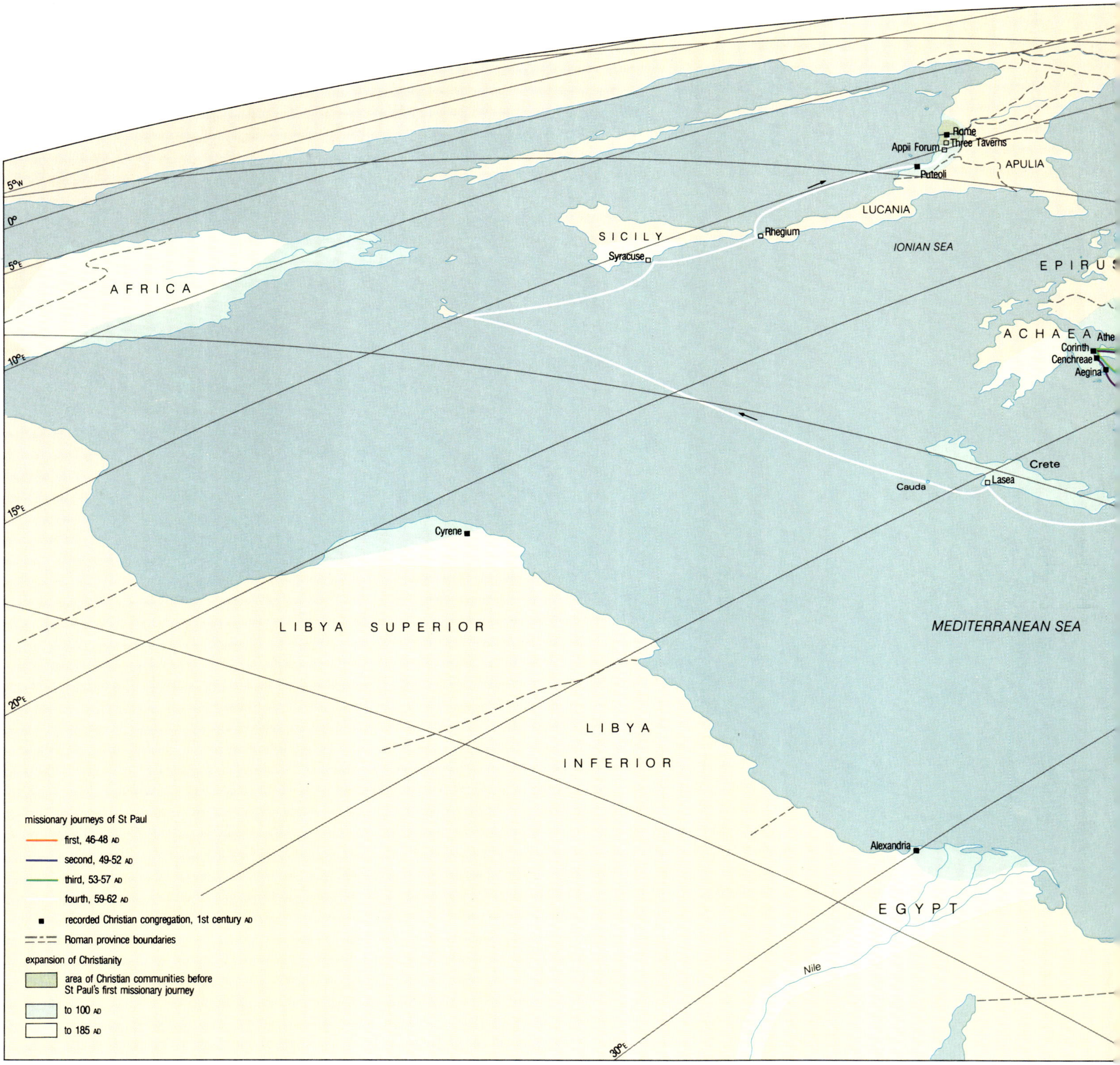

had no written law; so the source of Abraham's righteousness was the faith God gave him. Now again the Law of Moses, essential in its time, is no longer the universally valid expression of God's will for all humanity. Religious Jews are right in believing their people specially chosen for a world purpose. Now, says Paul, through the community "called out" of all the world (*ecclesia*), this purpose is being realized.

If both observant Jews and unobservant Gentiles were to be members of the same community, breaking bread together and pouring out wine in a solemn weekly memorial of Jesus' death and a participation in his redemptive, risen life, then tensions could not be avoided about traditional Jewish food laws. At Antioch in Syria (probably elsewhere too, to judge from Paul's complaints), where the Gentile mission had its initial springboard, a compromise came about by which Gentile Christians observed Jewish food laws. The compromise was disliked both by Paul and by rigorists on the opposite pole. The churches in Galatia, in Asia Minor, at Corinth, were for a time influenced by the Antioch compromise. To the young Christian community in Rome Paul sent a long manifesto of his position, presupposing a

Paul's missionary journeys
Authority in the earliest Church was at Jerusalem, shared between the holy family represented by James, the Lord's brother, and the 12 apostles led by Peter and James and John, sons of Zebedee. The Gentile mission of Paul transformed the Church from being a particular group within Judaism centered upon Jerusalem to being a European society aspiring to universality and looking for leadership to the bishops of great imperial cities, especially Rome. There both Peter and Paul suffered martyrdom under Nero.

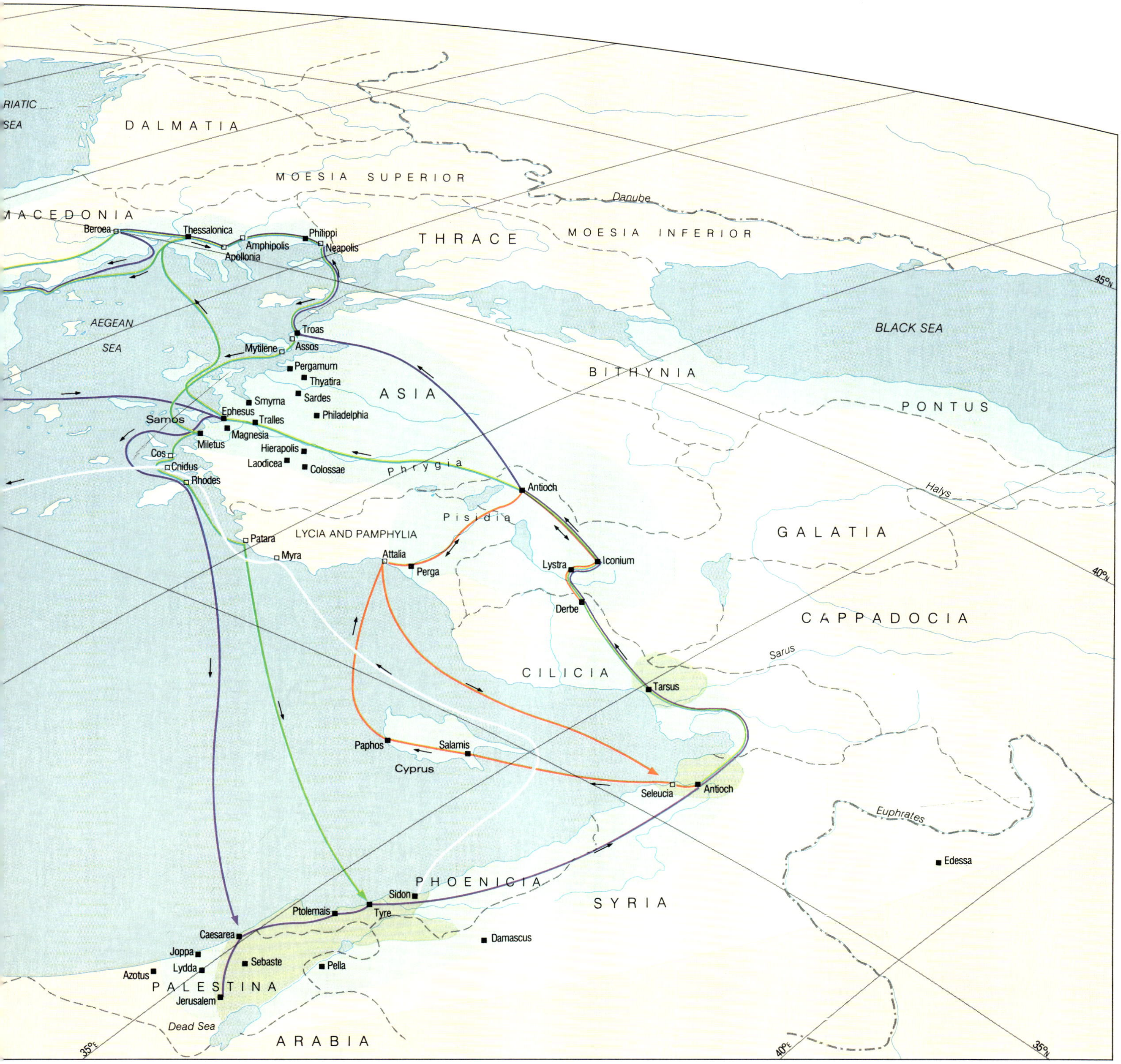

The extant Pauline letters are to churches not only in Asia Minor but also in Europe (Philippi, Corinth, Rome); and the move across from Asia Minor was seen as momentous (Acts 16:9). St Luke saw the geographical extension of the Church as an extraordinary triumph in face of opposition (but with the partial support also) of Jewish synagogues, Greek intelligentsia and Roman government officials, somehow bringing Paul to preach not only to philosophers at Athens (Acts 17) but to the great city of Rome itself.

special position for the capital of the Gentile world in the thought of the apostle to the Gentiles.

Christianity and Platonism

In the Gentile world outside the closed-community tradition of Judaism, the Old Testament assumptions were entirely absent. It was a world of local cults, all mutually tolerant of each other, the function of which was a performance of rites and ceremonies to keep the gods propitious to the tribe and the individual. The common driving force of ancient cult was the need to ensure survival and prosperity, fertile crops and spouses, success in love affairs or commercial ventures, protection against sorcery deployed by one's enemies, perhaps even against fate. To these ends, belief in astrology and magic had become widespread at all levels of society.

The ancient classical world of Greece and Rome did not divide time into periods of seven days as the Jews did. The Christians, however, celebrated Jesus' Resurrection in the early morning after the Sabbath and so took with them the observance of the week. This was reinforced by astrologers who placed each day of the week under the baleful presidency of a different planet. By 200 AD Christians began to see special symbolism in the coincidence of the sun's day with their thanksgiving (*eucharistia*) for the rise of the "Sun of Righteousness." Though some Christians used the planetary names for the days of the week, stricter believers spoke not of Sunday, but of the Lord's day (*dominica, kyriake*), and used numbers for weekdays.

This mixing of myths and religions, in the belief that they all say the same things in different ways, was common in the Gentile world to which the Christian missionaries went. Tolerance sometimes broke down, however, and syncretism (attempted reconciliation) might become an expression of religious imperialism and dominance: for example, the priests of Isis advanced claims that she was indeed the supreme mother deity, and all other cults were inferior versions of hers. More commonly, it expressed relativism or skepticism, that is the view that to the believer all cults are equally true, to the philosopher equally false, and to the magistrate equally useful.

In the Greek world of 500 years before the advent of Christianity, religious beliefs had been the object of critical discussion among philosophers. The myths that portrayed the gods as angry, proud or lustful outraged Plato, who expelled Homer and the poets from his ideal state. Plato saw the soul as being not at home in this material world. Platonism saw this world ambivalently: its beauty reflecting a higher, external and unchanging beauty, yet the continual flux and decay of things also making it a treadmill to which, by reincarnation, we are fated repeatedly to return—unless, by active suppression of physical appetite, we can liberate the soul to realize its affinity with heaven and escape to the vision of God.

Plato regarded the cosmos as a duality, where the good and spiritual pervade matter; in much the same way, on a microcosmic scale, the human soul pervades the human body, and with the same consequence that evil (which is material) is in constant painful abrasion with the good. A pessimistic dualism along these lines offered a philosophy to people who brooded on the unfairnesses and miseries of human experience. Fatalist myths, which told of the repeated reincarnation of the soul in body after body, or the soul's fall into matter, where it has become trapped by its attachment to the things of the body, provided a framework for a world-rejecting ethic.

Not only Plato spoke of the soul's fall. The book of Genesis pictured the human condition as resulting from an act of human free will against God's laws. In esoteric circles teachers claimed to reconcile all religions and philosophies, and to reveal the inner mystery of human destiny. Such circles proliferated on the margins of Judaism, fascinated by ingenious interpretations of recondite texts, mystical numbers and bizarre names of angels. Provided that adherents observed the Law, there was no censure attaching to cabalist speculations.

Jewish apocalyptic told the devout that despite sufferings and injustices there was a divine vindication coming and therefore a hidden meaning to history. The conflict between good and evil was cosmic, a war between primary forces, good and evil angelic powers, in which the good God is no omnipotent, and his providence is not in ultimate control.

The 2nd-century challenge

Out of the heady mixture of Platonic metaphysics and apocalyptic, a pessimistic dualism and determinism emerged. It took many forms which have been given the common label of Gnosticism. For Christianity this Gnostic religiosity presented painful problems. The main Christian body of "the Great Church" (as a 2nd-century pagan called it) rejected the sects on its periphery, largely on two grounds. First, while the Christians spoke of redemption as deliverance from an alienated world, they knew that their Redeemer is the Creator, one God, the Father Almighty; therefore the physical world has not originated in a precosmic smudge or embarrassing hiccup in the process of divine emanation, but has a positive and good purpose which redemption is to restore, not to eliminate. The outcome is secure. Secondly, the Gnostics were fatalists, and held that whether one is lost or saved depends on predestination, not on one's ethical behavior, not on any supposedly "free" act of faith or intentionality. The "Great Church" did not think human responsibility could be pushed aside and rejected determinism, though the subject has remained controversial throughout the history of the Church.

The 2nd-century Christians, Justin at Rome and Irenaeus at Lyon, argued that reason and freedom are inalienable in human nature. Some Gnostics sought to eliminate the particularity and the historical element in Christianity by assimilating it to mystery cults like those of Attis, Mithras or Isis.

In the 2nd century the Roman Christians became conscious of guarding the tradition of their martyred apostles. Monuments were erected c. 165 to Paul on Via Ostiense, to both Peter and Paul on the Appian Way, to Peter in a necropolis on the Vatican hill (reconstruction *left*). Constantine erected and endowed the basilica of old St Peter's (destroyed by Bramante to make the present building), placing the altar above the 2nd-century shrine held to mark Peter's grave (reconstruction *below left*). Access for pilgrims was by a curved passage. Before Constantine's time popes were buried at the catacomb of Callistus to the south of the city in a special vault (*below*). The first pope to be buried at St Peter's was Leo I (d. 461).

The orthodox insisted that Christianity is what it is, not something else.

The Gnostics, vehement rivals to each other, haunted the Church throughout the Mediterranean world—Saturninus at Antioch, Basilides in Egypt, Valentinus in Rome, and many others. To Rome also came a radical critic of the Old Testament, Marcion, excommunicated in 144. The communities he founded lasted long. Reading Paul, he saw the apostle's opposition to those for whom Christianity was no new thing but just a continuation of Judaism in a wider context, and the hints that the Jerusalem Church and the Twelve were compromisers with old custom. He read how Jesus asked for new wine to be in new bottles. The true message of Christ, he concluded, had been misunderstood in the apostolic age except by Paul; so the Gospels and Epistles had been audaciously interpolated, representing Paul too as a man of compromise, accepting Old Testament authority, which in Marcion's mind the real Paul could not have done. Resort to allegorical interpretations he rejected as a dishonest escape. To Marcion the truth was that the Jewish God was an inferior vengeful deity, creator of a defective world (as the malaise besetting human sexuality proved), giver of the Mosaic Law, and quite other than the loving Father announced by Jesus. Marcion produced a "corrected" edition of the apostolic writings purged of the large interpolations he detected. This view of the Bible persisted in dualist heresies well into the later Middle Ages and beyond, for example in notions that heretical apocrypha are more truthful than canonical texts accepted by the Church. The Gnostics claimed that their esoteric theosophy was a higher knowledge beyond the mere faith taught in ordinary church services. But this knowledge was not acquired by natural reason. It was a mystery.

The Gnostics were not the only 2nd-century writers to accuse the Church of making too many concessions to uneducated members of low-class origin. As early as the First Epistle to the Corinthians Paul had to deal with tensions in the Corinthian Church between the relatively small elite of upper-class and educated believers and the majority in the local community who were simple folk. A pagan attack on Christianity was written about 177–80 by a Platonist named Celsus who was offended by Christian belief in a divine intervention in this world, in miracles like the Virgin Birth and the Resurrection of Christ (the one he thought a cover story for illegitimacy, the other the result of "female hysteria"), in what seemed to him an irrational demand for faith, in the preaching of hellfire for unbelievers, in the incompatibility of their monotheism with any recognition of pagan cult sanctioned by immemorial social custom. Celsus thought the Christian mission was succeeding (to his great alarm) by exploitation of the uneducated and of women, not by the intellectual power and coherence of its doctrines or by its moral revolution and high ethical demands. In his eyes the Church consisted essentially of low-class people propagating an unreasonable superstition which a handful of intellectuals dishonestly made respectable by sophistical arguments and allegorical interpretation of awkward passages in the Bible. A massive reply to Celsus was written 70 years later by Origen, for whom the proportion of educated to uneducated in the Church corresponded to that found in society as a whole; in short, the Church is simply a cross-section of society in which garbage collectors are more numerous than grandees because there are more of them.

The Greek philosophers had succeeded in bringing their moral exhortations only to the educated elite. It seemed unreasonable to complain if the Christians were bringing a high morality to the rejects of ancient society, to the women, the poor, the underprivileged. No doubt such people did not always join the Church for what Origen would have thought the right reasons; some came for prosperity or health in this world, to please a patron, to be touched by the miraculous in terms other than the transformation of their inner character. Before Constantine, however, there was little social advantage to be had from conversion.

Christians in Ancient Rome

In 4th-century Rome public ceremonies of Christian worship and celebration matched the public celebrations of the old civic religion. On 29 June, the day of the old festival for Romulus, founder of Rome, a great festival for Peter and Paul was celebrated with pomp and long processions. The old and the new continued side by side in Christian Rome. The emperors enforced toleration. There was no outlawing of pagan ceremonies. Instead they were held in Rome under imperial protection. The emperor Valentinian (364–75) liked neither black magic nor Manichaeism, but it was possible for Augustine to meet the Manichees in 383 when he came to Rome from Africa. The state authority was ready to intervene in church affairs and this was natural enough; Rome was run by its great families, who were accustomed to influence. Damasus was criticized for the extravagance of his entertainments as pope (366–84), but they did something to make the great upper-class families of Rome feel at home as Christians. In a similar way, Damasus was able to imitate the great in the secular world and act as a patron of the arts within the Church.

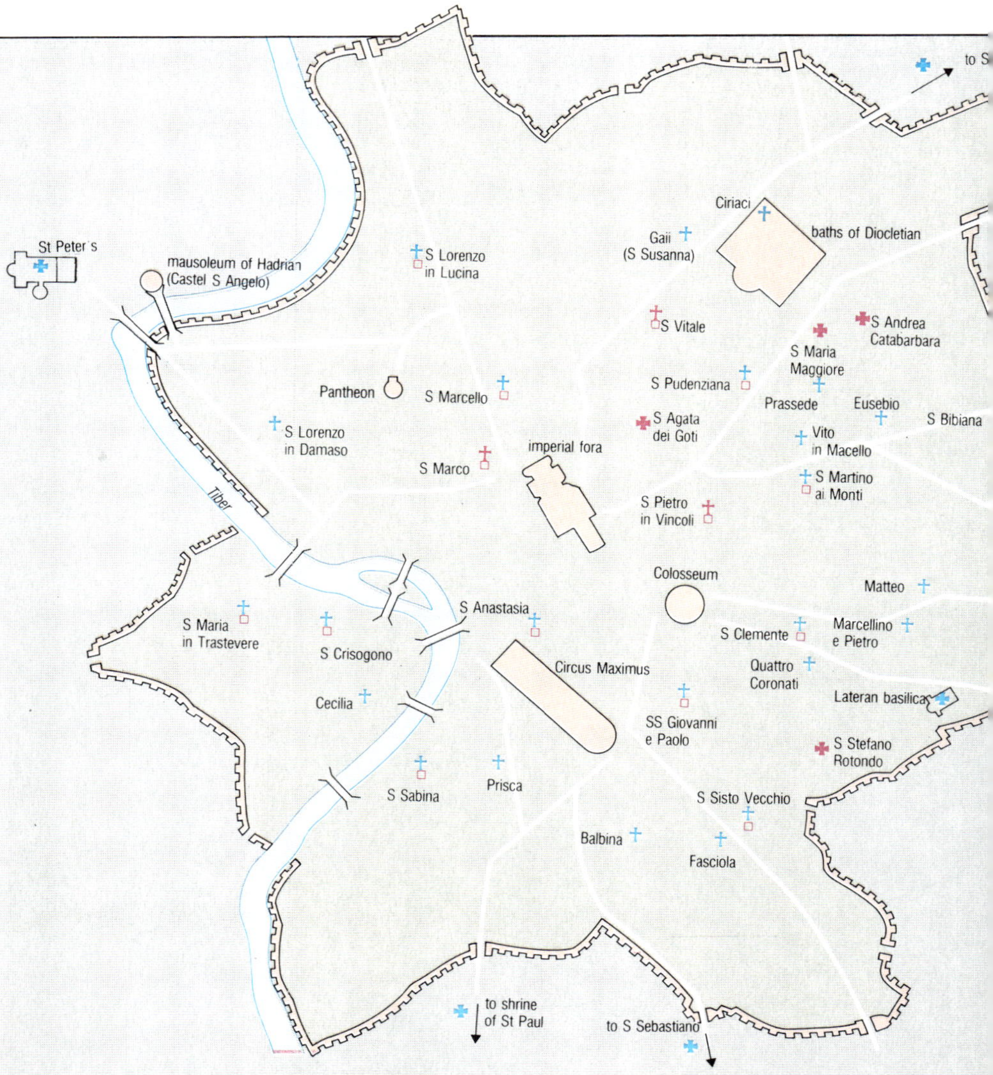

Above right The figure of Christ as a shepherd, or that of Peter, took the place in sculpture of figures from the past who had had a juridical or military glory in the public mind. In sculptures and mosaics Peter is shown as a new Moses, giving the new Law, or as the leader of the soldiers of Christ. In this sarcophagus from the Vatican Christ is shown as a young shepherd with the 12 apostles on either side. The sarcophagus, of 375–400 AD, was found near the church of San Lorenzo in Rome. The legs of the sheep have been restored. Biblical scenes, such as this relief of Adam and Eve (*above*), were also used to decorate the sarcophagi, as in this example from Syracuse.

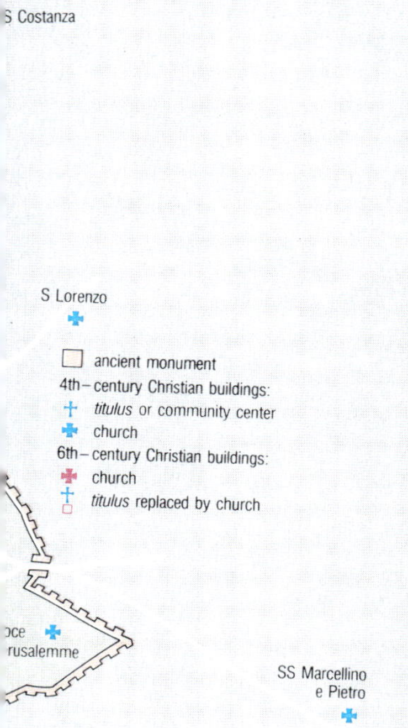

Below At the 4th-century shrine of the martyred exorcist Peter and the priest Marcellinus in Rome, Christ is portrayed between Peter and Paul; below, the Lamb of God between four martyrs, Gorgonius, Peter, Marcellinus and Tiburtius.

Far left From about 355 AD a mausoleum was built by the Via Nomentana in Rome to hold the porphyry sarcophagus of the princess Constantina (Santa Costanza). A century later the sarcophagus was moved and a baptismal piscina constructed; at that time mosaics were added portraying Moses receiving the Law and Christ giving the new Law to St Peter. But the original mosaics (*left*) remained on the barrel vault, with all-too-exciting vintage and Bacchic scenes, conventional motifs in pre-Christian funerary art. In early Christian art, where spring symbolized the Resurrection, this theme and style continued but the Bacchic revelry became rather more sober.

Above This portrait of a Christian family comes from the cross of Galla Placidia in Brescia. Women were an important influence in bringing Christianity into Roman homes. St Jerome wrote to a number of women who wanted advice on how to live a Christian life. One of these, Marcella, was a wealthy woman who used to hold Hebrew classes in her palace on the Aventine, where Jerome taught, and everyone prayed together and sang Psalms.

The Christian apologists

The necessity of meeting the Gnostic challenge on the one hand and the pagan intellectuals on the other forced the Christians to articulate their position. They needed to show that there was indeed a higher understanding of the Gospel lying beyond mere simple faith, and yet that this higher understanding was not a mishmash of Gnostic theosophy. A series of well-educated and thoughtful Christians wrote intelligent vindications of their faith in which they fought a battle on two fronts against both pagan critics and Gnostic heretics: Justin, a lay teacher at Rome, martyred in the 160s, Tatian, writing in Mesopotamia around 170, Irenaeus, bishop of Lyon about 180; at Alexandria Clement around 190, and Origen (184–254) who moved to Palestinian Caesarea about 232; at Carthage Tertullian about 190–215, and Minucius Felix. They published tracts in defense of Christianity as the true philosophy realizing the moral truth after which Plato and the Stoics had aspired, and they combined their defense with strong attacks on polytheism as no longer commanding the belief of philosophically educated people and as being a source of moral weakness to society. Clement spoke of Christianity as a river formed by the confluence of Greek philosophy with biblical faith and indeed, historically speaking, that is exactly what was happening in the process of finding technical terms and formulas in which Christian beliefs might be expressed.

A more immediate reaction against Gnosticism came from Montanus (160–89), a charismatic in Asia Minor who, with two prophetesses, Prisca and Maximilla, uttered oracles of the imminent 1000-year reign of Christ in the new (Phrygian) Jerusalem. The prophetic trio believed themselves to be the very mouthpiece of the Holy Spirit, calling for puritan abstinence in sex, food and drink and rigor in discipline. The Montanists expected all the Lord's people not to be prophets, but to acknowledge that they were.

In Asia Minor the charismatic "New Prophecy" became divisive. The reluctance of bishops to enthuse about the cause led Tertullian, recruited about 207, to deduce that the Church is constituted only by "spiritual men" and needs no ordination by apostolic succession. In the west Montanism was short-lived, but in the east Phrygia remained its citadel until the age of Justinian.

Reaction to Gnosticism and Montanism not only encouraged new thinking about Christian doctrine but also accelerated the formation of the canon of the New Testament, a process in the main complete by 180–200. The Bible by itself was insufficient to articulate unambiguously some essential points of Christian belief in opposition to heretical distortion. But the 2nd-century Church was strongly conscious of being custodian of a sacred tradition of which the Scriptures were a major but not the sole constituent. In the Rhône valley Irenaeus wrote a *Refutation* to insist on the Church's apostolic faith in the unity of creation and redemption, and therefore of both Old and New Testaments, in which Christ as second Adam brings renewal to a lost humanity. Many Gnostic sects accepted the authority of at least part of Scripture, but Irenaeus (and Tertullian after him) stands on the Church's tradition of interpreting its written records and on philosophical reason. Against heretical appeals to the Bible it was necessary to affirm that Scripture found its authoritative interpreter in the living tradition of the Catholic Church.

Irenaeus and the Rhône valley Church had close links with the community in Asia Minor. He much regretted the divisiveness of the Montanist movement. In youth he had sat at the feet of old Polycarp, bishop of Smyrna, martyred at the age of 86 perhaps about 162 (the evidence for the date is conflicting), and could recall Polycarp speaking of St John the Apostle at Ephesus. He felt himself to be in some sense the living embodiment of the authentic tradition and among the last to belong to the apostolic age of revelation and divine wonder.

His influence is measured by the debt of his followers, especially Tertullian in Carthage, the first person to put theology into Latin, and Hippolytus of Rome (died about 235), who wrote Old Testament commentaries (Daniel, the Song of Songs, Proverbs etc.), an Easter Table, a chronicle of world history, a church order with priceless liturgical information entitled the *Apostolic Tradition,* and above all a *Refutation of Heresies.* Like Irenaeus, he saw Gnosticism as speculative theology, not rooted in biblical faith. He tried to show how Gnostic sects originated in misunderstandings of old Greek philosophers.

Tertullian shared the opinion that pagan philosophy was mother of heresy; that is, that the hallmark of faith is obedience to the self-disclosure of God in Christ. Thirty-seven works by him survive in Latin (he published Greek editions of some), written in vigorous, torrential prose. He boldly coined the technical language of western theology, which owes to him its terms (such as "Trinity," "one substance in three persons," Christ as "one person in two natures" or substances). Tertullian also formulated the problem of "original sin"—of the "fault in origin" inherited by Adam's posterity, the collective cupidity which conditions and vitiates all human endeavor after justice and goodness.

Clement and Origen

The struggle against heresy with the aid of selected philosophical tools is again the background of the writings of the Christian Platonists of Alexandria, Clement and Origen. Clement (died before 215) came to Alexandria to study under a Christian named Pantaenus, a free-lance teacher noted for combining instruction in Stoicism with Christian faith. Clement's main achievement is seen in his trilogy: (a) *Exhortation* (*Protreptikos*) to conversion, (b) *Tutor* (*Paidagogos*), a guide to morality and etiquette, with much intriguing social comment, (c) the *Miscellanies* (*Stromateis*), a deliberately unsystematic work which is carefully designed to lead the reader by a zigzag path up to the language of the mystic's vision of God. These three works correspond to the three stages of spiritual pilgrimage—from the initial act of faith to understanding, with the suppression of distracting passion, and so to passionless ecstatic union with God. To Clement his ascent is an unending advance into the infinite mystery of God's being. If God held out the choice of a possessed salvation in his right hand and a ceaseless advance in knowledge in his left, Clement declares his choice of the left hand. Correspond-

Left An ivory (c.400 AD) from Munich shows three Marys at Christ's tomb addressed by a wingless angel; a figure in toga in a niche, and olive tree behind; above to the right on a hill, Christ, scroll in hand, ascends grasping God's right hand stretched from clouds. Two apostles bow at his feet.

Right A fresco from the catacomb on the Via Latina, Rome, of the 4th century shows Samson routing the Philistines.

Below right St Paul under arrest, from the sarcophagus of Junius Bassus, prefect of Rome in 359 AD, who was baptized on his deathbed.

Below A 3rd-century fresco in the crypt of Lucina, catacomb of Callistus in Rome, shows the good shepherd carrying a bowl of milk (perhaps with honey also), received by the newly baptized as symbol of entry to the Promised Land.

ingly, the wrath of God of biblical language signifies an educational process by which, like a surgeon or schoolmaster, God teaches humanity to love the right way. The "consuming fire" of God purges away evil to make his rational creation fit for his presence.

His successor at Alexandria, Origen, startled his contemporaries, Christian and pagan, by his exceptional erudition and mastery of philosophy. The martyrdom of his father at Alexandria in 203/4 permanently marked him with a deep opposition to the paganism of the culture in which he was, by education, simultaneously at home. The main body of Origen's voluminous writings consists of biblical homilies and commentaries. The first Christian to speak of the Bible as a single book (and perhaps one of the first generation of Christians to have seen the entire Christian Bible copied in a single codex), Origen's interpretations sought a middle course between the unrestrained and unorthodox allegories of Valentinus and other Gnostics, and those like Marcion who rejected all allegory. In *On First Principles* he rejected all pessimistic dualism and determinism. The immutable, transcendent, good Creator made free rational beings to love him, but by neglect of the divine they cooled. As a place of discipline, the Creator made this material world, reflecting its maker's power and glory by its beauty and order (which are to be discerned in the smallest and greatest of God's creatures) but at the same time sufficiently beset by uncertainties and pain to make souls realize that their true home must be in a higher world. Origen followed Platonic tradition in seeing the evil of this life either as the consequence of misused free choice, or as explicable by the diversity of function of the different constituents of the world. Because of Gnostic exploitation, the Platonic notion of evil as resulting from recalcitrance in the matter used for creation did not attract him. He preferred to say God created everything, including matter, out of nothing. So providence sends earthly inconvenience or even disaster to prevent souls supposing materialism to be their ultimate destiny. The Old Testament prophets initiated a process of redemption with its focus in the Incarnation of the divine Word, the immanent Reason ordering all things, whose work is continued by the Spirit in and through the saints of Christ's Church.

In Origen exalted language about the holiness of the Church and the bishops and presbyters to whom is committed "the power of the keys" is fused with astringent expressions of deep disappointment at the practical reality. Nevertheless the Church is the means by which God's reconciling work continues in this life; and the process of God's refining fire continues hereafter, burning away the wood, hay and stubble that weak believers erect on the baptismal foundation laid by Christ. God's goodness never despairs; even in the worst there always remains some spark of goodness. Love never fails, and at the end God will be all in all. Indeed if the Devil is a fallen angel, one must say that even Satan is evil only by will, not by created nature, and retains the capacity to have his will turned towards repentance and salvation. Hellfire is assuredly significant of real suffering but its moral purpose is remedial, not merely retributive, if it is to be worthy of God.

THE SPREAD AND STRUCTURE OF THE EARLY CHURCH

One of the factors making for the coherence of the early Christian churches was the remarkably early development of their ministerial and pastoral structure. That the people of God need shepherds to care for them, to lead the congregation in worship and mission, and to exercise discipline, is a principle plentifully attested in the New Testament writings (for example Ephesians 4). Christ's apostles, 12 in number and therefore symbolic of the renewed Israel and embodiment of the Church, received from him a solemn charge to preach, and at the Last Supper were commanded to continue the memorial of his redemptive sacrifice. As the apostles passed from the scene, the locus of authority became a matter of regional dispute. At Corinth the congregation assumed that, since it had had a part in the election of its clergy, it possessed a democratic power to get rid of them when it preferred more gifted and eloquent preachers. The Church of Rome wrote by the hand of Clement, its presiding presbyter, a letter of protest, insisting that, unless there has been some grave moral fault, the clergy, appointed by their standing in succession from the apostles, and sanctified by the holiness of their liturgical function are not disposable at the will of the laity. In the Epistles to Timothy and Titus it is laid down that the ministers who preside, teach and preach have a right to financial support from the faithful. They also have special responsibility for safeguarding the authentic tradition in teaching. Soon after, Ignatius, bishop of Antioch, asserted that the bishop, apparently now distinct from the presbyters flanking him at the celebration of the Eucharist, is to be the unique focus of order in the local church; there is no validity in a Eucharist celebrated in opposition to him. At the end of the century Tertullian regarded it as a mark of the Catholic Church over against heresy that "we receive the Eucharist from none but the president."

Pastoral structure of the Church

Tertullian describes in his *Apology* (39.1–6) how he and his fellow Christians worship together. We meet, he says, in a gathering and congregation, so as to approach God in prayer together. We pray for emperors, for their ministers and those in authority, for the security of the world, for peace on earth, for a postponement of the end of the world (to allow time for repentance).

There is reading of the Bible, intended to bring out of the text of Scripture any prophecy relating to the present time, anything which will make Christians see the circumstances of the day more clearly. The Bible reading also feeds faith, lifts the spirits to hope, strengthens confidence. And it inculcates God's commandments and precepts.

There is preaching, too, and rebuke of the members of the congregation. Judgment is passed on those who have sinned, "and it carries great weight, as it must among men certain that God sees them."

Finally, once a month, each member of the congregation "brings some modest coin . . . if he can; for nobody is compelled; it is a voluntary offering."

Many communities of Christians felt the need to set out the essential points of Christian belief in a summary. The new Christian stated his beliefs in front of the whole community and each member was reminded at the same time of the beliefs he himself had professed when he became a Christian. The service of baptism helped in this way to hold the community together and to keep its faith pure and intact. The exact form of words varied from place to place, but the main points were very similar. The convert who came for baptism in Rome about the year 200 was told to renounce Satan and all his servants and all his works as Tertullian describes, and when the presbyter had anointed him with oil in token of the driving out of evil spirits, he asked him: "Do you believe in God the Father Almighty? Do you believe in Jesus Christ, the Son of God, who was born by the Holy Ghost of the Virgin Mary, and was crucified under Pontius Pilate and was dead and buried, and rose again on the third day, alive from the dead, and ascended into heaven, and sat on the right hand of the Father, and will come to judge the living and the dead? Do you believe in the Holy Ghost, the holy Church and the resurrection of the flesh?"

Left A woman with hands raised in prayer from a necropolis at Tarragona, Spain, c.400.

Above: The spread of Christianity

The rapidity of Christian expansion amazed the Church itself. Christian communities were urban, moving only slowly into the countryside. While some saw the empire as diabolical and secular, most allowed it a providential role. The mission passed beyond the frontier. Armenia became Christian well before 300. In the Greek east (more slowly in the west), the Church quickly gained

a substantial proportion of the people. Causes of success were the universalist assertions of monotheism with its powerful ethical concern; a bias to the poor and readiness to share goods; the acceptance within one community of both married people and dedicated frugal ascetics; the assurance of forgiveness now and eternal life with Christ hereafter; a coherent social framework led by clergy in assured succession; the capacity of Christian intellectuals to combine biblical faith with openness to philosophy and to a positive evaluation of the empire.

Relations with pagan society

The Church's gradual permeation of high Roman society, especially among women, received a jolt in 251. Barbarian attack, civil war, trade recession and drastic inflation brought instability for which Christians were blamed. Cyprian, bishop of Carthage from 249 to 258, had difficulty upholding episcopal authority in time of severe persecution. Who had power to reconcile those who had offered idolatrous incense to the gods of Rome? And should the terms of reconciliation be rigorous or mild? At Rome itself the issue created division: two rivals were elected bishop, Cornelius (lax) and Novatian (rigorist). Cyprian rejected Novatian and all his sacraments as outside the one communion of which Peter's teaching chair is symbol. "He cannot have God for his father who has not the Church for his mother." But in 256 a new pope, Stephen, sharply disagreed asserting that sacraments, if duly given even by schismatic clergy, are valid, and that those baptized outside the Catholic Church are by tradition admitted by imposition of hands and not baptized again. Stephen implied a distinction between heretic and orthodox schismatics already adumbrated by Origen when discussing in which category Montanists fell.

Heresy derives from a Greek word signifying a private choice over against the consensus of the

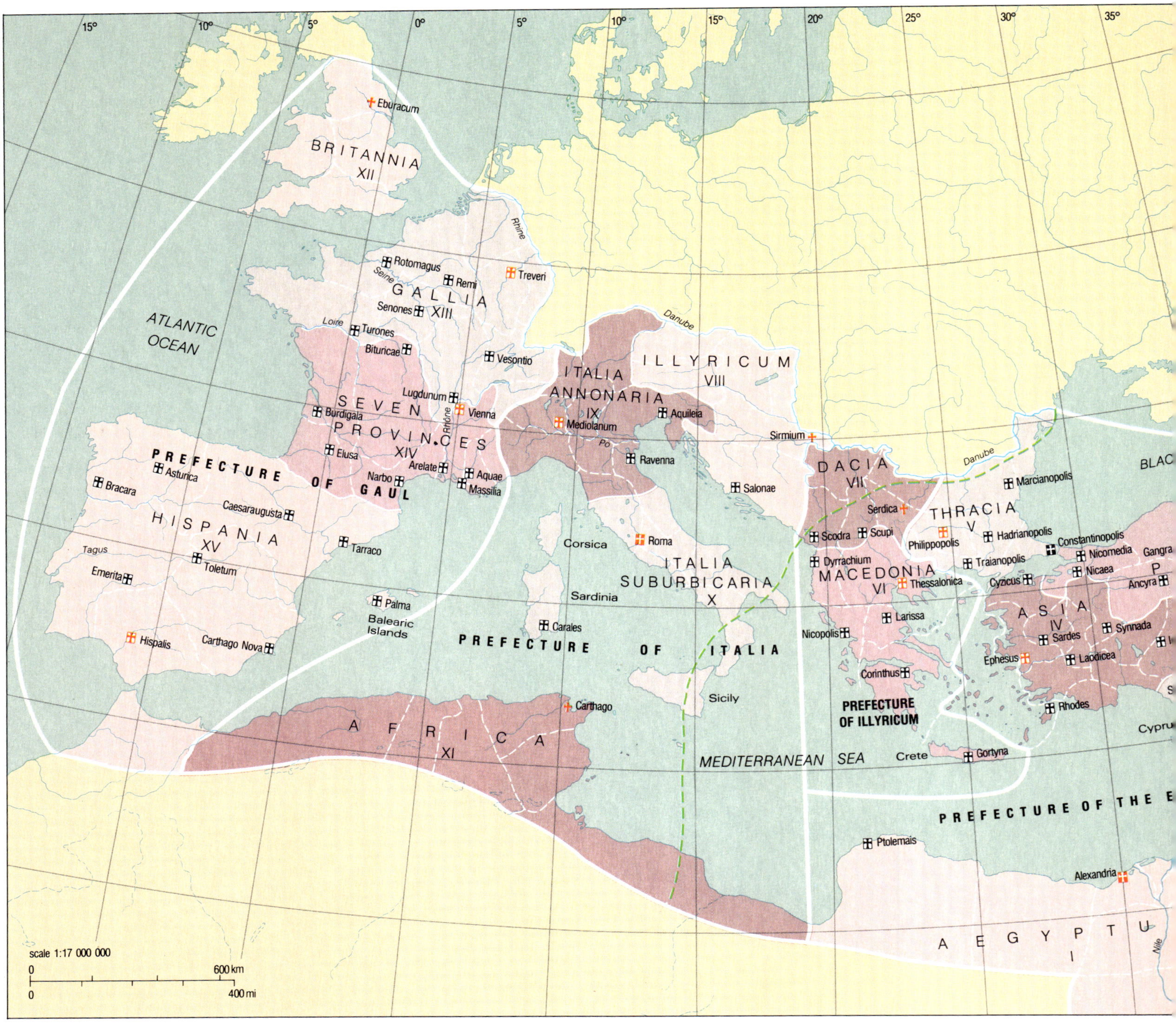

community. Justin Martyr and Hippolytus opposed not only Gnostics but heretics ("modalists") who denied any real distinction in God between Father and Son, a view soon associated with the Roman presbyter Sabellius. To another group it seemed that the Father sent his power, the Spirit, to inspire Jesus the Son. In the 260s the advocacy of this view by Paul of Samosata, bishop of Antioch, led a synod to condemn him, especially for worldly conduct unfitting in a bishop.

About 180 Celsus, pagan critic of Christianity, pleaded for more participation by Christians in public and intellectual life. Third-century Christians increasingly participated, and the more they did so, the more tense relations with pagan society became. In North Africa militant Christian bands attacked pagan shrines and festivals. The Neoplatonic school of Plotinus tended to split into two, one side welcoming rapprochement with Christianity, the other side (especially represented by Porphyry) embittered and hostile. Christians had penetrated into the senior ranks of the army and the court. Diocletian, who died in retirement at Split where the Catholic cathedral is his mausoleum, reorganized the empire militarily, politically, administratively and economically. Court soothsayers consulting the entrails to discuss the future felt their efforts neutralized by Christian army officers making the sign of the Cross (a mark of Christian devotion going back at least to the 2nd century, especially associated with the baptismal renunciation of evil). The decisive battle of the Milvian Bridge outside Rome in 312, which put Constantine on the way to supreme power, was won after invocation of "the God of the Christians" and a dream directing him to put on his shield a monogram of Christ and the words, "By this sign conquer."

Above: The Church and the Roman state
From apostolic times the churches prayed for the emperor and governors, on whose prudence and power depended justice and peace, roads, seas free of pirates, law and the good order which missionaries needed. Just as the early communities were based on towns, so the imperial provinces became units of church administration; the presiding bishop of a province was either (as in Africa) the senior by date of ordination, or, more commonly, the bishop of the civil metropolis. Bishops of great sees (Rome, Constantinople from 330, Alexandria, Antioch, Jerusalem from 451) provided a court of appeal for groups of provinces called patriarchates, analogous to the jurisdictions of praetorian prefects.

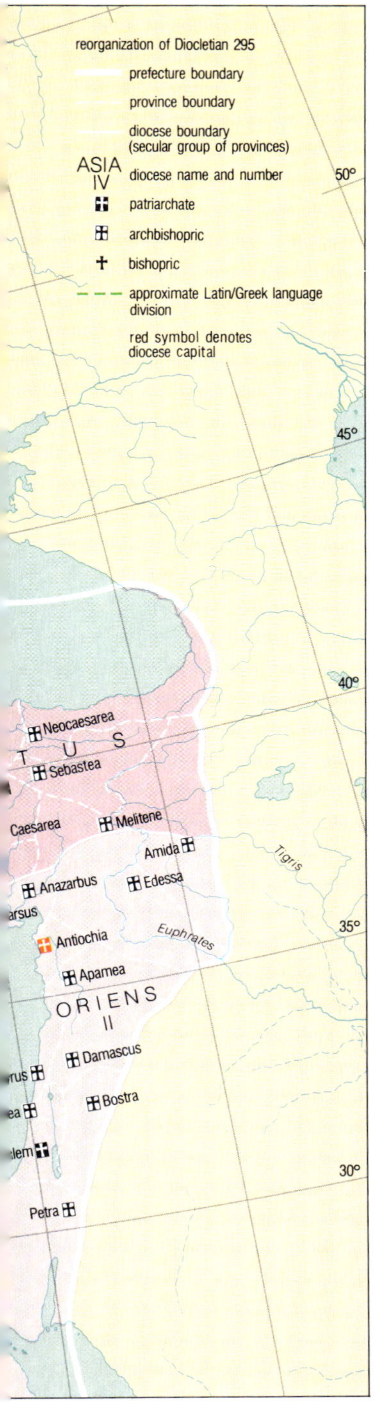

Greek east and Latin west: the gap widens

Constantine, with his sense of divine mission, felt threatened by Christian dissension in North Africa and Alexandria. The aftermath of the persecution left the community divided in Carthage between believers who saw it as an uncompromising battle against Satan and those who wished to lie low until the storm passed. The tensions led to schism, one side standing for unity with the Catholic Church overseas, recognized and supported by the emperor, and the other, soon led by Donatus, intransigently standing for ritual holiness and total separation of Church and state.

In Alexandria a dockland presbyter Arius distressed his bishop (but delighted others) by preaching that if the Son of God was crucified he suffered as the supreme Deity cannot do, and is therefore distinct in order of being from the transcendent Father, first cause of all things, from whose will he is derived. The resulting conflagration led Constantine to call a large synod of 220 bishops to Nicaea in Asia Minor, which included representatives not only of many Greek provinces, but two presbyters representing Silvester of Rome. The Council of Nicaea thereby became the first worldwide or "ecumenical" council. Its creed rejected Arius' theses and affirmed Son and Father to be "identical in being," "of one substance."

Ambiguities in the term "identity" contributed to half a century of controversy. Greek bishops feared it failed to allow for the distinction of the Son from the Father. Athanasius, bishop of Alexandria from 328 to 373, ensured the west's support for the defense of the Creed, but with the consequence that the gap between Greek east and Latin west was widened. The wrangles between different factions, each with its own slogans, became barbershop gossip and a music-hall joke. The principal pagan historian of the 4th-century empire, Ammianus Marcellinus, acidly commented on the ferocity of inter-Christian struggles, which contributed to the apostasy of Julian (emperor 361–63). Julian's death in battle against Persia was a sharp blow to his revival of polytheism, to which the majority of citizens still adhered at heart. Theodosius I (emperor 378–95) decided the Arian controversy in favor of the orthodoxy of the Creed of Nicaea, revised at the Council of Constantinople

Right A fresco by a popular artist Symeon Axenti (1513) at the church of St Sozomenos, Galata, Cyprus, showing the emperor at the Council of Ephesus in 431 exiling Nestorius and another heretic. Synods decided questions first of discipline, then of doctrine, issuing positive creeds fortified by negative anathemas. Some problems could not be settled without multi-provincial councils or even "ecumenical" assemblies where the Greek majority were joined by representatives of Rome. All the seven ancient ecumenical councils were summoned by east Roman emperors: Nicaea (325), Constantinople (381 – responsible for the eucharistic creed), Ephesus (431), Chalcedon (451), Constantinople (553), Constantinople (680–81), and Nicaea (787 on icons).

(381). He forbade pagan sacrifice and closed temples (391), many of which were later, like the Parthenon, transformed into churches. The fall of Rome to Alaric's Goths (410) had a more emotional than political significance at the time. Nostalgia for the old gods as protectors of Rome provoked Augustine, bishop of Hippo (= Annaba in Algeria) from 396 to 430, to embark on *The City of God,* a long vindication of Christianity against imperialist ideology and Platonic philosophy.

Augustine's conversion at Milan (386) owed much to the combined influence of his mother Monica and the able philosophical mind of Ambrose (bishop of Milan 374–97). Ambrose had been (unbaptized) provincial governor before becoming bishop of Milan where the emperor lived. He upheld the Church's independence and a Christian emperor's duty to protect it – for example, by refusing to reinstate the Altar of Victory in the Senate house at Rome. In close cooperation with the contemporary pope, Damasus (366–84), Ambrose made strong claims both for the Church's independence of the imperial power and for the western churches over against the eastern. Aristocrats vied with each other in adorning noble shrines of martyrs. Public processions celebrated high festivals.

In the mind of Ambrose the destinies of the Church and empire were bound together by providence. When Theodosius, irritated by the citizens of Thessalonica, ordered a massacre, Ambrose required him to do penance. Fourth-century emperors understood themselves to be autocrats above the law. For Ambrose the emperor as son of the Church had duties not only to natural morality but to the defense of true religion against demonic polytheism. In the invading Goths (375) he saw Gog and Magog assaulting God's city of Rome.

Schism in the east

The Church's independence of the imperial power in matters of faith and morals was not so easily asserted in the Greek east, where Christian political theory, formulated by the historian and scholar Eusebius of Caesarea (died 339), stressed the status of the Christian emperor as both priest and king. This was qualified by the requirement that orthodoxy be upheld. A Byzantine emperor countenancing heresy was sure to meet vehement conflict.

Nevertheless when Archbishop John (Chrysostom) of Constantinople (398–408) began to demand of the emperors behavior comformable to Christian morality, he found himself losing the support of the court. The bishop of Alexandria, Theophilus

Above: Monasticism
Monk means loner. But man is a social animal, and the Gospel commands love to one's neighbor. In the Nile valley c.320 Pachomius created communities for mutual support with an economic base as rural cooperatives, enclosed by a wall to make a sacred precinct. Similar societies were founded in Egypt in the Wadi Natrun, in the Judean desert, in Asia Minor (by Basil of Caesarea in 370–79), in North Africa by Augustine who had met such houses in Milan and Rome. The new foundations were usually away from towns, and transformed the social and economic life of the countryside.

Right At Ravenna from 404 western emperors found a safe citadel. The church buildings are among the noblest of late antiquity with mosaic and marble. At the nearby port of Classis the basilica dedicated to the patron saint of Ravenna, Apollinaris, was built in 549. The apse mosaic represents Christ's cross with Moses and Elijah and the sheep of paradise—symbolic of the glory of the transfiguration of Christ and his coming in triumph.

+SANCTVS
APOLENARIS

(385–412), led by Egyptian monks into condemning admirers of Origen, was nettled when John protected them; he came to Constantinople and, with the help of many alienated by John's reforming zeal, obtained his synodical condemnation.

John's fall was politically an unhappy manifestation of rivalry between Alexandria, by old tradition the second city to Rome, and Constantine's city at Byzantium on the Bosphorus, founded in 330 to be the New Rome. This civic rivalry affected the churches and from 429 it became entangled with thorny debates about the way in which Jesus Christ is both God and man. In the 360s Apollinaris of Laodicea (Syria) solved this problem by saying that in Christ there is no duality since the divine Word replaced the human mind. He thereby incurred censure for denying the solidarity of the Redeemer's humanity with ours.

He was opposed by the "school of Antioch," whose principal theologian was Theodore, bishop of Mopsuestia (died 427). Theodore understood redemption as achieved by the perfect obedience of Christ as pioneer of salvation (a theme of the Epistle to the Hebrews). The Alexandrian school disowned Apollinaris but insisted that no mere man can save the world of which he is part. The debate became a major conflict between Cyril, bishop of Alexandria (414–44), and Nestorius, bishop of Constantinople (428–31, died c. 449) and pupil of Theodore.

Nestorius was condemned at the stormy third ecumenical council at Ephesus (431), as failing to affirm the fundamental unity ("hypostatic union") of the person of Christ. Cyril spoke of "one nature after the union." Nestorius spoke of "two natures united in one person." This "two-nature" formula was offensive to Cyril's more extreme followers. At a second council at Ephesus (449) it was condemned, but the decisions of 449 were overthrown, under a new emperor, at the fourth ecumenical council at Chalcedon (451).

The Council of Chalcedon agreed on a definition that retains classical status, largely a mosaic of phrases from Cyril of Alexandria, except that Christ is said to be one person made known "*in* two natures." Cyril would have said "of" not "in." This preposition offended many in Syria and Egypt, mainly because, though the council censured Nestorianism, its formula was one a moderate Nestorian with a strong stomach might stretch his conscience to sign.

Two main factors helped to spare the west the worst agonies of the Christological controversy, which racked the Greek east with schism. The acknowledged leadership of the see of Rome was exercised by Pope Leo I (440–61), not only as a court of appeal from local synods, but as a positive teaching authority in St Peter's name. Secondly, the Latin west had had a series of first-class minds – Hilary of Poitiers (c. 315–67); Ambrose of Milan; the scholarly monk Jerome (347–419, resident at Bethlehem from 386) whose biblical commentaries and revised Latin Bible (the "Vulgate") were works of high scholarship; above all, Augustine.

Augustine, one of the greatest of Plato's disciples and critics, especially in *The City of God* and *On the Trinity,* towered intellectually above his contemporaries. Against the Manichees he vindicated the proper place of authority in harmony with reason ("I would not have believed the Gospel unless the authority of the universal Church had constrained me"). Against the Donatists he argued that the authentic Church cannot be in just one province. In controversy with the British monk Pelagius (from 412) he defended the inability of man to please God without the inward grace of Christ – *sola gratia.*

Left Augustine (354–430), a bookish country boy from the (now Algerian) hills, became a master of Latin oratory and a Platonist. Converted, aged 32, he was baptized at Milan (387) by Ambrose; returning to Africa (388) after burying his mother Monica at Ostia, he became presbyter (391) then bishop at Hippo (Annaba) 395–96. All his greatest works were composed after 396, including the *Confessions*, the *Trinity* and the *City of God*, with numerous masterful letters and sermons. His influence on the west has been and remains great.

Below Roughly contemporary with Augustine's birth is a find of Christian silver from Water Newton, Huntingdonshire, now in the British Museum. The treasure includes a number of triangular plaques resembling pagan votive offerings but stamped with Christian symbols. Illustrated is a silver bowl inscribed "I Publianus, humbly trusting in you Lord, honor your holy altar."

PART TWO

THE MEDIEVAL CHURCH

THE CHURCH IN THE EAST

Justinian and Theodora

Justinian I (527–65) was not the first Byzantine emperor to claim to be appointed by God, or to believe that he had a divine mission to enforce correct worship. Sweeping claims had been made for the authority of emperors from the time of Constantine the Great onwards, and steps had already been taken by Theodosius I to bring the law of the empire into line with Christian teachings. Justinian claimed to be God's mouthpiece and even "divinity walking upon earth."

Anxious to avert God's wrath and to gain his favor for himself and for his empire, he collected imperial edicts and systematized the law of his empire. "If we strive by all means to enforce the civil laws, whose power God in his goodness has entrusted to us for the security of our subjects, how much more keenly should we endeavor to enforce the holy canons and the divine laws which have been framed for the salvation of our souls!" "One empire, one law, one Church" was his motto.

Justinian clamped down on conspicuous deviations from the Christian norm, "Orthodoxy" (Greek *orthos* = "correct," *doxa* = "opinion, doctrine") as he understood it. Jews were persecuted, and those remaining pagan, or simply unbaptized, came under severe pressure. (The most famous blow struck against pagan intellectuals was the closing of the Academy of Athens in 529.) But there was work to be done in the countryside, even in areas such as Lydia, which had longstanding Christian traditions. John, the titular bishop of Ephesus, claimed to have converted 80 000 people in the mountain districts of western Asia Minor, destroying temples and building many churches in their stead.

Justinian was also concerned about the life and morals of Christian clergy. On the grounds that the purity of the clergy "brings great favor and increase to our commonwealth, whereby it is granted to us to subdue the barbarians," he forbade clergymen from gaming or going to the theater or the races. For Justinian, as for other Byzantine emperors, the Church was not a thing apart, or a wholly separate institution which could be run on its own lines. Justinian regarded it as, in effect, a department of state, charged with functions of unique importance to the common weal.

Neither Justinian nor any other Byzantine emperor claimed the right to administer the eucharist or to perform the other functions which were the special responsibilities of the priesthood. However, Justinian expected, as patron and protector of the Church, to exert influence over top appointments to bishoprics and patriarchates, and he expected discipline, attention to "the public interest," and often downright obedience from churchmen, dismissing even patriarchs, if their conduct displeased him. Above all, Justinian proclaimed as his right and duty the upholding of Orthodoxy. He formally undertook always to support the decisions and authority of priests, but added suggestively: "God's true dogmas and the priests' dignity are therefore our first concern." Such critics as Pope Vigilius objected to his issuing edicts which defined Orthodoxy and then calling synods to rubber-stamp them. In response, Justinian's *sacra* to the ecumenical council of 553 elaborately lists the precedents for imperial intervention in matters of dogma. When Vigilius still showed signs of truculence, he was simply declared to have been removed from office. The practical limitations on Justinian's power were shown up most starkly by the Monophysites (*monos* = "one," *physis* = "nature"), who believed that the incarnate Christ had a *single*, indivisible, nature, although coming *from* two natures, divine and human. They rejected the official doctrine upheld by the Council of Chalcedon (451) that the incarnate Christ was in *two* natures, divine and human. Such a doctrine, they claimed, divided Christ's person into two.

Below Image as message: emperors and churchmen used pictures to express claims and ideas. This medallion of Justinian (struck between 534 and 538, copy) celebrates Byzantium's reconquests in the west. Justinian is shown as a warrior, wielding a spear, preceded by a Victory. In reality, Justinian left the campaigning to his generals.

Right Monastery as time-machine. St Catherine's, Mount Sinai, founded by Justinian c.557, is still an Orthodox monastery today, containing icons from its first centuries and priceless manuscripts. Its plan—the church at the center of the community, surrounded by a high wall—was standard in Byzantine monasteries.

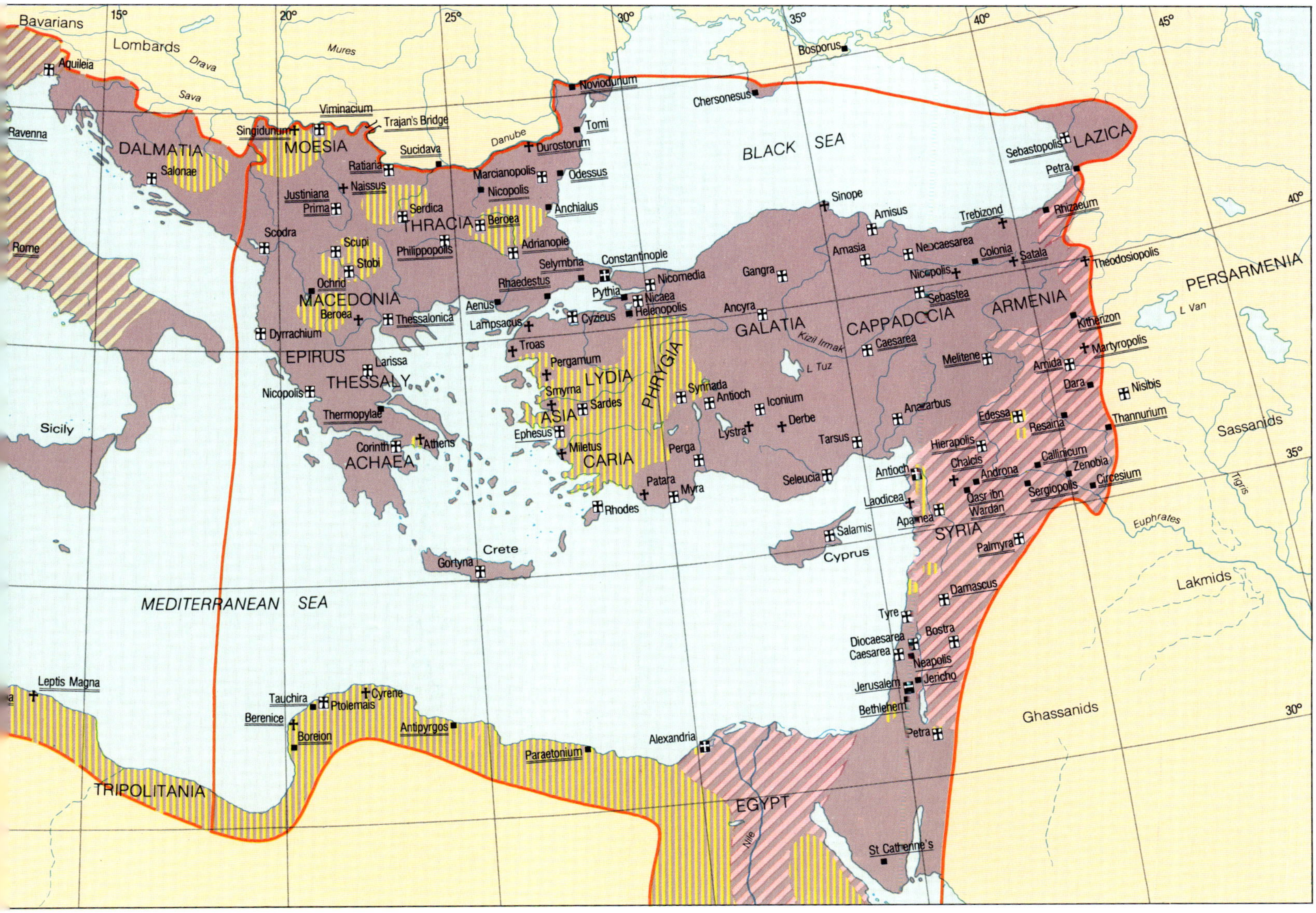

Below: Justinian's empire Justinian projected his rule as absolute and his state as Christian and united, but in reality paganism lingered in out-of-the-way areas and bitter doctrinal controversy divided the Middle Eastern provinces from those closer to Constantinople. The majority of the population in Italy, although sharing Constantinople's religious persuasion, lay beyond Justinian's reach at the time of his accession in 527. They were ruled by the Ostrogoths, who were Christian but heretics (Arians). Justinian failed to get his churchmen to agree about the true nature of Christ, but flamboyantly expanded his empire and tried to protect it with an ambitious building program. He also commissioned many churches as a means of leaving the imperial mark on his sprawling territories.

Monophysites and Chalcedonians

In the 6th century Monophysitism enjoyed widespread support in Byzantium's Middle Eastern provinces—Syria, Egypt and eastern Asia Minor. In Constantinople a luckless Syrian monk was mistaken by the mob for the Monophysite leader, Patriarch Severus of Antioch. The citizens, Chalcedonians, seized the monk and he was put to death. On the other hand, ordinary people in some regions were loth to accept communion at the hands of Chalcedonian clergy, whom they regarded with almost physical revulsion.

Justinian was the man in the middle, trying to conciliate Monophysites and Chalcedonians. For all the pomp and circumstance of rhetoric and imperial art and ritual, his leeway was limited. If he tried coercion against the Monophysites, he faced tumult in an area which lay beneath the shadow of his mightier neighbor, King Chosroes I of Persia. The great city of Antioch fell to Chosroes at a touch in 540. Monophysite fuses were short. The mere dismissal of some Monophysite bishops in Egypt in the early 540s caused an outcry of "persecution." Yet when Justinian tried to make concessions to the Monophysites, he risked the wrath of the Chalcedonian majority in Constantinople, and the destructive force of the mob, as well as the fragility of Justinian's hold on his capital, was demonstrated in the opening years of his reign. In 532 a riot in the hippodrome, provoked by dissatisfaction with the government's heavy taxation and strong-arm tactics, almost toppled Justinian from his throne. Too generous a concession to Monophysites might provoke a similar outrage. Yet the bellies of the Chalcedonian citizenry were filled with corn grown by Nile peasants, many of whom were Monophysite. Egyptian townsmen, too, tended to be of the Monophysite persuasion, and the patriarch of Alexandria was, like the patriarch of Jerusalem, Monophysite. Already in the last years of Justinian's reign, the Monophysites of Syria were forming themselves into a separate Church with its own organization.

The disputes over the nature, or natures, of Christ raged on after Justinian's death, and emperors vacillated from tolerance to persecution of the Monophysites. The Chalcedonians in the 590s sought the active support of Pope Gregory the Great. More often than not, Gregory declined invitations to involve himself in the theological wrangles of the eastern Christians.

It is difficult to tell how far the lives of ordinary Christians were affected by the disputes over the nature of Christ, or by the dissolution of the eastern empire, which had already begun before the Arabs swept in from the deserts of the south. As in the west at the time of the barbarian invasions of the 5th century, bishops effectively came to replace the representatives of the government as leaders in their local communities. Moreover, their people were increasingly attached to the honor of saints and of protective miraculous icons, a veneration especially promoted by the monks but also important for bishops, particularly if their see was at a shrine favored by pilgrims. While Justinian might regard them as state employees, permitting them to exercise certain jurisdictional powers over laymen, they were in many respects virtually autonomous and self-sufficient. Bishops of country dioceses possessed extensive landed estates while in the cities the Church drew ground rents and market tolls. Senior imperial officials such as town governors often held office for only a short time. They tended to regard their jobs as, so to speak, "cash dispensers," mulcting their charges by arbitrary levies or taking exorbitant fees and bribes. They seldom had the time, experience or inclination to reform or assist the communities which they governed. Everyday local matters such as bridge or road repairs and the regulation of markets fell to the bishop. Bishops were much more often than not honest and competent, possessing resources and a sizable staff of clerks. Many bishops were of local origin, and they tended to come from landowning families, and to have some background knowledge of estate management. Perhaps most advantageous of all was the fact that the bishop normally lived with his flock for life. As a man could be consecrated bishop from the age of 30 onwards, his episcopate could last many years, and a bishop could expect to see out the terms of several governors. He could thus face imperial officials on more or less equal terms.

Above This great church at Qalaat Seman, Syria, was built at the end of the 5th century in commemoration of St Simeon the Stylite (c.390–459). The cross-shaped church was built around the pillar which Simeon had made his home. The base of the pillar can still be seen, at the center of the church. Simeon lived atop his column for 30 years, wearing a chain and iron collar around his neck, presumably to lessen the risk of falling off. He championed Chalcedonian Orthodoxy.

Left In the opposite, Monophysite, camp is the Coptic monk shown on this limestone relief of the 6th or 7th century, hands raised in prayer. "Copt" is the Arabic distortion of "Egyptian." See below, p.169.

Right: In the shadow of Islam
During the 7th century Byzantium was transformed from a world empire bestriding three continents and four patriarchates into a regional power lodging only one patriarchate. The Arabs, united by zeal for "holy war" (*jihad*), swept into Byzantine provinces riven by theological controversies. The Christian life of the Monophysite majority carried on in the churches and monasteries under Muslim rule. It is probably no accident that Asia Minor, the region which withstood the Muslims, was predominantly Chalcedonian and thus united. After the early 8th century the Arabs seldom tried to conquer Byzantium, settling for seasonal raids into Byzantine territory. These were launched from well-organized bases southeast of the Taurus mountains. In the 9th and 10th centuries Muslim pirates added to the miseries of Byzantine provincial life. The bishops' sees were little more than glorified—and fortified—villages. The Church in the provinces was enfeebled as an institution by the relentless Muslim raids.

Not every see had its St Demetrius or its St John the Almsgiver. Nor were there many sees as prosperous or secure as Alexandria or Thessalonica. John the Almsgiver cared for refugees from the Persian invasion of Syria. There were many bishops among them. In Syria and Palestine the souls left unattended were most likely to come under the spell of "holy men." Often these were "accidental pastors," extreme ascetics in remote desert places or nooks of the countryside who attracted the curiosity, and then the pious devotion, of local folk. Such wind-blown recluses as St Symeon the Stylite had already been exciting popular veneration in the 5th century. Now there was a new motive for deliberate proselytization – the fierce rivalry between Monophysites and Chalcedonians.

John of Ephesus describes the good deeds done by the holy men and holy women in the metropolitan see of Amida (Diyarbakir) on the Upper Tigris near the Persian frontier. They braved Persian invasions and Chalcedonian oppression, feeding the poor and tending the sick "in peace or in persecution, in city or in exile." From the opposite camp, John Moschus in the early 7th century wrote in praise of Chalcedonian ascetics. While some spent many years in total silence without even seeing anyone, others competed with Monophysites. Moschus tells, for example, the edifying tale of two stylites, one Monophysite and the other Chalcedonian, who lived a mere 10 kilometers apart. They were constantly at odds with each other, the Monophysite continually trying, through messages, to win over the Chalcedonian. One day, the latter requested a portion of the Monophysite's communion bread. On receiving it, he tossed it into a boiling caldron, and soon it dissolved. Then he threw into the caldron a portion of "the holy Host of the Orthodox Church." The caldron immediately grew cold and the Orthodox host "was safe and unmoistened, and he has kept it to this day, and showed it to us when we visited him." With equal relish John Moschus relates how a stinking and bedraggled pigeon appeared sitting on the head of a pious-seeming Monophysite monk as he chanted verses in constant prayer. Other tales

of Moschus relate how Monophysites were prevented by God-sent apparitions from worshiping in the Holy Places of Jerusalem.

The fluctuations of emperors' policies created crosscurrents in this troubled situation. Whatever were their views on the merits of Monophysitism as a doctrine, emperors were anxious to secure the goodwill of those who lived near the Persian frontier. It has recently been shown that Byzantine emperors in this period were sending church decorators, precious gifts and even annual subsidies of gold to the monastery of Qartmin in the Tur Abdin. As a result of imperial benefactions, the monks might have been expected to use their considerable influence over the ordinary people of the district, to support the emperor's side and no doubt to endure all the exactions and requisitions which the presence of Byzantine frontier forces entailed.

The Council in Trullo

The Council in Trullo of 692 was attended by representatives of all the patriarchates except Rome. Since the pope refused to confirm its canons, it was not a full ecumenical council. (It is usually known as the Quinisext Council, as it supplemented the fifth and sixth councils, or as the Council in Trullo, because it met in the domed hall (or *trullus*) of the imperial palace.) The council issued strict rules for the morals and conduct of priests. For example, it repeated the ban on gaming laid down by Justinian I, and the penalties were made harsher than ever. Some canons criticized western customs, for example the celibacy of parish clergy, and reflected awareness and disapproval of differences manifest in the wayward Christians of the west. The laity was put firmly in its place, being forbidden to expound the Scriptures in public, and the use of chapels in private houses was to be strictly regulated. Priests were instructed to model their sermons on those of the Church Fathers, rather than write their own.

The Council in Trullo also attempted to bring order to the life of monks. Here, too, it repeated the legislation of the first Justinian, while making further attempts to bring monks under the supervision of the church hierarchy. A four-year probationary period in a cenobitic (communal) house must now be undergone before a man could be deemed suitable for the life of a hermit, and the authorization of the local bishop must be given. Anyone seeking to become a monk must undergo investigation: "so his profession of the life in accordance with God must be already firm, and made with knowledge and judgment"; a novice was therefore to be at least ten years old. The council still upheld an "open-door" policy in the case of those wishing to enter a monastery: "it is permitted to every Christian to choose the ascetic life and to put aside the tumultuous storms of everyday life and enter a monastery and to be shaven according to the monastic way, of whatever fault he may have been found guilty." Nonetheless, canon 42 of the council shows impatience at the ease with which dubious characters could lay claim to pious clothing: "Concerning the so-called eremites, who wear black clothes and, letting their hair grow long, wander around the towns, in touch with laymen and lay women and mocking their own profession, we decree that if they opt to shave their heads and to accept the habit of the other monks, they should settle in a monastery and be numbered among the brothers, but if not, they should be driven right out of the towns, and inhabit deserted places . . ."

Iconoclasm and after

The Council in Trullo was intended by Justinian II to codify the sprawling materials of earlier church councils and to provide for the strict observance of the Christian life. Although it was convened at a time when the Arab tide had ebbed somewhat, the underlying assumption of its canons is that barbarians will continue to harry the Christians and to disrupt society in general. Its canons form, even now, probably the most important collection of the Orthodox Church, but it is also significant as a prelude to the Iconoclast crisis which rocked the Church and empire a few decades later. For it shows the emperor keenly interested in religion, and casting a watchful eye over minute details of ritual and worship, as well as great theological issues. Even as a consensus over the nature of Christ began to emerge under the emperor's aegis within the shrunken empire, disagreements arose over matters of ritual, such as the role of icons.

A sense of duty to ensure order in the religious life of the empire, and also to minimize the disruption caused to it by barbarians underlay the canons of the Council in Trullo. A similar sense, heightened by the Arab siege of Constantinople in 717–18 and by the tremendous underwater eruption of a volcano near the island of Thera (Santorini), decided Leo III against the continued use of icons in 726. Icons now began to seem to him to be mere idols. Worship of them had, in recent years, been bringing down God's wrath upon the Byzantines, his new Chosen People, as once the golden calf had brought his wrath upon the Israelites. Leo saw it as his duty to guide his people out of error, and to preserve the Christian empire.

The Iconoclast (*eikon* = "image," *klazo* = "shatter") emperors benefited from the enfeebled condition of the Byzantine Church. The patriarch Germanus pondered over Leo III's proposal to ban the use of icons in worship during the late 720s and eventually rejected it. Leo was, however, able to convene a synod which deposed Germanus and issued a ban on icons. He was, of course, supported by some churchmen from conviction. Between 726 and 730 at least three letters were written by Patriarch Germanus, reprimanding Bishops Constantine of Nakoleia, Thomas of Claudiopolis and John of Synnada. These three bishops from Phrygia in western Asia Minor had expressed hostility towards the veneration of "handmade" objects, but there is no firm evidence of an organized "party" of Iconoclast churchmen in existence before 726. The first steps against icon worship seem to have been taken by the emperor, and the scantiness of clerical resistance to them is a mark of the emperor's power over the Church. In fact Leo III declared, "I am priest and king."

Imperial power in the Church was most fully exploited by Leo's son, Constantine V (741–75). He was more vigorous and more thorough in rooting out Iconodules (supporters of the icons) and in the physical destruction of representations of Christ

Right Photius at bay, 886 AD. Arms raised, perhaps in denial, the old man sits hunched before his accusers. The charges were trumped-up ones, brought by a court clique anxious to blacken him further, even after he had resigned his patriarchal office. The new emperor, Leo VI, had pressed him to do so. Photius had many enemies within the Church, but the young emperor anyway had no time for his strict former tutor. Leo made his own brother, Stephen, the new patriarch. Thus when the political circumstances were favorable an emperor could have his way in the Church, particularly in matters of appointments. The claims made by Patriarch Photius in his preface to the *Epanagoge* (see below, p.40) could not save him from banishment to a monastery.

Below The basilica of St Demetrius in Thessalonica is thought to have been built in the mid-5th century. It housed the saint's *ciborion*, which the citizens (if not the senior clergy) believed to be his tomb, and to which they directed their prayers. The church is large—over 60 meters long—and stands in the center of the medieval town. Its size and numerous galleries show that St Demetrius' cult was already flourishing at the time of construction. The cult, promoted by local worthies and the bishops of the city, enjoyed enormous popularity. The account of the *Miracles of St Demetrius* shows him as a healer but above all as military guardian of the citizens against the barbarians. Lying on the rim of the Balkans, Thessalonica long needed St Demetrius' protection, but not even he could prevent its sack by Muslim pirates in 904 (see map, p.35).

and the saints and apostles in human form. He wished to show that Iconoclasm was in accord with true doctrine, and tried to prove this by means of carefully constructed arguments. He convened a council of the Church for the purpose of establishing the doctrine. In 754 most of the bishops within the empire assembled at the Council of Hieria (near Chalcedon). Constantine V was the driving force behind the council, and the Definition itself, arrived at after long discussion, declared that the holy emperor had been moved by the Holy Spirit to destroy the new idolatry which the Devil had inspired. Constantine, a highly intelligent man, probably supervised the drafting of the Definition. His reign marks one of the high points in imperial power over the Church. The clauses of the Definition of 754 give a leading role in the suppression of icons and maintenance of order in worship to the imperial authorities. Anyone making an icon or worshiping it, or simply hiding it in a church or private house, "shall, if he be layman or monk, be anathematized and deemed guilty under imperial law as a foe of God's commands and an enemy of the doctrines of the Fathers."

Care was taken to prevent random destruction of the churches' furnishings. Thus if a man wished to efface images from church vessels or altar cloths, "he shall not presume to do so without the consent and knowledge of the most holy and blessed ecumenical patriarch and permission of our most pious and Christ-loving emperors, lest under this pretext the Devil dishonor God's churches." Soon after the Council of Hieria Constantine V issued an edict that all heretics would be treated as rebels against the state. Church and empire were now more nearly one than they had been in the *belle époque* of Justinian. It was at the instigation of the ruler that icon worship was restored at the Seventh Ecumenical Council in Nicaea (787), banned again by a council in 815, and finally restored by a council in 843. There were protests on the occasion of all these "U-turns," especially the first two, but imperial power always carried the day with the church hierarchy, whose more obstinate prelates could, as a last resort, be deposed.

The era following Iconoclasm was also one of bitter personal dispute among churchmen, which sprang ostensibly from the question of how former Iconoclasts should be treated. The champions of icons, very many of whom were monks, expected to play a leading role in the religious life of the empire. They objected vehemently to church appointments which disappointed their personal ambitions or offended their sense of rectitude.

When Photius was made patriarch in 858 after a career of many years spent as a government official, pursuing his scholarly interests, the imperial government, now directed by Bardas Caesar, undoubtedly hoped that Photius, as a former civil servant with unimpeachable Iconodule credentials, would be both pliable and at the same time acceptable to monks and other self-appointed guardians of Orthodoxy. But Photius proved to have an exalted view of his function as patriarch, while monks, notably those from the great house of St John of Studios, rallied to the cause of the ousted Ignatius whom he had replaced as patriarch. In the words of a contemporary saint's *Life*, monks from Studios and elsewhere "split up into many groups, just numerous enough to make true the Lord's promise that he would be with those gathered in his name, and thus scattered to various places in various lands." Photius himself described the church scene rhetorically but authentically: "Those who should have been for their people the preachers of peace, waged against each other a merciless war; those who should have set the flock an example of charity and union bred hatred. He who struck hardest was considered the best priest. The whole thing was absurd: pontiffs and priests fighting with priests and pontiffs." Their arguments raged over the validity of ordinations and depositions, but personalities and power were at the root of matters.

Church and state in the time of Photius

These events have three notable implications. First, the power of an emperor over the patriarch and the Church was extensive but not absolute, and it varied according to the political circumstances of the emperor, and according to the personalities involved. Emperors were able to depose Ignatius and Photius and to depose bishops who persistently objected to such actions, but they thereby incurred odium and the ensuing ructions brought anything but stability. Indeed, Basil I seems to

Icons and Iconoclasm

The Greek word *eikon* ("image") retains, even in its restricted sense of "religious image," the implication of a true resemblance. In the 6th and 7th centuries the cult of saints, holy persons and their images intensified. This development marks the success of Christianity in reaching ordinary people, who sought a personal, visible focus for their prayers. But it also reflects a quest for supernatural aid, as the Byzantine empire succumbed to waves of barbarian invaders and to natural disasters. Emperors themselves patronized some cults. Some of our earliest surviving icons come from St Catherine's Monastery, Mount Sinai, a foundation of Justinian I. The Council in Trullo (692) laid down rules for the painting of icons, as well as for many other aspects of worship. Justinian II's coinage reflects the council's interest in images. He was the first emperor to place an image of Christ on his coins.

In 717–18 the Arabs besieged Constantinople. Byzantines such as the later chronicler Theophanes attributed the siege's failure to "the assistance of God, through the intercession of the wholly immaculate Mother of God." However, the Arab invasions of the empire continued. Some wondered whether the icons, far from acting as lifelines to the

Below This encaustic icon, showing the Virgin Mary with the infant Christ in her lap, was probably painted in Constantinople, in the 6th or 7th century. The cult of the Virgin as special protector of Constantinople against attackers was developing then.

Left This bust of Christ, believed to date from the 6th century, is kept in St Catherine's Monastery, Sinai. Christ's right hand blesses while his left clasps a bejeweled gospel book. Christ's features are rendered in human terms, but their expression is majestic and aloof. The icon was painted at a time when disputes raged over the relationship between Christ's divine and human natures. The belief that Christ's divine nature could not be represented pictorially underlay the Iconoclasts' hostility towards icons. In this 11th-century manuscript illumination (*right*) Iconoclast churchmen are shown spearing an image of Christ. Images could take the form of ivories as well as paintings. This 10th-century ivory (*below*) was probably originally the center of a triptych. The enthroned Christ is shown above the 40 martyrs of Sebaste. Their writhing bodies, while conveying the sharpness of death in icy waters, evoke the forms of classical antiquity.

Below This gold solidus of Leo III (717–41) was struck between 720 and 732. Leo is wearing a crown topped by a cross and an imperial cloak (*chlamys*). He holds in his right hand an orb, also topped by a cross, while his left holds an *akakia*, a scroll-like bag with closed ends containing a handful of dust, and thus intimating mortality. Around the rim are Latin letters making up the inscription: "To the lord Leo, perpetual Augustus, many years." On the reverse of the coin is Leo's son, Constantine V, wearing a similar crown and cloak, and holding the same insignia. Like father, like son—piety goes with power.

saints, might not actually be incurring God's wrath: the Arab onslaught could be divine punishment for idolatry. Leo III himself had his doubts. These seem to have been crystallized by a colossal submarine eruption in the Aegean in 726. The image of Christ over the palace's Bronze Gate was removed and the cult of icons was formally banned. Those who actively resisted were persecuted. The Definition of Doctrine on Icons (754) summed up Iconoclast objections to the "confusion" and "vain fancy" of icon painters' renderings of Christ. The Definition complained that "the images of false and evil name have no foundation in the tradition of Christ, the apostles and the Fathers, nor is there a holy prayer that might sanctify an image, and so transform it from the common to a state of holiness." The only authentic "likenesses" or holy objects were, in Iconoclast eyes, the sacraments of the eucharist, churches, which had been formally consecrated by bishops, and the sign of the Cross, given by God to the first Christian emperor Constantine, which resembled in form Christ's own cross. Perhaps the insistence of Leo III and Constantine V on good church order reflected their background as military men. But their concerns had much in common with those of the 7th-century church councils—the minute prescription of conduct for priests and the virtual regimentation of worship. Individual laymen's veneration of icons could spawn abuses. If these abuses were not eradicated, God's wrath would fall upon his people, as night follows day.

The destruction of icons and persecution of their venerators seems to have been most thorough between 760 and 775. Icon veneration was rehabilitated at the Council of Nicaea in 787, only to be banned again in 815, after the empire had suffered another bout of defeats and humiliations, reminiscent of those of the early 8th century. It was finally restored by Empress Theodora in 843.

have been unable to purge the Church of all the bishops loyal to Photius after 867.

Second, the emperor's influence over appointments to bishoprics and other posts in the Church did not give him control over the monks. These could, and did, maintain a barrage of criticism against patriarchs and other churchmen of whom they disapproved. They did not usually pitch their abuse directly at emperors. However, their accusations of unjust, and uncanonical, dismissals and refusals to accept new ordinations as valid implicated the emperor and upset his direction of church appointments.

A third implication is the ambivalence of the relationship between emperor and patriarch, not only in practice but also in theory. The words of Photius, in the preface to "a revision of the ancient laws," the *Epanagoge*, which Basil I commissioned, so often quoted by historians, are less a statement of actual practice or of a generally accepted theory than a gauntlet flung down before monks, emperors and subordinates in the patriarchate alike (a parallel perhaps with the *Dictatus Papae* of Gregory VII, see pp. 66–67). "The emperor is a legal authority, a blessing common to all his subjects, who . . . behaves like an umpire making awards in a game." "The end set before the emperor is to confer benefits: this is why he is called a benefactor; and when he is weary of conferring benefits he appears, in the words of the ancients, to falsify the royal stamp and character. The emperor is presumed to enforce and maintain first and foremost all that is set out in the divine Scriptures; then the doctrines laid down by the seven holy councils; and further, and in addition, the received Roman laws." "In his interpretation of the laws he must pay attention to the custom of the state. What is proposed contrary to the canons [of the Church] is . . . not accepted as a pattern [to be followed]."

Photius's sketch of the role of the patriarch is drawn with more vigor and enthusiasm. "The aim of the patriarch is, first, to guard those whom he has received from God, in piety and soberness of life; to turn to Orthodoxy and the unity of the Church, so far as he can, all heretics . . ." "The end set before the patriarch is the salvation of the souls entrusted to him, and that they should live for Christ and be crucified to the world." The patriarch should, says Photius, be a teacher and a just judge and "he should lift up his voice on behalf of the truth and the vindication of the doctrines [of the Church] before an emperor and not be ashamed." "The patriarch alone must interpret the canons passed by the men of old, and the decrees enacted by the holy councils." "The supervision of all spiritual matters is reserved for the patriarch."

However, so long as the empire was united and strong, and the emperor rich and secure, the emperor would have the upper hand even in church affairs. Photius himself acknowledged the emperor's role in the Church when he referred to his own election as patriarch by not only the senior clergymen but also "the emperor, who with them is the upholder of the true Faith and of Christ." The emperor's special relationship with God, claimed so eloquently by Justinian, was still the centerpiece of Byzantine ideology, and solemnly recognized by churchmen.

There was no clear-cut body of canon law in the eastern Church. Law-making capacity was spread uncertainly between synods, church councils and the emperor. Synods of senior churchmen were normally called by the patriarch, but they could be convened by the emperor, and important decrees of the synod were often confirmed by him. The Church's need for an authoritative "umpire" long continued. Even in the 12th century, when new currents were beginning to run through the Church, an expert on church law, Theodore Balsamon, summed up the emperor's watchdog role thus: "Because it is a legal principle that no one shall suffer injury from another, if the patriarch himself commits sacrilege or is unorthodox or errs in any other way he shall be subject to the judgment of the emperor, the disciplinarian of the Church."

While Photius in his preface to the *Epanogoge* exaggerated the status of 9th-century patriarchs, he was near the mark when he wrote: "the peace and prosperity of the subjects in body and soul depend on the unity of mind and feeling and concord of the emperor and the archpriesthood in all things." No friction could be prolonged without serious damage to them both, as if a feud were to rage between Siamese twins. Their residences were close together, unlike those of German emperors and Roman popes, which had the Alps between them. Constantinople was a heavily policed city, and so, most probably, were such other sizable towns as the empire possessed. It may well be that expressions of religious dissent or heterodoxy were soon spotted and quelled, in the same way that malpractices of churchmen came to the attention of government officials, even though their correction was the task of the church authorities. We should not conclude from the glassily smooth surface of civic and ecclesiastical life in middle Byzantium that stagnation was "natural" or inevitable. The state and the church apparatuses were constantly on the lookout for signs of rebellion, dissent or heresy. The state was interested in ecclesiastical affairs in part out of a concern for order.

Patronage and monastic expansion

The ruling family of the late 11th and 12th centuries, the Comneni, maintained the tradition of patronage, even while deploring the increase in monasteries and extension of monastic estates. Alexius I Comnenus (1081–1118) cultivated St Cyril of Phileas, seeking his prayers for the empire's well-being and his own victories. Manuel Comnenus (1143–80) showed some signs of reversing the tradition of open-handed patronage. All the same, one should not be surprised that the occasional legislation curbing or banning new monastic foundations was ineffective, and as the state apparatus weakened in the 12th century, its ability to regulate the monasteries was still further impaired. Already in the empire's heyday, the legislation of Nicephorus II banning new monastic foundations was a dead letter, and soon repealed.

No ban could alter the fact that the monks' powers of intercession with God were highly prized. A chrysobull of Basil II issued in 978 enthuses about the monks of the Lavra on Mount Athos: "For who doubts that often what sword, bow and military might have been unable to bring

Above The church of the Dormition, Orchomenos, seen from the northeast. Built in 874, it lies about 30 kilometers northwest of Thebes and is a rare example of major church construction in Greece in the early Middle Ages. The building materials were blocks of stone from a nearby classical theater and column drums from a temple of the Graces. Byzantine builders often "cannibalized" classical structures, as did their counterparts in the medieval west.

Right The church of Qalb Louzeh, showing the west end. This basilica is one of the most beautiful churches in Syria, having very rich decoration: classical moldings jostle with crosses and other Christian symbols. Built c.460, it owes its good state of preservation to its inaccessibility. Although only about 50 kilometers from Antioch as the crow flies, it is located in hill country and in the 1970s could still only be reached by a mule ride over rough ground. In the vicinity of Qalb Louzeh are some of the "Dead Towns" of northern Syria. They are mostly difficult to reach and so have suffered only from the spoils of time, since their inhabitants deserted them at the time of the Persian invasion and the Arab conquest in the 7th century.

about, prayer alone has easily and brilliantly accomplished? . . . And if God has often been propitiated by the holy prayer of a single [monk] and has unstintingly bestowed that which was prayed for, who doubts that through 150 prayers and perhaps even more [i.e. the prayers of all the monks of the Lavra] these things will come about all the more? Therefore to every individual, and especially to the empire in its times of crisis, the prayers of good men are very beneficial and of great assistance.'' These sentiments, which resound through many other imperial donation charters, were not less heart-felt for being formulaic.

The number of houses on Mount Athos proliferated in the 11th century, and many were endowed with sprawling estates in the region adjoining the peninsula, but the mushrooming of monasteries was not confined to Athos; nor was the initiative always due to lay patrons. Charismatic holy men founded small houses, where there were facilities for those deemed spiritually worthy to live alone in a cell. Other monks founded larger houses, where all the brothers were expected to lead a communal—cenobitic—life. These were expensive to run, and large estates were needed to support them. Here, lay patronage *was* essential, and complex legal devices specifying the various rights and powers of laymen over their foundations were invented during the 11th century. The proliferation of monks and monasteries seems to be characteristic of the whole Byzantine empire in the 10th and 11th centuries.

A pure Byzantine culture?

The infirmities of their position made the Byzantines ever wary of foreigners, suspicious of their intentions towards the empire and disinclined to give them the benefit of the doubt. This attitude was not mitigated by the fact that, to a considerable extent, the Byzantines were themselves a nation of immigrants, portions of which were still unassimilated. The ruling elite could hardly be unaware of this heterogeneity. Michael III is even said to have urged Cyril to undertake a mission with Methodius to Moravia by pointing out, ''You are Thessalonicans, and everyone in Thessalonica speaks flawless Slavonic.'' Far from ''liberalizing'' educated Byzantines' outlook towards other cultures and languages, the presence of barbarism in their midst actually stiffened their resolve not to lower standards by compromise. They turned their backs on the cultures of the contemporary world around them, concentrating on conserving their own culture. This culture was itself an amorphous mélange of the Scriptures; the Church Fathers and later Christian writings such as saints' *Lives;* classical Greek historians and subsequent Greek-language histories of the world; classical Greek rhetoric and miscellaneous lore and literature, especially the works of Homer; laws and ceremonial inherited from the Roman empire. The bookends holding, as it were, these various works together were the ''purity'' of the Greek language and likewise the preservation of church doctrine undefiled by heresy or innovation. Also central to the Byzantines' living culture was their church liturgy, in which the theology and teachings of Orthodoxy received dramatic expression.

In Byzantine eyes, purity of language and purity

The houses of Mount Athos
Athos has good claim to be the true center of the Orthodox commonwealth. Founded in the 10th century, the high noon of Byzantine power, it early attracted foreigners—some for short stays, some for life. Although easily accessible by water, the peninsula offered solitude and harsh beauty. Slav and Georgian monks, living in their own monasteries there, translated Greek works into their native languages. These monasteries also acted as seminaries, sending monks back to set high monastic standards in their home countries. As the Byzantine empire decayed, Serbian, Wallachian and other Orthodox rulers offered funds and patronage for the houses on "the Holy Mountain." Athos maintained its international ties and reputation for piety in the 15th and 16th centuries, recognizing Turkish overlordship and even giving one sultan a ceremonial welcome. In return, Athos retained its status as a self-governing federation of monasteries.

Left The monastery of Dionysiou teeters at the top of a rock, more than 75 meters above the Aegean Sea, secure from earthly foes. Founded in the late 14th century by the Greek emperor of Trebizond, Dionysiou is one of the more important monasteries on Athos, having striking murals in its church and a splendid library with 804 manuscripts and over 5000 printed books.

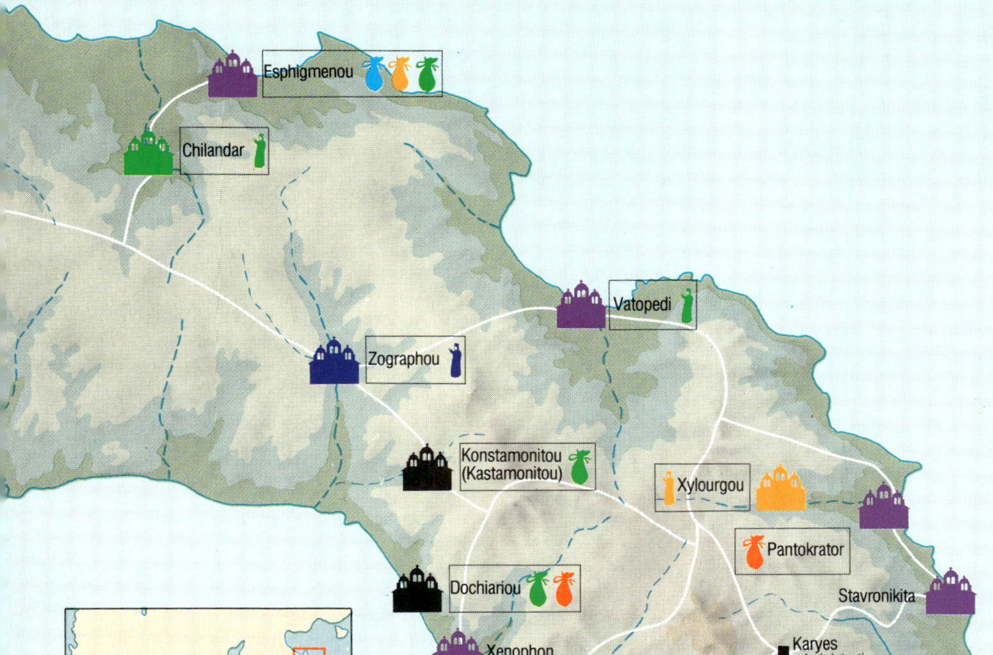
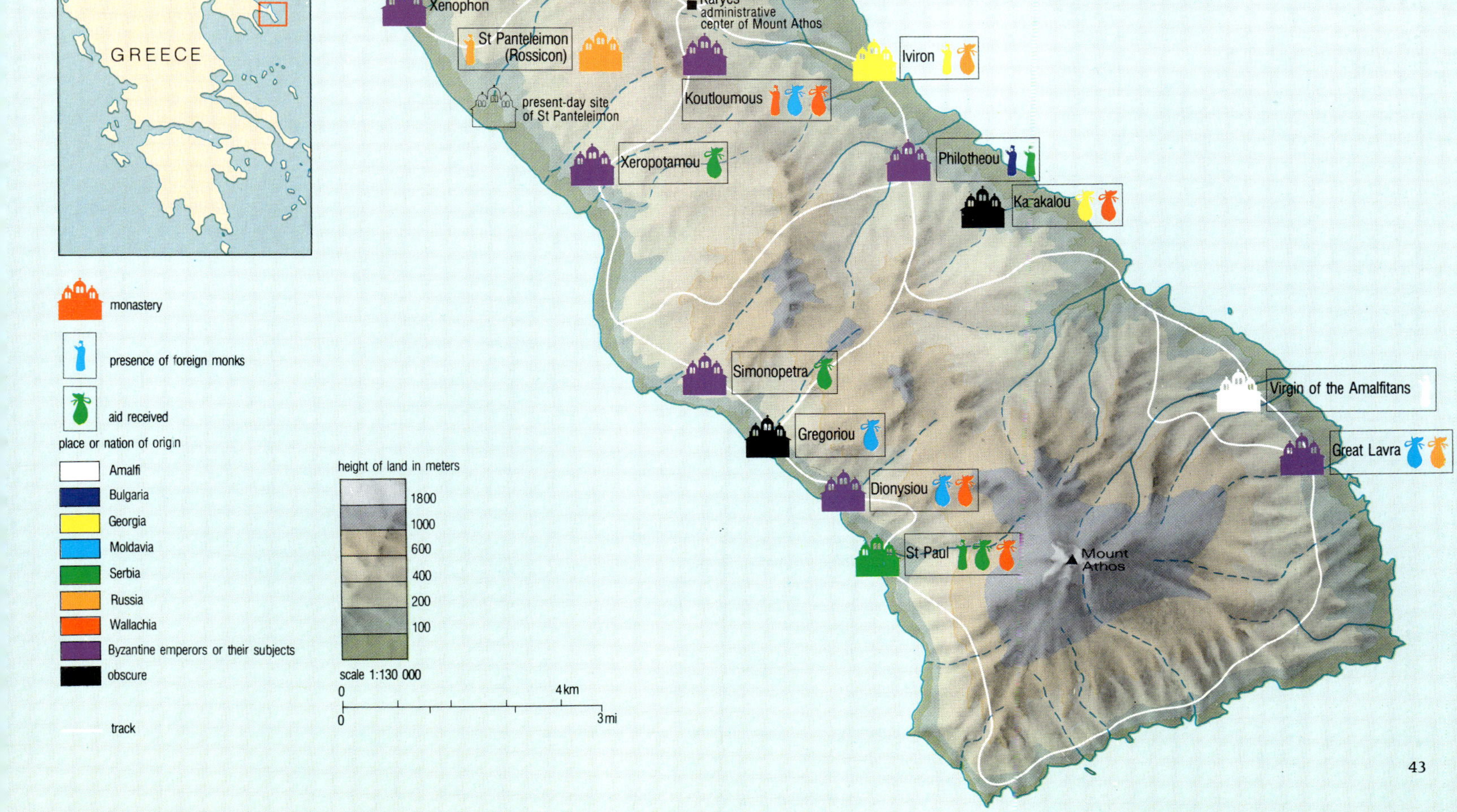

of doctrine were close-allied. It was observed of the 11th-century philosopher John Italus that, being half-Norman by origin, his pronunciation was imperfect and his writings "were liberally sprinkled with solecisms." Italus was also held guilty of heresy and, according to Anna Comnena, "he belched out doctrines foreign to church teaching; in the presence of church dignitaries he persisted in ridicule and indulged in other things of a boorish and barbaric nature." Barbarism, poor Greek and doctrinal error went together. It was therefore not solely out of concern for her style that Anna apologized for giving the Slav and Turkic names of rebel leaders on the Danube, "spoiling the tone of my history."

Similar apologies were made by a late 11th-century archbishop of Bulgaria, Theophylact of Ochrid. He wrote in letters to friends that "the Bulgarians' nature is foster father of all evil," and deplored the barbarity of the local Slav place-names. Theophylact was, in fact, probably the author of the *Life* of St Clement. In this *Life* of a Slav-born missionary, Theophylact actually makes sympathetic references to the use of Slavonic by churchmen, as being an emanation of the Pentecostal gift of tongues. Pastor grappled with mandarin in Theophylact, and perhaps in other Byzantine churchmen who found themselves among barbarians; but it can hardly be denied that the mandarin in him won. Even in his later letters, written after many years in Ochrid, he shows a distaste for "the rustic way of life" he now led.

By the end of the 11th century the Slavonic liturgy and religious literature were a *fait accompli* which the Byzantines had to accept, even after they reabsorbed Bulgaria into their territorial empire, as they did in 1018. But it was a begrudging recognition, and it is noteworthy that the *Life* of Clement is written in Greek, not Slavonic. Even for a conscientious missionary such as Theophylact, Greek was the medium of culture, and civilization was the preserve of a single city, Constantinople.

The mandarin in Patriarch Photius is more overt, and typically Byzantine. The *Life* of St Methodius depicts him, wishfully, as well disposed towards the Moravian mission, and undoubtedly he did take an interest in some mission work, when it was in strict accord with cultural decorum and with the empire's interests. His letter to Boris of Bulgaria and his pride in the work of the first Byzantine mission to the Viking Rus' in about 867 bear witness to this, but it is necessary to recall that his *Library* is one of the great monuments to Byzantine infatuation with classical antiquity. The classical scholar and rival of the ancients were the moving spirits in Photius. For him there was only one language of intellectual thought and piety—Greek. The distinguished Czech scholar V. Vavřínek has drawn attention to a letter of Photius to Catholicos Zacharias of Armenia, in which Greek is treated as the language chosen by Christ for spreading the faith: "When our Lord . . . had ascended to his Father, he entrusted the prophetical tradition to the holy apostles, enjoining them to spread it to the Greek countries and, through them, to all pagan countries." In his commentaries on Paul's Epistles, Photius discusses the role of the word in conveying concepts precisely. His assumption that Greek was the medium for precise communication is all the more telling for being unstated.

Cultural chauvinism permeates Byzantine literary works. Foreigners are mentioned usually only when they attack the empire or otherwise threaten it, the sort of activity to be expected from "barbarians." Even then, they are seldom mentioned by their contemporary names. Instead they are decked with the names of their precursors as threats to the Roman state in antiquity. Thus the Normans are disguised as "Celts," northern steppe nomads as "Scyths" and Oriental foes as "Persians"! A 10th-century eyewitness description of a campaign against Viking Rus' on the Danube is more concerned to digress on the resemblance of some of their customs and beliefs to those of the ancient Scyths than he is to relate the details of the actual campaigns which these Vikings fought. The cautious may say that all this merely denotes a penchant for classical lore, but there is surely more to it than that. The Byzantines invested the events of their present day with an air of "make-believe" such as their ceremonial and diplomatic protocols also conveyed. In a way, nothing of significance to Byzantine literati had happened for centuries, or ever could happen outside the empire's, indeed the city's, limits.

So although "apostolic" and "universalist" ideals were paraded in official Byzantine ideology, they were not dominant or influential in molding the policies of Byzantine rulers. The prevailing cultural current flowed inwards, towards court and capital, and referred backwards, towards a Christian "digest" of classical antiquity. There was little drive to take on the world, to expand outwards and civilize the barbarians or to graft their customs onto the Byzantines' own. In fact, Byzantine official interest in "the lesser breeds without the law" seldom extended beyond strategic considerations.

Monks and missions
Byzantine court culture was inward-looking, but Byzantine emperors did respond to the many initiatives of foreign rulers who sought the blessings—earthly and heavenly—of conversion to Christianity. Missions were sent as far afield as Moravia and the Lower Volga. Within the empire, the Slavs of the Greek hinterland were assimilated into Byzantine society by means of missionary work. Monks made the most devoted missionaries, some being sent by the emperor to proselytize, others going of their own accord. To wander without material encumbrances was at once the glory and the bane of eastern monasticism—it unraveled discipline, yet itinerant holy men could serve as inspiring "accidental missionaries." Individual Orthodox and Armenian monks wandered far into the Latin west, as well as through the lands of the Slavs.

BALTIC SEA
RUSSIA
to northern Russia
Pripyat
Elbe
Vistula
Oder
Prague
Sázava
MORAVIA
Vladimir, Monastery of the "Holy Mountain"
Kiev, Monastery of Caves
Dnieper
Volga
Sarkel
Khazars
Dniester
c. 860-70
c. 988
c. 920
Alans
Visegrád, St Andrew
Veszprém, Convent of the Mother of God
Pentele (Panteleimon)
Tihany, Monastery of Caves
Magyars
Drava
Sava
Oroszlámos, St George
Marosvár, St John the Baptist
Tmutarakan
Cherson
860
c. 910
BLACK SEA
PADOLIRONE
Venice
Po
Vidin
Belgrade
Sirmium, Szávaszentdemeter
863
c. 952
Danube
Dristra
Preslav
Narentans
c. 870-90
Raš
Niš
Lipljan
Sofia
SERBIA
BULGARIA
Prizren
c. 860-80
870
864-65
Skopje
Rila
Philippopolis
Constantinople
ROME
Grottaferrata
MONTE CASSINO
Dyrrachium
Ochrid
Prespa
Thessalonica
Mt Athos
Mt Olympus
ARMENIA
Amalfi
Rossano
Patirion, St Mary
c. 860-90
Sicily
Syracuse
Mt Latmos
Antioch
PELOPONNESE
Cyprus
Crete
MEDITERRANEAN SEA
Jerusalem
Alexandria
Nile
St Catherine's
10°
15°
20°
25°
30°
35°
40°
45°
50°
45°
40°
35°
30°

THE CHURCH IN THE WEST

The fall of Rome and the survival of Christianity

The fall of the Roman empire in the west brought to a number of Christians a sense that the end of the world was imminent and that it was coming at a time of high emergency for the faith. Gregory, bishop of Tours (born about 540), wrote a *History of the Franks* up to his own day, when, he claims, "churches have been attacked by heretics" and "the faith of Christ which used to glow in men's hearts has become a feeble flicker." He believed it to be of the first importance that there should be a record which set out two things: a clear statement of orthodox faith, which he gives at the beginning of Book I, and a chronological narrative which went back to the beginning of the world, so as to put recent events into their place in the divine scheme and support "those whose hearts fail them as the end of this world comes close."

The threat to the faith seemed to come in two

In this panel of the mid-11th century two Frankish noblemen are shown with upraised hands on either side of the figure of John the Baptist. He holds a representation of the Lamb of God, to which he is pointing. The hands of the noblemen indicate their acceptance of the Christian faith and their conversion from paganism, in a gesture like that of blessing.

forms among the barbarians who were invading the empire. Some were followers of Arius; their triumph would, to the eyes of catholic Christians, have meant the perversion of orthodox belief. Those who were pagans threatened to obliterate Christianity altogether in the lands they conquered.

Although Christianity had been the official religion of the empire since the days of Constantine, its hold was slight in the outlying provinces. Neither empire nor Christianity had progressed beyond the Rhine. In the west, in north Gaul where Gregory was bishop, in Britain and in Ireland there had been some conversions, but Christianity in Britain seems to have suffered gravely under the invading Saxons as they drove the Britons into Wales and Strathclyde. In Gaul the Christian population did not retreat, but stayed on, at first precariously, under the conquerors. As Gregory of Tours puts it: "The fathers respected the bishops of the Lord and listened to what they said; their sons not only refuse to listen to them, but even persecute them. The fathers gave gifts to enrich the monasteries and churches; the sons lay them waste."

The barbarians were, however, in some cases, open to conversion: if, for example, they could be persuaded that the God of the Christians was a powerful ally in war to those whose cause was just. As early as the end of the 5th century the Christian queen of the Frankish ruler Clovis "did not stop urging the king to accept the true God and give up his idols." But her words had no effect until he was involved in a battle with the Alemanni in which he suffered heavy casualties. "The king saw what was happening and his conscience troubled him." He believed that the Christian God was angry with him. He appealed to Christ, much as the emperor Constantine had done nearly two centuries earlier. He said that if he won the battle he would be baptized. Victory followed, and not only the king but more than 3000 of his soldiers too were baptized, perhaps in 496. The motive force was identical with that which had brought about Constantine's conversion, and its political consequences almost as important for the survival of Christianity in the west as that of Constantine had been for its position in the empire.

The conquests of the barbarians were often brutal; but the converted pagan rulers sometimes took an interest in the foundations of the faith they had adopted, which makes their Christianity more than the recognition of a powerful God as a backer in campaigns. Gregory of Tours describes how King Chilperic, in the late 570s, "wrote a treatise on the Holy Trinity." He said that the Trinity should be understood to be only one God, the Father the same as the Son, the Son the same as the Father, and the Holy Spirit the same as the Father and the Son. It seemed to him improper that God should be called a "person" like an ordinary man. Gregory himself tried to explain to him that this could not be the case. Only the Son was incarnate, and so he could not be the same as the Father. He wanted Chilperic to understand that the word "person" was being used in a spiritual sense. Chilperic was very angry and said that he would talk to wiser men.

Where the conquerors were Arians, their attitude to Catholic Christians was sometimes violent. Gregory describes how the Vandal King Trasamund began a persecution of the Christians, "and tried to compel the whole of Spain to join the wicked Arian sect by torture and by various forms of murder."

Perhaps the most generalized effect of the conquests was the one to which Gregory refers at the beginning of his *History*: the cultural and administrative decline of the old Roman system. Gaul had its educated men—Gregory himself and, among his contemporaries, Venantius Fortunatus, a learned Gallic bishop and poet who had been educated in imperial Ravenna and who became a focus of Roman culture at the Frankish court—but they were few and growing fewer. The Christianity of the empire had been very much a Roman Christianity, and this decay of old standards and the loss of a Roman flavor in things meant that it had to alter its assumptions, not doctrinally, or administratively, but culturally and politically.

Invasions, migrations and missions

St Paul's decision to go out to the Gentiles and convert them to faith in Christ was one of the decisive points in the history of Christianity. Within the Roman empire, as long as it lasted, there were conditions which fostered the further spread of the faith. Christian soldiers took their beliefs to the edges of the empire. With the breakdown of empire, and the retreat or disappearance of many Christian populations, something more purposeful was needed. In 600 Europe was heathen from what is now Belgium to the Balkans, but after a time salvage became repair, and repair became fresh enterprise, and something new began to grow out of the ruins. Christianity was slowly transformed from a Mediterranean to a European religion.

Catholics, heretics and barbarians in the late 6th century
The map shows the extent of the Arian incursions into the Christian Roman empire during the 6th century. The invasions of the Visigoths and Lombards were able to penetrate where the empire was strategically weakest; the result was a political rather than a religious change of color, in the sense that the conquered peoples were not necessarily converted as individuals to the Arian viewpoint. The kingdom of the Franks is another matter. Here Christianity made a real difference of commitment in people's lives, as it did in the Celtic lands.

Sometimes this was a natural growth, sometimes a deliberate planting by missionaries. We have seen how in some cases the Christians of the conquered lands converted the pagan barbarians and were able to give them the benefit of their clerical and administrative skills. The mission-bishops, too, sat down with the elders of the tribal courts and helped them to put their customs into written law codes and adapt them to the requirements of a Christian community.

Pope Gregory the Great took an active interest in ensuring the survival and expansion of Christianity on the edges of Christendom. He looked with an eye of pastoral concern to the welfare of the slaves which were purchased in the outermost empire. In a letter to Candidus, a priest who was being sent on papal work to Gaul, he instructed him to try to buy English slaves so that they could be given to God and brought up in monasteries. Gregory knew that such boys would be pagans and therefore unbaptized, and so he tells Candidus to make sure that there is a priest with them, so that if they become ill before they are received into their monasteries they may be baptized at once and their salvation assured.

The year after he wrote this letter, in 596, Gregory sent a party of 40 monks to travel from Italy up the Rhône valley to Tours, Paris and England. Gregory chose as their leader Augustine, trained in the *familia*, or episcopal household, of the bishop of Messina and well briefed for his task by Gregory himself. "Do not allow the hardships of the journey or the evil tongues of men to stop you," he wrote in a letter of encouragement and support. "Although I cannot labor beside you, yet because I long to do so I shall enter into the joy of your reward."

The Church in England

Gregory's idea of mission was above all pastoral; he did not want the pagans of the empire to remain in their sin. It was also gentle and unforceful. Bede describes in his *Ecclesiastical History* how Ethelbert of Kent received Augustine's party in a friendly spirit because he had a Frankish wife, Bertha, daughter of the Merovingian king of Paris, who was a Christian. She had a bishop at court whom her parents had provided to be a support to her. Augustine and his missionaries were given somewhere to live, where they "began to imitate the way of life of the apostles." "They were constantly engaged in prayers, vigils and fasts. They preached the word of life to as many as they could." Some of the people were so impressed by their example, "their simple and innocent way of life and the sweetness of their heavenly teaching," that they were baptized. The king, too, was converted in this way.

The new Church in England needed a liturgy as a basis for its services. Gregory suggested that Augustine should select from the patterns of worship of the Gallican Church and any others known to him those elements which he thought best for English use. Augustine was to introduce them gently and "let the minds of the English grow accustomed to them." This policy of mild and gradual introduction of Christian practices was extended to the use of former pagan temples as churches, and the substitution of one ceremony for another. The temples of the English nation should not be destroyed, Gregory wrote to Augustine. "Let the idols in them be destroyed, but let the temples be washed with holy waters and altars built with relics set up in them . . . so that the people . . . may the more readily resort to such familiar places and, removing error from their hearts, come to know and adore the true God, and since they have become accustomed to . . . sacrifices to devils, let some other ceremony be substituted on such occasions as the days of Dedication or the nativities of those holy martyrs whose relics are deposited there . . . No longer shall they offer beasts to the Devil, but kill cattle for eating to the glory of God, returning thanks to the Giver of all gifts for their provisions. If they are allowed some outward indulgences, they may the more easily accept the inward comforts of the grace of God. For it is surely impossible to erase everything from their obstinate minds at one stroke."

Gregory encouraged Augustine to allow the young clerks in minor orders in his *familia* at Christchurch, Canterbury, to marry if they wished. The plan was to train a native clergy in the *familia* in the usual Roman way, so that the English Christians might maintain the religion for themselves.

Left A 15th-century conception of Augustine of Canterbury (d. 604 or 605) from a stained-glass window at St Mary's, Stowting, Kent. Augustine led the mission sent by Pope Gregory the Great to convert the Anglo-Saxons to Christianity. He is shown here serene in late medieval episcopal vestments, but the mission itself was a work of some courage and required an energetic and pioneering spirit. Augustine was apparently a practical man rather than a scholar, but he dealt with local pagan prejudice with intelligence, sensitivity and common sense.

Right The Celtic Christians had developed an art of high elegance and sophistication. This page from the Lindisfarne Gospels (c.696–98) shows St Mark the Evangelist at work, with his symbol the lion above. The lion is blowing a trumpet to represent the Word he is uttering and carrying the Gospel itself, as is the human figure below. The symbolism is clear and simple but powerful, with the characteristic Celtic tangle of lines and beasts.

Above This earliest known surviving portrait of Gregory the Great (c. 540–604) was painted in the 7th century. Jerome (c.342–420) is on the left and Augustine of Hippo (354–430) in the center. Gregory's inclusion with them is a notable early recognition of his work as a Father of the Church.

imago leonis

Christian land
Muslim land
Christian mission with person and date where known
important place visited by Christian mission
invasions of the 9th and 10th centuries
Norse
Saracen
Magyars
political boundaries c.900
NORWAY
SWEDEN
DENMARK
BALTIC SEA
NORTH SEA
SCOTLAND
IRELAND
WALES
ENGLAND
Iona
Columba 563
Bangor
Dublin
Lindisfarne
Aidan, Cuthbert 635-64
Wilfrid, Willibrord 678, 690
Willibrord
Malmesbury
London
Glastonbury
Canterbury
Boniface 716
Utrecht
Ewalde
Suidbert
Hildesheim
Magdeburg
Corvey
Erfurt
Fulda
Aachen
Mainz
Trier
Elbe
Oder
Vistula
Rouen
Reims
Paris
Seine
Columban 590
EAST FRANKISH KINGDOM
Kilian
Rhine
Regensburg
Danube
BOHEMIA
AUSTRIA
Vienna
Salzburg
Reichenau
Luxeuil
WEST FRANKISH KINGDOM
Loire
Tours
Poitiers
ATLANTIC OCEAN
Gallus 614
Chur
CARINTHIA
HUNGARY
Drava
Sava
UPPER BURGUNDY
Lyon
ITALY
Aquileia
VENICE
CROATIA
Po
Bobbio
Ravenna
Rhône
Garonne
PROVENCE
Arles
SERBIA
Methodius 869
PAPAL STATES
Methodius 867
Rome
Naples
León
LEÓN
NAVARRE
Ebro
Duero
Corsica
Sardinia
Toledo
Tagus
CALIPHATE OF CORDOBA
Lisbon
Balearic Islands
Cordoba
Seville
Carthage
Sicily
MEDITERRANEAN SEA
scale 1:12 000 000
0
600km
0
400mi
10°
5°
0°
5°
10°
15°
20°
25°
60°
55°
50°
45°
40°
35°

Above This fine ivory cover (c. 870), probably from the Prayer Book of Charles the Bald, shows the psalmist David entering the House of the Lord. The hand of God appears from the cloud above and a lively army cavorts below. Style, wit and iconography reflect contemporary Frankish miniature painting.

Left: Invasions, migrations and missions from the 7th to the 10th century
The movement of the Christian missions ran broadly counter to that of the invasions of Europe from north, east and south. From Ireland came the Celtic missionaries into Wales and Scotland and mainland Europe. From northern England missionaries went out into the low countries and Scandinavia. From the great monasteries of central Europe and from other centers, missions drove east in the face of the invaders, and from Rome too there was a move east into Magyar and Byzantine lands. The Muslims were left largely untroubled in the south. The bulk of western Christian effort was directed to the conversion of northern Europe.

Augustine's was not the only attempt to convert England. The Celtic monks from Ireland began rather earlier. Ireland had maintained its Christianity since the conversion of the country in the 5th century by Palladius and Patrick. There had been no interruption by invasion, although the Irish were far from isolated and had contacts with the Copts and with the Greek world. The Irish tradition placed great emphasis upon the idea that this life was a journey to heaven. The Irish monks who converted northern England set sail in a pilgrim spirit, and preached where God brought them to land.

When Oswald of Northumbria, who had been baptized and educated at the Irish Celtic monastery of Iona, won back Northumbria in 635, the monastery of Lindisfarne under Aidan became the center of Celtic Christianity in the north. Aidan himself spent much of his life on preaching journeys in Northumbria. Irish customs were followed there; the Irish style of manuscript illumination was copied. The Celts' small rectangular churches with a space at the end for an altar were easier to build than the basilicas of southern Europe and they set the style for much later English church building.

Tension arose between Augustine's flock and the Celtic Christians over the date of Easter and the shape of the clerical tonsure. The "Roman" party even refused to accept the validity of Irish ordinations. By the mid-7th century reconciliation became essential. In 664 King Oswy convened a synod at Whitby. He heard both sides of the case and decided that Rome was in the right. The result was a triumph for the Roman side. The tribal, monastic bishops of the Celtic tradition were replaced by a continental episcopate based on geographical, not tribal, division of sees. Five years later the Greek monk Theodore arrived from Rome to be archbishop of Canterbury. He brought with him an African monk, Hadrian, who became abbot of St Augustine's abbey in Canterbury. Theodore traveled England visiting the kings and bringing the bishops under his authority. He reorganized the sees of England, grouped under Bishop Wilfrid at York and Bishop Chad at Lichfield. (The division into the provinces of York and Canterbury was not established until 735.)

The conversion of Germany

The conversion of Germany was largely achieved by missionaries from England. When Bishop Wilfrid of York was sailing to Rome to appeal against the division of his bishopric, he was shipwrecked on the coast of Friesland and spent the winter preaching there. More conversions were brought about by Willibrord, another monk from Northumbria who had visited Ireland and been fired there with the missionary zeal which had brought the Irish to England. He was sent to the continent by Egbert, a priest whom Bede describes as "living a life of exile in Ireland . . . so that he might reach his heavenly fatherland" and who had himself planned to be a missionary and to perform "the apostolic task of carrying the word of God . . . to some of those nations who had not yet heard it. He knew," says Bede, "that there were very many peoples in Germany from whom the Angles and Saxons who now live in Britain derive their origin . . . There are also many other nations in the same land who are still practicing heathen rites." He was prevented from going in person "by divine revelations and interventions."

When Willibrord arrived with his party, they visited the duke of the Franks; he received them well and gave them the support of his royal authority, so that they could preach unmolested. One of the workers with Willibrord was Boniface. He had been a child oblate, who had entered monastic life by his own choice and against his father's will. He was made a priest when he was over 30, in order to become a missionary. In 722 he left Willibrord and visited Hesse and Thuringia, where he won over large numbers to Christianity. Then he traveled to Rome, to take an oath of obedience to Gregory II and to be consecrated bishop so that he could ordain priests among his converts. Under the protection of Gregory II and Charles Martel and his son Pepin the Short he went on to the Saxons and the Frankish Church, where he preached and founded monasteries and pressed for reform where the Frankish Christians had fallen into laxity.

He died in 754 at the hands of a gang of pagans. He left in the mind of Pepin the Short the idea that mission was important, but Pepin went on to convert by the sword.

EAST AND WEST DRIFT APART

In the west, great changes had to be accommodated after the fall of the Roman empire. The east saw no such direct break with the past. In his awareness of continuity with and direct descent from the Early Church, and in the vagueness of his use of the term "Church," which he uses indiscriminately of patriarchates, peoples and cities such as Corinth, Theophylact of Ochrid (archbishop c. 1090–1125) probably represents many unfanatical, devout churchmen of the east. It is above all to longstanding custom and apostolic tradition that Theophylact appeals. For all his moderation of tone, and general desire for humility and tolerance, Theophylact is adamant that he is following the practices and the spirit of the Early Church. To pious Byzantines, the Early Church seemed comprehensible and immediate, even if it had had no room for an emperor. Simple facts of geography and language, so obvious that we often overlook them, lay behind this outlook.

The New Testament was written in Greek comprehensible to any educated Byzantine, and most of the recipients of the letters of St Paul lived in the Byzantine world, in Thessalonica, Corinth, Ephesus, Philippi and Colossae. These and other places were the scenes of many of the Acts of the Apostles. Tradition, to the Byzantines, meant a lifeline to the age of the first miracles and of the book of Revelation, written by St John on the island of Patmos, where in 1088 the monk Christodoulos founded the monastery of St John the Divine. Tradition held the key to truth. Change or innovation separated one from practices known to the apostles or from doctrines laid down by the Fathers in councils of the whole Church. So for eastern Christians change meant schism from the Early Church.

Authority in the Church: east and west

In east and west alike Christianity took root in towns and cities first, and only afterwards in the countryside. By the middle of the 5th century it was usual for a group of Christians in a city to have a bishop at their head, with his *familia* of clergy. The *familia* was modeled on the household of a noble Roman. In it the priests and deacons of the diocese were trained. Their work covered the city itself and some territory around it: normally a small area in Italy and in those parts of the east where there were numerous cities close together, and a larger area in the western parts of Europe where there were few cities. It was already usual for sees to be grouped in provinces, with a metropolitan bishop in charge of the whole.

Within this structure bishops exercised authority over their own clergy and people. When a see fell vacant a new bishop was chosen by the clergy, nobles and people who had lost their bishop and the metropolitan bishop supervised the election. The metropolitan bishop also summoned meetings of the bishops of the province and at these synods he and his bishops discussed points of doctrine which were causing difficulty locally, or problems of discipline, and then he made a ruling. Such rulings, the "canons" of synods and councils, set standards and made rules by which the Church was governed.

It was of the first importance that these local units should be one with other local bodies of Christians, so that the Church remained one and did not become divided. This was achieved in part by a still higher level of unification, of provinces under patriarchates. The patriarchs held sees in cities of outstanding importance in the world, where the apostles had preached: Antioch, Jerusalem, Alexandria in the east and Rome in the west – with the addition of Constantinople whose position in the empire gave it a claim to be the New Rome. General councils had been held in the first Christian centuries to help preserve unity and to make it possible to arrive at a definitive formulation of points of doctrine.

The Church remained primarily a conglomeration of local communities, administering themselves, but the trend towards centralization which was necessary if unity was to be preserved also tended to encourage the emergence of a single central authority in the Church. In the west the bishop of Rome naturally emerged as leader, as the head of the only western apostolic see. In general, churchmen in the eastern patriarchates were prepared to recognize that some special dignity belonged to the Roman pope, as being the occupant of the old imperial capital, and a longstanding and articulate authority on doctrine and Church discipline, but they regarded an ecumenical council, presided over by the emperor, as the supreme body, representative of all the Church. It alone was qualified to enunciate doctrine and to adjudge other matters of outstanding importance to the Church. Such had been the seven ecumenical councils at which all five patriarchs, or their representatives plenipotentiary, had been present. At the seventh, in 787, Iconoclasm had been renounced and anathematized.

From at least the 9th century onwards, eastern churchmen showed enthusiasm for the concept of the Church as a "pentarchy." Acting as a college, the five patriarchs could preserve the true faith and, in the event of major controversy, offer a redefinition. Prominent among the advocates of this ideal were Patriarch Nicephorus I (806–15) and Abbot Theodore of the monastery of Studios at Constantinople. Their concern with doctrine was stimulated by the Iconoclast controversy, and Theodore in particular proved ready to seek the judgment of the Roman pope when he was dissatisfied with the policy of the emperor; but not even Theodore regarded the pope as more than the senior patriarch, whose word was the weightier because he was beyond reach of the emperor's coercive powers. Theodore referred repeatedly to

View from the fortress-like monastery of St John the Divine, Patmos, of the surrounding village. The houses are mostly modern, but built in the traditional manner. Walls are painted white and windows are small. The flat roofs serve to collect the rare and precious rainwater. The monastery was founded by Christodoulos in 1088 and received full exemption from taxes and other

state charges from Emperor Alexius I Comnenus. These privileges were renewed by later emperors up to the end of the Byzantine empire. The monastery very soon became famed for its library, and remains so to this day. A school of theology, founded in 1669, still flourishes.

"the five-headed body of the Church," by which he clearly meant the five patriarchates acting in concert. No single patriarchate was presumed to have a monopoly of truth.

The apostolic succession

Nicephorus did not merely lay stress on collegiality. He also assumed that all five patriarchates had "apostolic" origins. "It is an old law of the Church that, when doubts and controversies appear in the Church, they are resolved and settled by an ecumenical council with the consent and approval of the illustrious patriarchs who occupy the apostolic thrones." In contrast, the papacy was ready to acknowledge only Antioch and Alexandria as "apostolic" besides Rome itself, in that they too had had close associations with St Peter.

However, the idea of apostolicity, of patriarchs "inheriting" their sees from apostles as if by a legal right of succession, was not central to eastern thought. Many Byzantine ecclesiastical writers followed Origen, who held that, essentially, St Peter was merely the first "believer." It is open to others to imitate Peter, and to believe. They, too, will then receive the keys to the kingdom of heaven. A 12th-century Greek writer in southern Italy stated: "The Lord gives the keys to Peter and to all who resemble him, so that the gates of the kingdom of heaven remain closed for the heretics yet are easily accessible to the faithful." Other Byzantine writers regarded bishops as the teachers and guardians of the faith in each community and therefore as continuing the task enjoined by Christ to Peter. Gregory of Nyssa's view that Christ "through Peter gave to the bishops the keys of heavenly honors" was shared by many Byzantines through the ages.

In the 12th century Nicholas of Methone wrote concerning the "grace" of episcopacy. He argued that, after being conferred on an individual at his consecration, it remained with him even if he resigned his see. His argument rested on the idea of the apostolic succession, whereby the grace of episcopacy was transmitted from generation to generation. Such ideas continued to be echoed, and indeed to be reinforced, in the last centuries of Byzantium. The very existence of a protracted divergence of opinions on the basis of authority within the Church indicates that the Orthodox hierarchy was not especially tight-knit, and that an eastern patriarch's authority was not as all-embracing or precisely formulated as that of a Roman pope. In the west the pope remained for many centuries the ultimate authority in the Church. Supreme among the popes who exercised their authority in this way were Gregory VII, of whose reforms we shall hear more later, and Innocent III (1198–1216), an autocrat who did much to enhance papal power, called two crusades, set up the Inquisition of heretics in the south of France, and hedged himself about with lawyers.

There was, however, a movement within the Church of the west in the later Middle Ages which argued that papal power could not be legitimately exercised without consultation, that councils were still a necessary part of ecclesiastical government and doctrinal decision-making. Innocent himself called a council in 1215, whose pronouncements were held to have the force of those of the early councils. The "conciliar" movement did much to create a hierarchy of higher clergy and to limit the direct power of the pope – and to reinforce the principle established in the 11th century that he must be chosen by the cardinals as well as by the Christian community. The movement began in response to a specific difficulty: the repudiation of Urban VI in 1378 by the majority of the cardinals who had elected him. They elected a rival pope, Clement VII. The affair revealed the lack of an organ of government in the Church capable of deciding a disputed election. It raised urgently the question: where does ecclesiastical authority reside? In the whole people of God, as Ockham said? In the pope, as Giles of Rome said? Or in the college of cardinals?

A vast literature was produced by the controversy. Nicholas of Cusa (1401–64) says that a general council is the only adequate representative of the universal Church, and rules the whole Church. It may depose the pope, as well as binding him by its decrees. Jean Gerson (1363–1429) sees the general council as the supreme authority in the Church, not as representing the whole body of the faithful, but because it is an assembly of the whole episcopate, who, he believed, can control and judge the pope in exceptional circumstances, when he is endangering the *res publicae ecclesiae* by his actions. Opposed to this view were those who sought to make the college of cardinals, in connection with the pope, the supreme governing body of the Church, above laity and episcopate alike.

Schism

To the Greek east it seemed self-evident that the patriarch of New Rome (Constantinople) should exercise an appellate jurisdiction parallel to that of Old Rome in the west, and should be accorded a place of honor after the pope. The Fourth Ecumenical Council at Chalcedon (451) passed a resolution on this, in the absence of the Roman legates. Canon 28 offered a compromise formula which placed Constantinople almost, but not quite, on a par with Rome: "The Fathers rightly granted privileges to the throne of Old Rome, because it was the imperial city, and 150 most religious bishops [at the Second Ecumenical Council, 381 AD], having the same considerations, gave equal privileges to the most holy throne of New Rome, justly judging that the city, which is honored with the presence of the emperor and the senate and enjoys equal privileges with the old imperial Rome, should, in ecclesiastical matters also, be magnified as she is and rank next after her." This declaration is bland and leaves much unclear. It omits any mention of the papal claim to be the sole successor to St Peter. This canon was rejected by Pope Leo the Great, but it remained valid in the eastern Church. Later attempts were made to find a generally acceptable definition of the respective roles of the two leading patriarchal sees. At the end of the Acacian Schism between Rome and the east (484–518) it was agreed that "the Catholic faith was kept inviolate by the apostolic see." But this acknowledgment of the papal role in safeguarding doctrine never achieved the status of a canon of an ecumenical council. Only a generation later, Justinian was proclaiming the "oneness" of Church and empire, and expecting compliance even in matters concerning doctrine from the papacy.

The last indisputably "ecumenical" council, attended and subsequently ratified by delegates of all five patriarchates, was that of Nicaea in 787, but papal envoys attended the council of 861, which confirmed the deposition of Ignatius and the election of Photius as patriarch. Pope Nicholas I disavowed his envoys, and formally pronounced Photius to be deposed, upholding the cause of Ignatius. Although it was at first only a matter of

Left St Luke reading by lamplight: an illumination from a 10th-century Byzantine gospel book. The style does not purport to be "realistic." The artist is less concerned with capturing the appearance of a man sitting at a table than with presenting St Luke (or other apostles or saints) in familiar guise, writing his name above his head for good measure. The decoration of manuscripts was confined to a narrow range of texts, such as the Gospels, the Psalter and a few works of the Church Fathers. Even plain books, lacking any illuminations, were very expensive.

ecclesiastical discipline, the case broadened out into a controversy over the nature and extent of papal authority, and Patriarch Photius accused the western Church of errors in the liturgy and condemned the use in the west of the *filioque* clause in the Creed as being an unwarranted and heretical addition. A circular letter from Photius, paying special attention to the *filioque,* was sent to the other eastern patriarchs.

In 907 the forceful and devious patriarch Nicholas (901–07; 912–25) denounced the marriage which the emperor Leo VI proposed to contract with his mistress Zoe "of the coal-black eyes" (Carbonopsina). Zoe had borne to Leo a male heir; Leo was anxious to marry her, and make the child legitimate. This would, however, be Leo's fourth marriage and Nicholas refused to sanction it. For third marriages, let alone fourth, were contrary to canon law. As the patriarch later wrote in a tract: "If the lawgiver [i.e. the emperor] is the first himself to make nonsense of what his own law prescribes by scorning its command, is it not evident that he encourages the public to transgress the law rather than to observe it?" Small wonder, then, that Leo VI looked to the other four patriarchs of the Church for support, setting greatest store by the message of approval of a fourth marriage which he received from the pope.

It was upon the news of the approach of "representatives and writs issuing a saving dispensation from the pope from Old Rome" that Leo moved against Nicholas. He had him exiled and deposed, and the papal emissaries confirmed the deposition of Nicholas and installation of his successor, Euthymius. Nevertheless Nicholas emerged from the affair as a martyr. He enjoyed the backing of many churchmen, and he was reinstated as patriarch in 912. The schism within the Byzantine Church between Nicholas's supporters and the supporters of the now deposed Euthymius

Below A money bag for Christ. Christ sits between Emperor Constantine IX Monomachus and Empress Zoe in this mosaic in St Sophia, Constantinople. Constantine's hands cradling a full bag recall the fact that in the 1040s he made an enormous donation to St Sophia. This display of his piety and generosity was all the more necessary because he owed his crown not to inheritance but to the fancy of Empress Zoe, who took him as her third husband. The mosaic originally showed Zoe and her first husband, Romanus III Argyrus (1028–34). The latter's memory was, in effect, purged by the new head of Constantine IX.

continued until 920, when a "Tome of Union" solemnly reconciled the two parties and concluded with a series of resounding anathemas: "All that has been written or spoken against the holy patriarchs Ignatius, Photius, Stephen, Anthony and Nicholas – anathema!" The emperor was to be bound by church canons on matters of morality, without acknowledgment of any flexibility required through *raisons d'état*.

While the "Tome of Union" formally ended the strife between Byzantine churchmen, its anathemas were at variance with the dispensation for third and fourth marriages made by the papacy. The pope's name had been absent from the Constantinopolitan diptychs since Nicholas's reinstatement as patriarch in 912. Both Romanus I Lecapenus and Nicholas seem to have been keen to restore correct relations with Rome – Romanus from a desire for a counterweight to his untrustworthy patriarch, and Nicholas from a need to guard his flanks against fanatical foes lingering in the Church.

The papal coronation of Otto I as "emperor" in 962 raised fresh complications, but once Otto had spent his strength in trying to capture Bari and overrun other parts of Byzantine Italy, he proved willing to scale down his initial demand for a Porphyrogenita and to accept as bride for his son, Otto II, Theophano, the niece of the reigning emperor, John Tzimisces. Later the Byzantine government was uneasy at Otto II's incursion into Byzantine Calabria and at the extent of the Saxon emperors' attempts to take Rome in hand. Otto III's bid to tighten his control by making his cousin, Bruno, pope seems to have caused particular concern to the imperial government.

It was not, however, the relationship between pope and emperor which principally offended Byzantine churchmen or ideologists. Papal claims resting on the "Donation of Constantine" probably made little impression on the Byzantine government or Church, while Saxon pretensions to be "Roman" emperors seldom needed to be taken as a serious threat to Byzantium's claim to be *the* successor state to imperial Rome. What caused the deterioration in relations between Byzantium and the papacy in the 11th century? The deeper cause may well have been the drastic amplification in the west of papal claims concerning the rights and duties of the papal see.

The reformist zeal of the emperors Otto III, Henry II and Henry III brought to Rome a new breed of churchmen, trained (usually as monks) north of the Alps, tempered by the stricter discipline of the houses in Lorraine and, in some cases, of Cluny, and eager to impose the standards of the cloister on the papal curia. They were impatient with the slackness and corruption which still prevailed there. Working relations between the papacy and Byzantium had required some measure of worldly compromise. Odilo, abbot of Cluny, wrote unsympathetically of Theophano, the Byzantine wife of Otto II, and made dark (and false) insinuations concerning a plot which involved Theophano, John Philagathus "and other toadies" against other members of the regency during the minority of Otto III. Other reform-minded churchmen showed disapproval of the Byzantine government's use of bribery at the papal court, and regarded it as having a corrupting influence on the papacy. However the immediate cause of estrangement seems to have been the introduction into the Creed used in Rome of the *filioque* clause.

Differences over the *filioque* clause

The "Nicene" Creed, as revised at the Council of Constantinople (381 AD), stated that the Holy Spirit proceeded "from the Father." Some time in or before the 7th century Spanish churchmen well read in Augustine took to adding the words "and from the Son" (in Latin *filioque*). The addition was adopted in parts of Francia and Germany, and northern churchmen introduced it at Rome. The papacy did not positively endorse the *filioque* clause, but in the 860s it rejected Photius's claim that the addition was theologically unsound. Only in the opening years of the 11th century does the papacy seem to have begun regularly to use this supplemented version of the Creed. The initiative then seems to have come from German churchmen. The supplemented version was solemnly sung at the coronation of Henry II as emperor in Rome in 1014. It was probably used in the declaration of faith sent by Pope Sergius IV to Constantinople in 1009, in the routine "systatic" letter sent by new patriarchs to their confreres.

An indication of awareness that something was amiss comes in 1024. The Constantinopolitan patriarch wrote to the pope proposing a formula of agreement: that "with the consent of the Roman bishop the Church of Constantinople shall be called and considered universal in her own sphere as that of Rome is in the world." This studiously ambivalent formula was acceptable to Pope John XIX and to the papal curia. It seems to have been the prominent reformer, William of Bénigne, who objected most vehemently. He wrote a letter to Pope John, reproving him for his readiness to share out his universal, indivisible authority. John thereupon revoked his agreement to the formula. The episode suggests that the difference over the *filioque* had soon reopened other issues, such as authority in the Church, and that Byzantium was now trying to paper them over. The formula proposed by the Constantinopolitan patriarch would presumably have comprised a tacit agreement to differ over the validity of the *filioque* clause in the Creed. Significantly, the opposition came not from Roman clergymen but from northerners, intent on clarity and truth as they saw it, and impatient with the politics of compromise and respect for longstanding conventions, which they deemed corrupt.

If Byzantium took no known steps towards an agreement with Rome after the 1020s, this can hardly be the result of difficulties in communications. The full conversion of Hungary to Christianity and the ebbing of the Muslim pirate menace made travel between east and west safer in the mid-11th century than it had been since the 7th century. Byzantine church and government leaders were probably content to wait for the storm from beyond the Alps to abate, and for the papal curia to resume its stance of accommodation, which John XIX's initial response to the compromise formula had intimated. There was, moreover, another element in the calculations of Byzantine diplomacy. Up to the early 1040s the Byzantine state was hopeful of reconquering Sicily from the Muslims and consolidating its authority over southern Italy. Had the various campaigns which it launched succeeded, its ability to put pressure on the papacy to reach an accommodation, or simply to ensure general cooperation, would have been powerfully enhanced.

New directions in the papacy

If Byzantium temporized, the west fermented. Norman adventurers, some of them former mercenaries employed by Lombard princelings or the Byzantine army, began seizing lands and lordships throughout southern Italy. Italian maritime cities such as Venice, Pisa and Genoa began to win the initiative against Muslim corsairs and themselves to mount successful raids against Muslim bases. Churchmen showed a new readiness to assert their separate status from laymen and to envisage "the Church" as a discrete order in society, giving instruction to laymen rather than letting them control many church appointments. These rising winds of change found both a vent and a machine to drive in a new direction in the papacy, when Bruno of Toul, a leading church reformer, was appointed pope by Emperor Henry III in 1049. Leo IX, as Bruno became, immediately began to revitalize the papal curia, staffing it with energetic, austere northerners of his own stamp, seeking to eradicate the buying of offices and simony in all its forms, and concubinage, not just from monasteries but from the Church as a whole. Uniform standards were to be imposed on the Church, and the standard-setter was to be the pope. There was a flurry of church councils in the west, at which individual simoniacs and simony in general were condemned. A clarion call was sounded at the Council of Rheims in 1049. Besides 12 canons on the correction of clerical abuses, one of the council's edicts declared that the pope alone was "the primate and apostolic (*apostolicus*) of the universal Church." This edict had been preceded by the reading of "sentences on this matter formerly promulgated by the Orthodox Fathers."

The speed with which the reforming papacy came to blows with the patriarchate of Constanti-

The papal states
The "patrimony of St Peter" was enlarged through generous grants of King Pepin and his son Charlemagne. In return for military assistance Charlemagne was crowned "emperor" in 800. The emperor was expected to protect the pope and his possessions. The papacy found a forceful new protector in Otto I of Germany, whom Pope John XII crowned emperor in 962. The "patrimony" was less a solid bloc of property than a patchwork of rights and powers. The Gregorian Reform movement allowed popes little time to consolidate their holdings in central Italy and their adversaries were able to stir up dissidence among the towns there: the citizens anyway needed little prompting. It was the colossal achievement of Innocent III (1198–1216) to bring order, first to his own city of Rome, then across central Italy, to the Duchy of Spoleto and the March of Ancona. Papal control there remained imperfect, and still more so in the Pentapolis, but now at last the papacy had a large, effective power base in Italy and drew ample revenues from it. The price, however, was ever deeper entanglement in political wrangles.

Christians in Medieval Constantinople

Medieval Constantinople was perhaps the most Christian city the world has ever known, teeming with monks, monasteries and churches. Not all the inhabitants were Byzantine Orthodox or even Christian—Jews lived there, and there was at least one mosque. But the official ethos of the "God-protected city" was emphatically Christian. It was proclaimed month in month out at religious services and imperial ceremonies, functions which were intertwined. While many of these were performed behind the closed doors of the palace or St Sophia, others took place in the main streets. Ordinary citizens seem to have appreciated the public forms of worship, especially the cult of the Mother of God, the special protector of the city against successive waves of barbarians. Personal piety is difficult to gauge, but we hear of ordinary people flocking to consult or be healed by holy men living outside the city.

Below Sts Sergius and Bacchus, interior of the dome. The church was commissioned by Justinian and dedicated to two Syrian soldier saints, martyred under Diocletian. Part of the Greek inscription running along the epistyle (above the capitals) on the ground floor is visible in the photograph: "Other rulers have honored mortals whose works were useless, but our sovereign Justinian, as an encouragement to piety, has honored with a superb building Sergius . . ." Justinian was demonstrating his reverence for Syrian saints, and the octagonal groundplan owes much to Syro-Palestinian martyrs' shrines.

Above The narthex of St Sophia, looking south. This is part of the original building put up by Justinian. The slabs of multicolored marble facing on its walls are framed by borders of white marble. The doorways on the left lead into the nave and aisles. Through the middle one of these, "the royal door," imperial processions passed into the church.

Right These three adjoining churches, seen from the east, served the monastery of Christ Pantocrator, founded by John II Comnenus (1118-43). The church to the north (right) was dedicated to Christ Pantocrator himself, that to the south to the Merciful Mother of God. They are linked by a funerary chapel of St Michael. John Comnenus intended the chapel to become the burial place for his dynasty, and several emperors were buried there. The monastery also maintained a home for old men, a hospice and a large hospital with separate wards for different types of ailment.

nople is a reflection partly of the stridency of papal claims, and partly of the closeness of relations between papacy and empire hitherto: they were likely swiftly to register any significant change in the position of either party. Furthermore there is reason to suppose that change was afoot in the Byzantine Church too in the mid-11th century.

The papacy did not, in fact, immediately seize on the opportunity which the Normans presented to impose Latin customs on the churches and monasteries of the Greek rite in southern Italy. Leo IX later claimed that Rome had shown great tolerance towards the Orthodox: "Although there are to be found very many monasteries and churches of the Greeks inside Rome and outside, none of them has hitherto been disturbed or banned from observing its ancestral traditions or customs, but rather has been urged and admonished to observe them." "Behold, how much more discreet, moderate and clement in this area is the Roman Church than you!" It seems to have been Patriarch Michael Cerularius (1043–58) who acted first, closing down the Latin churches in Constantinople when they failed to heed his demand that they observe Byzantine usages. He was then engaged, with the emperor's cooperation, in trying to impose Byzantine ritual, such as the use of leavened bread in communion, on the Armenian Church. This was part of the government's program for incorporating the Armenians fully within the empire.

Paradoxically, it was a rapprochement between Rome and Byzantium that laid their differences bare. The papacy regarded the Norman freebooters as barbarous intruders. After failing to gain effective help from Henry III, Leo IX looked for aid against them to the same power that John X had enlisted in 914–15—Byzantium. At about the same time, in 1052, Michael Cerularius induced Archbishop Leo of Ochrid to write a letter to be passed on to Leo IX and other western prelates. In his letter Archbishop Leo vigorously criticized the westerners' use of unleavened bread (*azymes*) for the sacrament. He also denounced various other western ("Latin") customs, such as fasting on Saturdays "like the Jews," and the eating of strangled meat. Leo urged his addressees to renounce these practices, "so that you may all be with us through the true and immaculate faith one flock of the one true and Good Shepherd, Christ." Soon after this letter was dispatched the Normans inflicted crushing defeats on both the Byzantine army and the papal army in Italy, taking Leo IX prisoner. It is a signal mark of the strength of the habits of collaboration between the papacy and Byzantium that Leo still looked eastwards for military aid, even while seeking compliance from the patriarch of Constantinople. Early in 1054 Leo IX sent legates to Byzantium, charged with answering the tract of Archbishop Leo of Ochrid, bringing Cerularius sharply to heel and negotiating a military alliance with Constantine IX Monomachus.

The imposition of mutual excommunications

Among the legates were such top members of the curia as Cardinal Humbert, the chief papal secretary, and Frederick of Lorraine, chancellor of the Roman see and a future pope (Stephen IX). The seniority of their rank suggests that their mission was regarded as important at the time. So does the profusion of documents which they took with them. Among them were two letters addressed to Cerularius and one addressed to Emperor Constantine. Although these letters seem to have been composed by Humbert, there is no reason to doubt that Pope Leo approved them or that they expressed the general sentiments of the reformist curia. The emperor was urged to emulate his great predecessor, Constantine the Great, in his devotion to the apostolic see: "Beloved son and most serene emperor, deign to work with us to the relief of your mother, Holy Church, and to the recovery of her privileges . . . and patrimony in the areas under your sway." In contrast, Leo's letter to Michael Cerularius upbraids his "insolence" and "arrogance": "Surely a foot or a hand does not consider the glory or disgrace of its head to be its own?" The head is superimposed on the body and the senses.

This papal call to obedience met with a cool reception from Patriarch Michael, who certainly did not aspire to the role of hand or foot of the papacy. The legates' presence in Constantinople evoked various expressions of hostility from Byzantine churchmen to western practices. A monk of the Studios monastery wrote a tract criticizing the Latins' use of unleavened bread, and adding new topics to the dispute, such as the Latins' ban on married priests. In Byzantium the existence of married priests was permitted and customary, as it still is in the Orthodox Church today.

The summer of 1054 at Constantinople presents a bizarre, even comic, spectacle: the beginnings of a sort of pamphlet warfare; the slinging about of charges, many of them trivial or utterly baseless; and the cluckings of the emperor, as he tried to smother the dissension by restraining the Orthodox churchmen.

On 16 July 1054, after a quite a lengthy wait, Humbert activated, so to speak, his "time-bomb," and placed a bull of excommunication on the main altar of St Sophia. The papal legates left the city soon afterwards, after giving the "kiss of peace" to Constantine IX, who received them in his palace. A synod was held on 20 July 1054. Constantine IX's decree ordering that the legates' bull be burned was read out, and those responsible for the bull were anathematized. Four days later the anathema was repeated and a copy of the offending bull was burned in public. Cerularius's anathema fell on "those who produced and wrote this [bull], and who gave approval or advice on the drafting of it."

These mutual excommunications gave a new, sharper definition to the estrangement which was already discernible before 1054. Both sides took some steps to leave loopholes through which some future compromise might be worked, but such care itself suggests consciousness of the likely repercussions of their actions. Indeed, there was an ominous declaration in the papal legates' anathema of Michael Cerularius, Leo of Ochrid and their followers, as pronounced aloud at the emperor's court: "Whoever shall contradict obstinately the faith of the Holy Roman and Apostolic See and its Host, let him be anathematized and not be held a catholic Christian, but a heretical prozymite [i.e. advocate of leavened communion bread]!" The mutual excommunications were eventually lifted in 1965.

SCHISM AND UNION

The crusades
The aim of the First Crusade was to aid the Byzantines against the Seljuk Turks and to liberate Jerusalem. But the Byzantines suspected that their own empire was the crusaders' real goal. The presence of Normans on the crusade fueled their fears: the Normans had attacked Byzantium in 1081–85. The First Crusade made it easier for Emperor Alexius I Comnenus to recover western Asia Minor, but Byzantine suspicions of crusaders remained keen. Unfortunately for Byzantium, it straddled the land route to Palestine and when members of the Second and Third Crusades suffered disasters, they blamed them on the Byzantines. The Fourth Crusade attempted to take a sea route to the Holy Land, but ended up at Constantinople through the manipulation of some of its leaders. Confused, poor and few, these crusaders eventually sacked Constantinople, abducting its relics.

The Fourth Crusade (1204), and the imposition of Latin ways on the Greeks until 1261, left lasting anti-western feeling in the Byzantine Church. The Greeks turned out the westerners from Constantinople in 1261, but in the long term emperors had to stave off the conquering Turks, and could hardly succeed without Latin help. That was available at the price of church union, which meant Orthodox submission to papal jurisdiction. The implacable opposition of the Greek Church to the "heresies and pride" of the Latin west made it difficult for emperors to make concessions to the west which they could hope to deliver. The Fourth Crusade and its aftermath left the Church strong, the emperors relatively weak. They still appointed patriarchs and in some cases deposed them if outspokenly critical of palace policies, but the attitude of the faithful and the monks to western control was a decisive obstacle to imperial initiatives. The prestige of the Church rode high, monasteries continued to attract benefactions. The times generated many important works of Greek theology and spirituality, and an outstanding vitality in painting and mosaics. In an age when political life might hold few attractions, when some emperors and patriarchs resigned office to become monks, otherworldly mysticism and the great silences of Mount Athos were of supreme value. While a few powerful intellects in the Greek Church were strongly impressed by the theological achievements of western theology, in the quietist or Hesychast movement on Athos Greek spirituality took a form profoundly divergent from that of the west.

Patriarchal power

The majority of late 13th- and early 14th-century patriarchs had served long apprenticeships as monks before attaining their high office, and several in the 14th century were former monks of Athos. One of the outstanding monkish patriarchs was Athanasius I (1289–93; 1303–09). In his efforts to enforce ascetic standards on the clergy under his charge he received support from Andronicus II, who called a synod to denounce as rebels any clergymen who resisted the patriarch's measures against simony and other abuses. Athanasius

The Crusades

The crusading period, at its height from about 1095 to 1204, the time of the first four crusades, was a compound of real piety and honest devotion with greed for land and the acting out of old hostilities, often with the utmost mercilessness and rancor. The first crusaders included many younger sons without an inheritance in western Europe looking for a new life in a new world. They had no intention of returning, and indeed communities of westerners did grow up in the Holy Land during the century.

But, in conception, the crusade war was not merely a just war but a holy one. The recapture of the Holy Places from the Muslims was of immense importance in an age when those places were thought of as points of intensely real contact with the life of Christ, and the earthly Jerusalem as a face of the heavenly Jerusalem. There had been pilgrimages to the Holy Land for many centuries, and the crusaders saw themselves as pilgrims too. They were soldiers of Christ fighting a war which was spiritual as well as physical and bloody, exiles coming home to heaven.

The mixture of high idealism and crude self-interest which characterized the crusades does not make them a less remarkable phenomenon. For over a hundred years large numbers of people forgot their internal squabbles and set off on a journey of unimaginable danger and difficulty in the belief that they were doing work for God and bringing the kingdom of heaven nearer.

Bottom The crusading period coincided with the building of stone castles in western Europe and the new approach to defense policy that went with them. The Holy Land was filled with castles, too, as the most secure means of holding the newly conquered territories strung out along a thin coastal line. The most famous of these castles, Krak des Chevaliers, is shown here. It fell by treachery.

Below The Fourth Crusade was obliged to hire ships from the Venetians and in return the Venetians insisted that the crusaders should travel by way of Constantinople and sack the city of their major trading rivals. They took it in 1204 and set up a Latin rule there, but never completed the crusade.

Below Urban II is shown here preaching the First Crusade at the Council of Clermont in 1095. He promised those who undertook to save Jerusalem from the Muslims that they would be freed from the penalties due for all their sins. (He discouraged members of religious orders from going, because they were fighting a spiritual war for the kingdom of heaven already.) The response was enormous and eager and instantaneous.

Below Fighting tactics developed in the west as a result of the crusaders' encounter with the superior skills of the Turks and Arabs. The crusaders were used to pitched battles. They had heavy horses and swords wielded with two hands. The Saracens had maneuverable horses and short, curved scimitars which could be used at a gallop from horseback to slash the enemy. This late medieval jousting picture of Richard and Saladin glosses over the difference. Richard the Lionheart and Saladin were the figures of the Third Crusade who most captured the popular imagination as dashing heroes.

Below Crusaders were said to "take the cross" when they offered themselves to go on crusade. Their vow was fulfilled when they reached the Holy Sepulcher. The picture shows crosses carved on the wall at its entrance by crusaders.

Below center The First Crusade took a mainly land route, marching through the territories of the eastern empire, where Anna Comnena, a royal princess, called them an uncivilized rabble, and down through Asia Minor, where they fell ill with dysentery. Subsequent crusades made greater use of ships.

Below The crusaders' principal idea was to capture Jerusalem by besieging it. They applied the same technique at Antioch and elsewhere on their way. It was a slow and wearisome business and almost as costly in stress and hunger to the crusaders as to their enemies. In this 15th-century reconstruction various devices for getting into the city can be seen disposed around the walls.

repaid him for his pains with frequent and hectoring advice on various affairs of state and public policy. Athanasius warned Andronicus not to contemplate making a request for aid from the Latins, as more and more lands in Asia Minor fell under Turkish control: "Do not think that we shall prevail by means of armed expeditions . . . even if the entire west, if it were possible, were to join and help us. What then is the solution? Turning towards God and repentance to the utmost of our ability, for which he is waiting patiently." In another letter to Andronicus, Athanasius supposes that the boot is, so to speak, firmly on the patriarchal foot: "For priesthood was not granted to Christian people for the sake of empire, but empire for the sake of priesthood, so that if the empire in a manner pleasing to God supported the Church with the secular arm and honored and protected her, the empire in turn would be supported and protected and increased by God." Athanasius pressed the emperor to show greater concern for the welfare of the refugees from the Turks who were crowding into Constantinople. The patriarch set up soup kitchens, while the emperor appointed an official to regulate food prices. The patriarch's role would have seemed familiar to John the Almsgiver.

Fourteenth-century patriarchs seem often to have taken a casual view of the responsibilities of their office – an *insouciance* which did not preclude their making pronouncements upon public affairs,

Not a baroque ceiling, but mosaics in the monastery of the Chora (Kariye Cami), Constantinople. The monastery church was rebuilt and decorated by Theodore Metochites, the leading statesman of his day. He wrote, in Homeric verse, that his aim was "to relate, in mosaics, how the Lord Himself . . . became a mortal man on our behalf." Appropriately, this mosaic shows the genealogy of Christ—39 of his ancestors wheel around the dome beneath him. Their poses and gestures are all individual, a mark of the vitality of early 14th-century Byzantine art.

in the tradition of holy men of the middle Byzantine period. Patriarch Athanasius was in the habit of roaming the streets of Constantinople in sandals and a hairshirt, exuding a foul smell. Patriarchs whose hearts were not really in their jobs were liable to lay down the burdens of office with equanimity, resuming an exclusively monastic way of life, as Athanasius did in 1309. They therefore had few qualms about speaking out when displeased with the behavior of emperors, or of any other members or sections of society. Quite often emperors felt obliged to depose them, but they had to put up with far more outspoken, and less predictable, patriarchs in the 14th century than had their predecessors before 1204.

The specters of another "martyr"-patriarch in the pattern of Arsenius (1254–60, 1261–64), and of another acrimonious church schism, stood before them. They also had to reckon with the difficulty of finding a reputable churchman or monk willing to become patriarch, for many who were offered the job refused it.

Imperial impotence

The tale of the successive attempts of emperors to elicit military aid from the papacy through promises of union has a muted tone. It no longer greatly mattered what the emperor believed or proposed: he would not be able to impose it. In moments of desperation, emperors tended to attach a talismanic significance to gaining an agreement with Rome, and to the assistance which this might bring them against the Turks. Even the otherwise strictly Orthodox Andronicus II raised the question of union in his last years, when embroiled in a civil war against his grandson and unable to prevent further Turkish encroachments. So did John VI Cantacuzene, at particularly desperate junctures of his rule. John V Paleologus seems naively to have supposed that church union was feasible and that it would bring a solution to his woes. In a personal letter to the pope, John V proposed eventually to submit himself to the holy father, but admitted that he dared not force union on his subjects for fear that they would revolt against him.

A few Byzantine courtiers and intellectuals shared and encouraged John's interest in the west. Of these, the liveliest and most articulate was the chief minister, Demetrius Cydones. Having learned Latin from a Dominican, he translated works of Thomas Aquinas into Greek and conveys in his writings a sense of excitement at discovery of the range and quality of western thought. Cydones urged his fellow countrymen to give up their age-old idea of the world as divided into Byzantines and ignorant barbarians: "Previously, there was no one to persuade our people that there is any intelligence in the Latins, or that they are able to raise their minds to consideration of anything more exalted than shipping, trade and war." In fact, the Byzantine Church and people remained unpersuaded.

When John V Paleologus, anxious to clinch an agreement so as to bring about a crusade against the Turks, was received into the Roman Church in St Peter's, Rome, in 1369, there was a notable lack of repercussions. Not a single Byzantine churchman accompanied John to Rome, and he made no attempt to impose the Roman teaching on the *filioque* or Roman ritual on his subjects. John had had ample experience of the limitations on his ability to direct church policy. Himself out of sympathy with the mystic and severely ascetic aspects of the Hesychasts, he had to endure a succession of patriarchs who were of the Hesychast tendency. According to Demetrius Cydones, the imperial palace was full of Hesychast monks wandering around and displaying their beards, their theology and their ignorance. The urbane Cydones joined the Roman Church, as did a number of other teachers and thinkers. Some of them became

Turkish advances, Latin possessions and Byzantine retreat
Michael VIII Paleologus recovered Constantinople for Orthodoxy in 1261, but had to contend with rival Orthodox rulers in the Balkans, with Frankish warlords dominating southern Greece and with the Turks. The reconstituted empire made some territorial gains, notably in the Peloponnese, but economic weakness and internal quarrels beset the Paleologan family and in the mid-14th century the Serbian ruler Stephen Dušan won a brief but brilliant mastery over much of the Balkans. Above all, Byzantium had to reckon with the Turks. The Osmanlis (Ottomans) were in the early 14th century just one group of Turks, a small border emirate in northwest Asia Minor. The Ottoman rulers' championship of holy war against the Christians helped to extend their power over other Turkish potentates in Asia Minor. Having occupied Gallipoli in 1354, they made very rapid gains. The victory of Timur (Tamburlaine) over the Ottomans in 1402 fragmented their power, but by the 1430s they were reunited. Their reserves of fanatical manpower and undeniable fighting skills soon overwhelmed the scattered remnants of Byzantine imperial power. In 1453 Constantinople, "queen of cities," fell.

Dominican friars, for example, Manuel Calecas, a pupil of Cydones.

The influence of Latinizing emperors and intellectuals was, however, negligible, for all the profusion of their writings. The fact that so many of the intellectuals interested in western thought went over to Rome suggests that there was no tenable middle ground between Orthodoxy and western modes of thought. Counterblasts against Latin practices and beliefs were issued by many Orthodox churchmen in the 14th and 15th centuries.

The decline of Byzantium and the act of union

In the 15th century the military and economic situation of the Byzantine empire became ever more pitiful. Byzantium was now little more than a city-state on the Bosphorus, with Peloponnesian appendages. Senior churchmen and monks crowded into Constantinople from regions stricken by the Turks. They were able to command respect from many of the citizens and to let forth barrages of criticism against imperial policies of which they disapproved. The final fall of Thessalonica to the Turks in 1430 and the sultan's regular exaction of tribute from Constantinople instilled a desperate, and often erratic, note into imperial policies, and began to shake lingering assumptions of many churchmen concerning imperial power.

Emperor John VIII Paleologus (1425–48) was encouraged to pursue the chimera of union by the newly mild and conciliatory overtures which came from the western Church. The latter was itself divided between the papacy and the conciliar movement, and popes and conciliarists competed for the prestige of winning the Byzantines to their cause. An ecumenical council had normally been a Byzantine precondition for negotiations since the days of Alexius Comnenus. Now a council was being proposed by the pope himself, and a fleet was even dispatched to ferry the penurious emperor and his delegation to attend it. The tantalizing reward of a massive western expedition to assist Byzantium proved irresistible and in 1437 John VIII, the aged and ailing patriarch Joseph II, and representatives of the other three eastern patriarchates and senior Byzantine prelates set sail on the papal boats.

Several years earlier, Archbishop Symeon of Thessalonica had warned against the holding of a council, which was already then being mooted. He warned that it "would become a cause of disturbance rather than of peace," and himself voiced stern condemnations of the Latins. "True peace" was not to be had through acquiescence in the wishes of the unionists. It entailed "that we should be with the Fathers." "We are both servants and disciples of our Fathers who were earnestly devoted to the true traditional faith of the Church, and we ever remain inseparably united to them." A continuance of the rift with Rome was preferable to a breach with the Orthodox faith and with the tradition running back through the Church Fathers to the apostles.

Symeon's sentiments are reminiscent of those of Byzantine churchmen in past centuries. His forecast that a church council would work more havoc than concord proved prescient. The large Byzantine mission to the council which began in Ferrara and continued in Florence did eventually decide almost unanimously in favor of union. All the Byzantine delegates except Mark Eugenicus signed the act of union, which was proclaimed in Greek and Latin on 6 July 1439. The monks of Constantinople and the ordinary clergy of the capital were not impressed. Some of the bishops who had subscribed to the act of union faced such hostility from their diocesan clergy and laity that they withdrew to Italy. In 1451 Patriarch Gregory III Mammas himself migrated to Italy and the patriarchal throne stood, in effect, empty.

The brother of John VIII, Constantine XI (1449–53), pursued the same illusion of union, while recognizing that he could not impose the Latin faith or ritual on the citizens of Constantinople, let alone on the Orthodox Christians outside his sway. In 1452 a poignant ceremony occurred in the great church of St Sophia at Constantine XI's initiative. The union decree was read out by Cardinal Isidore, another former Orthodox delegate to Ferrara-Florence, and a Roman mass was cele-

Above The monastery of the Pantanassa (Queen of the World), Mistra, founded in 1428 and still inhabited by nuns today. It is just one of the many monasteries and churches, large and small, which throng the hillside of this spectacular Byzantine town in southern Greece. They were all built in the 14th or 15th century. The "despots" who lived in its "palace" were relatives of the emperor in Constantinople and ruled on his behalf those parts of the Peloponnese still loyal to him. Mistra fell to the Turks in 1460.

Left: Christianity in Kievan Russia
Russia came late to Christianity. Its ruler, Prince Vladimir of Kiev, converted to Byzantine Orthodoxy and imposed it on his subjects c.988. Bishoprics were founded, at first mainly in the region of Kiev. Their numbers were increased in the 12th and early 13th centuries by new sees in the west and the northeast, reflecting the rise of new principalities in those areas. Senior churchmen were usually deeply beholden to princes. The map shows the distribution of finds of a type of cross-encolpion in Russia. The encolpia, showing the Crucifixion on one side and the Mother and Child on the other, were usually worn on a chain suspended from the neck. Cast in bronze from molds, they were produced for the popular market in the 11th-13th centuries. They were merely one among many types of encolpion, but their distribution pattern acts as a kind of tracer of personal piety at grassroots level in Kievan Russia.

brated in the almost empty building. Many of the emperor's own officials stayed away. From a practical point of view, the protracted wooing of Rome was futile, since the papacy was, in the wake of the conciliar movement, incapable of launching a crusade equal to the might of the Ottoman Turks. But even if western aid had been more effective, it would still have been unwelcome to most Byzantine churchmen and laymen. The most famous expression of revulsion against the Latins was made by Constantine XI's own chief courtier: "Better to see the Turks' turban reigning in the midst of the city than the Latin miter." These words were voiced shortly before the Turkish guns were hauled into position for the final assault on Constantinople in 1453.

Christianity under Turkish rule

In the 14th century the Constantinopolitan patriarchate was able to reassert its authority over Russia, which had slackened over the last 150 years, since before 1204. Liturgical practice was codified at Constantinople under Patriarch Philotheus Kokkinos. Almost immediately it was transmitted to Russia. But in this, as in so many other ways, the patriarchate's expertise and moral authority were closely associated with monasticism, especially Hesychasm. Philotheus Kokkinos (1353–54; 1364–76) and Kallistos (1350–53; 1355–63), who did much to implement their claims of "universal leadership" for the patriarchate, were themselves former Hesychast monks from Athos. But in lands where no Orthodox princes or influential local churchmen were available to follow the lead which Byzantine spirituality still offered, the Church as an institution broke up. Philotheus bemoaned the loss to the Turks of "the great Nicaea, Prousa, Nicomedia and Chalcedon, those ancient adornments of the Church and the Christian empire."

An early 14th-century list of bishoprics, unofficial and confused as it is, seems to show a fairly healthy state of numbers, thanks largely to the Lascarid and Paleologan revival and support for the Church—112 metropolitanates, albeit often with only one or two suffragan (subordinate) bishoprics apiece. A memorandum composed in 1437 tells a different story: 67 metropolitanates, many of them lacking any suffragans at all. Of these metropolitanates, only 15 were on territory still ruled by the Paleologan family, and 36 were on Turkish territory. There is abundant evidence that, while some metropolitanates continued to function under Turkish lordship, the quality of pastoral care, and of Christian life in general, declined.

Conditions for those who persisted in adhering to Orthodoxy in Asia Minor were, on the whole, wretched. Life for those who were Muslims was more secure and carried a lighter tax burden. In fact, the western coastal areas of Asia Minor prospered from agriculture, and a lucrative trade in grain, cattle and slaves was conducted with Italian merchants. The material advantages of apostasizing to Islam were therefore great, and they probably accounted for the rapid Islamicization of former Christian regions as much as did the Turks' religious persecution and attempts at peaceful persuasion to win converts. Already in 1303 Patriarch Athanasius lamented: "Not only have certain people, in an excess of wickedness, repudiated piety of their own accord, but also countless numbers—even more than the grains of sand—of unwilling people have been driven to this by irresistible necessity." Such an apparent stream of desertions then makes it rather surprising that there were still enough Christians left in Asia Minor in the later 14th century for Demetrius Cydones to report that "every day floods of Christians are drawn off into unbelief." But while one may cavil at the exaggerations of Byzantine rhetoric, the general pattern of the shrinkage of the Christian congregations and the retreat of the church hierarchy in Asia Minor is unmistakable, and a connection between this and the decline of the Byzantine empire is undeniable.

A similar reign of unbelief seemed to be descending on the European centers of Orthodoxy in the first half of the 15th century. Archbishop Symeon of Thessalonica constitutes an example of a prelate enjoying high prestige and wide-ranging powers in his community, and there was a profusion of monasteries in the late medieval city. Symeon does, however, also attest the precariousness of the Church's position in the face of the Ottoman Turks' advance, and his conventional pieties concerning imperial power are all the more poignant for this.

Symeon's writings reveal that in Thessalonica itself many people favored bowing to what they regarded as the inevitable, and surrendering to the Turks. In 1413 a delegation had been on the point of handing the city over to Sultan Musa when St Demetrius intervened in defense of his city and caused Musa to be killed. In 1422–23 Symeon himself had to contend with "the majority" of the citizens, who "actually declared that they were bent on handing . . . over to the infidel." Symeon, and others in authority, were calumnied for not being concerned with the welfare of the population as a whole. The citizens had suffered terribly from the Turkish attacks and blockade. Archbishop Symeon's response to those who wished to surrender was to denounce their "laziness" and "pusillanimity," and their desire "to be fed like farm animals and to lack none of those things which fatten the flesh and bloat it, and which bring in money and turn men into grandees." Symeon's unbending opposition either to surrender to the Turks or to a Venetian occupation of the city earned him general opprobrium: the people "demonstrated publicly against me myself, continually gathering in a great crowd, rioting against me and threatening to pull down the churches, and me with them, if I refused to do as they wanted."

Many in the Thessalonican mob were probably rioting in pursuit of capitulation and bread, rather than contemplating positive apostasy to Islam. But their indifference to the values of strict Orthodoxy is plain. In fact the unremitting chain of hardships which befell the last Byzantines seems to have shaken the faith of many ordinary lay folk. When Gregory Palamas found himself a prisoner of the Turks in Lampsacus, many of the local men, women and children crowded around him. Some were firm in the faith, "but the majority were demanding the reason for God's desertion of our race."

CHURCH AND STATE

Established practice in the west

The emperor Charlemagne wrote to Pope Leo III as to the principal bishop of his realm, and in his empire bishops acted as royal administrators, collecting taxes, going on diplomatic missions for the emperor, working for him as judges. Throughout the Carolingian period the king or emperor appointed bishops, invested them with lands and castles and with their churches, in England, France or Spain as well as in the empire itself. Even the synods of the Church itself often had royal or imperial presidents. In 1046, at the synod of Sutri, Henry III presided while the synod deposed two popes, saw a third abdicate and elected yet another.

The system worked well enough, principally no doubt because it resulted in a hierarchical arrangement—Church subordinate to state—which made it possible to resolve the majority of practical difficulties where the two authorities might have come into conflict. It was an effective means of reinforcing one authority with the other. It remained so until in the 10th and 11th centuries the lay and clerical magnates in much of Europe began to grow more powerful in relation to king and emperor. Local nobles sometimes created bishops; kings sometimes took the revenues of the Church for their own use; bribery and simony became prevalent.

The reforms of Gregory VII

In this situation there arose a pope who chose to dispute established practices. Hildebrand, Gregory VII, was a reformer not only of laxities within the Church, but of a pattern of Church–state relations which he saw as quite the wrong way around. He asserted all that was claimed in the "Donation of Constantine," a document of Carolingian manufacture which purported to be a grant from the emperor Constantine to the pope of many of his imperial rights, and was intended to justify the papacy's aspirations to political power in the west. He searched the papal archives in his reform of the papal chancery and found documents to confirm and extend the "Donation."

Gregory drew up a list of claims (which survives in one of his letter books, almost as though it had lain on his desk as a series of jottings and had been gathered up by a busy clerk and copied with other papers). It is not a formal document, but is perhaps the more powerful for its brevity and point. This *Dictatus Papae* includes the following claims:

That the Roman Church was founded by God alone.

That [the pope] alone may use the imperial insignia.

That of the pope alone all princes shall kiss the feet.

That a sentence passed by him may be retracted by

"The Donation of Constantine." The emperor Constantine is shown kneeling before Pope Sylvester, who is blessing him as he hands over his crown as a symbol of the donation of secular authority to the spiritual authority in the world. This "Donation of Constantine" was in fact a Carolingian forgery, but much rested on high medieval faith in its authenticity during the debates of the investiture contest.

Church and state in the Middle Ages
The map shows the degree to which political and spiritual jurisdiction coincided in the Middle Ages. These ecclesiastical "provinces" differ from political ones in area chiefly where disputes had moved political boundaries significantly: Burgundy, Serbo-Croatia, for example. Christian bishoprics persisted under Muslim domination in the south of Spain.

no one; and that he himself, alone of all, may retract it.
That he himself may be judged by no one.
That the Roman Church has never erred; nor will it err to all eternity, the Scriptures bearing witness.

These assertions met with a hostile response from the emperor, the young Henry IV, who had succeeded as a minor and was beginning to assert his own rights in the 1070s. The pope disputed Henry's power to invest bishops with ring and staff; these, he said, were the spiritualities of the sea, and only a priest could confer them. As Henry was engaged in pressing his right to appoint bishops in imperial Italy, the conflict was a sharp one. Henry was excommunicated; he elected a pope of his own and declared Gregory deposed; there was an exchange of letters and open warfare. Circumstances in Germany, however, made Henry's position there uncertain, and to save his throne he came over the Alps in winter to Canossa to beg Gregory to lift the ban of excommunication which made his subjects free to look elsewhere for a monarch. Gregory kept him waiting in the snow and made him kiss his stirrup in a gesture of feudal humiliation before he accepted the reconciliation.

The extent of Gregory's power was not far short of his claim in the letter of excommunication he sent to Henry: "God has given me through blessed Peter, chief of the apostles . . . the power of binding and loosing in heaven and on earth. Relying on this article of belief . . . I prohibit Henry the king, son of Henry the emperor, who has risen up against your Church with unexampled arrogance, from ruling in Germany and Italy. And I release all Christians from the oaths which they have sworn or shall swear to him; I forbid all men to serve him as king . . . and I bind him with the bonds of anathema" (February 1076). While there were disaf-

Left The relationship of Church and state in the Holy Roman empire looked back to the model of Constantine and Sylvester I in the early 4th century, when the empire first became a Christian state. It became customary for emperors to have themselves crowned by popes at Aix-la-Chapelle (Aachen), as Charlemagne had done, or in Rome. The picture shows the coronation of the emperor Frederick III by Pope Nicholas V in 1452 in Rome. This was the last crowning of an emperor of the Holy Roman empire in Rome.

Right: Monastic reform, experiment and expansion Monasticism began with a period of experimentation, especially in eastern Christendom; but since the 6th century in the west the Benedictine Rule had been followed by almost every community. It had been necessary to reform standards more than once. The most notable of these reforms, of Cluny in the 10th and 11th centuries, was followed late in the 11th century by a further move for reform and experiment, which produced the Cistercians. They followed the Benedictine Rule, but with great austerity and with an emphasis on a balance of labor, prayer and reading which they felt the Cluniacs had got wrong. Their popularity led to a wide spread of Cistercian houses. The canons, priests living under a rule, but free to work in the community, also multiplied in the shape of Victorines and Premonstratensians in the 12th century.

fected and ambitious subjects, and especially while magnates were looking for means of extending their own powers and diminishing those of their monarch, such threats were not empty. Besides, as Gregory pointed out in a letter to the bishop of Metz in 1081, there are things a man needs *in extremis* which only a priest can supply: "Every Christian king on his deathbed seeks as a pitiful suppliant the help of a priest so that he can escape hell's prison . . . and stand at God's judgment seat absolved from the bondage of his sins. What layman, to say nothing of priests, has ever in his last hour asked an earthly king's help for the salvation of his soul?"

Temporal and spiritual power disputed

The dispute went on for some decades until it was brought to a rough working settlement at the concordat of Worms in 1122. It was agreed that kings and emperors should have the power to confer the temporalities of a see, while the Church retained the right to confer the spiritualities. Calixtus II grants to Henry V "that the elections of the bishops and abbots of the German kingdom, who belong to the kingdom, shall take place in your presence, without simony and without any violence." Henry V grants in return "that in all the churches that are in my kingdom there may be canonical election and free consecration."

This did not by any means bring the dispute to an end. Recent events had upset the balance of centuries, and the relative positions of emperor and pope, Church and state, were to be discussed with no little anxiety and urgency by a succession of later medieval writers. In the middle of the 12th century Otto of Freising wrote a sequel to Augustine's *City of God* in which he took stock of the history of *The Two Cities* since Augustine's day. He believed that something important had recently taken place, a breakdown of an old working relationship between empire and papacy, which was a sign of impending disaster. He had some hopes of the new Staufen emperors, whose line began with the accession of Frederick Barbarossa in 1152, but there were to be further periods of conflict. The minority of Frederick II coincided with

NORTH SEA
ATLANTIC OCEAN
Cluniac reforms 910-1150
main center of reform
other foundation reformed from Cluny or Cluny-derived influence
spread of Cluniac reform
scale 1:12 000 000
0 300km
0 200mi
Bermondsey
Lewes
Ghent
München-Gladbach
St Trond
Liège
Malmédy
Stablo
Cologne
Siegburg
Hersfeld
Fulda
Hildesheim
Merseburg
St Vaast
Brogne
Fécamp
Rouen
Seine
Paris
Verdun
Metz
Gorzé
Lorsch
Rhine
Feuchtwangen
Regensburg
Niederalteich
Danube
Hirsau
St Blaise
Ebersberg
Tegernsee
Einsiedeln
Inn
Fleury
Loire
Auxerre
Vézelay
La Charité
Dijon
Souvigny
Cluny
Sauxillanges
Rhône
Fruttuaria
Po
Drava
Sava
Garonne
Moissac
Marseille
Sahagún
Ebro
Classe
Farfa
Rome
Subiaco
Monte Cassino
Corsica
Sardinia
Sicily
MEDITERRANEAN SEA
Elbe
NORTH SEA
Rievaulx
Fountains
Roche
Chorin
Amelungsborn
Clairmarais
Savigny
Royaumont
Longpont
Clairvaux
Morimond
Pontigny
Fontenay
Bebenhausen
Danube
Citeaux
La Ferté
Loire
Inn
Drava
Sava
ATLANTIC OCEAN
Chiaravalle
Po
Obazine
Garonne
Rhône
Fontfroide
Corsica
Fossanova
Las Huelgas
Ebro
Poblet
Sardinia
MEDITERRANEAN SEA
expansion of the Cistercian order 12th and 13th centuries
main center of reform
other Cistercian foundation
spread of Cistercian reform
missionary route
area of Cistercian preaching to the Albigensian heretics
scale 1:16 000 000
0 300km
0 200mi
10°
0°
10°
20°
50°
40°
30°

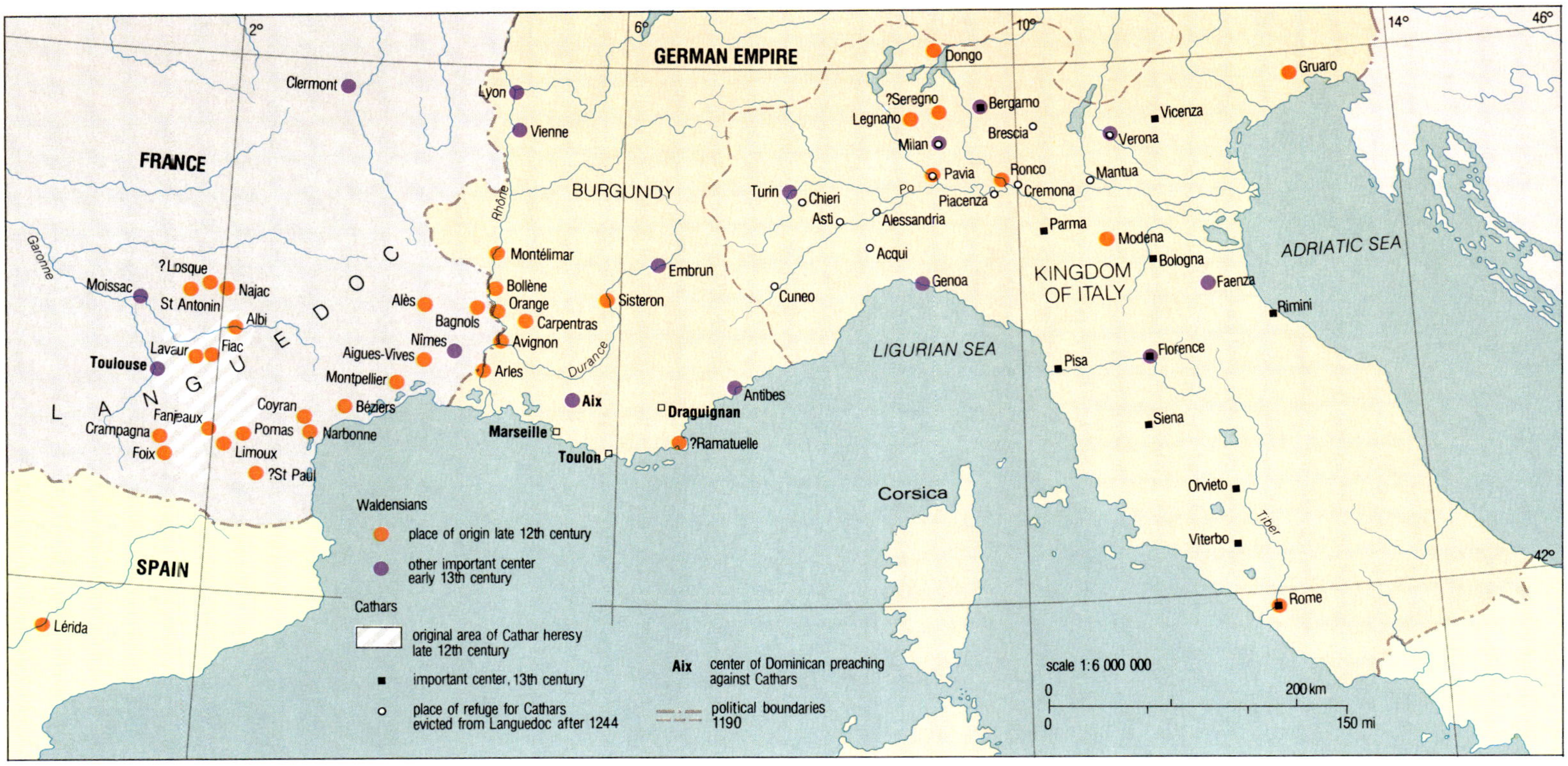

Above: Heresy and dissent
The map shows the concentration of popular heresy in the south of France, northern Spain and north Italy. Several varieties of heresy were common in these areas, particularly dualism (Catharism), whose followers belonged to the school of thought of earlier Gnostics and Manichees and held that the universe is ruled by two powers, one good, one evil, locked in eternal conflict. Anticlericalism fired other popular groups, such as the Waldensians or "Poor Men of Lyon," to reject the sacraments and to argue that the Christian need do no more than renounce worldly wealth and follow Christ.

the pontificate of Innocent III, a pope of determination and learning, a lawyer and a patron of lawyers, who supported German princes to weaken the central authority of the emperor. Frederick II responded by encouraging the cardinals to think of themselves as "successors of the apostles" who had a right to demand "equal participation in whatever he who presides over the see of Rome proposes as law or promulgates as official." In the long term moves of this kind were to curtail papal claims and a system of councils was to hold the papal monarchy in check.

The apologists for the Church's claims tended at first to see matters in the light of the great war which was going on in the universe between good and evil, spiritual and temporal, and to think of Church and emperor as one in waging that war. Bernard of Clairvaux, father of the multitudes of Cistercian houses which spread across Europe from the 1120s, wrote a letter in five books to Pope Eugenius III, who had been a Cistercian monk, and of whose capacities Bernard had some doubts. He encourages Eugenius to think of himself as lord of the world. The apostles said to Jesus at the time of his arrest: "Behold, here are two swords" (Luke 22:38). Jesus answered: "It is enough." On this text was founded a doctrine of the "two swords" which came to a new popularity in the circumstances of the disputes of the late 11th and 12th centuries. Bernard tells Eugenius that both swords, "that is the spiritual and the material, belong to the Church; however, the latter is to be drawn *for* the Church and the former *by* the Church. The spiritual sword should be drawn by the hand of the priest; the material sword by the hand of the knight, but clearly at the bidding of the priest and at the command of the emperor . . . Now, take the sword which has been entrusted to you to strike with, and for their salvation wound, if not everyone, if not even many, at least whomever you can" (*De Consideratione* 4.3.7).

Dante discusses the point in an image which he

Right: The Church and learning
The Church was the principal patron of medieval learning, directly or indirectly, running cathedral schools, and employing in the ecclesiastical civil service the best of the graduates of the universities. The map shows the coincidence of cathedrals and university towns and the spread of schools across Europe.

Left In this 15th-century illustration of Dante's *Divina Commedia* Dante is shown with Beatrice, his guide in the circles of heaven, being introduced to a heaven which is both astronomical and spiritual.

important monastic school
Laon notable cathedral school
university founded before 1300
university founded 1301-1400
university founded 1401-1500
university founded 1501-1700
NORTH SEA
BALTIC SEA
ATLANTIC OCEAN
MEDITERRANEAN SEA
Uppsala 1477
Aberdeen 1494
St Andrews 1411
Edinburgh 1582
Glasgow 1451
Lund 1688
Copenhagen 1478
Königsberg 1544
Jarrow
Wearmouth
Rievaulx
York
Dublin 1591
Kiel 1655
Rostock 1419
Greifswald 1456
Franeker 1585
Groningen 1614
Peterborough
Cambridge 1209
Amsterdam 1631
Harderwijk 1648
Osnabrück 1630
Helmstedt 1576
Magdeburg
Oxford c.1190
Leiden 1575
Utrecht 1636
Hildesheim
Wittenberg 1502
Paderborn 1614
Halle 1694
Corvey
Leipzig 1409
Canterbury
Louvain 1426
Cologne 1388
Marburg 1527
Erfurt 1379
Jena 1558
Fulda
Krakow 1364
Tournai
Giessen 1607
Prague 1348
Mainz 1476
Bamberg 1648
Olmütz 1573
Trier 1473
Würzburg 1402
Caen 1432
Bec
Rouen
Beauvais
Laon
Worms
Reims
Speyer
Heidelberg 1385
Regensburg
Mont St Michel
Savigny
Paris c.1150
Pont-à-Mousson 1572
Metz
Ingolstadt 1459
Tyrnau 1635
Chartres
Nancy 1572
Tübingen 1477
Dillingen 1549
Linz 1669
Vienna 1365
Pressburg 1467
Orléans 1235
Fleury
Strasbourg 1567
Clairvaux
Freiburg 1457
Salzburg 1623
Buda 1389
Nantes 1460
Angers 1337
Tours
Basel 1460
St Gall
Bourges 1464
Besançon 1485
Graz 1585
Poitiers 1431
Citeaux
Dôle 1422
Cluny
Pécs (Fünfkirchen) 1367
Vicenza 1204
Treviso 1318
Vercelli 1228
Milan
Padua 1222
La Chaise Dieu
Grenoble 1339
Pavia 1361
Turin 1405
Bordeaux 1441
Valence 1452
Piacenza 1248
Parma 1502
Ferrara 1391
Ravenna
Cahors 1321
Orange 1365
Bologna 1100
Avignon 1303
Reggio 1188
Urbino 1564
Santiago de Compostela 1506
Oviedo 1604
Orthez 1561
Toulouse 1229
Montpellier 1289
Aix 1409
Pisa 1343
Florence 1349
Siena 1246
Perugia 1308
Perpignan 1349
Arezzo 1215
Palencia 1208
Huesca 1354
Valladolid 1346
Zaragoza 1474
Lérida 1300
Corsica
Rome 1303
Monte Cassino
Salamanca 1243
Barcelona 1430
Coimbra 1290
Alcalá 1499
Sigüenza 1489
Naples 1224
Salerno 1173
Toledo
Sardinia
Valencia 1500
Palma 1483
Lisbon 1290
Cagliari 1626
Evora 1550
Balearic Islands
Palermo 1637
Messina 1549
Monreale
Catania 1434
Seville 1254
Granada 1540
Sicily
Elbe
Oder
Vistula
Seine
Loire
Rhine
Danube
Drava
Rhône
Po
Garonne
Ebro
Duero
Tagus
Guadalquivir
scale 1:12 000 000
0
400 km
0
300 mi

Christians in Medieval Paris

Paris in the 12th century became perhaps the premier school and university center of Europe. The school of the cathedral of St Geneviève, the school of the house of Canons at St Victor and numerous masters and their pupils vying with one another for reputation made it attractive to ambitious young students. Many of them intended to make a career in the Church or the ecclesiastical civil service. In the 13th century Paris became the focus for the teaching of Scholasticism, and a number of colleges including the Sorbonne were founded to provide accommodation for poor students.

Left This court scene in Paris shows graphically one of the problems of 12th-century Church–state relations. In England Henry II quarreled with his archbishop Thomas Becket over the question of their respective jurisdictions in law. Church courts tried the clergy, and could not impose the death penalty. Those who were not clergy were anxious to prove that they were and get the benefit of clemency. The king attempted to impose restrictions on these would-be escapees from his jurisdiction. Here in Paris the clerical estate is present in court, in a body of bishops, while the king presides.

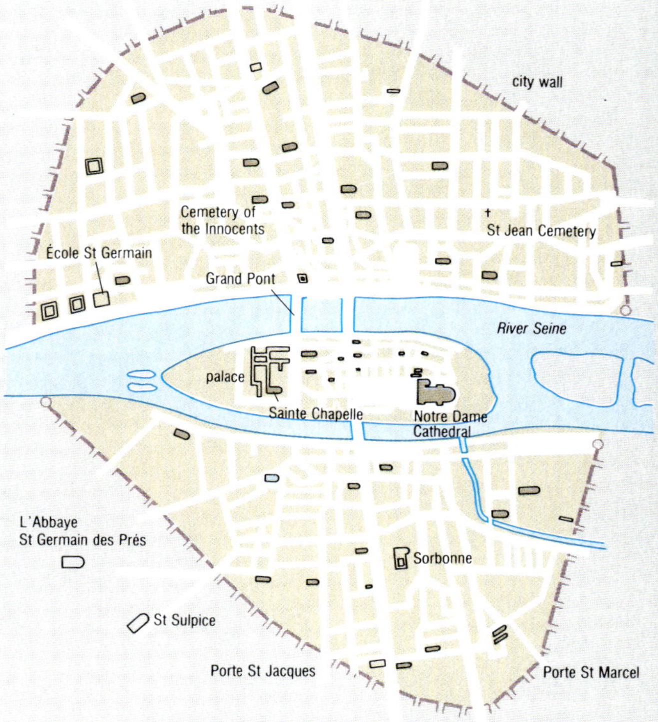

This 13th-century relief from the cathedral of Notre Dame at Paris is one of a series of pictures of student life. It shows the lecturer and his students. Lectures consisted of a systematic commentary on the set texts. In the 13th century the

pupils could hire the text a few pages at a time from booksellers, but many would listen without a copy to help them follow what was said, and most masters were careful to read the passage which was being discussed.

uses in his *De Monarchia* (3.4): those who argue that the empire's authority is subordinate to the Church's say that, "according to Genesis, God created two great luminaries, a greater and a lesser, one to govern the day and the other the night. This, they say, is an allegory for two types of power, spiritual and temporal. Then they argue that as the lesser luminary, the moon, has no light of its own except as it receives it from the sun, so temporal power has no authority, except as it is derived from spiritual." Dante himself was not quite certain where he stood on the matter, and other scholars of the later Middle Ages took such images and made them serve quite different arguments from those for which Gregory VII and St Bernard had used them. John of Paris, for example, writing *On Royal and Papal Power*, disposes of the "Donation of Constantine," not on the grounds that it is a forgery (its spuriousness was not realized until the end of the Middle Ages), but on the grounds that it affected only a specific portion of the empire, and was invalid for reasons which may be found in the gloss on the civil law (Ch.21). As to Bernard's argument in his letter to Eugenius III, that "the power of forgiving sins" is greater than that of "dividing estates," John answers that in "temporal matters the temporal power is greater than the spiritual, and in these matters is in no way subject to the spiritual since it is not derived from it" (Ch.5). Indeed, kingship came first in time, for there was no true priesthood before Jesus, and there were certainly kings before Jesus (Ch.4).

The matter of Church–state relations became academic, but it was never solely an academic issue. It became urgent again in the 16th century, again as a result of pressure from the Church, at the time of the Reformation.

Above In this miniature from a Hussite manuscript in Prague the painter shows the pope as he appeared to dissenters—vaingloriously wearing the triple crown and surrounded by monks who bow and scrape to him.

Below Christ's vicar on earth, the pope, is judging heretics. The fire of punishment is the burning of heretics. Hell is the imprisonment into which the condemned are being shepherded on the right. The picture emphasizes the authority given by Christ to his vicar.

This late 9th-century mosaic over the imperial doorway in St Sophia, Constantinople, shows Christ in majesty being adored by the emperor Leo VI, in token of the submission he owes to God.

Emperors and patriarchs in the east

At Constantinople and at Antioch, in the period of Byzantine rule there from 969 until the 1070s, there was to hand an alternative to patriarchal authority—the emperor's. His role overlapped, and sometimes clashed, with that of the patriarch. He too was entrusted by God with safeguarding the faith, and he had a particular duty to propagate the faith among infidels, bearing the epithet "equal of the apostles." He was also described as "the living law." The western concept of the pope as the maker of law was therefore not congenial to the Byzantines, even though emperors sometimes found it expedient to appeal to Rome for judgment against the patriarch of Constantinople. The western concept of the pope as an "emperor-maker" was also alien to the east. The "Donation of Constantine" extended to the secular and political sphere. The authority was founded on the text which papalists interpreted as Christ's bestowal of absolute authority over his Church on Peter. "You are Peter, the Rock, and on this rock I will build my church." "I will give you the keys of the kingdom of heaven; what you forbid on earth shall be forbidden in heaven, and what you allow on earth shall be allowed in heaven" (Matthew 16: 18–19).

No such claims to keys or kingdoms were made by any of the other patriarchs. In fact the role of the Constantinopolitan patriarch in the making of Byzantine emperors was modest. The patriarch normally placed the crown on the head of a new emperor, but did not have a monopoly in the conduct of inauguration ritual. The act of crowning associates as co-emperors was performed by existing emperors. No anointing took place in the middle Byzantine period, and the crowning did not acquire legal significance as the key act of conferment of authority. Neither did the patriarch exact any more precise undertaking from the crowned man than a general profession of the Orthodox faith. The emperor was in no way the patriarch's earthly lieutenant. The emperor was often termed "God-crowned" and was sometimes depicted as being crowned directly by Christ, the Virgin, or the hand of God. Such representations indicated that the elevation of an emperor was by the will of God and no single churchman was the special agent of that will. Even ambitious patriarchs such as Nicholas Mysticus referred to the elevation of an emperor as being by the "inscrutable" ways of God. Nicholas had his reasons for thus glossing over the rise to power of Romanus Lecapenus, but his avoidance of any formal claim to a right to make emperors is significant. Formulations of patriarchal authority could not easily be made in a state where a churchman, Theophylact of Ochrid, wrote of an emperor as "crowned by God and, if I may say so, God of the universe"!

Byzantine imperialists and many Byzantine churchmen were, then, speaking a different language from Roman papalists.

PART THREE

TO BE A PILGRIM

Holy Pilgrimage

Left This little medallion worn by a Greek pilgrim shows a simple representation of the Virgin and Child. It was found in the church of St John at Ephesus. This shrine, where St John was believed to have spent his old age, was an important center of pilgrimage until the Turks invaded the area and the shrine at Patmos replaced it as the focus of pilgrimage to the saint. Ephesus also had the first church dedicated to the Virgin.

The idea of pilgrimage rests on two conceptions which are very ancient in Christian tradition. The first is the idea of the soul of man on earth as an exile, traveling home to God. The whole of life is thus a pilgrimage to heaven. The second is the belief that certain objects and places are in some way a focus of holiness, where the spiritual world can be touched. To visit a shrine of a saint, where the saint's relics are kept, or to go to a place such as Rome or Jerusalem, was to come closer to God. So strong were these two notions that in simple people's minds in the Middle Ages to travel to Jerusalem on earth seemed little different from traveling to Jerusalem above, the heavenly Jerusalem or City of God itself. To go on pilgrimage was a way of getting to heaven.

Some of the earliest pilgrims, like the 4th-century Egeria, were something of pioneers, finding their way to holy places which were scarcely "on the map" and along dangerous and ill-defined roads. By contrast, in or before the 11th century mass pilgrimages became increasingly popular. Alongside true piety ran a holiday spirit. These medieval package-tours included entertainment and souvenirs. Something of the flavor of one later medieval English pilgrimage can be got from Chaucer's *The Canterbury Tales*.

Certain pilgrim shrines became great and important. The three most notable in Europe throughout the Middle Ages were Rome (St Peter), Compostela in Spain (St James) and Jerusalem itself, together with the other places in the Holy Land especially associated with the life of Jesus. In the second quarter of the 12th century St Bernard of Clairvaux wrote a book for the newly founded Knights Templar, soldiers living under monastic rule and dedicated to the service and protection of the Holy Places. He took them on a "guided tour" of the Holy Places, pausing before each and reminding them of its meaning. In addition, other shrines, such as that of St Thomas Becket at Canterbury, became internationally famous. Becket was archbishop of Canterbury in the reign of Henry II of England and fell out with the king, who had appointed him because he was an old friend, over the respective rights of jurisdiction of Church and state. Becket was murdered within the cathedral in a horrifying breach of the peace of a holy place (sanctuary), by men anxious to win the king's favor. The public reaction was of such horror and disgust that Henry had to do public penance to save his throne. Becket was canonized, and the affair became so notorious throughout Europe that the shrine of Becket drew pilgrims from everywhere.

Shrines became wealthy because of the tourist trade they attracted, and the churches and cathedrals which house them are often particularly splendid. At Lourdes, for example, the fine church of the Rosary was built beside the church over the grotto between 1883 and 1901. At Santiago de

Below A male and a female pilgrim travel together here, their headgear marked with a cross, their eyes meekly downcast, hands clasped in prayer or held to the breast. A 15th-century fresco from the workshop of Ghirlandaio in the church of San Martino, Florence.

Below In this 13th-century window in the Trinity Chapel of Canterbury Cathedral bare-headed pilgrims are shown with wallet, water bottle and staff. This evidently non-military garb was a protection for pilgrims in foreign lands, where they were normally given safe conduct.

Compostela and at Canterbury the cathedral buildings reflect the importance of the shrine in their magnificence that was felt to be only proper, a mark of respect for the saint, and an appropriate way to use the funds which flooded in in the form of gifts and offerings from the pious.

The miraculous cures which sometimes took place at shrines were another major and consistent factor in the history of pilgrimage. It sometimes happened in the Middle Ages that when an abbot or bishop died his bones effected such a cure by chance. Then a campaign would be mounted for canonization and the shrine might become an established center of pilgrimage for many generations. The most striking modern example is perhaps the spring in the grotto at Lourdes.

Lourdes belongs to a group of pilgrim centers associated not with the life of Jesus on earth or with saints but with the Blessed Virgin. At a number of places she has appeared in visions (especially to children or young girls), or a statue of the Virgin (often of no special importance artistically) has appeared to move. A case of a moving statue of the Virgin recently in Ireland has begun to draw large numbers who hope to see the miracle recur. The importance of these Mary shrines in popular piety attests to her special place in the affections of Orthodox and Roman Catholics worldwide, as an example of mercy and gentleness and as deserving special honor as the Mother of Our Lord. At Tinos in Greece the shrine draws those in search of a miraculous cure just as Lourdes does in the west, and the sick sleep outside the church all night, waiting to visit the shrine.

In the modern world pilgrimage has often had a strong element of witness—that is of a public manifestation both to the Church and to the world of the fellowship of the Christian community in every place and in every age. The millions of pilgrims who criss-cross the globe each year meet in polyglot crowds at the shrines. A group of Americans dressed in timeless white robes can be seen crossing St Peter's Square with airline bags on their shoulders. Another party carries a banner which informs the world that it comes from a parish in Venice. The silent or singing patient queues have eyes and hearts fixed on a place of proven holiness and they wait without squabble or disorder. Their witness to peace and fellowship is perhaps largely unconscious, but sometimes their banners declare it clearly. (See, for example, the Christian CND marchers on p.184.)

To some Protestants the notion of a local focus of holiness in this world associated with a saint or with the Blessed Virgin is an unacceptable distraction from the centrality of faith in Christ, and a distraction too from the spiritual to the material. There is, however, an important sense in which it is a help—and not only to the simple—to be able to use an object or a place which can be seen and touched as a way of concentrating prayer. Just as a flower or a landscape can lift the soul to God (as Gerard Manley Hopkins understood better perhaps than any other modern poet), so a holy place or a holy thing may act as a step to spiritual understanding.

The tradition and the practice of such devotion are very ancient. The Paduan Gabriele Capodilista, who made a pilgrimage to Jerusalem in 1458, recorded in his diary his meditations on gospel events at the relevant holy sites and sometimes the prayers that he said there. More formal devotions were not neglected. Nearly five centuries later the poet T.S. Eliot made a pilgrimage to the obscure Cambridgeshire village of Little Gidding, which forms the subject of the last of his *Four Quartets*. In this place in 1625 Nicholas Ferrar founded his small family-based community devoted to prayer and works of charity. Eliot touches upon the way in which the visitor's sense of the continuity of worship in a particular place nourishes his own prayers and meditations there:

> You are not here to verify,
> Instruct yourself, or inform curiosity
> Or carry report. You are here to kneel
> Where prayer has been valid.

The physical activity of journeying to God can also be a help to the mind in making its own journey. Those who join processions of witness, those who march in support of peace or good causes, those who go on sponsored walks to raise money for charity, are all engaging in this sort of pilgrim activity.

Polish pilgrims on an Easter pilgrimage in the rain at Kalwaria Zebrzydowska, hunched under umbrellas.

Left Easter pilgrims in St Peter's Square, Rome, in the Holy Year of 1975.

Below The sick brought to Lourdes in hope of a miraculous cure maintain a long tradition of healing at the shrines of pilgrimage. Lourdes is the site of the visions of Bernadette Soubirous, a 14-year-old peasant girl, in 1858. She saw the Blessed Virgin in a grotto in the rock and a spring burst out of the rock. Those who bathed in the waters were healed. By 1862 the place was recognized by the Church as a pilgrim shrine and since then Lourdes has become a major center for pilgrims in search of healing, millions going there every year, especially on the anniversary of the apparition (11 February).

Bottom A Palm Sunday procession going down from the Mount of Olives, Jerusalem.

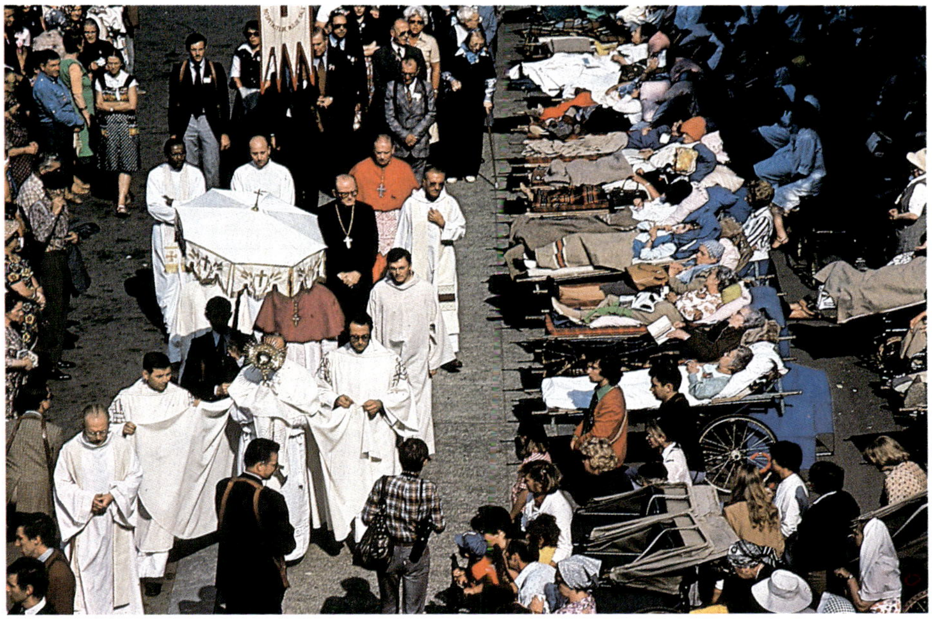

Above A circle of pilgrims at a service in the snow outside the Orthodox church at Souzdel in Russia.

Opposite At Fatima in Portugal three children saw a vision of the Blessed Virgin in May 1917. She appeared to them six times. On her last visit she explained to them that she was "Our Lady of the Rosary." She told the children to say their rosary prayers every day and she asked for a chapel to be built for her at that place. Only one of the children survived to grow up. She became a Carmelite nun and later wrote an account of the visions. She gave the "threefold message of Fatima": penance, the importance of saying the rosary prayers, and devotion to the Immaculate Heart of Mary. This site has become a major pilgrim shrine. In the picture the pilgrim embraces the cross he has carried, his face transfigured by devotion.

Right A procession of pilgrims to the shrine of Our Lady at Copacabana in Argentina.

Overleaf The shrine at Loreto is another of those which belong to the Virgin, but whereas Fatima is very new, Loreto is an old site of pilgrimage still attracting large numbers today. The shrine, near Ancona in Italy, is on the site to which the house in which Mary was believed to be living at the time of the Annunciation was, according to legend, miraculously brought by angels from Nazareth. The first record of the story, about 1470, is contemporary with the great basilica built in Mary's honor. Loreto is a center of pious pilgrimage for Roman Catholics from all over the world.

PART FOUR

REFORM AND REACTION

THE LATE MIDDLE AGES: VITALITY OR DECLINE?

Call a period "the age of Reformation," or of "Renaissance," and that immediately preceding it will automatically be thought of as one of corruption or decline. The religion of Europe in the years before Luther's revolt is therefore always considered in the light of what was *wrong* with it. But no religion can be understood unless we look at its positive content as well as its defects, and there are important ways in which the years before 1517 can be seen as years of great spiritual vitality. We need to see both sides of the coin.

The late medieval papacy

To look first at the negative side. The most spectacular ill of the Church was the papacy. The fantastic network of patronage, legislation and taxation which had been perfected under Innocent III and his successors persisted, but the prestige of the pope as the religious leader of Europe was at an all-time low. From 1378 to 1417 there were two lines of popes demanding the allegiance of a bewildered Europe, and the attempt by the Council of Pisa in 1409 to resolve the problem led only to the election of a third pope. Inevitably, uncertainty led to the dwindling of the importance of the papacy in men's minds, and to the emergence of theological speculation about the problems of a divided or corrupt papacy. The conciliar movement, based on the belief that a general council was superior to a pope and could depose him, became increasingly attractive, and it was a council, that of Constance in 1417, which ended the schism. No subsequent pope ever accepted the notion of limited monarchy by which the conciliar movement tried to interpret the papacy but it remained a potent force in men's minds at the beginning of the 16th century.

Other lessons had been learned from the schism. It was an age in which the claims of national governments were growing, and secular powers were eager to extend their competence. The monolithic Church of the high Middle Ages had been the chief challenge to this growing claim to omnicompetence, and many rulers had welcomed the divided papacy, as offering a less formidable challenge. Lorenzo de Medici was not alone in thinking that "if it were possible without scandal, three or four popes would be better than a single one." One of the main attractions of Protestantism to 16th-century rulers would be this very division of the center of religious authority into units more easily controlled than the papacy had been. "Christendom" was dissolving.

The greatest weakness of the papacy, however, was the character of the popes themselves. The 15th century had seen great popes, but increasingly the see of Peter was occupied by men who were Italian princes rather than universal spiritual leaders, and some of them were of vicious character. Sixtus IV (1471–84) is one of the key figures here, for his ambitions were essentially those of a temporal prince. Locked in a series of power struggles with Lorenzo de Medici, with Ferrara and with Venice, he promoted his horde of impecunious and rapacious nephews on a scale and with a blatancy unprecedented even in the history of Rome. The most notorious of these Renaissance prince-popes was the Spaniard Roderigo Borgia, who as Alexander VI presided at his daughter's wedding and flaunted a young mistress within the Vatican itself. His son, Cesare, the model for Machiavelli's *Prince*, gave a party in the Vatican in 1502 at which 50 prostitutes danced naked, picked chestnuts off the floor with their teeth and were competed for by the men present.

Yet none of these men was without redeeming features, considered even as pope. The venal and ambitious Sixtus IV was the second founder of the Vatican library, built the Sistine chapel and was a generous patron of charitable institutions and churches, while even Alexander VI set up in 1497 a commission of cardinals to draft a scheme of reform for the Church. But their virtues were secular virtues, as in the splendor of their patronage of the arts, especially under the warrior-pope Julius II, for whom Raphael decorated the Vatican and who engaged Michelangelo as architect for the rebuild-

Loyalty during the Great Schism 1378–1417
The division of the papacy divided western Christendom politically for a complex of reasons, as rulers played upon the situation. From 1309 to 1377 the popes resided at Avignon. After the papal court returned to Rome in 1377 "antipopes," rivals to the pope in Rome, continued to hold court there, first "Clement VII" and then "Benedict XIII," who was deposed by the Council of Constance in 1417. This period came to be known as the Great Schism. It began after the election of Pope Urban VI when the future "Benedict XIII," Pedro de Luna, changed allegiance and supported the rival candidate, the antipope Clement. When Clement died in 1394 "Benedict" was chosen as his successor, promising to bring the schism to an end. Once enthroned, he was no longer willing to give up his own claim, and successive attempts were made to depose him. Schism between rival papal claimants was nothing new, but this episode came at a time when the

papacy was under assault from dissenters who saw corruption in papal claims to plenitude of power. France was loyal to the Avignon papacy for geographical reasons. Her traditional enemies supported Rome (England, northern Italy). The southern Italians and Sicilians lined up against their old enemies the northern Italians. The German princes played their long-standing game of alternating their support for rival papal claimants.

Right Despite his pious posture in Pinturicchio's picture, Roderigo Borgia, Pope Alexander VI (1492–1503), was the most notorious of all the popes, an extravagant womanizer intent on enriching his children. Responsible for the torture and burning of the reforming friar Savonarola, Alexander is believed to have died of a poison he had intended for one of his cardinals.

Far right Leo X (pope 1513–21) became a cardinal at 13, and pope at 37. He was the younger son of Lorenzo Medici (Lorenzo the Magnificent). He was a wily and dishonest politician and an extravagant patron of the arts. His desperate financial needs (he once had to pawn his furniture) led to the sale of the indulgence against which Luther posted his 95 theses. He was the pope who awarded Henry VIII the title Defender of the Faith, for his book against Luther. English monarchs have used the title ever since.

Right Sixtus IV (pope 1471–84) represents the contradictions of the Renaissance papacy. Personally pious, a fine preacher and competent theologian, he was a devoted client of the Virgin Mary, founded the Sistine chapel choir and built many churches. But his extravagance plunged the papacy into debt, and his family entanglements (one nephew became Julius II) involved the holy see in Italian power politics. In this fresco from the Vatican library by Melozzo da Forli he is shown receiving the humanist Bartholomeo Platina (1421–81) whom he made his librarian, despite rumors of Platina's heresy and even paganism. Yet Sixtus IV was also the founder of the Spanish Inquisition!

ing of St Peter's. That rebuilding itself symbolized much about them. At one level it was an act of piety and a celebration of religious truth, at another it was an act of *superbia*, of breathtaking arrogance and extravagance involving the destruction of the central shrine of Christendom.

The products of a new confidence in man and his capacities, of a commitment to this world and a belief that in its beauty lay not the snares of the devil but the good things of God, they are men only to be understood in the context of the Italian Renaissance. It is no accident that from 1480 the business of the papal Curia was no longer transacted in the universal lingua franca of Latin but in Italian. Non-Italian observers were very conscious of this trend. Reform treatises, like the German "Concerning the filth of the Roman Curia," reflect it, and so devout a Catholic as Thomas More could remind his king that the pope was not simply the head of the Church, but an Italian prince, to whom allegiance, even religious allegiance, should be given with caution.

Corruption and degradation of the Church

The rest of the hierarchy was hardly better. The fabric of the medieval Church was riddled with inconsistencies, inequalities, inefficiencies. Of the 670 bishoprics of Europe over 300 were in Italy, while for the whole of Germany and central Europe there were only 90. Remote and tribal Ireland, with 35, had more than England, Wales and Scotland put together. Among bishoprics there were wild variations of income and resources. The bishops of Winchester in England and Rouen in France had incomes rated in the papal chancery at 12 000 florins, while the bishop of Ross in Ireland or Ruvo in Italy had a beggarly 33 florins. The greater sees were eagerly sought by noble families for their younger sons, and were bought and sold. Ludovico Sforza sought the archbishopric of Milan for his nine-year-old bastard son, and the Medici pope Leo X became a cardinal at the age of 13. Many prelates, like Cardinal Wolsey, were great officers of state, who held numerous ecclesiastical posts and therefore neglected all of them. Both popes and secular princes used bishoprics and other ecclesiastical offices to reward their civil servants. At various points in the 14th and 15th centuries the archdeacons of Buckingham, Leicester, Northampton and Oxford were all either French or Italian cardinals.

At the humbler level of the parish clergy things were no better. There were virtually no seminaries, so clergy could only be trained in the universities or cathedral schools, or by apprenticeship to a working priest. Only the elite went to college or school, and they were siphoned off into secular or ecclesiastical administration. Most aspiring clerics learned rubrics and the smattering of Latin necessary for the services from a priest who had himself had little or no training. Examinations for ordination were perfunctory, and the great 15th-century preacher St Bernardino of Siena tells of a priest who only knew the Hail Mary, and used it even at the elevation at mass. Concubinage was widespread: impecunious clergy with a houseful of children, presiding over a half-coherent liturgy on Sundays and indistinguishable from their parishioners as they worked their farmland the rest of the week, were common all over Europe. Absenteeism was rife. A quarter of the parishes of the diocese of Strasbourg were without resident clergy by the 1520s, while in the diocese of Geneva, a wild mountainous area certainly, and therefore worse than many, the figure may have been as high as 80 percent. Yet here, as everywhere in Europe, there was a glut of clergy—Geneva had 2000 priests for its 453 parishes. Most of these were "mass-priests"—chaplains serving the non-parochial altars of churches or chantries given over to the celebration of masses for the dead.

The monastic life shared in the general decline. In England comfortable mediocrity prevailed. Elsewhere, as in Italy and parts of France, there were many openly scandalous houses. There was everywhere a decline in numbers, and handfuls of monks lived in luxury on incomes intended to maintain hundreds. Sexual laxity was not uncommon, though probably few bishops can have encountered figures like the south Italian abbot who had a concubine and five children, whom he refused to send away because, as he told the bishop, he was fond of the children, and his physician had prescribed sexual intercourse for his gallstones!

The situation was perhaps worst in convents of nuns. Most nuns were the surplus daughters of well-to-do families, who found the modest entrance payment to a convent cheaper than a marriage dowry. Few had vocations, and the enforced idleness in which they lived bred mischief—backbiting, worldliness and, inevitably, sexual intrigue. It was a common joke, with a core of truth, that half the relics of the Holy Innocents, found all over Europe, were in fact the bones of murdered monastic by-blows.

The friars and lay piety

There were of course exceptions to all this. "Reform" or "observant" groups existed within all the religious orders, and there were edifying monasteries like the London Charterhouse. There were saintly bishops, like Archbishop Antonino of Florence. The voice of reform sounded throughout the 15th century, in the conciliar movement and in figures like the German Cardinal Nicholas of Cusa, or the Dominican Savonarola. It was an age which was avid for preaching, and vernacular sermons by Franciscan or Dominican friars, often leading to spectacular if sometimes short-lived mass conversions, were a regular feature of 15th-century town life. Savonarola, St Vincent Ferrer, a Spanish Dominican, and St Bernardino of Siena, an observant Franciscan, are only the best-known of many popular preachers. St Bernardino even taught that sermons were more important than the mass itself.

It would be easy to give a description of late medieval lay piety in terms of its constituent parts and in a way which would emphasize its oddity and the element of "magic" or "superstition." Such an account would stress elaborate rituals, "rites of passage," processions, pilgrimages and vigils at shrines, the cult of relics and dependence on the saints, above all the obsessive concern with death and the afterlife which had contributed to the multiplication of masses and altars (and thereby clerical overpopulation), and the eagerness

Right: Pilgrimage in the Middle Ages
Medieval pilgrim routes depended upon reasonable safety of travel. They were often closely associated with trade routes, trade following pilgrims and pilgrims trade, as mutually beneficial in a practical way. In the Holy Land, where there was danger of attack by the "infidel" as well as of highway robbery, the Templars, or Knights of the Temple, were founded in the early 12th century to protect traveling pilgrims and ensure their safe conduct.

Below Devotion to the saints in the Middle Ages focused on their graves, or on portions of their bodies, "relics," which were believed to mediate power and healing to the believer. Relics, like the Blessed Sacrament, represented in the most concrete way imaginable the medieval Catholic conviction of the universal presence of the divine in human life. In this 14th-century Italian reliquary the relics (exposed in the center of each panel) are surmounted by images of the Incarnation and Passion of Christ, the mysteries from which the saints derived their power.

of men and women to acquire indulgences which would release their relatives and themselves from the tortures of Purgatory. But there is a danger that such a list will miss the heart of the religion of the late Middle Ages—its concern with community, with social relations, with the role of the sacred as the ground and support of human community. Christianity was emphatically concerned with building up "the unity of the Spirit in the bond of peace."

This communal concern is evident above all in the preoccupation with the dead. It was believed that even good Christians died imperfect. Every man, woman and child must therefore endure unspeakable tortures in Purgatory for the imperfectly repented and expiated sins of a lifetime. This torment could be shortened by the prayer of the saints and of living friends and relatives, by masses for the dead, by the papal pardons known as indulgences. It impinged on every aspect of lay piety. Testators left money for masses to be said at their funerals, at their "month's mind," on the anniversary of their death. Bereaved families prayed for their relatives, as they hoped to be prayed for in turn.

Confraternities and the cult of the saints

The most vital religious institutions of the time were the "confraternities," religious brotherhoods of lay people dedicated to a patron saint, to the Virgin or to some aspect of Christ's Passion or glorified humanity (the Five Wounds, the Precious Blood, the Blessed Sacrament). Every parish had at least one of these brotherhoods. In 15th-century Norfolk there were over 900. These groups, run usually by laymen, attended the funerals of members, paid for masses, dispensed charity to orphans and widows, gave doles to the poor whose prayers for the dead were believed to be especially pleasing to God. Thus the whole community was drawn into mutual concern, rich and poor, saint and sinner.

The confraternities and guilds promoted community in other ways too. In Italy in particular there were many confraternities concerned with works of mercy—to the dying, the poor, to prisoners—and this "civic Christianity" produced a flood of orphanages, hospitals and almshouses. Elsewhere trade guilds united craftsmen and workers in a sense of corporate identity. The cycles of religious plays celebrated in many late medieval cities were organized by trades, or "mysteries," and were crucial in the maintenance of peace and the social pecking order. The guild processions on festivals such as Corpus Christi served the same function. The sacramental presence itself was an expression of *communal* awareness. At Provins in France the confraternities organized a Corpus Christi procession and mass. The cultic celebration of Christ's body was then followed by a celebration of the social body, with street parties, games and dancing, and "by this means they maintain peace, concord and amity with one another . . . the poor as well as the rich . . ." That these celebrations expressed a real aspect of the Gospel is evident; it is equally clear that such junketings could produce less respectable results, and clerical reformers took a jaundiced view of them which historians have too readily followed.

The cult of the saints reflected similar concerns. If the ordinary dead needed the prayers of the living, the living needed the prayers of the holy dead. Every Christian had his own patron, whose name he took at baptism. Villages had a communal patron, whose relic or image was kept in the parish church or local shrine, and which might be carried in procession around the parish in times of social crisis such as disease or harvest failure. This cult of relics and holy images helped localize the sacred; it made visible and concrete the eternal significance of the daily preoccupations and afflictions of mankind. Earth and heaven were thus bound up in a great community of concern.

Of course much of this was "superstitious" and "magical." Few of the clergy were educated enough to be able to exercise any corrective influence, and attempts by reform-minded bishops or preachers to regulate the more dubious aspects of lay religious observance were resented, resisted or ignored as foreign interference. Sacramental belief toppled over into animism. Holy water, dust from the altar steps, even the stolen sacramental bread were used to conjure illnesses. The multiplication of saints' cults and the huge inflation of relics tended to the debasement of the holy.

The "domestication" of the sacred which took place is reflected charmingly in the familiarity with which the saints were treated—addressed as "Monsieur St Claude, my godfather," or portrayed in sculpture and glass in the everyday clothes of the period and with peasant faces or hands. Its less charming dimension is reflected in incidents like that of the Florentine who slashed a picture of the Virgin because she had not brought him luck in gambling, or in the perverted sense of the omnipresence of the supernatural associated with the growing fear of witchcraft. It is typical of the ambivalence of late medieval religion that the chief propagator of the tender and evangelical devotion of the rosary in Germany, the Dominican Jacob Sprenger, should have been also one of the authors of *Malleus Maleficarum*, the horrifying treatise which became the basis of the growing pogrom against witches.

The *Imitation of Christ* and Christian Humanism

Mention of the rosary makes it clear that the spiritual energy of the late Middle Ages found expression not only in corporate religiosity. This was especially true in northern Europe, where there had arisen a fervent, introspective piety based in meditation on the Gospels and mysteries of religion, the *Devotio Moderna*. It emphasized the simple life of prayer, self-denial and practical works of charity. It has been called a "commonsense mysticism," and its classic expression was Thomas à Kempis's *Imitation of Christ*. This little book, published in 1418, embodied much that was most characteristic in late medieval Christianity, for example its concern with death and judgment and its penitential character, its reverence of priesthood and the sacrament of the altar. It contained also, however, much that ran counter to the trends already described, as in Thomas's dismissal of the "many" who "hurry about from place to place to visit the relics of the saints . . . and to gaze at the spacious churches built in their honor and kiss their sacred bones all from mere human curiosity and the novelty of the sight." Such exercises, he thought, were barren, and men would do better to approach with love and devotion the sacrament on the altars of their parish churches. Thomas was urging an inner pilgrimage of repentance and devotion in opposition to a religion of externals.

This is the religion of a bookish individual, to be pursued in the silence and privacy of one's own room (and only the prosperous, it should be noted, had a room to themselves in late medieval Europe). It found an echo in a movement equally at odds with much in the contemporary religious scene, that of Christian Humanism, the religious dimension of the Renaissance.

Above Processions were (and in many places are still) a fundamental part of Catholic piety. They enacted the notion of life as a journey, enabled the Christian community to display its solidarity, order and orthodoxy, and sanctified the physical boundaries within which it lived.

Above Erasmus, the most influential critic of late medieval religion, is portrayed here by Dürer ten years before his death, ink pot and pen in hand, surrounded by his writings, and with an inscription in Latin and Greek; the engraving is effectively an icon of the patron saint of the new learning.

Left Throughout Christian history intellectuals and reformers have been uneasy about the excesses and abuses of popular religion. In the younger Holbein's marginal sketch in a copy of Erasmus's reforming satire *Praise of Folly*, a foolish traveler seeks to guarantee a safe journey by appealing to St Christopher. It was widely believed that if one looked at a picture of Christopher, no harm could come to one that day.

The Renaissance has often been seen as an anti-religious movement, a revival of classical pagan values, a preoccupation with this world, its beauty and its power, a vision of man not as the fallen sinner of medieval piety but as lord of creation to whom all things were possible. Renaissance art glorified the body, often the naked body. It lavished on palaces and townhalls the riches and grandeur which the Middle Ages had reserved for cathedrals. In fact the more positive view of human potential which lay behind the great flowering of creative energy which began in Florence was rooted in Christian thought, in particular in the writings of the Neoplatonic tradition as found in Christian writers like Origen and St Augustine, and in traditional exposition of the story of the creation of man in Genesis. Renaissance art was overwhelmingly religious in character: it has been calculated that only 13 percent of the works of art produced in Italy from 1420 to 1539 were of secular topics. The elaborate religious processions which punctuated the life of the great cities of northern Italy, and the eagerness with which the hard-headed rulers of Venice acquired expensive relics, testify to the importance religion had for them. So too does the extraordinary effect of Savonarola's apocalyptic preaching in Florence in the 1490s, when he became virtual ruler of the city, and numbered Botticelli among his converts.

Erasmus and the religious Renaissance

But it was above all in northern Europe that the Renaissance took its most directly religious form. There the quest for a return to the pure sources of culture, the "classics," led to a desire to force the pure impulse of Christianity from the accretions of ritual and oversubtle theology which had turned it from a living spirit to a system. Men like Johannes Reuchlin (1455–1522) in Germany or Jacques Lefèvre d'Étaples (1455–1536) in France moved from the study of the pagan classics and philosophy to the study of scripture in its original tongues. Reuchlin's Hebrew grammar and lexicon revolutionized the study of the Old Testament and provoked a furious attack on his orthodoxy by the Dominicans of Cologne which became a set-piece confrontation between traditionalists and humanists.

In Desiderius Erasmus (1466–1536) northern Humanism found its most characteristic expression. Educated by the Brethren of the Common Life, the propagators of the *Devotio Moderna*, Erasmus combined the practical internalized piety of the *Imitation of Christ* with the new learning. His editions of the works of St Jerome, Irenaeus, Ambrose, Augustine and other Fathers was an attempt to go behind the complexities of medieval theology to the "classical" sources. Above all, his edition of the Greek New Testament with a modern Latin translation (1516) sought to bring before men "Christ speaking, healing, dying and rising." Christ was, for Erasmus, "our only teacher . . . What will you find in Thomas, in Scotus, compared to his teaching?" He wanted to see the scriptures in the hands of "the farmer, the tailor, the traveler and the Turk," to hear the plowman at his plow singing the Psalms.

Himself a displaced person, traveling from the Netherlands to Paris, to England, to Rome, to Switzerland, a man who lived inside his head, he had no sympathy for the religion of place and community. Relics, pilgrimage, monasteries, hierarchy, even the sacraments were all to him at best secondary, and more often than not substitutes for true Christianity, the spirit of Jesus. In the manual of the Christian life he published in 1504 he wrote "Of what use is it to be sprinkled on the outside by holy water if you are filthy inside? If you want to please Peter and Paul, imitate them. I do not condemn you for venerating the ashes of Paul, but if you neglect his living image, speaking in his letters, your devotion is preposterous. You make much of a fragment of his body, boxed up in a shrine: do you admire the whole word of Paul shining through his epistles?"

In a stream of comic and serious works Erasmus attacked the monastic orders for their greed and laziness, the hierarchy and the clergy for their ignorance and immorality, even the papacy itself in an anonymous satire in which Julius II finds himself locked out of heaven by St Peter, who does not recognize in the warrior-prince his own successor. Erasmus offered instead a religion of sweet reasonableness, a contempt of technical theology, an insistence instead on the imitation of Jesus which reveals his indebtedness to the *Devotio Moderna*. He had no wish to overturn, only to reform. Patronized by popes, by churchmen like Archbishop Warham of Canterbury, by scholars and statesmen like Thomas More, by kings like Henry VIII and Charles V, Erasmus's influence was immense. Learned Europe roared with laughter at his *Praise of Folly* and *Julius Exclusus*, prayed with his *Enchiridion*, discovered in his translation of the New Testament reasons to doubt much of the teaching and practice of late medieval religion. Where the official version (the Vulgate) had Jesus say in Matthew 4:17 "Do penance, and believe the Gospel," Erasmus translated "Repent (be sorry) and believe the Gospel." If Erasmus's translation was right, Jesus was calling men to change their hearts and minds, not to go to confession or perform acts of penance. Here, in elegant Latin, was revolution.

The religion of the late Middle Ages, then, was a rich and complex thing. Decline is evident in many of its institutions, but more striking are its vitality and diversity. Indeed it was that very diversity which made its balance so precarious. The papacy pursued its artistic and political aims, resented by the Germans and English who were expected to finance it. Bishops and enlightened administrators sought to impose order and proportion on the anarchy of popular celebrations, and cast suspicious or despairing eyes on the individualist enthusiasm of southern hermits or northern mystics. Diocesan clergy denounced the preaching friars who drew away their parishioners and therefore their income. Local religious loyalties cut across external structures and official orthodoxy. Humanists flailed the corruption of hierarchy and the abuses of the ignorant. Princes in pursuit of territorial consolidation and juridical independence sawed away at the bonds of obedience and obligation which were the sinews of Christendom. Here was a tinder barrel waiting for the match. In 1517 an obscure theology professor in a German provincial university lit it.

REFORMATION: THE FOUNDATIONS SHAKEN

Martin Luther
Martin Luther (1453–1546) is in many ways a medieval figure. Born of peasant stock in one of the least civilized areas of Germany, he never entirely shook off the mental world of the peasant. His conversion to the monastic life after a university training for the law could have come from a saint's life in the *Golden Legend*, for it was the result of a terror-stricken vow to St Anne taken in a thunderstorm. Yet if he is in one sense a product of the concrete wonderworld of the late Middle Ages, a man of sign and symbol, in another he embodies the solvent individualist culture of the word, represented in different ways by the northern mystics, by the *Devotio Moderna*, and by Erasmus. Both elements contributed to the character of the Lutheran reformation.

Luther was a model monk, quickly rising to positions of authority in the Augustinian order. In 1511 he became professor of philosophy at the new university of Wittenberg. Here terror surfaced again. His deep-seated sense of unworthiness before the wrath of a just God drove him to extravagant penances and obsessive daily confessions. He became a gaunt, wild-eyed figure, as can still be discerned in his early portraits, suffering from scruples, a morbid condition recognized in the confessional textbooks, in which the penitent became preoccupied with his own inadequacy rather than God's mercy in the sacrament. With inspired insight his confessor persuaded him to take on the Bible chair at Wittenberg. Between

Right Cranach produced a striking series of propaganda images of Luther throughout his life, culminating in a bizarre portrait of the reformer on his deathbed. Here he is engraved at the beginning of his career as reformer, but still wearing tonsure and cowl. In many such representations Luther has been given a halo, and the dove of the Holy Ghost hovers over him. Mass-produced, such images helped create a Luther myth.

Right In an age of mass illiteracy, visual images were vital to Reformation propaganda. In this elaborate Lutheran print of 1545 the "true" Protestant Church is contrasted with the papal Church of Antichrist. On the left, Luther preaches, while the pious Elector John Frederick listens. He is carrying the cross, as a good Christian and a good prince should. Lutheran ministers, surrounded by a devout and well-educated laity, administer the two evangelical sacraments of baptism and the Lord's Supper. Notice that the communicants receive communion in the traditional manner, direct into the mouth, kneeling, that one of the ministers wears traditional Catholic mass vestments, and that the altar is surmounted by a crucifix. On the right the devil puffs lies into a monk's ear as he preaches (in contrast to the Holy Spirit who inspires Luther). The pope does a roaring trade in indulgences and false pardons, while, in the background, various aspects of Catholic ceremonial and observance are satirized. Above, an angry God showers down fire and brimstone, which the merits of the saints, symbolized by St Francis's stigmata, are powerless to avert.

Left Hieronymus Bosch's extraordinary picture of the Seven Deadly Sins depicts in vivid contemporary detail late medieval man's sense of the variety and power of human evil. It is a striking example of the way in which the Church's moral teaching could be communicated in a non-literate culture. Reading anticlockwise from the bottom, we are shown Anger, Pride, Lust, Sloth, Gluttony, Avarice and Envy. In the center is the figure of the wounded Christ, the Man of Sorrows. A constant theme of late medieval piety was the attempt to move men and women to repentance by contrasting the loving generosity of Christ, pierced for our sins, with humanity's hard-hearted ingratitude. Surrounding the picture are representations of the deathbed, judgment, hell, and heaven, the "Four Last Things."

1513 and 1518 Luther preached and lectured his way through the Psalms and the Epistles to the Romans, Galatians and Hebrews in their original languages. In the process he found spiritual peace and evolved a revolutionary theology.

Luther's fear of God was based on the notion of divine justice with all its medieval connotations of doom. He discovered that the biblical concept of justice meant rather the goodness and righteousness of God himself, freely given to those who trusted in him through Christ. In the Pauline saying "the righteous shall live by faith" he found the reassurance he sought. The saint was not a man who no longer sinned; he was a sinner who put all his trust in Christ. Good works contributed nothing to salvation. Faith, a childlike dependence on God, was all. There was a place for moral striving and good works in the Christian life, but this effort was the grateful response of the redeemed man to a loving God, an attempt to become what in God's eyes he already was. A phrase from his lectures on Romans puts the matter pithily—"always a sinner, always a penitent, always right with God."

Luther was indebted to many sources—the northern mystics, St Augustine and his German commentators, the nominalist philosophy in which he had been trained. But he went far beyond any of them in his insistence on man's total corruption and helplessness before God. On this issue he was to break, spectacularly, with Erasmus in 1525, but Humanism too played a crucial role in his development, for it was with the aid of Greek philology and Erasmus's New Testament that Luther arrived at his interpretation of St Paul. Like Erasmus Luther recognized that the New Testament bade men "repent," turn around in heart and mind, and not "do penance" in the sense of works of satisfaction. Unlike Erasmus he grasped clearly that if this were so, then the whole medieval fabric of penance and merit, and above all the practice of indulgences, must collapse.

The practice of indulgences

An indulgence was originally a dispensation from the penance or satisfaction required of a penitent. A man might be permitted, for example, to commute a pilgrimage to the Holy Land to a gift of alms to the poor, or to a church, and the performance of some less rigorous pious act. Theologians gradually elaborated this notion. Christ had acquired a boundless "treasure of merit" for mankind. The pope could apply this merit to repentant sinners, like a banker transferring money from a rich man's deposit to a bankrupt's cash account. And cash became crucial. Over time alms to the poor became payments to the pope, an indispensable source of papal revenue. Popular imagination distorted the doctrine. It was widely believed, and came to be taught, that indulgences could take away sins, and could be applied to the suffering souls in Purgatory. Indulgences attached to relics, shrines, prescribed prayers, multiplied.

Luther, like other intellectuals, had criticized this development several times, but in 1517 it was forced on his attention in a new way. Prince Albert of Brandenburg, at 23 archbishop of Magdeburg, had also become archbishop of Mainz and primate of Germany. The bribes and fees spent in achieving this were huge, and he was in the hands of the great banking house of Fugger. To pay off his debts he promulgated in Germany Leo X's indulgence for those who contributed to the rebuilding of St Peter's in Rome. Half the proceeds were to go to the pope, half to Albert and his bankers. Even by the standards of the day, the "hard-sell" patter of the indulgence pedlar, the Dominican Tetzel, was outrageous:

> Place your money in the drum
> The pearly gates open and in walks mum.

Luther, still fresh from his own spiritual breakthrough, saw this as a cruel and blasphemous confidence trick on the ignorant. He printed a set of 95 Latin propositions for academic discussion, attacking the abuse of indulgences though not the practice itself. Translated into German, the "theses" became a best-seller, and Luther found himself the talk of Germany.

In the debate that followed he published a series of pamphlets which, as the church authorities moved against him, became increasingly ferocious. Abandoning the indulgence question, he launched an attack on the whole range of Catholic teaching and practice. If only faith counted, and faith came only by hearing the word preached, then men's reliance on pilgrimage, relics, saints, on good works, on the priesthood, on the sacraments themselves, was all in vain. Confronted with the gulf between his teaching and Catholic tradition, he denied both the primacy of the pope and the infallibility of general councils. Condemned by the pope in 1520, he was summoned to answer heresy charges before the Emperor Charles V at the Diet of Worms in 1521. Luther made an emotional speech refusing to retract, and was outlawed and solemnly excommunicated. He went into hiding.

The role of the printing press

Luther was a gifted popular writer, and the late Middle Ages had seen a marked growth of literacy in Germany. For the first time the printing press became a vehicle of mass persuasion. By 1521 a third of a million of Luther's books were in circulation. His message fell on receptive ears. Germany's political coherence under Charles V was precarious, with many areas governed by tin-pot local

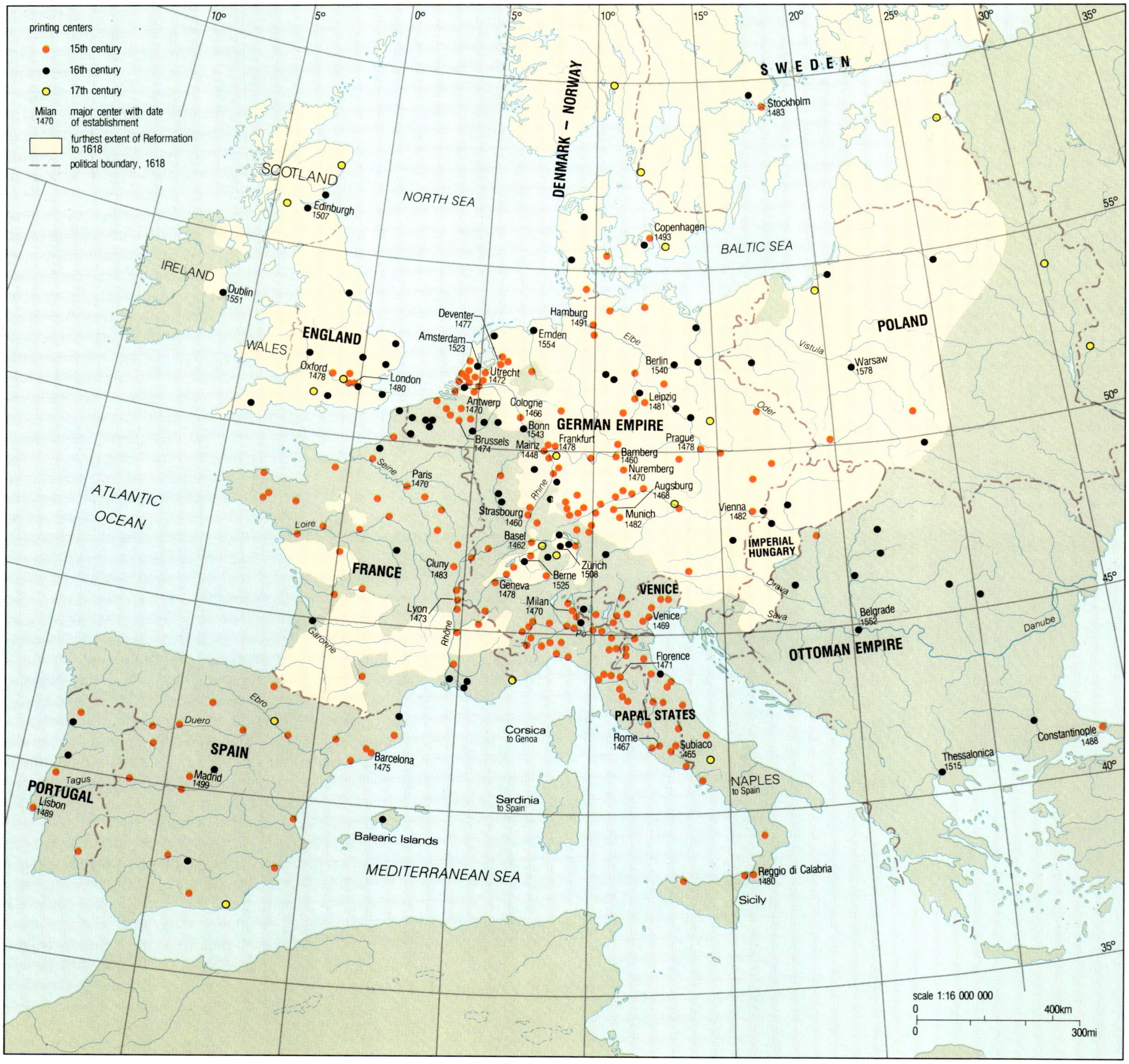

Above Luther's German Catechism became the basis of religious education in Lutheran schools, and was imitated even by Luther's Catholic opponents. Normally based on the Creed, Commandments and Lord's Prayer, catechisms became a vital instrument of indoctrination for both Catholics and Protestants, and helped transform Christianity from a ritual and ethical system to a doctrinal or ideological one.

Left: Centers of printing
Printing played a key role in fostering and spreading humanist ideals in the last years of the 15th and early part of the 16th centuries. By the end of the 15th century almost a quarter of Europe's books were being printed in Venice; next in importance came Paris, Lyon, Florence, Leipzig, Deventer, Milan, Strasbourg, Cologne, Augsburg, Nuremberg and Basel. England was still to a great extent dependent on the importation of books from abroad. The number of German cities in this list witnesses to the astonishing printing boom there at the turn of the century, which was to be crucial to the success of the Reformation.

knights no better than bandits, eager for an excuse to shake off their allegiance. Its borders were being nibbled away to east and west. Foreigners were deeply resented, and papal officials most of all, with their perpetual financial demands. Luther's polemic played on that xenophobia. The cities of the empire, too, were powder kegs awaiting a spark. Riven by tensions between the ruling oligarchies, trade guilds and the voiceless unskilled laborers, they were united only in a concern for unity, and a loathing of the clergy with their legal and tax exemptions and their loyalties to ecclesiastical overlords outside the city. Here above all Luther's message struck roots.

His sweeping away of the expensive paraphernalia of medieval religion, his assertion that *all* believers were priests, his insistence that no one could impose laws on a Christian's conscience, that if laws cut across Gospel liberty they should simply be ignored, his attacks on scholastic theology and high finance appealed to humanists and intellectuals. Even more, they appealed to those at the bottom of the social pyramid, to whom attacks on law and talk of Gospel freedom had resonances perhaps unintended by Luther. In the thousands of illustrated pamphlets and broadsheets of the period Luther entered the folk imagination as a Jack-the-giant-killer, pitted on behalf of the downtrodden against papal and clerical greed. Luther's attack on religious begging, his proposal that rulers or local communities should take the ordering of the Church into their own hands, his suggestions about the merging and confiscation of monastic property appealed to town rulers eager to bring the clergy to heel. Luther's message was spiritual, but its implications were nothing if not concrete. City after city declared for the Gospel.

Reform runs riot

As preachers and printers spread Luther's message over Germany, it drew other theologians to him. At Wittenberg his lieutenant was the pacific humanist Philip Melancthon (1497–1560), whose *Commonplaces* (1521) were the first Protestant systematic theology, and who drafted the Confession of Augsburg of 1530 which was to become the standard Lutheran confession of faith. But Luther's movement was being swept into a vortex of social and political upheaval which was anything but peaceful. While he was still in hiding after Worms, another of the Wittenberg professors, Andreas Carlstadt (1480–1541), took the Reformation into his own hands. The mass was abolished, communion in both kinds introduced, organs silenced, monks and nuns brought out of their cloisters and married. Rioting students ransacked images and altars and rabbled the clergy. Carlstadt began to go barefoot, to dress like a peasant and call himself "Brother Andreas," to denounce learning. A group of patriarchal "prophets" from Zwickau appeared in the town, proclaiming the mystical indwelling of the Spirit, talking of dreams and visions.

Luther emerged from hiding and calmed the storm with a series of sermons urging charity and gradual reforms, but radicalism grew apace. Thomas Münzer (1490–1525) was a Saxon priest influenced not only by Luther but by the medieval millenarian and mystical traditions. He rejected the authority of the scriptures in favor of direct revelation by the Spirit and taught that the Church consisted only of the elect reborn in the Spirit. Münzer proclaimed the duty of Christians to take up the sword against the ungodly, and foresaw an apocalyptic struggle in which many of the righteous would suffer. He believed Luther was selling the Gospel to the ruling classes and denounced him as "Dr Easychair," "Dr Pussyfoot," "Dr Liar." Based at Allstadt, where he produced the first liturgy in German, he organized bands of workmen and miners to prepare for Armageddon. Carlstadt joined him.

In 1524 a series of risings by the oppressed and half-starved peasantry began, calling for a range of rights, from the abolition of serfdom to the choice of their own religious pastors. Though social grievances were uppermost, the religious dimension of the revolt was unmistakable. Lutheran pictorial propaganda had always portrayed the honest peasant with his flail as the chief supporter of the Gospel against worldlings and the papacy: now that rhetorical image was given terrifying reality, as peasant bands swept through central and southern Germany burning castles and monasteries. Münzer came forward as a theologian of revolt, calling on the peasantry to establish the kingdom of the saints—"on, on, spare not, pity not the godless, strike!" Luther was horrified, not least by the fact that his teachings were being blamed for the revolt. In a savage pamphlet *Against the Murderous and Thieving Hordes of Peasants*, he urged the princes of Germany to "smite, slay and stab . . . remembering that nothing can be more poisonous or devilish than a rebel." The revolt was put down in 1525, and Münzer was tortured and beheaded.

Luther's Gospel was irrevocably discredited among many of the peasantry, who believed that he had betrayed them. Certainly he was conscious of the dependence of the Reformation on the Protestant princes, in many of whom desire to mulct and dominate the Church was stronger than evangelical zeal, and none of whom would be impressed by suggestions that Protestantism and social upheaval were natural allies.

In the 1520s and 1530s Lutheranism too had its distinctive character. Luther had abolished all but the three sacraments of baptism, eucharist and penance, but much of the old church ceremonial, even Latin, remained. The heart of German worship was Luther's translation of the Bible and the rich collection of hymns he provided. In the *Greater Catechism* he produced a standard of doctrine for ministers, in the *Smaller Catechism* a superb and original combination of instruction in fundamentals with a prayerbook, all couched in simple and direct German prose. He was not greatly interested in church government. Episcopacy was allowed virtually to disappear, its essential administrative functions being taken over by mixed courts of ministers and lawyers, answerable to the prince. In general Luther's dependence on the Protestant princes, organized for mutual protection in the Schmalkaldic League, forced him to concede to the secular arm more say in church affairs than he wished. He taught that the prince could and must reform if the clergy will not—the prince was *Summus Episcopus*. Though he believed in a rigid demarcation of spiritual and secular juris-

Post-Reformation Diversity

Every early-modern state aspired to religious uniformity, for Catholics and Protestants alike believed that religious disagreements angered God and threatened the stability of government. The Reformation policy of the open Bible, however, made such uniformity impossible to attain, and caused many of the reformers, like their humanist predecessors, to rethink the wisdom of offering the Bible to the unlearned for them to interpret as the "Spirit" led them. After the Peasants' Revolt in the mid-1520s, Luther came to think that caution must be used in exposing ignorant men to the uninterpreted text, and the German Bible was not used in Lutheran schools, biblical instruction being confined to the upper classes and from the Latin New Testament. Such attempts to close the stable door could not, however, recall the bolted horse, and religious diversity became a permanent feature of European and British Protestantism. Only after most European states had failed to crush such diversity by force would notions of coexistence and toleration gain any wide currency, though such ideas had been very fully formulated by Erasmus in the 1520s.

Even within the Catholicism of the Counter-Reformation conflicting theologies and devotional styles coexisted, often uneasily, and all over Europe religious rigorists and Puritans came face to face, and often sword to sword, with those who took a laxer, or a more liberal, view of what the demands of the Gospel were.

Bottom left In England, as elsewhere, the Reformation found its energies deflected and divided by theological disagreement and social conflict, which erupted in the mid-17th century in a civil war in large part inspired by religious conflict. In this contemporary portrayal of the Dies Dominica, the Lord's Day, the activities of the godly (on the left)—praying, hearing sermons, meditating on the Bible, visiting the sick, relieving the poor—are contrasted with the works of darkness—roistering, drinking, gambling and breaking the Sabbath by servile work.

Below But religious divisions also had doctrinal roots. In this woodcut from a conservative religious pamphlet of 1641 the enemies of true Protestantism—Anabaptist, "Brownist" or Congregationalist, "Familist" and Papist—toss the Bible, symbolizing right religion, in a blanket.

Above Van de Venne's ironic canvas portrays satirically the way in which gospel zeal for souls had become competition for adherents to rival ideologies. Protestants and Catholics face each other across a river. On the right are the Catholics, theologians in the foreground, behind them, cane in hand, stands Philip III of Spain, and in the background the pope and cardinals. The Protestant heads of state on the left include Maurice of Orange, James I of England, Christian IV of Denmark, and the young Louis XIII of France, held to be favorable to the Reformation. In the water rival boats manned by priests and Protestant ministers try to drag naked swimmers into their control. Over all presides the rainbow, a traditional symbol of God's judgment.

The two images of Lutheran (*right*) and Calvinist (*left*) worship highlight the austere break with the Catholic past favored by Calvinism, contrasted with the doctrinal and ceremonial conservativism of the Lutheran churches.

dictions, political realities blurred the distinction and Luther himself came to justify the suppression of religious dissent by the magistrate, a thing he had condemned in the early 1520s.

Zwingli and the Swiss Reformation

From the early 1520s a distinctive form of Protestantism was emerging in the cities of the Swiss confederation, which was to dominate the reformed world in the second half of the century. Its originator was Huldreich Zwingli (1484–1531), from 1518 town preacher at Zürich. Zwingli was by temperament poles apart from Luther, a cheerful optimist, a passionate Swiss nationalist, a former army chaplain with at least one seamy love affair behind him. Soaked in Erasmian Humanism, Zwingli's Reformation was rationalist, critical, and pervaded by the order, discipline and community sense of his Swiss background. Unlike Luther he set about systematically eliminating every aspect of Catholicism which could not be shown to have explicit scriptural authority—the mass, clerical celibacy, fasting, saints' days, church music. Zwingli's humanist-didactic preoccupations were reflected in the introduction of "prophesyings," open seminars in which the Scripture was expounded and discussed by clergy and laity together. The town council cooperated closely with the ministers to police public morals, and the council was even responsible for excommunication. This collaboration between magistrate and minister in the enforcement of godliness was to prove one of the most characteristic and influential aspects of the Swiss Reformation.

Though Zwingli broadly accepted Luther's theological position, he took a more positive view of man's ability to cooperate with God, and even thought that good pagans such as Socrates might be saved. On one issue in particular they were diametrically opposed. While rejecting transubstantiation Luther emphatically insisted on the real presence of Christ in the mass. For him, Jesus' words "This is my body" meant exactly that. "If God speaks these words, do not search any higher but take off your hat." To Zwingli's rationalist mind this was rank superstition. Like Erasmus he lived in the head, and he had no real sacramental sense. The Lord's Supper was merely symbolic, a service of commemoration and thanks for an absent Lord. As political tensions mounted, this disagreement became a terrifying stumbling block on which the very existence of Protestantism might shatter. An attempt was made to resolve the problem at Marburg in 1529. Melancthon persuaded Luther to meet Zwingli, with the pacific Martin Bucer of Strasbourg to oil the wheels. Luther, however, truculently scrawled "This is my body" in chalk on the conference table, and the meeting got nowhere. Two years later Zwingli died in battle against the Catholic cantons of Switzerland with Protestantism still divided. His attempt to formulate a Protestantism with international appeal was, however, to be achieved in another Swiss city.

John Calvin

John Calvin had come to the turbulent fortress-city of Geneva by accident in 1536, intending to stay one night. With a three-year interval at Strasbourg, he was to remain there for the rest of his life. He was a humanist, trained in languages and the law, his first work a commentary on Seneca. Equally crucial to an understanding of his work is the fact that he reached intellectual maturity when the Reformation was already well established. Educated among the evangelical humanists of France, he made the transition from Catholicism to the reformed faith painlessly, a choice between two formed alternatives. Driven from France by the stepping up of royal action against "the Lutherans," Calvin published at Basle in 1536 the first edition of his summary of the Protestant faith, *Institutes of the Christian Religion,* optimistically dedicated to the king. He was to expand and revise this work till his death. In terms of its effect on contemporary thought and its impact on practical politics it has a fair claim to be considered the most important book of the century.

Calvin's theology differs in no essentials from that of Luther, whom he revered, but it is orchestrated into a far more consistent and formidable system, at the heart of which was Calvin's distinctive emphasis on the sovereignty and freedom of God. Man knows himself only in relation to God, and is ultimately an instrument for the working out of God's will. Thus his salvation is something predetermined, fixed in God's purpose before time began, to which he contributes nothing. "Eternal life is foreordained for some, external damnation for others." Calvin meant this horrible teaching to be a comforting doctrine; our salvation does not depend on our fickle nature, but on the fathomless will of God. His theology is focused on the figure of Christ, in whom God has joined himself to men, and he dwelt less on the negative side of predestination than many of his followers. He taught that we should live in hope, not seeking to probe the mysteries of election, conforming our lives as best we can to God's will.

In pursuit of this conformity, Calvin carefully spelled out a detailed pattern for the Church, governing every aspect of the Christian life. Order, discipline, godly living were prime objectives. Ministry was four-fold. Pastors cared for the Church by preaching, rebuke and encouragement. Teachers ensured doctrinal purity by expounding Scripture. Lay elders administered moral discipline, and with the ministers formed a court or consistory which punished backsliders, in the last resort by excommunication. Deacons dealt with finance and the poor. The element of censoriousness, the close scrutiny within the community of moral standards, in which spying as well as "fraternal admonition" was encouraged, is to modern observers one of the least appealing aspects of Calvin's system. It was deeply resented by the "libertine" party in Geneva. The city had originally gone Protestant principally as part of a rejection of the authority of its secular overlord, who was also the bishop, and to the end of his life Calvin, who did not readily brook opposition, could never count on carrying the city council along with him. Nevertheless it was precisely this

Right Calvinism broke decisively with the Catholic past. Churches were no longer sacred dramatic spaces, but auditoria in which people listened and learned. This picture of 16th-century French Calvinist worship strikingly illustrates the change. Notice the prominence of women, who played a leading role in promoting the French Reformation.

EMPLE DE LYON, NOMMÉ PARADIS.

"discipline" as a potent means of transforming the community at large into a "godly commonwealth" which made Calvinism so influential abroad. Coupled with the rigor and clarity of his exposition of doctrine, Calvin's reworking of the civic Protestantism of Switzerland became in his own lifetime the principal model for reformers elsewhere.

Like Zwingli, Calvin excluded all "non-scriptural" elements from worship. Thus although he shared Luther's emphasis on congregational singing, he forbade hymns, permitting only metrical renderings of Scripture. Like Zwingli he repudiated Luther's belief in the corporeal presence of Christ in the eucharist, though his teaching was subtle and allowed for a spiritual and "real" or "effective" presence. Indeed, he believed that the eucharist should be celebrated daily or at least weekly, but was never able to persuade the non-communicant Genevans to more than monthly celebrations.

By the time of his death, however, Geneva had come to heel. Though some of his experiments had failed, like the municipal grogshops where one could drink in small quantities while reading the Scripture texts on the walls, the town was orderly, sober and, at least on the surface, godly. The poor, sick and aged were well cared for, crime and immorality ruthlessly punished, and his academy and college (university and high school) had made Geneva a Mecca for Protestant Europe—what John Knox called "the most perfect School of Christ that ever was on earth since the days of the Apostles."

Protestantism was able to establish itself in northern and eastern Germany and over wide areas of central and eastern Europe largely because of external factors. Charles V, despite his image of himself as the divinely appointed defender of Catholicism, was unable to deal with the Protestant threat because of the great menace of Muslim invasion to the east and south, and the growth of Valois France to the west. Francis I had allied with both Turks and German Protestants, and by the time Charles was free to attack the Protestant Schmalkaldic League in 1546 it was too late. The capture of Wittenberg in 1547 was a brief triumph, but Charles was forced in 1555 to come to terms with the permanent existence of the Reformation.

Right Under the conservative Henry VIII the English Reformation had been ambiguous. Under his successor, the boy king Edward VI, there was a dramatic and radical shift towards Swiss-style Protestantism. In this propaganda picture the dying Henry points to the new order. Edward, flanked by his Protestant council, treads down the pope and his monks. Through the window can be seen the "cleansing" of the land from error and superstition, in the form of "iconoclasm," or the violent destruction of religious images.

Left: The religious state of Europe in 1560
Luther died in 1546, Calvin in 1564. By the latter date Europe had become deeply and, in the eyes of many, permanently divided by religion. The whole of northeastern and much of central Germany, as well as Denmark and Scandinavia, were Lutheran, and Lutheranism had also gained a strong base in parts of Bavaria, and in the Habsburg heartlands of Carinthia and Austria. Bohemia, Silesia and much of Poland also sheltered Lutheran communities. Zürich, Basel, Berne and Geneva formed a ''Reformed'' or ''Calvinist'' block, and Scotland established a church on Swiss lines in 1560. England, retaining episcopacy and many traditional religious practices, was a special case among Protestant churches, but its leaders in 1560 certainly looked first to Switzerland for inspiration. Calvinism, therefore, represented the future of Protestantism, and would expand in the Netherlands, Hungary, and central and eastern Germany. The failure of the Peace of Augsburg (1555) to recognize the territorial reality in Germany of this potent and expanding new force was to prove a long-term source of political instability.

By the Peace of Augsburg the principle of *cuius regio, eius religio* was established, giving each ruler the right to determine the religious allegiance of his territory. Calvinism was not provided for in the settlement.

Reformation in other parts of Europe

Lutheranism had quickly spread outside Germany. In Scandinavia it made rapid progress, with the backing of the Danish and Swedish monarchies and the inducement of confiscated church property. Progress was much slower in Norway, where the Reformation was, quite correctly, viewed as an instrument of Danish imperialism. To the south, Protestantism made little progress before the mid-century. France had many humanists and anticlericals, the Bible was available in French and the circle of ''evangelicals'' based at Meaux, of which Lefèvre d'Étaples was the chief, advocated many of the reforms achieved within Protestantism. But although Francis I carried on a political flirtation with the German Protestant princes, he had no desire for a break with Rome, and the silly incident of the posting of an anticatholic placard on his bedroom door at Amboise in 1534 led to a rigorous persecution of French Protestants, which set Calvin on the road to Geneva.

Italian Protestantism was even more fragile, associated with a handful of intellectuals and nobles, and in particular with the circle of the Spaniard Juan Valdes and the households of Cardinal Ercole Gonzaga and Vittoria Colonna at Naples. But Valdes's teaching was mystical and quietist rather than Protestant. Most Italian reformers kept their opinions to themselves while outwardly conforming, a ''Nicodemianism'' roundly condemned by Calvin. The great exceptions were the friars Bernardino Ochino and Peter Martyr, who fled Italy during the early 1540s. Both of them found their way to England, and Peter Martyr became Edward VI's Regius Professor of Divinity at Oxford.

The English settlement

England's Reformation was perhaps the most drawn out and uncertain of any in Europe. Erasmian Humanism had made a deep impact in England, and Lollardy, the native heretical tradition, doubtless predisposed some towards Protestantism. Henry VIII, however, was a pious Catholic, and won the papal title ''Defender of the Faith'' for his 1521 *Defence of the Seven Sacraments* against Luther. Though Lutheran books circulated, Tyndale's English New Testament appeared in 1526 and a colony of dons at Cambridge fostered Lutheran ideas, the Reformation made little headway until the king sought a divorce from his wife Catherine of Aragon, who had not managed to produce a male heir. Catherine was the aunt of Charles V, whose troops had recently sacked Rome and whose prisoner the pope was. The divorce was refused and Henry turned on the Church. Ties with

Left The age of Reformation, with its religious and political upheavals, wars and rumors of wars, as well as natural disasters like famine and epidemic disease, convinced many that the end of the world was near. Apocalyptic expectation fueled much of the religious radicalism of the period. The magnificent series of illustrations to the Book of Revelation engraved by Albrecht Dürer in 1498 conveys something of the spiritual and psychological anxiety of many in Germany on the eve of Luther's preaching.

Rome were severed and in 1534 Henry declared himself supreme head of the Church in England. Suppression of the monasteries followed. A few churchmen, including the greatest patron of the new learning in England, Bishop Fisher of Rochester, resisted and were executed, as was Henry's former lord chancellor Thomas More.

Initially there was little or no doctrinal or liturgical change and Henry persecuted Protestants and Papists alike. But under the patronage of the archbishop of Canterbury, Thomas Cranmer, and the secretary of the council, Thomas Cromwell, reformed ideas slowly made their way. With the accession of Edward VI the Reformation was given a free hand, the mass was abolished, and in two successive English prayerbooks (1549 and 1552) Cranmer gave the English Church a liturgy which retained medieval material, but by 1552 embodied an essentially Swiss theology. With the accession of Queen Mary, Catherine of Aragon's daughter, England returned to papal obedience and, with Mary's marriage to her nephew Philip of Spain, to the Catholic power bloc. Mary and her archbishop, Cardinal Pole, were preoccupied with restoring Catholic worship and discipline and harassing Protestant radicals. Three hundred were burned, including Cranmer. This unpopular campaign was never consistently pursued, and was not accompanied by any positive preaching. When, after only six years, Mary's Protestant sister Elizabeth succeeded, the process was reversed.

The Elizabethan settlement was ambivalent. The doctrinal standard adopted by the Church (the 39 Articles) was in part Calvinist; harder to label is the eucharistic teaching in the prayerbook, but episcopacy and the medieval system of church discipline were retained. The prayerbook contained much that to Genevan eyes seemed popish, and the clergy were required to wear Catholic vestments. Elizabeth was obliged to appoint to the episcopate many clergy who under Mary had fled to Switzerland, and who found in the settlement too many half-measures. This dissatisfaction (at all levels of the Church) was to prove deeply divisive. Most Marian clergy, however, continued in office and, although few people cared about the papacy, outside the southern and eastern parts of the country Protestantism probably made little real impression till the end of the reign.

Anabaptism

Most reformers sought territorial reformation, to transform their churches *en masse*. In Anabaptism the Reformation produced a radical strain which questioned the validity of regional or national churches. If men were saved by faith alone, then it might be argued that only adults capable of faith could be numbered among the elect. There were many who argued that only the elect could claim to belong in the Church, and that the Church was therefore wholly distinct from society at large. This was the basis of Münzer's teaching. At Zürich a group under Conrad Grebel followed the logic of this, rejected infant baptism and separated themselves from the town's worship. Zwingli's rationalist theology was in fact very vulnerable to their arguments, but he justified a vicious suppression of the group, many of whom were executed, with grim humor, by drowning.

As the Scriptures became generally available, separatist movements of this sort spread like wildfire among the urban and rural poor of many parts of Europe. The apocalyptic tone of much Anabaptist preaching, and the lowly social status of its adherents, alarmed governments who remembered the Peasants' Revolt. Anabaptist preachers were imprisoned or executed. These fears seemed vindicated in 1534 when Anabaptists took control of the city of Münster. Catholics and Lutherans fled, common ownership of property was declared. A Dutchman, John of Leiden, had himself made king, proclaimed the New Jerusalem, and established polygamy. King John took 16 wives, one of whom he beheaded for impertinence. Holy war was declared on all the ungodly. The city fell to the prince-bishop in 1535, and the leaders were tortured to death.

Anabaptism was not a single or a coherent sect but a hold-all term for those within the reformed camp who believed that the principle of justification by faith had not been fully realized within any of the classical forms of Protestantism or who sought a religion of the Spirit which was free of the formalism they perceived in the Reformation as much as in Catholicism. It incorporated mystical and apocalyptic influences as well as Renaissance rationalism, and many Anabaptists, most famously Michael Servetus and Fausto Sozzini, rejected traditional teaching on the Trinity. The differences between all these groups are more significant than their resemblances, but all were discredited by the Münster episode, which was to haunt the imagination of both Protestant and Catholic Europe for over a century.

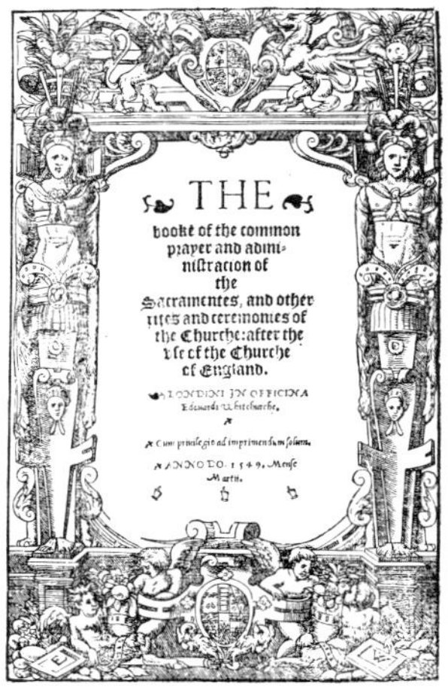

THE
booke of the common
prayer and admi-
nistracion of
the
Sacramentes, and other
rites and ceremonies of
the Churche: after the
use of the Churche
of England.

Above Cranmer's *Book of Common Prayer* (1549) introduced English into the mass and other public services. It was however sufficiently traditional to win some Catholic support, though it provoked armed revolt in the conservative West Country (Devon and Cornwall). It was replaced by a more Protestant book in 1552.

THE COUNTER-REFORMATION

Attempts at Catholic reform

The Reformation was largely a northern phenomenon. It was paralleled in the Catholic south by a transformation hardly less profound, which had begun even before Luther's revolt. Humanism was itself a manifestation of this quickening of the Catholic religious impulse, and received striking embodiment in the Spanish peninsula. Under the austere Cardinal Ximenez de Cisneros (1436–1517), primate of Spain, a concerted reform was inaugurated, beginning with his own Franciscan order, reduced to strict observance by 1506. To raise clerical standards he created the university of Alcalá, one of a rash of such new foundations all over Europe. In 1502 Ximenez set his professors at Alcalá to produce a critical edition of the Scriptures in seven languages, the *Complutensian Polyglot* (printed 1514–17). He invited Erasmus to come to Spain, and although he never did so, his influence was a major factor in the emergence in the peninsula of a humanist milieu which made the Spanish clergy among the most edifying in Europe. Ximenez forbade the preaching of indulgences in his diocese of Toledo, but he was nevertheless a rigidly orthodox Catholic, and was Grand Inquisitor from 1507.

The search for renewal in a return to scriptural sources was experienced also in Italy, and a new religious seriousness is evident in the painting of the period, in the tranquil adoration in Raphael's Sistine and Grand-ducal Madonnas (1513 and 1505) or in the decorations Michaelangelo provided for the roof of the Sistine chapel between 1508 and 1512. The same spirit which inspired these works appears in the Oratory of Divine Love, founded in Rome during the pontificate of the pious but easy-going Leo X. This aristocratic group of devout clergy and laity was led by a fiery Neapolitan bishop, Giovanni Pietro Caraffa, later Pope Paul IV, and Count Gaetano da Thienne, later canonized as St Cajetan. Out of the Oratory grew the Theatine order, an experimental group of secular clergy who dedicated themselves to poverty and a heroic observance of the apostolic priestly life. The Theatines were never a large group, but they became a byword for piety and established themselves as a model for clerical reformers.

None of these early attempts at Catholic reform, however, could even begin to meet the challenge posed by Luther. Even Adrian VI, the austere Dutchman who succeeded Leo X and who lived the life of a monk in the Vatican, saw reform in terms of the cleansing of the Curia and the city of Rome, and seems not to have grasped the full seriousness of what was happening in Germany. However, the sack of Rome by imperial troops, many Lutherans among them, marked a turning point. In a frenzied eight days in May 1527 northern soldiery raped, pillaged and burned their way through Rome. Four thousand citizens died, and the rest deserted the city. The shock of this incident brought a new and somber note into the ethos of Renaissance Italy, a new pessimism about human nature and a quickening of the religious pulse of the city. To compare the Sistine *Last Judgment*, painted when this new seriousness and pessimism was well established, with the ceiling above it, is to get some sense of the change.

Pope Paul III and the Spirituali

In this period there emerged a circle of reform-minded churchmen who included Giovanni Matteo Giberti, bishop of Verona, Caraffa, the Venetian layman Gasparo Contarini and the Englishman Reginald Pole. Consistent advocates of reform, they found the atmosphere of Rome uncongenial. Vested interests within the Curia resisted change, and the papacy proved itself unwilling to summon the general council everyone now believed to be necessary. The accession of the Farnese Pope Paul III, however, at last changed this. In 1536 he established a commission to propose reforms. Not a single Curialist was appointed, and the commission was dominated by reformers – Bishop Giberti, Contarini, now a cardinal, Caraffa, Pole, the humanist Jacopo Sadoleto – all to be raised to the purple at the end of the year. The report, presented to the pope in March 1537 under the title *Consilium de Emendenda Ecclesia*, was staggering. In the bluntest of language it blamed all the ills of the Church, including the Reformation, on the corruptions of the papacy, the hierarchy and the clergy. In unrelenting detail the abuses of the time were listed and the religious orders in particular were attacked; the report even advocated allowing many of the orders to die out, and the merger of the rest. Inevitably, this report was stone-walled by the Roman clerical civil service, and disastrously a copy was leaked to the press. Luther published a German version with a lip-smacking commentary, and the ensuing publicity scotched any chance of its implementation. But it was clear now that reform was in the air.

The reform party, however, was deeply and tragically divided. All were agreed that the Church was sunk in corruption, and must be cleansed. But there were many, like Contarini and Pole, who believed that this corruption was not simply in the Church's practices but in its teaching. On the matter of church authority and the sacraments Luther was deeply and sinfully wrong, but on justification he was right, and was recalling the Church to its true and ancient teaching. Soaked in the Pauline and Augustinian revival which had grown alongside Humanism, they accepted justification by faith, though not the negations of Catholic tradition which Luther based on it. As Pole wrote, "Heretics are not heretics in everything." They therefore worked for reconciliation with the Lutherans

These men, known as *Spirituali*, believed themselves to be good and loyal Catholics. The ambiguity of their position however is clear from the

Left The Inquisition symbolized for Protestants all that was repressive and cruel in Catholicism. The Roman Inquisition, founded in 1542, was in fact largely concerned with the punishment of moral offenses like incest, and modern research suggests that those accused before the Inquisition were likely to get a fairer trial than in any secular court. The Spanish Inquisition, controlled by the monarchy, not the papacy, was founded to deal with false converts from Judaism and Islam in Spain – racialism was more central than heresy hunting. Nevertheless, the Inquisitions became part of the "Black Legend" of Counter-Reformation Catholicism. Berruguete's painting of an *Auto de fé*, the solemn ceremony in which heretics either repudiated their errors and did penance, or were executed, actually portrays a medieval Inquisition punishing Cathar heretics. It contains, however, all the conventional negative stereotypes of domineering clerics, ritual humiliation and death by fire.

Above The Council of Trent, portrayed here in session, was much interrupted by disease and war. It was also dogged by internal divisions and jealousies, and by the rivalry of France and the Habsburgs. Nevertheless its doctrinal formulations were accepted by all the Catholic states of Europe, and represented a remarkable consolidation and clarification of traditional teaching. Its reforms in the training and discipline of the clergy, and the regulation of the lives of the laity in such matters as marriage, were to remain the framework of Catholicism until the 1960s.

content of the little devotional tract *Beneficio di Christo*, which circulated in the early 1540s. Teaching justification by faith, it was enthusiastically welcomed by the Spirituali, and one of them, Cardinal Morone, later to be papal legate at Trent, read it "avidly" and circulated it in his diocese. It has now been shown to be largely a paraphrase of the second edition of Calvin's *Institutes* of 1539!

Opposed to the Spirituali were uncompromising figures like Caraffa who also accepted the need for moral and institutional reform, but rejected all moves towards Luther's doctrine as rank heresy. To Caraffa, the Spirituali increasingly came to seem a fifth column. The doctrinal issue should be settled not by discussion, but by ruthlessly hunting down all heretics. His party gained an enormous victory in 1541, when talks between Contarini, Melancthon and Bucer at Regensburg failed. Contarini returned to Italy deeply disillusioned, and died in the following year. Now Caraffa was given his head. Asked by Paul III "what remedy must be devised for this evil," he proposed an Inquisition to "suppress and uproot the errors . . . permitting no vestige to remain." Appointed one of six inquisitors general in July 1542, he fitted up a prison at his own expense with bolts and chains. In the atmosphere of suspicion thus created, two of the leading preachers of the Spirituali party, Bernardino Ochino and Peter Martyr, fled to Switzerland and became Protestants. Both had been protected by Contarini and Pole, and their apostasy closed the door against doctrinal reform. Caraffa's intransigent outlook was to triumph completely in 1555 when he became pope as Paul IV. It was he who introduced the Roman Index of Prohibited Books, and one of the first he put on it was the *Consilium de Emendenda Ecclesia*!

The Council of Trent

It was against this background that the Council of Trent met. Men had been calling for a council to pacify the Church since the early 1520s. The popes, fearful of a revival of conciliar ideas and of an attack on the Curia, had temporized. Now Paul III acted, and the council met in the Italian Alps at Trent, in December 1545. It was to drag on until 1562, with interludes, including one of ten years, caused by war. It was from the beginning a controversial and divided assembly. There were only 31 bishops at its opening, and only one of them was German; even at its largest there were only 270 bishops present, and never more than 13 of those were German. From the start undue papal influence was feared – one French bishop said that if the Holy Spirit attended the council he must come in the pope's mailbag, though it should be remembered that after the council no Catholic state in Europe questioned its doctrinal formulations.

The emperor wanted the council to tackle practical abuse, leaving him to negotiate doctrinal issues with his Protestant subjects. The pope wanted Catholic doctrine reaffirmed, and reform of abuses left to him. The French Crown wanted to avoid any outcome at the council which would pacify Germany and thereby release Charles V's energies to attack France. In the event the council produced formulations on all the major controverted areas calculated to alienate even moderate Protestants. Transubstantiation was reaffirmed, as were the seven sacraments, Purgatory, the sacrifice of the mass, indulgences and the invocation of the saints. On the crucial issue of justification the council, while insisting that man is justified wholly by grace, and can do nothing of himself to merit justification, nevertheless taught that he can and must cooperate with grace by freely assenting to it. The council rejected Luther's distinction between sanctification and justification, and with it the notion that justification is merely extrinsic, leaving man still a sinner. The grace of justification changed a man, infusing hope and charity as well as faith into the soul, and endowing his subsequent good works with the power of pleasing God which is to merit reward. This careful formula successfully avoided Pelagianism, but it dashed the hopes of the Spirituali for a reconciliation with Protestants.

The doctrinal work of the council ensured that Protestant and Catholic now faced each other over an unbridgeable divide. Its disciplinary and practical program presented a blueprint for the reconstruction of a militant Catholicism. The council put forward a vision of the Church as a well-disciplined army, its personnel strictly organized by parish and diocese, the Christian life regulated by the Church's rules, its central principle that of hierarchy. So bishops were to be resident and to preach, and must hold regular visitations and synods. The religious orders were to be brought under episcopal control, only preaching with the bishop's permission, subject to his canonical visitation. The parochial clergy were to wear clerical dress, reside, be serious, modest and devout. Churches were to be maintained, worship purged of irreverence, simony and superstition. The laity were to be instructed by sermons and catechizing. Above all, seminaries were to be established in every diocese to produce a clergy who would be conscientious, pious, chaste and educated.

The council was in fact setting itself quite consciously to combat the religious anarchy of Catholic, just as much as the heresy of Protestant, Europe. Over the next century and a half churchmen were to seek to impose on the religion of the people a disciplined and authoritarian framework which often brought them into conflict with popular religious feeling and with secular government. The parish was to be the center of the layman's religious life. Therefore, religious activities which led him away from his parish were to be discouraged or at least controlled. Trent gave bishops control over all confraternities, even those run by laymen or possessing exemptions of any sort, and many bishops would seek to suppress independent confraternities, replacing them with parochial brotherhoods under clerical control. In its decree on relics and images the council reaffirmed the pious use of such things, but attacked popular abuses surrounding them, such as "boisterous festivities and drunkenness" at festivals, or "unusual images" in churches. This decree was used from the 1570s onwards to control the content of religious paintings, excluding anything "superstitious, apocryphal, false, idle, new, unusual." This led to a narrowing of spirit. Painters like Veronese were to find themselves before the Inquisition for deviation from scriptural literalism in portraying Gospel scenes. Michelangelo's work on the Sistine chapel roof was attacked for its inclusion of classical figures, while a succession of popes had draperies added to cover the nakedness of the figures in his *Last Judgment*. It also brought bishops and clergy into conflict with their flocks. Nicholas Pavillon, a 17th-century bishop of Alet in southern France, spent 20 years trying to stamp out half-pagan celebrations at the graves of local holy men in his diocese, only to have the population recognize his sanctity by celebrating the same festivities at his grave when he could no longer protest.

The ministry of Charles Borromeo

The Tridentine model of Christianity can be seen at work in the ministry of Charles Borromeo, archbishop of Milan from 1562 to 1584. Borromeo was Pius IV's nephew and had played a crucial role in the direction of the later stages of the Council of Trent. He settled in his diocese in 1566 after Pius's death, the first resident bishop of Milan for 80 years. Austere, self-denying, he wore a hair shirt and lived in poverty, selling even the curtains in his palace for the poor. Borromeo ended the easygoing regime he found in the Milanese monasteries and convents; the rule was rigorously enforced and nuns were once more locked behind their grilles. He inaugurated a series of diocesan synods and visitations to purge the slack and dissolute among the clergy, created a series of schools and seminaries for new priests and founded a congregation of clerks regular like the Theatines called Oblates of St Ambrose, whom he used to staff his educational and pastoral enterprises. Over 20 of the clergy he gathered around him themselves became reforming bishops.

Though he welcomed some aspects of popular religion, such as the pilgrimages to Loreto and the shroud of Turin, and himself carried the relic of the Holy Nail in a procession of supplication during the plague of 1576, Borromeo was implacably opposed to many manifestations of the anarchic folk-religious culture which he found among the laity. He tried, unsuccessfully, to suppress the Carnival, and was an active prosecutor of witches and sorcerers in the mountainous parts of the diocese. Schools or confraternities for catechizing on Sundays were introduced to combat ignorance, and missionaries were sent into the rural districts, especially the Swiss valleys. Borromeo paid particular attention to confession as a means of individual conversion and instruction. To replace the dozens of independent lay confraternities he inaugurated a diocesan confraternity of the Blessed Sacrament. To reduce liturgical variation he imposed a uniform liturgy, interestingly based on the Milanese Ambrosian rite, not on the Tridentine rite for which he himself had been largely responsible.

All this was not accomplished without opposition. The Spanish rulers of Milan were devoutly

Left The Counter-Reformation had much in it that was puritanical, and much of the humanist ethos of the Renaissance Church was repudiated. Michelangelo's statue of the naked risen Christ, in the Dominican church where Fra Angelico is buried, S.Maria sopra Minerva, carved in the liberal, art-loving papacy of Julius II, was subsequently made "decent" with a clumsy gilt-bronze loincloth.

Below In El Greco's painting, *The Allegory of the Holy League,* the religious struggle in Europe is portrayed. Philip II kneels between the Doge of Venice and the pope, leaders of the hosts of the Church militant. They are worshiping the holy name of Jesus, revealed in the heavens, while behind Philip the jaws of hell open to engulf Protestant error and wickedness.

Catholic, but where the new reforms cut across the interests of the state they resisted Borromeo. He was determined that key ecclesiastical posts should go to the best-qualified men, whatever their nationality: the Spaniards were determined that they should go only to those loyal to Spain. Moreover, Borromeo did not pursue his reforms armed only with pious exhortation. He had set up an episcopal court, and offenders against ecclesiastical law found themselves under arrest in the archiepiscopal prison. His attempts to abolish simony and to get rid of immoral clergy cut across patronage and property rights. Borromeo was obliged to use the pulpit and even excommunication and interdict to force the authorities to accede to his wishes. The clergy, too, resented his rigor, and in 1567 he was shot and wounded by a member of the order of the Humiliati, which he had reformed. Nevertheless, the pattern of priesthood and episcopate established by Borromeo swept Europe. His Synodal Acts and Visitation Articles were printed in his own lifetime as models for others.

Education of the clergy

Borromeo's success was by no means always matched elsewhere. Both the Spanish and French governments were jealous of papal interference in the religious affairs of their kingdoms, and the Spanish Inquisition itself was an instrument of royal, not papal, authority. Both governments claimed the right to restrict or even refuse the circulation of papal bulls and briefs in their kingdoms – the disciplinary enactments of Trent were not permitted in France, though its doctrine was enforced. The web of patronage, finance and law which bound Church and state together all over Europe prevented any easy or uniform victory for the radical simplifications of Trent. Even where these difficulties did not operate, sheer inertia, or the lack of money or adequate personnel might prevent change. This is nowhere more obvious than in the matter of clerical education.

Tridentine seminary legislation was certainly among the most momentous of the council's achievements. In Spain and the more prosperous parts of Italy it was quickly put into effect, and the papacy itself had taken the lead by founding or supporting missionary colleges to train priests for those parts of Europe which had succumbed to the Reformation, the English colleges at Douai and Rome among them. But elsewhere little was done. Trent stipulated that seminaries should be founded by appropriating a proportion of the revenues of cathedral, monastic and other benefices, and of confraternities, compelling the possessors "even with the aid of the secular arm." This was easier said than done, and even when finance was raised, suitably qualified staff were not always available.

In many Italian dioceses little was achieved before the end of the 16th century, and in France virtually nothing was done until the 1620s, when St Vincent de Paul introduced a series of ten-day crash-courses to instruct candidates for the priesthood in the basics of doctrine, moral theology, liturgy and canon law. Vincent's work sprang out of the realization of the desperate religious plight of the poor of rural France; the activities of his Priests of the Missions and Sisters of Charity were part of a major French pastoral renewal. Vincent's objectives were modest enough, and impeccably Tridentine—to establish in every village a pattern of regular attendance at confession and communion, and a laity well grounded in the Creed and the Commandments. His work to produce a clergy capable of sustaining this was taken up by others, notably St John Eudes, and by the end of the 17th century the French clergy were models for the rest of Europe. In all this the influence and example of Borromeo were central.

These efforts to educate the clergy mark a shift in perception of the priest's life. He was now less a ritual figure, the "mass-priest," and more of a teacher and preacher. This shift towards a more active understanding of ministry is nowhere more evident than in the greatest single success story of the Catholic Reformation, that of the Jesuits.

Ignatius Loyola and the Society of Jesus

The Jesuits were a new kind of religious order. That in itself is paradoxical, for most reform-minded men in the early 16th century, Catholic or Protestant, were talking about abolishing the orders, not increasing their number. But the Society of Jesus was simply the best example of a new flowering of the religious life: not cloistered and withdrawn, but embodying the sense of urgent action, of man's ability to cooperate with the grace of God to transform himself and his world, which Trent enshrined. It was, significantly, founded by a soldier, Ignatius Loyola (c. 1491–1556), a poverty-stricken Basque nobleman, converted after a battle wound in 1521. After his conversion Ignatius became a familiar medieval Spanish type, the holy beggar journeying from shrine to shrine. But a profound mystical experience and ten months' meditation in a cave above Manresa resulted in the formulation of a highly disciplined spiritual method, in which systematic and vivid evocation of Christ's life and passion led to conversion of the will and the choice of a way of life in God's service.

Ignatius got himself a university education, gathered companions and began teaching his *Exercises,* in the process incurring repeated arrests by a suspicious Inquisition. Unable to go to preach in the Holy Land because of Turkish ships in the Mediterranean, Ignatius and his companions traveled to Rome in 1538 and put themselves at the disposal of Paul III. In 1540 their constitutions were approved, and Ignatius became general of the new Society of Jesus. It was a highly unconventional order, whose members wore no habits, sang no common office, and whose rule was extremely flexible in all but their obedience to general and pope. Their special concerns were mission, to Protestant Europe and the pagan world alike, the education of youth, and the religious instruction of the poor. Their training was rigorous and prodigiously long, and the first two generations of Jesuits included some of the most gifted men of the century. At Ignatius's death there were 1000 Jesuits (though only 33 were fully professed). Within a century there were 15 000.

The centrality of the Jesuits in the work of the Catholic Reformation is manifest in the work of the Dutchman Peter Canisius in the German empire. Canisius entered the Jesuit order in 1543 at Cologne, where he led the Catholic counterattack on

SWEDEN
DENMARK - NORWAY
SCOTLAND
NORTH SEA
BALTIC SEA
IRELAND
ENGLAND
WALES
London
UNITED PROVINCES
GERMAN EMPIRE
Elbe
Oder
Vistula
POLAND
Vilnius
Braunsberg
SILESIA
Glatz
Kuttenberg
Krakow
Prague
Olmutz
Brünn
BOHEMIA
UPPER PALATINATE
MORAVIA
Krumlau
Trnava
Vienna
AUSTRIA
BAVARIA
Ingolstadt
Dillingen
Molsheim
Bamberg
Würzburg
Fulda
Mainz
Trier
Antwerp
St Omer
Douai
Liège
Mons
Rhine
Rouen
Seine
Reims
Paris
Verdun
Pont-à-Mousson
Nancy
ATLANTIC OCEAN
La Flèche
Loire
Bourges
Dôle
FRANCE
SWISS CONFEDERATION
Lyon
Rhône
Bordeaux
Garonne
Toulouse
Avignon
IMPERIAL HUNGARY
STYRIA
Graz
Neuhaus
CARINTHIA
CARNIOLA
Drava
Sava
OTTOMAN EMPIRE
Danube
VENICE
Milan
Po
Parma
Genoa
Ravenna
PAPAL STATES
DALMATIA
Rome
Naples
NAPLES
to Spain
Corsica
to Genoa
Sardinia
to Spain
Sassari
Cagliari
Santiago de Compostela
Duero
Valladolid
Ebro
Salamanca
SPAIN
PORTUGAL
Tagus
Toledo
Madrid
Lisbon
Valencia
Balearic Islands
Seville
MEDITERRANEAN SEA
Palermo
Messina
Sicily
to Spain
Malta
15°
10°
5°
0°
5°
10°
15°
20°
25°
30°
60°
55°
50°
45°
40°
35°
30°
major Jesuit center, 1640
Jesuit institution
Mons Jesuit seminary
political boundary, 1648
Catholic areas, 1560
areas reclaimed to 1648
areas lost after 1560
distribution of other religions 1560-1648
Protestant
Orthodox
Muslim
scale 1:15 000 000
0
400km
0
300mi

Above Ignatius Loyola (c.1491–1556), founder of the Jesuit order, was arguably the most important figure of the Counter-Reformation. A converted soldier of impoverished Spanish noble stock, he became a wandering pilgrim and spiritual guru, and was frequently imprisoned by the church authorities on suspicion of heresy.

Right Rubens's picture, *The Triumph of the Catholic Church* (1628), epitomizes the aggressive and triumphalist vigor of the Counter-Reformation. Holy Mother Church (in the chariot) is portrayed as a conquering general returning with captives. In her hand she carries the Blessed Sacrament, from which glory and power stream. Over her head is poised the papal tiara, and an angel postilion carries the papal keys of St Peter under a canopy. Error is led a blindfold prisoner, while the Church's enemies are crushed under the chariot wheels.

Left: Catholic recovery and Jesuit centers
By the mid-17th century Protestantism had lost much ground. The Habsburg triumph in the early stages of the Thirty Years' War led to the forcible reclamation of Carinthia, Styria and Bavaria to Catholicism. Poland, once a byword for rampant religious pluralism, had become monolithically Roman in allegiance, and the Reformation was now being squeezed into the northeast corner of Europe. One of the key forces at work here was the Society of Jesus. In the magnificent centenary celebration volume produced by the Society in 1640, the *Imago Primi Saeculi*, Jesuit schools, universities, colleges and houses were listed. Plotted here from that list, they are an eloquent symbol of the chronic vigor of Counter-Reformation Catholicism.

the archbishop who had recently joined the Lutheran camp. Canisius quickly gained a reputation as preacher and controversialist, and took part in the Council of Trent as theological adviser to the bishop of Augsburg. From 1549 he was involved in the attempt to halt the progress of the Reformation in the empire. Even in areas where Protestantism was not established, humanist views had a large influence, and produced a tolerant, slack Catholicism which was vulnerable to Protestant evangelism. At Ingolstadt, where Canisius went at the request of the duke of Bavaria in 1549, he found the undergraduates unconcernedly reading Luther, Bucer and Melancthon. Some of them even asked him to look after these books during the vacation, while the rector of the local seminary was a layman who collected Lutheran literature. At Vienna where he worked from 1552 no priest had been ordained for 20 years, and over 250 parishes in the surrounding area were vacant.

Canisius plunged into a relentless round of activity to reverse all this. He negotiated the entry of Jesuits into Holland, Bohemia, Tyrol, Prussia, Poland and Hungary and founded colleges and schools at Vienna, Prague, Munich, Innsbruck, Halle, Nijmegen, Mainz, Trier, Würzburg, Osnabrück and Münster. Canisius journeyed incessantly through the length and breadth of the empire, preaching in the universities, in cathedral cities, in mountain villages and at princely courts where he sought to secure the banning of Protestantism, "the root from which springs division, disorder, rebellion, insolence and all kinds of excesses." He was a tireless propagandist for the Council of Trent, spreading its message, defending its decrees, sending it ammunition in the form of parcels of Protestant books for refutation. But his most crucial contributions to the Catholic counterattack were his three catechisms, especially the *Shorter Catechism of Catholics* of 1558.

This book was charmingly and lavishly illustrated with woodcuts of the life of Christ and of the sacraments, ceremonies and saints of the Church. It was both a manual of Catholic doctrine and a book of prayers and meditations, drawing heavily on scripture, the Fathers and on the spirit of German mysticism, adapting traditional rhymes to render the material memorable. All subsequent Catholic catechisms were modeled on Canisius's work, and by his death there had been 200 editions in 15 languages, including Lowland Scots and Hindustani. In addition he published a stream of longer books, from editions of the Fathers to commentaries on the Sunday Epistles and Gospels. His work marks a turning point in the religious history of Germany and northeastern Europe: in Poland alone by the year of his death there were over 500 Jesuits. He had turned the universities of Ingolstadt and Dillengen into Catholic powerhouses while his influence over successive dukes of Bavaria established the pattern of coordinated action between the secular arm and religious evangelists which was to reverse the spread of Protestantism in the Habsburg domains.

Spiritual revival and papal renaissance

Aspects of Canisius's work can be paralleled in the careers of other Jesuits, like St Edmund Campion,

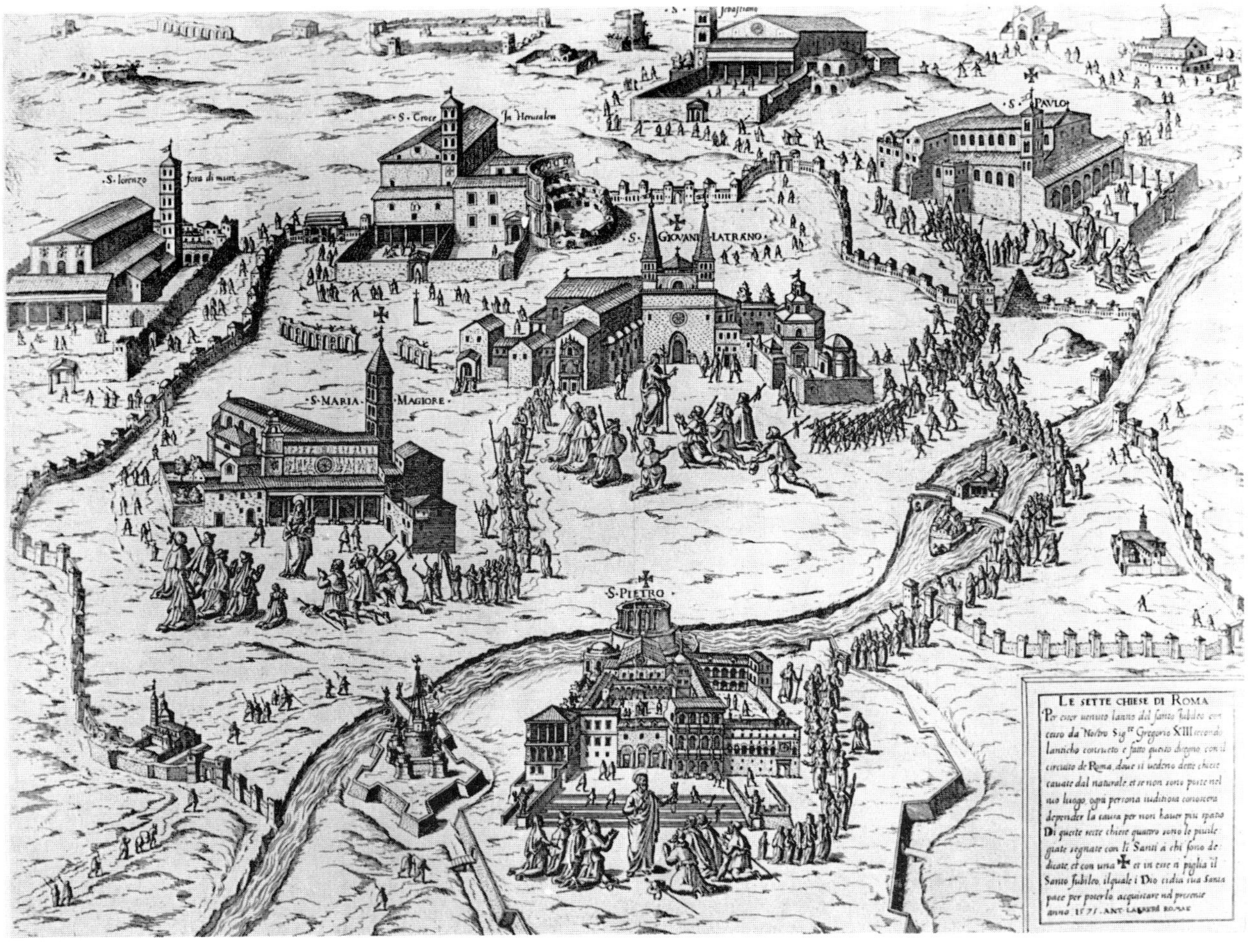

Antoine Lafrery's print of the seven pilgrimage basilicas of Rome was one of many publications associated with the Jubilee or Holy Year of 1575. Declared by Gregory XIII, the Jubilee represented a recovery of confidence in the spiritual authority of the papacy and a reassertion of the value of traditional Catholic practices such as pilgrimage and indulgences. Gregory's pontificate was marked by the expansion of the papal diplomatic corps and its use as an instrument of religious reform, and the creation in Rome of many seminaries and colleges (for Germany, England, Greece, Armenia and Hungary). He also protected and supported reformers like Teresa of Avila and Philip Neri. All this helped restore to the papacy the centrality it had seemed in danger of losing earlier in the century.

who preached and lectured at the Jesuit college at Prague before suffering martyrdom in Elizabethan England. But the order's influence was also less tangible, in the universal impact of Ignatius's distinctive piety on the religious sensibilities of Catholics and even Protestants. The *Exercises*, with their emphasis on the vivid evocation of religious images in order to arouse the mind and heart to a change of direction, and a new sense of religious purpose or resolution, gave rise to a multitude of devotional writings, many of them adapted by Protestants for their own use.

A revival of the inner life of the spirit was one of the most positive aspects of the militancy of Catholicism. If this was the age of the Inquisition and the Index of Prohibited Books, it was the age also of the mystics. In Spain Teresa of Avila and John of the Cross were only the two greatest of a rich variety of explorers along the inner journey of the soul towards God. Their writings, and Teresa's speedy canonization, established the spiritual life high in the priorities of a period whose passionate activism might otherwise have lost direction. In 17th-century France the lofty ideals of the Spanish mystical school were modified and domesticated, especially by Francis de Sales, the model bishop of Geneva, whose *Introduction to the Devout Life* (1608) emphasized the possibility of a saintly life lived in the world, and taught a warm and humane piety based in Ignatian meditation and frequent communion. It joined the *Imitation of Christ* in popular regard.

Perhaps the most remarkable transformation produced by the Catholic Reformation was the central place now occupied by the papacy. In a real sense Luther had saved the pope. Trent had been a papal council and the pope had been entrusted with promulgating its proceedings, embodying them in a catechism and reviving in its name a new uniform liturgy. It was the pope who now provided a symbol of unity around which the scattered forces of Catholicism could rally. Only papal authority could cut through the tangle of exemptions and privileges which paralyzed bishops in their dealings with cathedral chapters, monastic orders and lay confraternities. Only the pope could coordinate missionary efforts to the New World to the west, to the ancient civilizations to the east, to the broken remnants of the churches overwhelmed by Protestantism.

The papal Rome of the late 16th and 17th centuries was once again a center of pilgrimage and religious aspirations, the *Roma Sancta* to which pilgrims flocked during the Jubilee of 1575. Its churches rose from the ruins in the glory of the new Catholic baroque style, full of color, their restless outlines and gesticulating saints visible embodiments of the council's teaching that men must translate faith into action if they are to be saved, their cloud-painted, angel-covered domes proclaiming the omnipresence of the miraculous and the divine, breaking through the thin veils of external reality in the Church's teaching and its sacraments. Inevitably this focusing involved a narrowing, a rejection of the broad Catholicism of the preconciliar period, symbolized in the placing of all of Erasmus's writings on the Index. But if papal Catholicism was narrow, it was also strong. Under its attack the progress of the Reformation was halted, and then reversed.

WAR, SETTLEMENT AND DISUNITY

In the 16th century to reform the Church meant changing the world, for the Church was the world. Change of religion meant the upheaval of the state, or its settling. The Reformation might be seen as a way of uniting a state against all outside threats, as it was in the imperial cities of Germany, or as a potential solvent of the precarious ideological and spiritual unity of a kingdom, as it was in Spain. The savage pogrom launched by the Spanish Inquisition against heresy in the generation after Luther crushed the Erasmian movement which had promised so much for Spanish religion. It did so at the behest of the Spanish Crown, who saw in Catholicism not simply God's truth, but the cement of a society only recently welded together out of the kingdoms of the peninsula. Nowhere in Europe was religious toleration thought compatible with civil stability, and the few lone Erasmian voices who advocated it were drowned in the general call for religious uniformity, whether Protestant or Catholic.

The retreat and revival of Catholicism

By the mid-century it looked as if that uniformity was destined to be Protestant, and the Reformation seemed triumphant everywhere except in the Latin countries. Central and northern Germany were Protestant as were the Palatinate, Baden, Württemberg and Ansbach in the south. It seemed only a matter of time before the great prince-bishoprics of northern Germany went, despite the agreement at Augsburg known as the *Reservatum Ecclesiasticum* which stipulated that no further church lands should go Protestant. In Bavaria, Austria, Carinthia and Silesia the Habsburg lands were deeply penetrated by Protestantism. Most of this was Lutheran, but Calvinism was already showing itself the most militant of reformed faiths, passionately and

Protestantism in Germany
German Protestantism was, to begin with, Lutheranism. But in the second half of the 16th century Swiss-style Protestantism, with the greater ideological coherence given it by Calvin's *Institutes*, and its fighting refusal of compromise with traditional rituals and beliefs, became a potent force in Germany. Though the Peace of Augsburg gave no recognition to Calvinism, the principle of *cuius regio eius religio* gave to the prince the determining power over the religion of a state. This, and the volatile political state of Germany in general, could lead to wild variations: Baden Baden was Protestant in the 1550s, Catholic in the 1570s and Lutheran again in the 1590s. The Protestant Palatinate was Lutheran in the 1550s, Calvinist in the 1560s, Lutheran again from 1573 and Calvinist from 1580. Such fluctuations made uniformity impossible to enforce, and the religious map of Germany on the eve of the Thirty Years' War was a palimpsest revealing three-quarters of a century of religious upheaval.

crusadingly inimical to Catholicism. In Poland and Hungary it was growing rapidly alongside Lutherans, Bohemian Brethren and Anabaptists.

From the 1560s onwards, however, Protestant advance began to slow. To a large extent the Jesuits were responsible. Armed by Trent with doctrinal certainties as clear-cut as anything in Calvinism, the order brought to the flagging forces of Catholicism a new life. The work of Canisius bore fruit, not simply in an educated and preaching clergy, but in a new generation of ardently Catholic rulers, committed to the enforcement of Tridentine orthodoxy. In Bavaria successive dukes constructed a model for Catholic reform, with a rigidly orthodox university at Ingolstadt, an Index, a vigorous Jesuit presence, and a prince prepared to crush opposition. The Habsburg emperors were less wholehearted; their lands were a jumble of races and languages, where religious diversity seemed best managed by concession and compromise. Until the end of the century the prevailing Catholicism was humanist and tolerant. There was no Inquisition, no Index, and Trent was nowhere rigidly enforced, not least because imperial commitment to Catholicism, however real, was tempered by suspicion of growing papal influence. Nevertheless, the work of creating colleges, schools and printing presses, and of reviving monastic life went forward. By the end of the century Catholicism was immeasurably stronger in all the Habsburg lands than it had been 40 years before, and Protestants were girding themselves for battle with an enemy they had once thought to be in retreat.

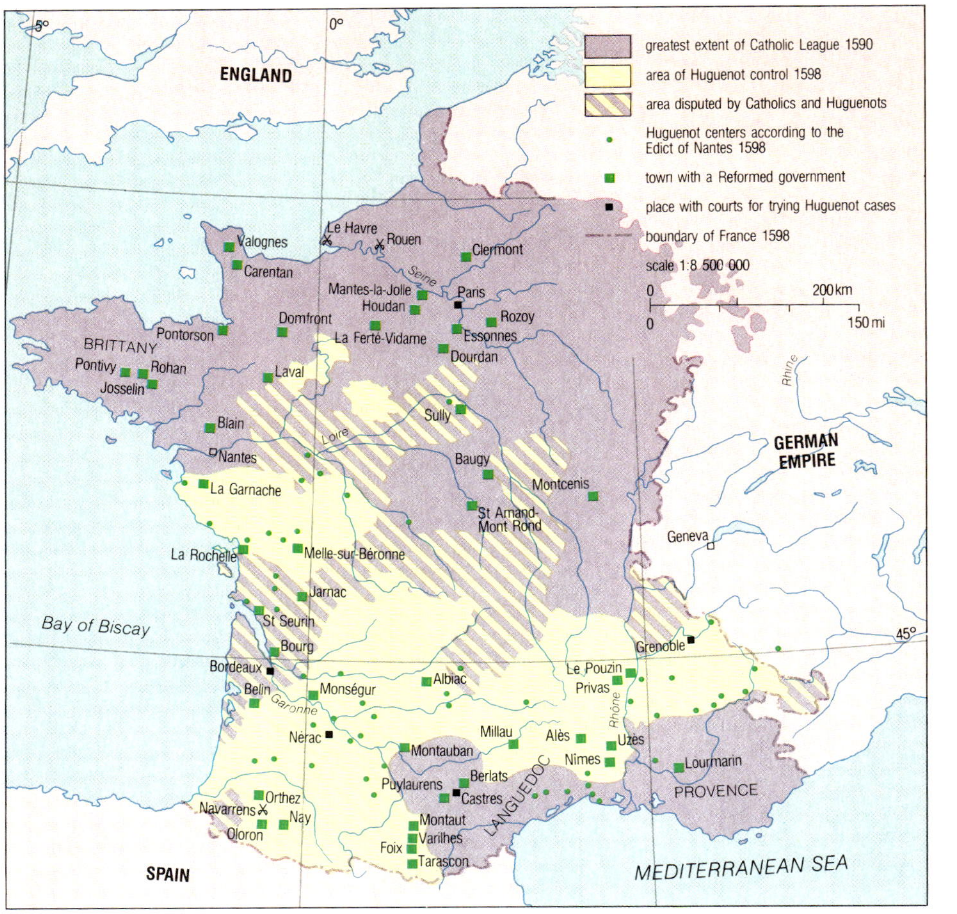

Above: Protestantism in France
The Calvinist mission to France, masterminded from Geneva, focused on the conversion of the nobility. Given the weak state of the monarchy in the second half of the 16th century, this was a recipe for social conflict and civil war. Militant Catholicism armed itself in the form of the Catholic League, which dominated much of northern France. Though some areas remained comparatively untouched by the conflicts which ensued (like Brittany) the religious wars between Catholics and Huguenots involved most of France. There were pitched battles and major sieges in places as wide apart as Navarrens, near the Spanish border, Le Havre and Rouen in the north. By the end of the century Protestantism had emerged as a permanent presence in the southern half of France south and west of the Loire; it was powerful also in Languedoc and parts of Provence.

The election of Archduke Ferdinand of Austria, first as king of Bohemia and then in 1619 as emperor, precipitated a crisis. Ferdinand had been educated at Ingolstadt by the Jesuits, and on attaining his majority in 1595 had set systematically about extirpating Protestantism in Austria. Bohemia, in which Calvinists, Lutherans and humanists had united to achieve large concessions from previous emperors, rose against its new king. The ensuing Thirty Years' War plunged Europe and Germany in particular into a bloodbath whose ideological origins became blurred by France's willingness to back Protestant armies against the Habsburgs. The major casualty however was, unmistakably, Protestantism. In imperial lands Catholicism became synonymous with political loyalty. When the war ended in 1648, the former Habsburg policy of compromise had been swept away. Teams of priests flooded the Protestant heartlands in Austria, Silesia, Hungary, followed closely by troops of soldiers: Protestant churches were closed, Protestant marriages and burials outlawed. In lower Austria 235 nobles converted to Catholicism in 1652 alone, and many parishes had more new believers than old. The religious orders were central to this, for good secular clergy were scarce. The baroque splendors of the abbey of Melk on the Danube testify both to the monastic role in the Catholic revival and to the breathtaking triumphalism that characterized it.

In all this brute force was often the decisive, but by no means the only, factor. Alone of all the countries of Europe, Poland had evolved a genuine policy of toleration. Lutheranism, Calvinism and all the varieties of Anabaptism had found a lodgment here, where the aristocracy saw religious diversity, at least among their own class, as part of their jealously guarded independence of the Crown. Despite a succession of sincerely Catholic kings religious freedom became the mark of Polish society, and Cracow became notorious throughout Europe as the center of the Socinian anti-Trinitarian movement. Catholic and Protestant zealots alike deplored what Calvin's successor at Geneva called this "Diabolical freedom of conscience." It was overcome not by coercion, but by the gradual drift of the gentry back to Catholicism, as their children were educated at the excellent Jesuit colleges, as the Crown's power of patronage exerted its sway, and under the growing pressure of the need for national unity against Protestant Prussia to the west and Orthodox Russia to the east. This process was complete by 1668, when the Polish Diet made conversions from Catholicism punishable by death and confiscation of property.

Wars of religion in France and the Netherlands

In western Europe the reformed faith had made deep inroads into French society; and around the mid-century large numbers of the nobility had embraced Calvinism. The religious vitality of French Calvinism was astounding, and by 1562 there were 2000 churches all over France, organized in consistories and synods. Missionaries from Geneva played a major part in this growth, and Calvin deliberately sought noble converts who could protect the churches against the Crown. Inexorably Calvinism was drawn into the power struggle of a disunited nation, and under the patronage of the Condé, Coligny and Bourbon families it became a major threat to national unity. France plunged into civil war, in which the Huguenots, as

Above In the second half of the 16th century France was torn apart by religious civil wars. The rise of Calvinism under noble patronage gave ideological and religious justification to the struggles of the great houses to control a weak monarchy. The massacre of the Huguenot leaders in Paris on the Feast of St Bartholomew, 1572, with the connivance of the court, triggered similar bloodshed all over France and printed on Protestant minds the indelible conviction that Catholicism was a bloody and treacherous religion. Gregory XIII ordered the celebration of a "Te Deum" of thanksgiving in Rome on hearing of the massacre, for he saw it as irrevocably committing the French monarchy to the suppression of Protestantism.

Below The succession of the Protestant king of Navarre to the throne of France as Henri IV terrified and angered Catholics, and the zealots of the Catholic League sought his overthrow. Henry conformed to Catholicism in order to pacify France, and by the Edict of Nantes granted his former fellow Protestants liberty of worship in certain towns and the right to maintain defenses for themselves. The existence within the kingdom of such Protestant fortresses as La Rochelle (shown here) was to prove intolerable to successive monarchs. The erosion of Protestant liberties continued throughout the 17th century, and was completed in 1685 when Louis XIV revoked the Edict of Nantes altogether.

the Calvinists were called, came close to winning control of the king, Charles IX, still a minor. The Massacre of St Bartholomew's Day in August 1572, when the queen regent and the de Guise factions butchered 3000 Protestants in Paris, spread into a national bloodbath, and France's agony was ended only when the Huguenot Henry of Navarre succeeded to the throne and, deciding "Paris was worth a mass," converted to Catholicism. By the Edict of Nantes of 1593 the Huguenots were granted their accustomed freedom of worship outside Paris, and permission to fortify at royal expense about a hundred small towns. This "state within a state" was precisely what every government, Catholic or Protestant, feared, and the Crown was to whittle away at Huguenot liberties until in 1685, after a policy of enforced conversion, the edict was revoked altogether by Louis XIV.

One of the most momentous products of the French wars of religion was a transformation of reformed attitudes to civil government. Calvin had sharply distinguished between the rights and jurisdictions of Church and state, while laying great emphasis on the duty of the magistrate to forward the Church's work. But he had insisted that the Christian's duty in the face of a tyrannical or unjust ruler was patient suffering obedience. Under the pressure of war this teaching collapsed, and Calvin's successor, Theodore Beza, formulated a theory of resistance to the prince not by individuals but by the "inferior magistrates," which others developed. This drove a wedge between Calvinism and other Protestants, and was a major factor in the appeal of Calvinism to militant minorities. Its ideological cutting edge was manifest in the revolt of the Netherlands against Philip II.

The revolt was complex in origin. Dissatisfaction felt by the traditional ruling nobility at their growing exclusion from power, resentment of town councils at royal intervention in their affairs, the social and religious grievances of the artisans and urban poor, the revulsion of moderate Catholics against Spanish persecution of heresy in the Low Countries, all played a part. Popular Calvinism in the Netherlands, manifested in the massive field preachings of 1566 painted by Brueghel, probably differed only in emphasis from the Erasmian and anticlerical religion of educated Catholics there. But the savage religious persecution launched by the duke of Alva in 1567 after an outbreak of Protestant iconoclasm polarized opinion. By the 1570s Calvinism had emerged as a fighting ideology in which the strength of the Dutch and French Protestants was seen as part of a worldwide confrontation of the forces of reformed light and Catholic darkness. Calvinism was successfully stamped out in the southern Netherlands, but entrenched itself within the defiant cities of Holland and Zealand.

Religious polarization and qualified contrasts

By the early 17th century, then, the religious polarization of Europe was well advanced. In Protestant England as in Catholic Spain religious deviants were harried, imprisoned, executed, though since England had no Inquisition, dissidents, whether Jesuit priests or sectarian Protestants, were executed under the treason laws.

It is tempting to see this polarization as extending into every aspect of society, and it would be easy to make a set of black-and-white contrasts. Catholic Europe was hierarchical. Its religion of external observance, of works of charity and the mediation of grace through the sacraments, was embodied in the flamboyance of the baroque style, of gigantic altarpieces portraying the miracles or merits of the saints. The Catholic ideal of the religious life was monastic and clerical. Catholic emphasis on authority was reflected in the Inquisition, and in the prohibition of freedom of thought or scientific inquiry as revealed in the condemnation of Galileo. Its characteristic form of government was absolute monarchy—Philip II of Spain, Louis XIV of France. By contrast, Protestant Europe characteristically emphasized the importance of the individual; its art was domestic. In this account of things, the peaceful paintings of Dutch interiors, the wise, lined faces of merchants and town governors who gaze out at us from Rembrandt's pictures, are an embodiment of the reformed emphasis on the priesthood of all believers, and in particular Calvin's insistence on the religious nature of every honest "calling" or state of life. Republicanism or constitutional monarchy is the characteristic political expression of Protestantism, and it is in Protestant countries that freedom of thought and scientific advance occur.

There is just enough truth in these contrasts to make them dangerously misleading. Certainly it is possible to discern Catholic and Protestant styles of worship and piety. The Counter-Reformation certainly attacked and attempted to refine the religion of the illiterate, to bind it more closely to church authority, to make it more Christocentric: the steady decline of shrines to the saints in the Spanish countryside from the end of the 16th century, and the steady growth of shrines and confraternities dedicated to Christ or to Mary as suffering witness of the Passion show that to a surprising extent this effort was successful. Nevertheless, the Counter-Reformation sought to harness and redirect *existing* forms of piety, and Catholicism remained a religion of ceremonial and of communal observance, centered not on the Bible but on sacrament and saint and pious work. By contrast the defining elements of Protestant piety were lay and biblical, focused as much on the home as on church. The archetypal Protestant figure is not the minister or priest, but the father of the household gathering his family about him to hear God's word and to sing his praises.

But one must beware of easy generalizations. In religion, above all other areas of life, men are conservative, and continuities and survivals complicate the picture. Here is a godly household: "Then [the father] sits at home with his good wife and his children and his serving folk, and he asks what they remember of the sermon, and tells them what he himself remembers. He questions them also whether they know and understand the Commandments, the deadly sins, the Lord's Prayer

Left: Protestantism in the Low Countries
Before the revolt in the Netherlands, religious dissent in the form of both Lutheranism and the more radical collection of beliefs known as Anabaptism had been present in the Low Countries, and had been the object of vigorous persecution. From the mid-century Calvinism had made its appearance in growing numbers, and was strongest in the southern provinces, and particularly in towns, such as Antwerp. Paradoxically, the effect of the revolt was to entrench the northern provinces, which had little popular support for Protestantism, as the stronghold of the Calvinist rebels. By 1618 Protestantism had been effectively abolished in its earlier southern territory, and Calvinism had been imposed in the United provinces, though there remained a very substantial Catholic population.

Right Fundamental to the Reformation almost everywhere outside Lutheran Germany was the purging or cleansing of the churches from every trace of Catholic "superstition." In this painting of a Dutch reformed church by Saenredam the congregation turn their back on the chancel, formerly the focal point of the church. They gather around the pulpit in a building stripped of all that could distract attention from the Word of God preached.

Below Though the grievances of the Netherlands against its Spanish rulers in the 1560s were not merely religious, the preaching of Calvinist radicals in the open countryside was a crucial factor in rallying support for the Dutch revolt. Brueghel's picture of *St John the Baptist preaching*, painted in the crisis year of 1566, vividly evokes the ministry of the Calvinist field preachers.

and the Creed, and teaches them. Finally he has a little drink brought in for them, and makes them sing a charming little hymn . . . and rejoices in God with all his household." But this is not in Elizabeth's England, or Calvin's Geneva, or Luther's Wittenberg; the passage is from a pre-Reformation work published in Austria. Within Catholicism, too, individual and family piety flourished, and the great spiritual revival in 17th-century France and beyond, which derived from the writings of Francis de Sales, was precisely a revival of lay, individual and household piety.

The broader contrasts, too, should be qualified. It was Calvinist ministers who developed the theory of resistance to tyrants—but that doctrine was also taken up and developed by Jesuits operating as missionaries in reformed territory, notably England, while 17th-century Huguenots were just as ardent in their devotion to monarchy as Catholics. The trial of Galileo and the notoriety of the Spanish and Roman Inquisitions have lent plausibility to the notion of a connection between Catholicism and scientific and philosophical obscurantism. But Galileo himself was a devout Catholic, who was silenced for incursions into theology rather than for his scientific theories, and his work was part of a revival of the natural and medical sciences in Italy which continued through the 17th century. Catholic as well as Protestant governments fostered practical technicological advances in optics, mathematics, astronomy, for these things brought material benefits. The most influential philosopher of the century, Descartes, saw his profoundly skeptical philosophy as providing invaluable apologetic ammunition for Christianity and Catholicism.

Divisions within Protestantism

Perhaps the most important qualification to be made to the real contrast between Protestant and Catholic civilization, however, is the fact of division within the opposing monoliths. Protestantism rejected the authority of pope and Church and replaced it with the authority of the Word of God in Scripture. The resulting diversity of interpretation within Protestantism was to prove endemic. This was not simply a question of sectarian activity at the fringe of the churches—Anabaptists in the first generation of reformers, the Independents or Baptists in early 17th-century England and Holland. As both Calvinism and Lutheranism congealed into orthodoxies, rival schools and critical reactions formed. Some of these were revival movements, intended to recall orthodoxy to its origins. The Pietist movement begun within Lutheranism by P.J. Spener in the 1670s was an attempt to revive an experiential understanding of justification by faith as the total rebirth and reorientation of the believer, rather than the merely forensic act it had been become in Lutheran orthodoxy. In fact the movement represented a new and moralistic interpretation of the doctrine, an emphasis on the Christian life as a wrestling with specific sins and the pursuit of virtuous action. Pietist dislike of confessional barriers, of dogma, of academic theology, above all its location of the reality of the Church within small groups of "awakened" Christians, made it the object of suspicion and opposition within the Lutheran Church at large. Pietist moderation, antipathy to dogma and theology, and interest in education as a means of reform made it in fact a vehicle for some of the forces of the Enlightenment, which in the following century would act as solvents of traditional orthodoxy.

Within the reformed churches, the rise in the Netherlands of the movement known as Arminianism was even more momentous. Arminius and his followers rejected the doctrine of predestination which had become so central to Calvinist theology, and asserted the freedom of man's will for good as well as evil. The consequences of this were enormous. Christ had died not for a God-chosen minority, the elect, but for all who chose to follow him. Here was escape from the inexorable grasp of Calvin's unfathomable God, and in its place was established a God who valued men for their actions. Morality, not faith, became the primary focus of the Christian life. And since God could be sought and found by all men, Arminians like Hugo Grotius (1583–1645) emphasized his reasonableness, stressed the rule of morality, of reason, of law, and saw the ordering of human society as reflecting the divine or natural order. The great gulf which Calvin had made between nature and grace disappeared. Here was a different sort of religion, cool, optimistic, playing down the mysterious and the supernatural, accommodating Christianity to the best instincts of mankind in all ages and places. Ruthlessly persecuted in Holland, the impact of Arminianism subtly but deeply penetrated Protestant Europe, cooling religious passions, making the dogmatic barriers of zealots seem foolish, the reunion of churches possible.

Arminianism had highlighted a deep-seated ambivalence within the Reformation. Was salvation for all men or for the elect? If for all, then the Gospel preached must accommodate itself to human weakness, its standards must not be set too high, and the human need for external and ritual activity must be met. If for the elect, then the godly were the norm by which other men should be judged, and the efforts of ministers must essentially be to gather the godly and help them to fulfill their calling. In Elizabethan and Stuart England that dilemma had lain at the root of the so-called "Puritan movement." Most Anglicans were Calvinists, but the Puritans were those who followed the doctrine of the elect to its logical conclusion, remaining within the structure of the national Church, but pursuing a piety which had the effect of marking them off from the ungodly. The godly household gathered on a Sunday afternoon to hear the Scripture read: as often as not outside would be the sound of their profane neighbors relaxing around the maypole or the village alehouse. Protestantism by its very emphasis on the Word tended to exclude what Richard Baxter called "the rabble that cannot read." At a profound level the reformed faith was inimical to popular religious feeling and culture, with its deep rhythms and ritual survivals which reformers saw as the rags of popery. The Puritan vision of the world was one in which compromise with worldly standards was apostasy, and it is this intransigence, this stark opposition of nature and grace, which explains its collapse after a brief moment of triumph during the English Revolution.

Divisions within Catholicism

The divisions of Protestants found an echo within Catholicism, for the Counter-Reformation was motivated by a multitude of energies rather than a single one, and they frequently came into conflict. Episcopal hierarchy was fundamental to the Tridentine vision of Catholicism. Orders like the Jesuits wholeheartedly accepted the value of the hierarchy, but their very nature as the storm troopers of the Catholic revival made them impatient with the ponderous structures and regulation which hierarchy involved. For this reason they sometimes opposed the introduction of episcopal rule in mission territory, and Cardinal Manning thought that there was "only a plank" between the Jesuits and the Presbyterians. When in the 1590s the Jesuit Robert Parsons drafted a plan for the recatholicizing of England he thought nothing of sweeping away the contemplative religious orders, diverting monastic revenue to educational, charitable and missionary use, and abolishing the parson's freehold in favor of an activist clergy who could be hired and fired at will.

The new Catholicism was a reaffirmation of the value of activity; its saints were achievers,

Right In a religion in which image and ritual were taboo, literacy and access to the written word became essential to salvation; Protestantism joined Islam as a "religion of the book." Gerard Dou's painting of an old woman absorbed in reading extracts from the Gospels arranged in a daily lectionary, with illustrations to help interpret the text, reflects this profound shift in Christian piety.

Below The 17th century in France brought with it a great wave of Catholic religious fervor, of which Jansenism, an austere and demanding form of Catholicism based in the later teaching of St Augustine, was one expression. The center of the Jansenist movement was the prestigious convent of Port Royal, to which devout men and women flocked, and which was eventually to arouse the fatal suspicion and enmity of the Crown. Champaigne's picture captures something of the austere repudiation of the ways of the world demanded by Jansenist piety. It portrays the artist's daughter, Catherine, a nun of Port Royal who was miraculously healed of paralysis in 1661 at the prayers of the prioress, Mère Agnes Arnauld (who kneels in the painting). The inscription on the wall behind her recalls the miracle.

founders of religious orders, of orphanages and hospitals, heroic missionaries to remote lands. But there were souls who found God not in action but in inwardness, and the mystics found themselves again and again objects of suspicion. In a church that taught the necessity of good works and the sacraments for salvation, the mystic's inward journey, his search for a God known without intermediary of any sort, might seem heretical. The most disastrous clash between these opposing energies came at the end of the 17th century, when the archbishop of Cambrai, François Fénelon, was condemned for Quietism. Fénelon taught a doctrine of "disinterested love." The most perfect love of God is unselfish; the Christian is passive before God, oblivious of any reward, even of his own salvation. To Fénelon's opponent Bossuet this doctrine led straight to the abandonment of moral striving, of the use of the sacraments. Fénelon readily submitted to the pope's reluctant rejection of his views, but the condemnation served to coarsen the fiber of Catholicism and to canonize spiritual self-interest as the mainspring of the Christian life.

The most profound rift within Counter-Reformation Catholicism showed itself in the Jansenist debate. Trent's teaching on justification and grace had not eclipsed the Augustinian tradition. There were many Catholics who believed that man was sunk in sin, that few could be saved, that only penitence and inner conversion befitted man's fallen state. These views were given extreme expression in the posthumous *Augustinus* of Cornelius Jansen, a Dutch theologian and bishop who had modeled himself on Charles Borromeo. Jansen's followers gathered around the convent of Port Royal, where their somber version of Christianity was given noble and increasingly famous embodiment. Jansen taught that only the predestined would be saved, that Christ had not died for all men, and that man was not free to resist God's grace. These views were condemned, but they were not the crux of the matter.

Jansenism stood for the repudiation of compromise with the world. Ardently Catholic in their veneration for the sacraments, Jansenists deplored the too easy access which sinners had to them. Absolution should be given only to those who could prove their repentance, communion should be approached with fear and trembling, and for most people infrequently. They hated the Jesuits, whose optimistic teaching on man pandered to pride, whose emphasis on frequent communion encouraged sinners to profane the most holy, whose absolutions were too casually given. Though Jansenist teaching contained much that was inspiring, and although they shared much common ground with the leaders of the French spiritual revival, the condemnation of the movement was both inevitable and necessary. Had their view prevailed, all attempts at mass evangelization in the European countryside and in the Asian, American and African missions would have been robbed of meaning. Jansenist bishops took the lead in attacking popular piety, and it is significant that St Vincent de Paul, whose personal religion had some affinities with the Jansenists', recognized them as enemies of his work among the "rabble that cannot read," and worked for the condemnation of the movement.

TO EAST AND WEST

The expansion of Christianity in the New World and the Far East began before the Reformation, for which it came to seem a providential compensation. Its advances, and even more its lets and hindrances, throw into stark relief the complexities, contradictions and weaknesses of organized Christianity in that age.

In a series of bulls issued between 1456 and 1514 successive popes had ceded to the Spanish and the Portuguese Crowns the task of converting the heathen peoples which exploration was bringing under their control. In 1493 Pope Alexander VI divided the world into two regions, west and east of the Cape Verde Islands, the Spaniards to rule in the west, the Portuguese in the east. The power thus granted to the monarchs of the Iberian peninsula was among their most treasured prerogatives, and in the Spanish case in particular bestowed on the Crown total control of the personnel and revenues of the Church in the largest empire the

Missionary voyages
The Iberian kingdoms played the key role in the initiation of early missionary enterprise, and the overwhelming majority of 16th-century voyages of evangelization, like their 15th-century predecessors, originated in the ports of Spain or Portugal. It was the Spaniards who took seriously the task of dividing the new territories into dioceses, since by and large the

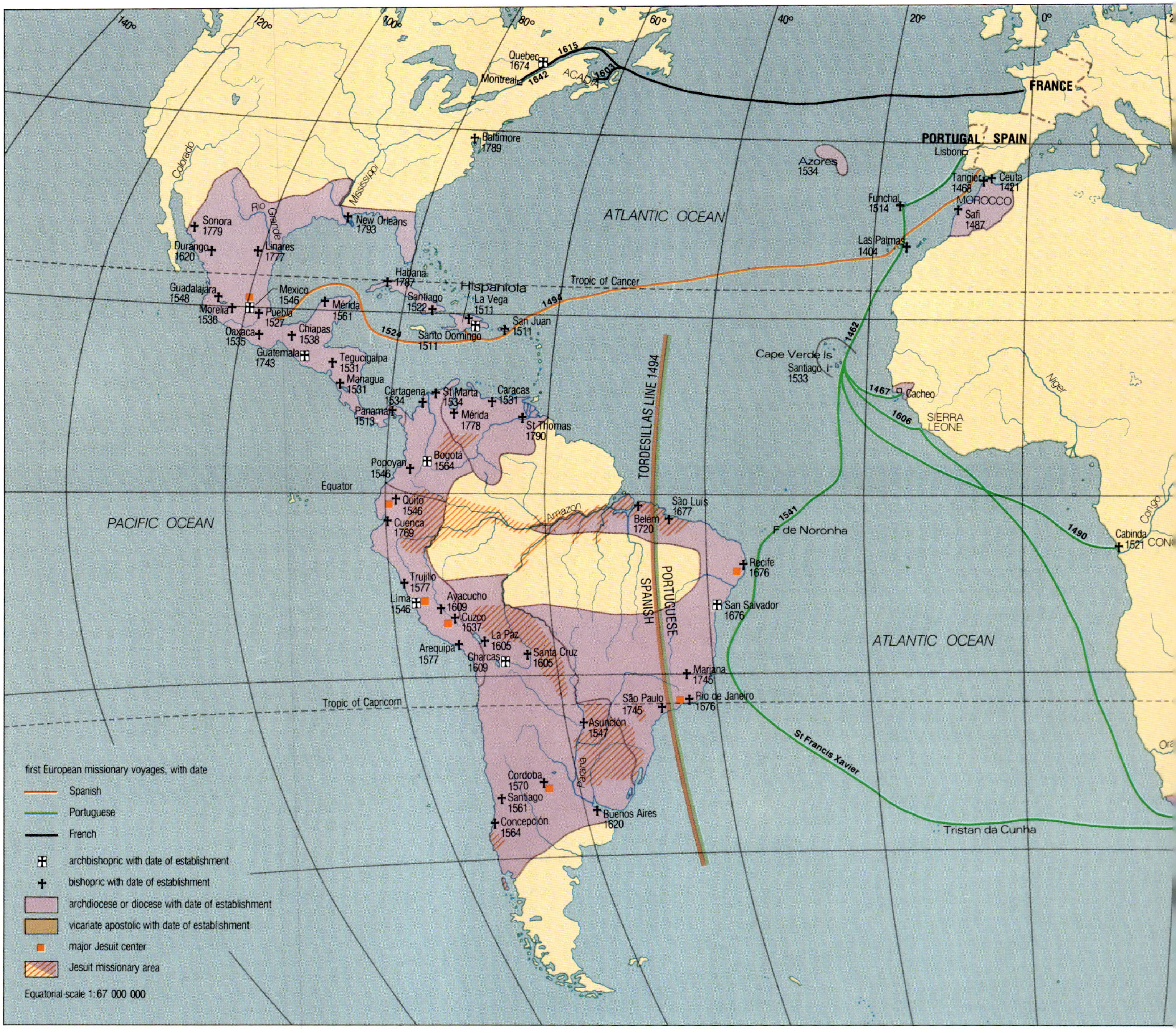

Portuguese saw missions more in terms of chaplaincies to colonial communities than in terms of the spread and indigenization of Catholicism. Both monarchies, however, jealously guarded access by non-national missionaries to their territories. By the end of the 17th century, the papacy was driven to the expedient of setting up Vicariates Apostolic which "poached" the territories of the Iberian overseas diocese, in order to break the Spanish and Portuguese monopoly – increasingly seen as a stranglehold – on missionary enterprise.

world had ever known. On the whole the Spanish Crown took its role as evangelist and custodian of the Church with great seriousness, and there is a marked contrast between the speed with which new dioceses were established in Spanish territory and the unimpressive record of Portugal in this respect. But in both cases the control of the missions granted by the papacy, when the scale of colonial expansion was as yet undreamed of, was to project onto a world screen the conflict of jurisdictions and interests within the Counter-Reformation which had provoked Borromeo in late 16th-century Milan, or launched the papal interdict against Venice in the early 17th century.

Mission was in this period almost exclusively a Catholic phenomenon. Protestantism, fighting for its political existence in Europe and with a permanent shortage of educated clergy, had little evangelistic energy to spare. There were tentative but short-lived English missionary efforts among the tribes of North America, and the Dutch sent clergy to the East Indies, though they largely confined themselves to proselytizing among Roman Catholics. Calvinism, with its deep hostility to ritual and symbolism, its stark exaltation of the Word, and its rejection of human philosophies or traditions, offered little leverage to non-European cultures by comparison with the luxuriance of Counter-Reformed Catholicism.

Spanish friars in New Spain

Spanish missionary activity in the New World began at an auspicious moment, for in the 1520s and 1530s the Spanish Church was at the height of the humanist reform inaugurated by Ximenez. Cortes had asked Charles V for a Franciscan mis-

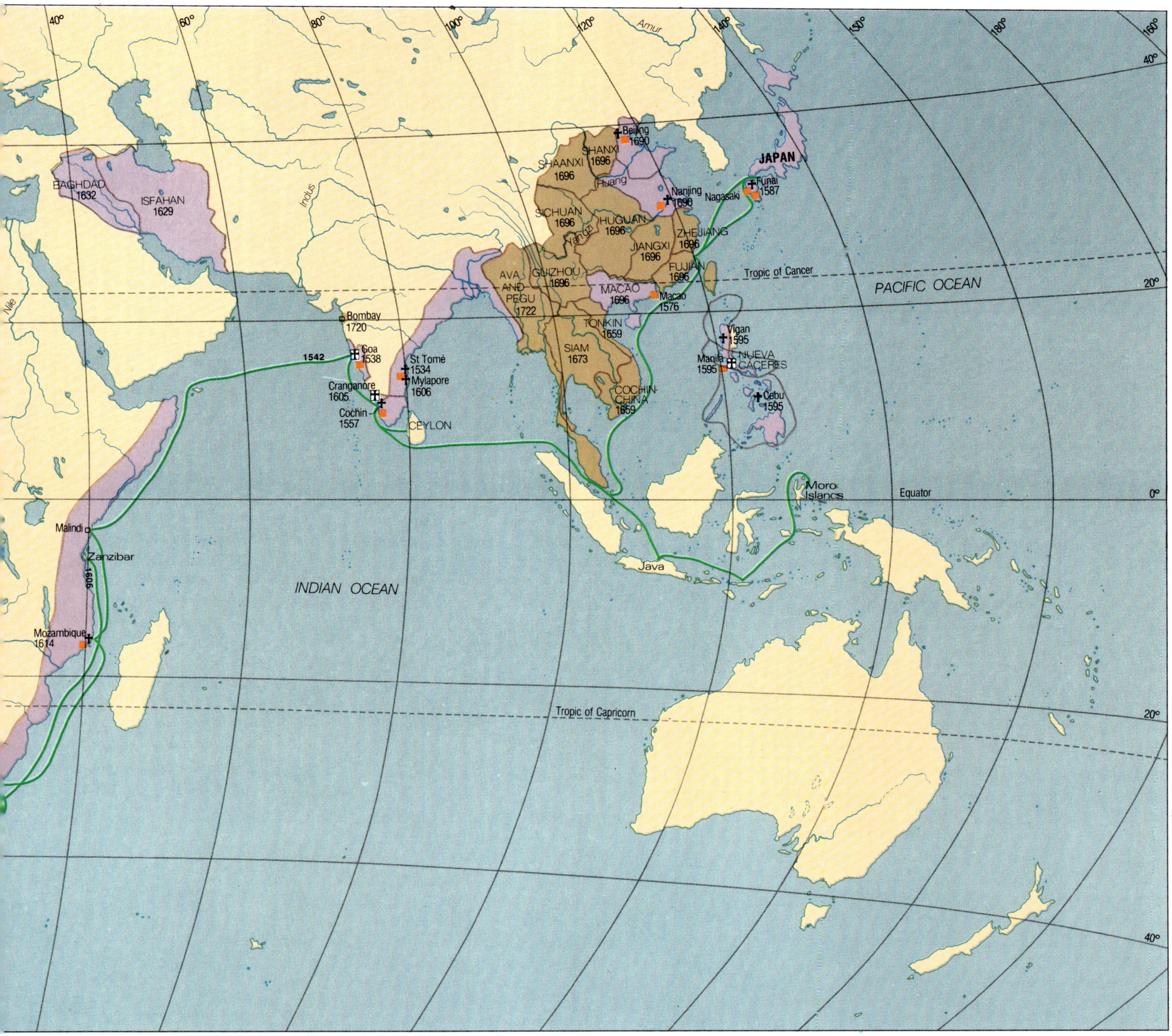

Left Oaxaca was the fourth diocese set up in the American continent by the Spaniards. It symbolizes much of the mixed motives of the conquest of Mexico, for its choice as a religious center was largely due to its rich gold deposits: Cortes took the title Marquis of the Valle de Oaxaca. The see quickly became the focus of more spiritual concerns, however, and houses of all the religious orders working in New Spain were established there, resulting in the building of a number of magnificently ornamented churches.

Above The interaction of European and pagan culture was always problematic, even when European influence seemed dominant. This 17th-century Mexican crucifix is carved with the conventional symbols of the Passion – nails, crown of thorns, pillar and scourge, ladder and lance, the cockerel that crowed three times, the eucharistic chalice and bread, and so on. But these impeccably orthodox elements have been molded into a superbly powerful but (to European sensibility) alien and equivocally Christian object.

sion, and the mendicant orders were to dominate American evangelization until the 1570s. The first friars in New Spain were radicals, men of austere sanctity and proponents of an ardent and biblical Catholicism. The Franciscan Juan de Zumorroga, first bishop of the diocese, introduced the printing press into the Indies, on which he printed catechisms and instructional works for the clergy, drawing heavily on Erasmus's writings and advocating the unlimited circulation of the Scriptures.

The friars were highly organized, establishing themselves in population centers in Mexico and Puebla, and quickly mastering the local languages. Preaching was deliberately simple, concentrating on a minimal and highly compressed set of essentials. The Franciscans in particular aimed at speedy conversion and baptism, to be followed up afterwards with catechism and individual instruction. Their preaching was astonishingly successful. Zumorroga claimed that more than a million converts had been made between 1524 and 1531; others claimed that by the mid-1530s five million Indians had been baptized. These mass conversions clearly needed reinforcement. For all their humanism the friars were implacably hostile to native religion. They set themselves to destroy every trace of it, and to substitute a culture soaked in the thought patterns and imagery of Catholicism, a religion of elaborate ritual, processions, lavish festivities and religious drama. Statues and shrines of pagan deities were systematically smashed, and on the sites of some of the larger temples Christian churches were erected. Zumorroga reported in 1531 that more than 500 temples and 20 000 idols in his diocese had been destroyed.

The spiritual achievement of New Spain was full of problems. The religion which the friars were attacking was woven deep into the structure of Indian society: to replace it involved the creation of an alternative social and religious system. The friars therefore often sought to gather the Indians into tightly controlled communities built around the church and convent, with a system of communal landownership. These communities were consciously modeled on Thomas More's *Utopia,* and represented a visionary humanist quest for a new start. They served to isolate the Indians from pagan influence, and, more importantly, from the European settlers whose moral lapses, and desire for slaves, were held to be equal threats to the new converts. The huge and elaborate churches built by these communities were an attempt to give visible expression to the benevolent theocracy envisaged by the friars.

The missionaries were engaged in a constant running battle to protect their converts against the colonists. The savage violence of the early *Conquista* was justified by the transparent fiction that the Indians were a bestial and unnatural race who had refused Christianity, thereby entitling the Spanish to force them to submit to Christian rule. In some instances the Spanish had gone through the farce of reading a formal demand for acceptance of the Gospel and submission to the Spanish Crown to uncomprehending Indians before massacring or enslaving them. Neither the Crown nor the Church was easy about this. In 1511 the Dominican friar Antonio de Montesinos had denounced the settlers on Hispaniola for their atrocities against the Indians: "Are they not men? . . . Are you not bound to love them as yourselves? In such a state as this, you can no more be saved than the Turks." Bartolome de Las Casas, the Dominican bishop of Chiapa, devoted his whole life from 1514 to 1566 to a tireless campaign to secure justice for the Indians and achieved the prohibition of enslavement of the Indians under Charles V's "New Laws" of 1542.

But the iniquities of the colonists were only one of the problems of the missions. Given the vast numbers involved, the grasp of most converts on their new religion was to say the least hazy, shot through with pagan beliefs and practices. It was therefore customary to withhold communion from all but the best-instructed and most pious natives. The result was a largely noncommunicant Church. Early hopes for a native priesthood faded, and the Franciscan college established at Tlatelolco in 1536 for that purpose was abandoned. By the mid-century the friars themselves were questioning the effectiveness of their own mission, and much of the earlier zeal evaporated. The settlement of the nine dioceses of New Spain, too, led to conflict between the religious orders and the bishops and secular clergy, quarrels over jurisdiction and title which frittered missionary energy.

Missions to South America

The conversion of New Spain had been nonetheless a major success story, excelled only in the Philippines, which had two million converts by the 1620s. South of Panama, in Peru, progress was hindered by the vast distances and more scattered tribes. By the 1540s the reforming fervor which had produced a remarkable first generation of missionary friars had been stifled by the panic reaction of the Spanish Inquisition to the Reformation. The Peruvian dioceses, under the archbishop of Lima, were huge, and evangelization inevitably superficial: the peasantry adopted Christianity as an addition to an already complex polytheism. The statues of the saints in procession on festivals frequently proved on closer inspection to be those of Indian deities, and the old religion survived alongside the new. The Peruvian episcopate found themselves, in the era of Trent, confronted with a conflict between official and popular religion infinitely starker than anything their brethren in Europe had to contend with, but without manpower or resources to make any deep impression on it. Peru found its Carlo Borromeo in Toribio de Mogrovejo, second archbishop of Lima (1579–1606), a tireless evangelist himself, who died in a remote Indian village during his third visitation of the diocese. In a series of diocesan and provincial synods Mogrovejo sought to control paganism, provided three graded catechisms, limited Indian access to communion, regulated the use of images in worship, and denounced the persistence of idolatrous rites and customs. But the Peruvian Church remained largely the Church of the Spanish and Hispanicized Indians, a thin veneer on a seething paganism.

Something of the difficulties involved in the encounter of two cultures in the Americas is evident in this depiction of the baptism of an Indian by an observant Franciscan friar, from the Codex Azcatitla. Here the depiction of the Christian sacrament is surrounded by images remote from Christian tradition; the New World was to present evangelists with formidable problems in assessing the reality and depth of the "conversion" of Indian culture.

The arrival of the Jesuits in South America brought a new vigor to missionary activity in the late 16th century. Their most spectacular achievement was the creation of a chain of missions to the Guarani Indians, in the valleys of the Paranã river, beginning in 1610. The Jesuits gathered the Indians into a series of "reductions" (34 by 1630, with a total of 100 000 inhabitants) in autonomous territory granted by the Spanish Crown. Subject to constant attack by Portuguese raiders seeking slaves, they armed the Indians, and in 1649 set up the independent republic of Paraguay which survived until the dissolution of the order in the 1770s. The reductions were Utopian communities, spacious, clean, well paved, where education was compulsory, democratic councils ruled, and the death penalty was unknown. There was no money, and all property was held in common. Orchards, sugar, cotton, tobacco were grown, and the Indians wore textiles, made iron, built clocks and operated printing presses. Music making and religious drama were given a central role. Though the Indians were given little room for initiative, and the fathers dominated their lives, the reductions were a unique attempt to realize a Christian society, and one of the most significant survivals of the humanist impulse in a post-Tridentine world.

The early missionaries to the New World had been predisposed to reject native religion as essentially inimical to Christianity by their experience of militant Islam. Many of the first Franciscans in New Spain had been involved in the spiritual reconquest of Granada, where they had used a similar *tabula rasa* policy. The collapse of Aztec and Inca culture under colonial ruthlessness left Christianity with no real rival. In India, China and Japan, however, European missionaries encountered cultures as sophisticated as their own, and religious systems which could not so readily be dismissed as barbaric or devilish.

The Portuguese in India

As Spanish conquest had been in the west, Portuguese exploration and trading were the principal vehicles for the mission to the east. Based at Goa from 1510, the initial religious concern of the Portuguese was to provide chaplains for their own communities, and to Latinize the indigenous Nestorian "St Thomas" Christians. In 1534 a bishopric was established at Goa, and serious missionary work began. Spectacular success immediately attended it. The Bharathus caste of fisher-folk on the coast of Coromandel had long been the prey of marauding Muslim raiders. Illiterate, poor and without organization, the Bharatas were helpless. They turned to the Portuguese, and the price of protection was conversion. The entire caste was baptized. News of tens of thousands of baptisms reached Lisbon, and prompted King John III to send missionaries to consolidate and extend this beginning. Chief of these was Francis Xavier, one of Ignatius's earliest companions, and the first and greatest of the series of Jesuit missionaries to the east.

Xavier was initially swept into a mission to Goa itself, an appalling sink of evil, where the Portuguese slave-owners counted blows on bastinadoed slaves on their rosary beads, and with a floating population of half-instructed converts who had become Christians "for the sake of a new hat, or a shirt, or to escape the gallows." For five months he worked in the city's three prisons, in the hospital and among the lepers. Moving to the coast of Coromandel, his only luggage an umbrella and a piece of leather to mend his shoes, he found the language barrier his greatest problem. He had the Creed, Commandments, Lord's Prayer, Hail Mary, Salve Regina and the Confession translated into Pidgin Tamil, which he memorized. Then gathering flocks of children by walking with a handbell, he taught them to chant the prayer. In one month of frenzied activity he baptized 10 000 people, and sent a barrage of letters to Ignatius at Rome and to the Portuguese Crown begging for helpers. "Experience has taught me that Your Highness has no power in India to spread the faith of Christ, though you have power to take away and enjoy all the country's temporal riches."

Jesuits in Japan

In 1549 he turned to Japan, where he believed he would find "a race entirely guided by the law of reason." Feudal Japan was experiencing a period of disorder and decentralization, and unusual openness to foreigners. The local warlords, or *daimyos*, were all-powerful and longed for contact with the west, with its superior armaments. Once again language problems hindered Francis's mission, but in his 27 months in Japan he grasped that the *tabula rasa* policy of obliterating local culture and religion, and substituting a western cultural setting for his preaching, was useless. Recognizing the nobility of much of Japanese civilization, he realized the need for highly trained missionaries who could build on this, and who would appeal to the educated and ruling classes.

The Jesuit mission to Japan was to last for a century, and to be astonishingly successful. Many *daimyos* were converted, and by 1580 there were over 150 000 Christians. The Jesuits built seminaries to train native catechists and priests, though the absence of a bishop prevented Japanese ordinations until 1601. Japanese students were sent to Europe to study and gain support. By the end of the century other orders, notably the Franciscans, had established missions. Rivalry between the various groups contributed to the disaster that befell the mission in the new century. The emperors came to believe that the widespread acceptance of Christianity would make Japan vulnerable to European conquest. From the 1620s onwards a horrifying persecution was launched, in which European priests and native converts were boiled, flayed, crucified or spiked. An English trader reported seeing "fifty-five martyred at one time at Miyako. Among them were little children of five or six years, burned alive in the arms of their mothers, who cried 'Jesus, receive their souls'. Very few return to their idolatry." By 1650 2000 Christians had been killed, 70 of them European priests. Christianity survived, but as an insignificant underground church.

Missions to China

The challenge of a high civilization to the missionary was encountered even more strikingly in China, off whose shores Xavier had died in 1552. The Jesuit mission to China was launched by a figure almost as remarkable, Matteo Ricci. Ricci had entered the society in 1571, and had studied mathematics under Clavius, the friend of Kepler and Galileo, and theology under Robert Bellarmine. In 1582 he was sent to Macao to prepare himself for the Chinese mission. There he studied Chinese language, philosophy and history, and when in 1583 he was permitted to enter China, he presented himself as an admiring student of Chinese culture. He adopted Chinese dress and life-style, even growing his nails to show his mandarin status, and gaining a reputation as a clock maker and painter, astronomer and cartographer. In 1601 he was allowed to come to the imperial court and given freedom to preach. Ricci's whole purpose was evangelistic, but he did not openly proselytize. He worked instead as an interpreter of the two cultures to each other, seeking Chinese literary equivalents for Christian terms, finding in Chinese customs as many parallels with Christian truths as possible. He adopted much Confucian teaching, and permitted apparently religious rites, such as ancestor worship, as merely civil or social ceremonies. By the time of Ricci's death in 1610 he had made only 2000 converts, but they included many scholars and members of the mandarin class, and Jesuit successors built on his work; by 1650 there were 150 000 Chinese Christians, and one Jesuit, Adam Schall, had become astronomer royal at the emperor's court.

But the Jesuit method of evangelization in China aroused furious opposition from other missionaries. For the Dominicans and Franciscans the whole notion of the accommodation of Christianity to a Chinese environment was anathema, a compromise with paganism and devil worship, obscuring the gulf between unregenerate nature and grace. The friars who marched through Fuzhou in 1634, holding crucifixes in the air, shouting that "the idols and sects of China are false, and deceits by which the devil leads them to hell forever," epitomized this deep rift. Chinese suspicion about the cultural imperialism of Christians increased; matters worsened as French missionaries, imbued with the Augustinian theology which formed the background to Jansenism, arrived in China, and European quarrels found fresh fuel in the missionary context. Accusation and counteraccusation

The Portuguese *padroado* in the east was a mixed blessing from the point of view of mission. The colonial clergy (*left*) saw themselves as chaplains to the Portuguese community, rather than as missionaries. They were often content, like Robert de Nobili's Jesuit colleague Henri Fernandes, to identify Christianity with being *parangi* (foreign). Missionaries such as Xavier and, later, Ricci were forced to free themselves from these associations and limitations. Where possible, however, they liked to keep on good terms with the colonial clergy, who could, if alienated, hinder their work. In the vignette above the map in this 17th-century idealization of Xavier's arrival in Goa (*above*), he is embraced by the local bishop (with whom he did in fact strike up a friendship).

Right It was in China that the most spectacular missionary accommodation to pagan culture took place, under the guidance of Matteo Ricci. In this picture of Ricci, in mandarin dress and carrying a fan, note the restrained character of the crucifix, the relatively more prominent image of the Madonna, and the decoration of the altar with words and abstract symbols rather than the vivid realism of the Counter-Reformation. The Chinese found baroque images of religious suffering and death offensive.

shuttled between China and Lisbon, Madrid, Rome. The debate was exacerbated by the hostility of the Portuguese authorities to missionaries who came under French or Spanish patronage. The emperor of China himself supported the Jesuits, but in 1704 Rome ultimately condemned the practice of "accommodation" with local cultures.

Roman policy towards mission

The "Chinese rites" quarrel illustrates the complexity and the often contradictory character of the Catholic Reformation. It was by no means unique, for Jesuit missionaries elsewhere employed similar methods, like Robert de Nobili in India, who cut himself off from all Europeans and became a Brahmin holy man teaching Christianity as the true fulfillment of Hinduism, and refusing to evangelize lower castes. The debates were not simply theological. Jesuit desire for a native clergy for example was frustrated as much by racist notions of "purity of blood," rooted in the confrontation with Judaism and Islam in the Iberian peninsula, as by any Augustinian theological problem. The Portuguese *padroado* or patronage of eastern missions proved a liability, as Xavier had early found, Portuguese nationalism and trade interests militating against either the free access of non-Portuguese missionaries or the emergence of an indigenous clergy. The papacy sought to wrest this monopoly away, and the establishment of the Congregation de Propaganda Fide in 1622 under its energetic secretary Francesco Ingoli provided a focus for an active Roman policy towards mission.

Ingoli was highly critical of Portuguese activity in the east, backing the native clergy in India and China against racism, attacking royal tardiness in appointing or filling bishoprics for the new churches, denouncing forced conversions. Ingoli circumvented the Portuguese Crown's monopoly on episcopal appointments by introducing episcopal "vicars apostolic" responsible directly to the pope, a device first used in Holland and England, where the governments were Protestant. In its first 25 years Propaganda founded 46 new missions, and had its own multiracial seminary and printing press in Rome. It relied heavily on French missionary clergy from the 1660s to undermine the Portuguese *padroado*. But vigorous as Propaganda was, it never succeeded either in mastering the royal patronage of Lisbon or Madrid, or in solving the problem of an indigenous clergy. Ingoli disliked the Jesuits, and although Rome gave the Beijing Jesuits some backing, even granting permission for the recitation of mass and breviary in Chinese, the strong presence of French clergy with Augustinian views in the Propaganda missions inexorably worked against accommodation, and led ultimately to the withdrawal of all such concessions. The combined obstacles of Latin and clerical celibacy prevented significant recruitment of non-European clergy. It is an added irony that the French clergy, employed to strengthen Rome's claims to missionary control against the Crowns of Spain and Portugal, themselves were increasingly imbued with Gallican ideas about the independence of the French Church over against the papacy. Here, as so often, the apparent monolith of the Counter-Reformation in fact consisted of an uneasy alliance of often opposed energies.

THE CHURCH IN NORTH AMERICA

The story of Christianity in the United States is a story of exploration, colonization, immigration and innovation. In the 15th but more especially in the 16th century, the North American continent along with the New World generally found itself a prize to be captured or quarreled over by the European powers—notably Portugal, Spain, Holland, France and England. A good part of the quarrel concerned religion. The Gospel should be planted in North America—but whose Gospel? Portugal and Spain, both Roman Catholic nations, had by the end of the 16th century made major inroads into Central and South America. France, another Roman Catholic power, had under the leadership of Jacques Cartier penetrated the Gulf of St Lawrence in 1534. England, the major Protestant power, was slow to accept the opportunities afforded for either national aggrandizement or Protestant expansion. The great propagandists and churchmen, Richard Hakluyt the Younger and Samuel Purchas, intended to change all that, Hakluyt calling in 1584 for England's monarchs to deserve their title of "Defenders of the Faith" and Purchas scolding his nation three decades later for being noted more for lethargy than for liturgy. By the beginning of the 17th century, however, it was evident that the

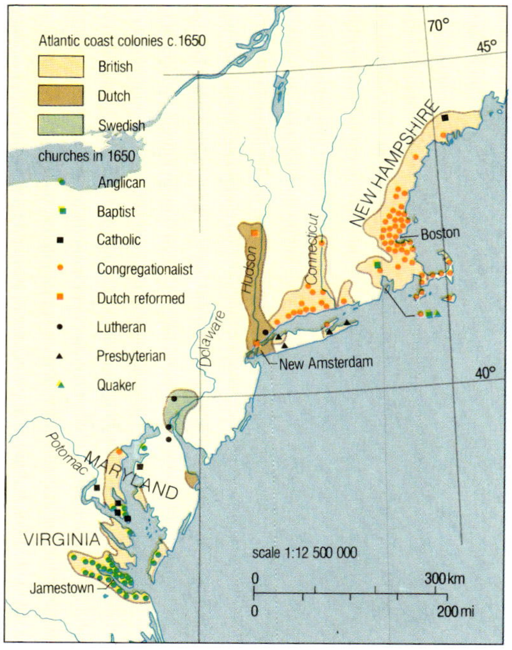

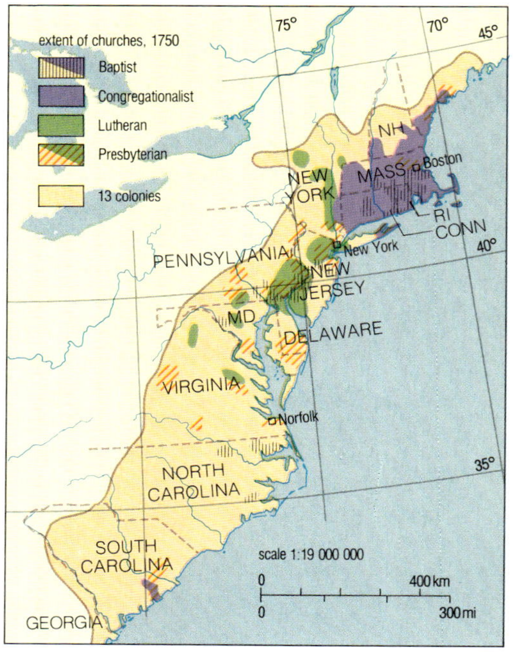

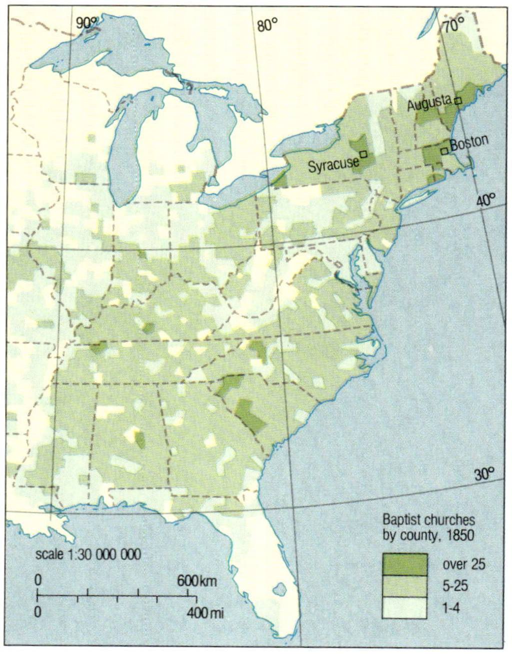

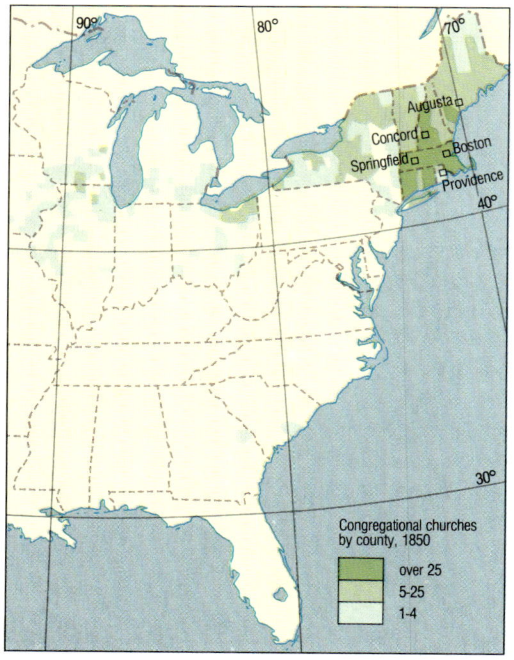

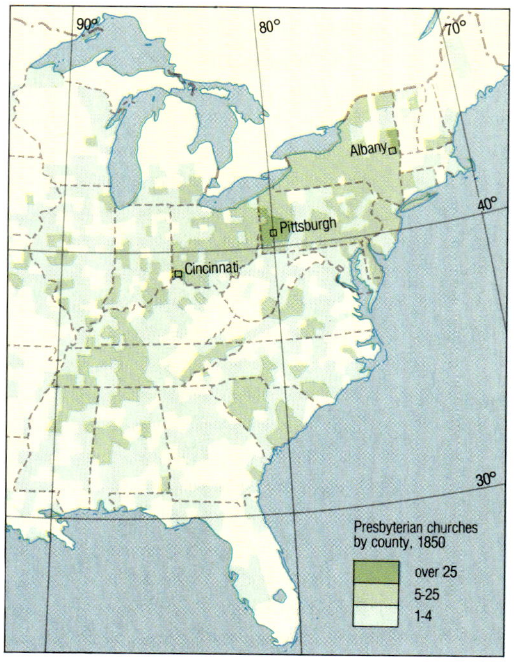

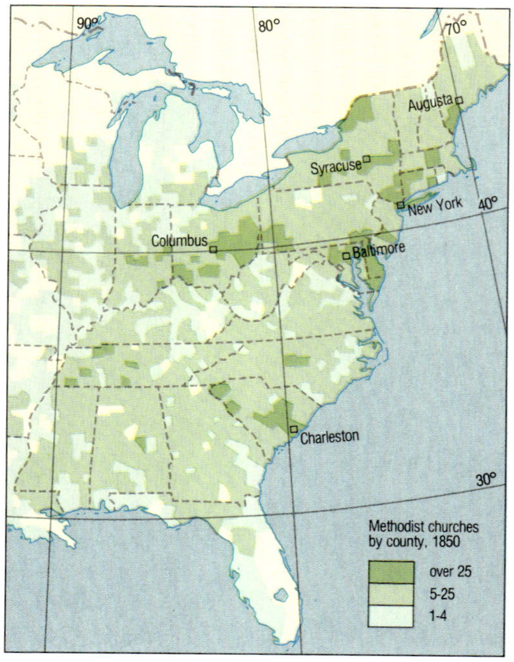

Right Jamestown was not necessarily the happiest choice for an English settlement early in the 17th century, but it did endure. In the New World, Jamestown gave both the English nation and its national church a point from which to expand along the broad rivers and into the Chesapeake Bay. The idealized scene here portrayed hardly hints at the internal quarrels among the English or the growing distrust and hostility between native Americans and arriving Europeans. The rivers, like the James, York, Rappahannock and Potomac, no less than the bay itself, proved to be the waterways of commerce and the avenues to settlement. Amid much difficulty, they also proved to be the chief determinant of parish boundaries.

Christianization of North America would not be left entirely to Europe's Roman Catholic nations.

Anglicanism in the Southern colonies

England's earliest efforts at colonization were abortive, and for a time the Jamestown (Virginia) settlement of 1607 did not look a great deal more promising. Enduring starvation, disgruntlement, Indian uprising and economic collapse, Jamestown did nevertheless survive and with it England's most populous colony on the North American continent. Steps were taken as early as 1619 to insure England's Church an official status in this, England's colony. Maintaining the Anglican way proved, however, to be most difficult. Money was scarce, ministers were few, and the modest population was widely scattered. An English observer writing in 1662 elaborated on that last point, explaining that Virginians settled not in towns but in plantations that stretched for many miles along the rivers. Parishes drawn up by the legislature covered a great deal of ground, but only a few people. "The Families of such Parishes being seated after this manner, at such distances from each other, many of them very remote from the House of God, though placed in the middest of them" (*Virginia's Cure*). The author proposed that towns be created anyway, in defiance of both geography and economy, so that an English parish would look as an English parish ought to. His plan failed, of course, as did his proposal for fellowships at Oxford and Cambridge that would ensure a better supply of better ministers to North America. (A more promising solution to the problem of ministerial quality and quantity came in 1701 with Thomas Bray's founding of the Society for the Propagation of the Gospel in Foreign Parts.) Despite the very real problems, Anglicanism was stronger in Virginia by the middle of the 18th century than it was anywhere else on the continent, having about one hundred churches at that time.

Elsewhere in the Southern colonies, the Church of England sought to improve or regularize its status. While Maryland was founded under the auspices of English Catholics in 1634, by the end of the century England's Church was officially established there. So also it enjoyed legal favor in South Carolina and North Carolina, though the latter colony was the despair of all true churchmen. North Carolina, in the words of Anglican Charles Woodmason in 1766, "is in a Stage of Debauchery, Dissoluteness and Corruption—and how can it be otherwise? The People are compos'd of the Out Casts of all the other Colonies who take Refuge there." Woodmason's picture is greatly distorted, but it does point to the major Quaker settlement and growing Baptist presence in North Carolina. The last of the 13 colonies which were to become the United States, Georgia, founded in 1733, also granted legal favor to the Church of England, but growth there lagged behind even that of the Carolinas. By the time of the American Revolution, Anglicanism dominated the South, especially the areas of earliest settlement: the tidewater region. That revolution, however, heavily damaged its prestige and appeal, with the result that within a generation Anglicanism was reduced to the status of a minority in all of the South.

The Congregational establishment in New England

The religious picture in New England differs dramatically from that of the South for demographic as well as denominational reasons. Patterns of settlement now were by towns, not by rivers; families maintained a close unity; slavery was a modest, even negligible, institution; life expectancy was much greater; and theological earnestness was far more evident. The migrations to Plymouth Colony and to Massachusetts Bay Colony

Left: The spread of Christianity in the USA
The spread of Christianity on the North American continent reflects the movement of the colonizers, at first predominantly English Puritan refugees, Presbyterians, Quakers, Anabaptists, Congregationalists as well as Anglicans, Lutherans and Reformed Christians from the continent of Europe. Because many had come to America for freedom to practice their religion, the denominational divisions proved persistent.

were of English Puritans whose main motivation was religious. The colonies of Massachusetts and Connecticut, therefore, were results of an "errand into the wilderness" in a way that the Southern colonies never were. A remarkable degree of Puritan homogeneity was maintained under the denominational tag of Congregationalism, the early distinction between those Puritans who had already separated from the Church of England and those who had not losing its point in America by the mid-17th century. Congregationalism, which also enjoyed legal favor, grew steadily with an ample supply of learned and able ministers, either from Cambridge in the first generation, or from Harvard (1636) or Yale (1701) in succeeding generations. A flush of revivalistic pietism in the 1740s intensified the fervor of New Englanders, though it also led to some separation or schism from the official Church. The American Revolution, receiving strong support from the Congregationalists, meant no sudden reversal of fortune for their Church as it had for the Anglican institution further to the south; indeed, the official character of the Congregational establishment managed to survive even after the Revolution, in Connecticut until 1818 and in Massachusetts until 1833.

Of course, homogeneity was never perfectly maintained in all of New England, not even in the two colonies named above. But it was the colony of Rhode Island and Providence Plantations that won the "prize" in New England for religious variety and a scandalous—to most of the western world in the 17th century—diversity. Puritan Roger Williams, exiled from Massachusetts in 1636, bought land from the Indians and launched a colony devoted to the "livelie experiment" of maintaining "a most flourishing civil state" on the fundamental premise that all its citizens shall enjoy "a full liberty in religious concernments." Williams, briefly a Baptist, was later aided by John Clarke, a Baptist for a great many years, in securing Rhode Island's charter and fixing its boundaries. Baptists were the first to profit from this colony's deliberate embrace of religious liberty, but Quakers were not far behind in establishing Newport, Rhode Island, as their principal New England base. By keeping itself open to all malcontents, dissenters, unchurched and unconcerned, Rhode Island unconsciously assisted the rest of New England in its efforts to protect and preserve the New England or Congregational "way."

Diversity in the Middle Colonies

In between the South and New England, the Middle Colonies presented no single religious pattern but the widest diversity: ethnic, national, linguistic, no less than denominational. The Dutch, early into the region now known as New York, brought Holland's own national Church with them. And while the Dutch flag was lowered in less than two generations in favor of the English flag (in 1664), the Dutch Reformed religion continued to be a strong cultural force in both New York and New Jersey—strong enough, in fact, to bring a Dutch Reformed college (Rutger's) into being in 1766. The Calvinist Dutch also joined heartily in the Calvinist-oriented Great Awakening of the 1740s, as did the Scottish and Irish Presbyterians of the Middle Colonies who had begun settlement in this region early in the 18th century. It is the Society of Friends or Quakers, however, who made the most dramatic entry into this part of America. Under the vital leadership of William Penn the large land grant of "Penn's woods" became a haven not only for the much-despised, much-persecuted Quakers but for all other religious dissenters as well. Though not founded until 1682 (long after Jamestown, Plymouth or New York), Philadelphia grew

Left With religious motivations much more clearly evident in the Puritan than in the Virginia migrations, population growth in the Bay Colony was also more assured and swift. The "Pilgrims" who settled at Plymouth and the "Puritans" who founded Boston soon melded into that denomination known as Congregationalism. The geographical strongholds of this Church (Massachusetts, Connecticut, New Hampshire and later Vermont) powerfully shaped what came to be called "the New England way."

Below So much of 19th-century American history is bound up with the voluntary migration of thousands across the Appalachian mountain chain, down the Ohio river, onto the rich lands of the Midwest—then, in a rush far beyond to the Pacific coast by the late 1840s. Religion took part in that grand march, building churches and founding colleges, reaching the ever-moving frontier through itinerant preachers, domestic missionaries and—most dramatically of all—camp meetings. The latter offered entertainment and education, companionship and courtship, all under the umbrella of a democratic gospel powerfully proclaimed.

rapidly, so swiftly indeed as to become the cultural capital of America by the mid-18th century and the political capital during the days of revolution and reconstitution.

By the end of the American Revolution in 1783, the strongest denominations in the newly independent nation were as follows: Congregational, Presbyterian, Baptist, Anglican, Lutheran, German Reformed, Dutch Reformed, Roman Catholic. As suggested above, these denominations were not evenly distributed up and down the Atlantic coastline; on the contrary, a significant geographical particularity is evident. Congregationalists, as noted, dominated New England, while Presbyterians were heavily concentrated in the Middle Colonies. Baptists, early in Rhode Island and Pennsylvania, after 1750 moved more strongly into the South, especially in the backcountry areas. Anglicans, proceeding from a strong Southern base, penetrated into Pennsylvania, New York and even New England but never without challenge and strong competition. Lutherans, primarily of German origin at this time, flourished chiefly in Pennsylvania, as did the German Reformed. The geographical concentration of Dutch Reformed in New York and New Jersey has been indicated, while the small minority of Roman Catholics lived mainly in Maryland, with the next largest concentration being in eastern Pennsylvania.

Revolution and "the voluntary principle"

The fact of nationhood did not obliterate all the colonial lines of religious geography. It did, however, open up vast new territories for religious conquest, and in 1791 it formally placed all religious groups upon an equal legal footing in their proselytizing pursuits. Both pietist and deist principles argued against any national church; moreover, no single church emerged as a politically possible candidate. Thus, either by necessity or by conviction, the churches adopted "the voluntary principle." Without governmental help, but also without governmental hindrance, each denomination was free to build its own schools, train and support its own personnel, print and distribute its own literature, organize and staff its own churches, recruit and sustain its own missionaries.

Aiding many of the denominations in these large tasks were such purely voluntary societies of the early 19th century as the American Bible Society, the American Sunday-School Union, the American Tract Society and the American Education Society. Presbyterians and Congregationalists joined together in a Plan of Union in 1801 to pool their resources in order to save the west from barbarism and for Christianity. A new arrival on the American scene, Methodism, proved particularly adept at reaching the opening west and serving the rapidly moving frontier; circuit riders or itinerant

Christians in 19th-Century Pennsylvania

By 1750 Pennsylvania had become the archetype of what virtually all America was to be: pluralistic, prosperous and regularly enriched by direct immigration from abroad. Avoiding some of the mistakes of earlier colonial adventurers, William Penn dealt honorably with the Indians, allowed no persecution of religious dissent and provided a realistic assessment to prospective settlers of the actual costs and hardships involved. While English Quakers constituted a majority of the first wave of immigration to the Philadelphia area (and other regions along the Delaware river), Germans and Scots soon made their way to this vast new and beckoning land. The resulting religious diversity shocked those unaccustomed to such a public display of the consequences of religious freedom.

York County's dominant ethnic flavor was German; within that ethnicity, Lutheranism was the major religious force in the 18th century as it has continued to be in the 20th. Happily, we have visual testimony to this German cultural life in general and religious life in particular by means of the *Sketches and Chronicles* of Lewis Miller (1796-1882). With sketch-pad in hand and with a curiosity that was unquenchable, folk artist Miller traveled, observed, drew. In that often frustrated search for those not of the elite nor in positions of great power, Miller rescues us from ignorance both in detail and in general outlines. Because of him, we can know and see so much more of the religious diversity and particularity of 19th-century rural Pennsylvania.

Right Miller identifies this drawing as that of "a country church, nine miles from Christiansburg, Va, and three miles from new River, facing the pike road." With characteristic precision, he dated his visit to this church as having taken place on 22 June 1856. That region was also heavily settled by Lutherans, generally migrating down from York County, southward into Frederick and Carroll counties in Maryland, then into the Shenandoah Valley of Virginia. This migration, through the Appalachians rather than across them, extended at least as far as Montgomery County, where Christiansburg is located.

Above Lewis Miller even helpfully "photographed" the altar and communion vessels of York's Lutheran church. His description is as follows: "a Silver Box artfully made to hold the Host . . . and a Gilded Cup to hold the wine . . . two Silver plates & two Silver Spoon, And a fine Cloth to cover over the Altar pieces."

Left Singing choir. Miller's sketch of a Lutheran church in York in the early 1800s emphasizes the music that was so vital a part of the congregational life of Lutherans—as also of the Moravians in Bethlehem and other Pennsylvania communities. The organ, dominating the upper right-hand corner of the sketch, is of a most impressive size, as is the "Singing Choir" of 16 voices.

Right Birth certificate. A fine example of the Fraktur technique, this "certificate of birth and baptism" shows the transition from German to English as being nearly complete by 1849. Tradition lingered on, not only in the German script, but in the richly decorative and widely familiar artistic symbolism.

preachers traveled every newly opened post road, providing a ministry even before there was a town. Baptists, less committed to a college-educated clergy than the Congregationalists, utilized the "farmer preacher" to maintain some degree of Christian ministry in rural hamlet or riverfront.

The vastness of the whole continent beckoned United States citizens after the Louisiana Purchase of 1803 and the Mexican American War of 1846–47. Such open territory demanded "new measures" of evangelization: the camp meeting, the "anxious bench" of the revivalist, the "retreat" of the Roman Catholic fathers, the simplification of theology, the elevation of the "Bible only" as sufficient rule for all, the blunting of denominational loyalties—all these and more. Sometimes new measures led to new institutions or associations. Under the leadership of Thomas and Alexander Campbell as well as Barton Stone, a restorationist impulse (to restore the pure Church of the apostolic age) created its own frontier church: the Disciples of Christ and related "Christian" churches. The untrammeled and traditionless west also suggested to many that here brave and daring experiments in Christian living could be carried out: the Shakers, the Oneida commune, the Owenites, the Rappites, the Theosophists, and—most successful of all—the Mormons. The west did not create all such groups, but the west gave them a home.

Growth of Catholicism in the 19th century and Orthodoxy in the 20th

Even as churches strained to meet the calls for resources, finances and personnel from the Great Plains and Pacific shores, these same institutions found themselves flooded with a heavy immigration upon their Atlantic shores. This was especially true after America's bitter Civil War, a war that took its toll upon both the evangelizing zeal and the moral concerns of the nation's churches. By virtue of the 19th-century immigration, the Roman Catholic Church moved from its minority status in the 1780s to become by 1850 the nation's largest single denomination. Its explosive growth (early in the century from Ireland and Germany; later, from southern and eastern Europe) created many internal strains, even as it aroused nativist fears of "Romanism" and papal threats to American liberty. Internally, the Catholic Church's leadership avoided the pressure for ethnic parishes with ethnic priests and ethnic bishops. Externally, that leadership—James Cardinal Gibbons (1834–1921), for example—labored unceasingly to convince a skeptical citizenry that Catholic polity and national liberty were wholly compatible. In the 20th century, while political suspicions declined, immigration pressures surged again, but this time not from Europe. Spanish-speaking Catholics from Central and South America as well as from the Caribbean islands presented a new challenge of assimilation to the Roman Catholic Church; ethnicity would not determine all structure, but neither would it be obliterated by a largely non-Hispanic structure.

Eastern Orthodoxy, though it had an early start on the continent in "Russian America," failed to capitalize on its 18th-century Alaskan beginnings. In the 20th century, however, significant immigration from abroad resulted in a visible, colorful presence in the United States of both Russian and Greek liturgies, as well as those of lesser size. Orthodoxy, while in the nation, has yet to move effectively through the bloodstream of the country. Its enclaves remain secluded and isolated; its internal divisions preclude a united voice on national concerns. In all probability, the 21st century will find Orthodoxy, as in the manner of so many other Christian groups that arrived before it, more fully assimilated, more thoroughly engaged in American affairs.

Proliferation of religious bodies

So much of the broad display of religious variety in the United States is merely the result of immigration: European, African, Asian, Latin American. Sometimes immigration in different time periods, as from Holland in the 17th century and Holland again in the 19th century, led to the creation of separate ecclesiastical entities. After granting much to immigration, however, it must also be acknowledged that the United States has been peculiarly fecund with respect to religious bodies. Some of the proliferation has come from schism, for where there is no establishment, nor even any hoary tradition, schism comes easily. In the 18th century Congregationalists separated into Old Lights and New Lights, Presbyterians into Old Side and New, Baptists into Six-Principle, Seventh-Day and Calvinist. In the 19th century the Civil War divided Methodists, Presbyterians and Baptists along the political lines of the north–south split (the first two having reunited in the 20th century). In the early 20th century the continuing fundamentalist-modernist debate provoked a series of ongoing and ever smaller separations. But in addition to schism, America has been the scene of much experimentation and innovation. Especially among the spirit-filled who wear their institutionalism lightly, a plethora of new denominations has been born: Assemblies of God, Churches of God, Church of the Nazarene, Pilgrim Holiness Church, Pentecostal Churches of many names and varieties. Religious liberty in America meant among other things a seemingly endless proliferation of Christian bodies, a mad dash in the direction of the goal foreseen by Emerson: every man his own church.

Yet ecumenism has in the 20th century slowed the pace of that dash. From over 20 separate churches of varying ethnicity, Lutheranism in America has moved to two major bodies. Methodists in 1939 and Presbyterians in 1983 healed the Civil War schism, but each in addition merged with others "of like faith and order" where the question of slavery or race was totally irrelevant. In 1962 an ambitious Consultation on Church Union spoke of a Christian Church "truly catholic, truly evangelical, truly reformed" that might gather most Protestants (only Lutherans and Baptists among the major groups have not been involved in some discussion) under a single church order. Ecclesiastical cooperation as opposed to organic union has also grown in the 20th century, from the Federal Council of Churches formed in the first decade (and reorganized as the National Council of Churches at mid-century) to the national Association of Evangelicals organized in 1942. Cooperation between Roman Catholics and Protestants has, moreover, markedly improved since the days of Vatican Council II (1962–65). Deep divisions and suspicions nonetheless remain, some based on divisions of race, some of class, some of theology, some of polity, and some of sheer accidents of history and geography.

Left Not all migration of American religion moved from east to west. For Roman Catholicism in particular, significant colonizing and missionary activity marched from the south (notably Mexico) toward the north (particularly into Texas, New Mexico, Arizona and California). Franciscan Father Junipero Serra (1713-84) established a chain of missions along the California coast, that chain ultimately reaching all the way from San Diego in the south to Sonoma in the north. San Luis Rey, here portrayed, lay about 50 kilometers north of San Diego. A move in the 1980s to canonize Father Serra ran into opposition from Indian groups and others on the grounds that his "mission policy" had destroyed more than it had preserved of Indian dignity and integrity.

A God-fearing nation

Through all of the division, schism and proliferation, a regularly repeated observation about American religion was that it *grew*. Church membership increased from somewhere around 15 or 20 percent at the nation's beginning to over 60 percent two centuries later. The wealth of the ecclesiastical enterprise grew so great as to arouse sharp criticism and pointed attack on the pervading policy of tax exemption for all that property and income. Politicians could be of almost any religious affiliation, but woe unto them if they were of none. Church attendance has for years averaged in the 40 to 45 percent bracket, well below registered membership but well above most

Below Sex and marriage proved troublesome to all utopian experiments and disastrous to some. The Shakers solved the problem by interdicting both. Segregation of the sexes was the pattern, and celibacy the rule. As long as frontier revivalism and camp meetings kept providing the Shakers with new converts, their membership grew. But when that source of new life dried up before the Civil War, Shakers entered upon a gradual but steady decline. As the religious life withered away, antiquarian and historical interest in the Shakers revived, much of it centered on their folk art and furniture design, their herbal medicines, and their ritual dancing and hymns.

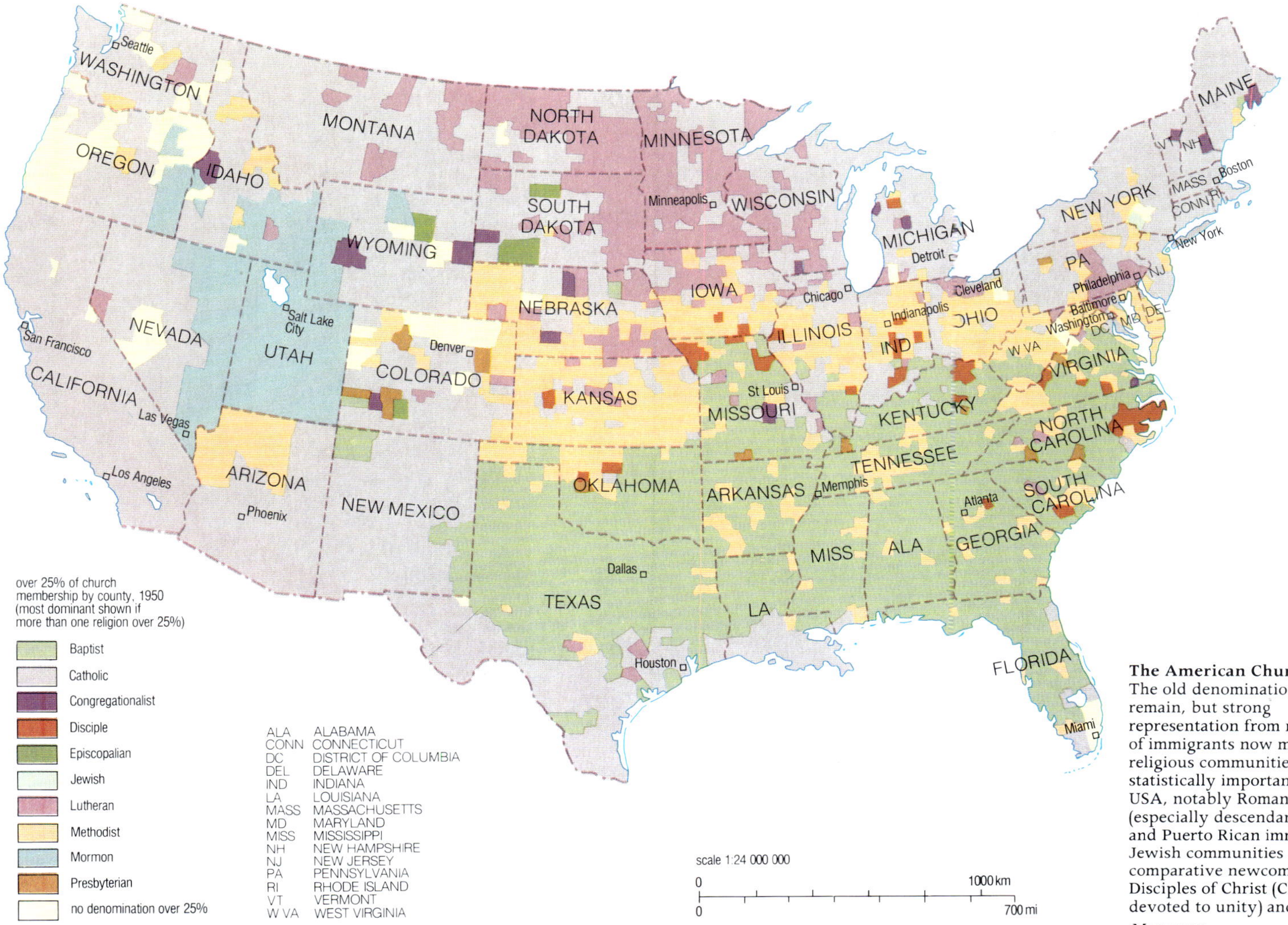

The American Church
The old denominational divisons remain, but strong representation from new waves of immigrants now makes other religious communities statistically important in the USA, notably Roman Catholics (especially descendants of Irish and Puerto Rican immigrants), Jewish communities and the comparative newcomers the Disciples of Christ (Christians devoted to unity) and the Mormons.

contemporary nations of the Western world. And even beyond attendance, contribution or membership, a staggering proportion of the national population (over 90 percent) identified themselves—whether by heritage, sentiment or affinity—with some religious group. America, like the Athens of St Paul's day, was "very religious."

Yet in the 1960s the growth rate of the older-established denominations leveled off, some even beginning to decline. That together with the rampant pluralism, the "success rates" of newer churches, the invasion of Oriental religions, the attraction to authoritarian communes, the competition of "the electronic church" and other para-ecclesiastical movements has thrown older Christian groups on the defensive. Not too much scholarly investigation was called for to explain growth: that was simply the American pattern. Decline, on the other hand, called for commissions, teams, grants, case studies and extrapolations to explain what went wrong. The decline, moreover, affected not only the domestic data, but missionary efforts (which for Protestantism had been so heavily Anglo-American) also receded abroad.

The "decline" can of course be exaggerated. Many of the well-publicized new religions are tiny in size and perhaps ephemeral in time. For the most part, the major denominational families still dominate the American landscape numerically, politically and socially. The Roman Catholic Church remains the largest single ecclesiastical entity in the nation, with roughly 25 percent of the population affiliated therewith. The largest Protestant family, the Baptist, counts about 15 percent of the population, both black and white, within its ranks. Methodists tally around 8 percent, Lutherans around 5 and Presbyterians around 3. Then, finishing out the top ten denominational families, are these five in gradually descending order: Christian (Disciples of Christ, Churches of Christ), Episcopal (Anglican), Eastern Orthodox, United Church (Congregationalists merged with Evangelical and Reformed Church), and the Mormons or Latter-Day Saints of Jesus Christ.

While all these groups have many decades of history in America behind them, they represent a quite different ranking from that of the colonial period. In that earlier time Congregationalism, Anglicanism and Presbyterianism were the leaders, this trio to be decisively replaced by another one of Roman Catholics, Baptists and Methodists. G. K. Chesterton once described America as the "nation with the soul of a church." In whatever sense that was, is, or shall remain true, the specific manifestation of that church changes over the course of American history and over the expanse of American space.

New Christian Groups in America

No single term satisfactorily encompasses all the religious movements spawned in the United States in the last century, or for that matter those spun off even in the last two decades. Nor does any single system of classification avoid all ambiguity, overlap or scholarly argument. The following is intended only to illustrate the wide variety, the remarkable fecundity within American Christianity. As such, it is suggestive only, not exhaustive.

Adventist and Millennial. The 19th century saw special emphasis placed upon the Second Coming of Christ: visible, dramatic, imminent. William Miller (1782–1849) and his followers looked forward to the year 1843 as the time for such an Advent. Charles Taze Russell (1852–1916) and his followers pinned their apocalyptic hopes on the year 1914. Seventh-Day Adventism, a recognizable entity by mid-century, is the best-known survivor of the Millerite movement, while the Jehovah's Witnesses, who began to take organizational shape in 1872, achieved worldwide attention less than a century later. By the 1980s the American membership of each group stood at around two-thirds of a million.

Communal. In American history, communities whose origin and purpose were manifestly religious enjoyed a notable flowering in the 1830s and beyond. The 1960s saw another spectacular burst of experimentation in communal living, some of this religious and Christian in nature, but much of it not. A representative example of the earlier communal types, the United Society of Believers in Christ's Second Appearing (popularly known as the Shakers), originated in England but flourished in the United States in the early decades of the 19th century. From a membership peak of around 6000 in the 1830s, the Shakers had reached virtual extinction a century and a half later. In the 1960s many communities showed the clear influence of eastern religion, though the "Jesus People" constituted a conspicuous reaction against exotic ideas and practices. One communal society, the Children of God, originating in Los Angeles in 1969, attracted widespread hostility and resistance as it incurred charges of brainwashing, heresy and idiosyncratic behavior. Apparently having crested by the 1980s, the Children of God have about 500 members scattered in 60 small colonies across the country.

Ethnic. Ethnicity has frequently defined community, proving stronger than theology or ecclesiastical authority. Early in the present century the Native American Church, gathering its membership from several Indian tribes and utilizing peyote in its sacramental observances, had by the 1980s attained a membership of approximately one-quarter million. With about the same number of members, the Polish National Catholic Church represents the most evident failure of Roman Catholicism in America to bridge successfully all of the ethnic diversity confronting it. Eastern Orthodoxy, on the other hand, has been far less successful in rising above ethnic divisions, these divisions still testifying to the powerful force of ethnicity in the 1980s.

Fundamentalist/Dispensationalist. This large category has many institutional manifestations in America, many of them tiny and fugitive. Among the better-known groups are the Plymouth Brethren, English in origin, but reaching the United States by the middle of the 19th century. Rigorously biblical and millennial by the numbers, this sect has suffered frequent schism and separation. Currently, all segments of this body in America have a membership of around 100 000. A far larger fundamentalist body, adding a conviction concerning the full autonomy of the local church to its biblical literalism, is the American Baptist Association (successor to "Landmarkism"), with a membership in the 1980s of over one million.

Holiness. Throughout the 19th century many Americans—notably those coming out of a Methodist tradition—gave particular attention to John Wesley's doctrine of Christian perfection. Soon this emphasis upon sanctification and "second blessing" seemed to require its own institutional expression. The results include the Church of the Nazarene, founded in 1895 and growing to half a million members by the 1980s; the Free Methodist Church of North America, which began a generation or so earlier but reached only about 100 000 members in 1980; and the predominantly black Church of God (Holiness), launched in 1914 and

Above The Baptist revival has been particularly strong among Blacks in the southern states. By 1968 there were as many as 26 million Baptists in North America.

Right The Jesus People are a community-oriented sect who live together once they have disposed of their material possessions.

Below right "I touch them, God does the rest." Michael Lord of Columbus, Ohio, a faith healer since the age of five, baptizes worshipers, heals the sick and leads his own cult in the mass.

Below Members of the Haitian community in Miami. Ethnic ties have often proved stronger than ecclesiastical authority in the USA.

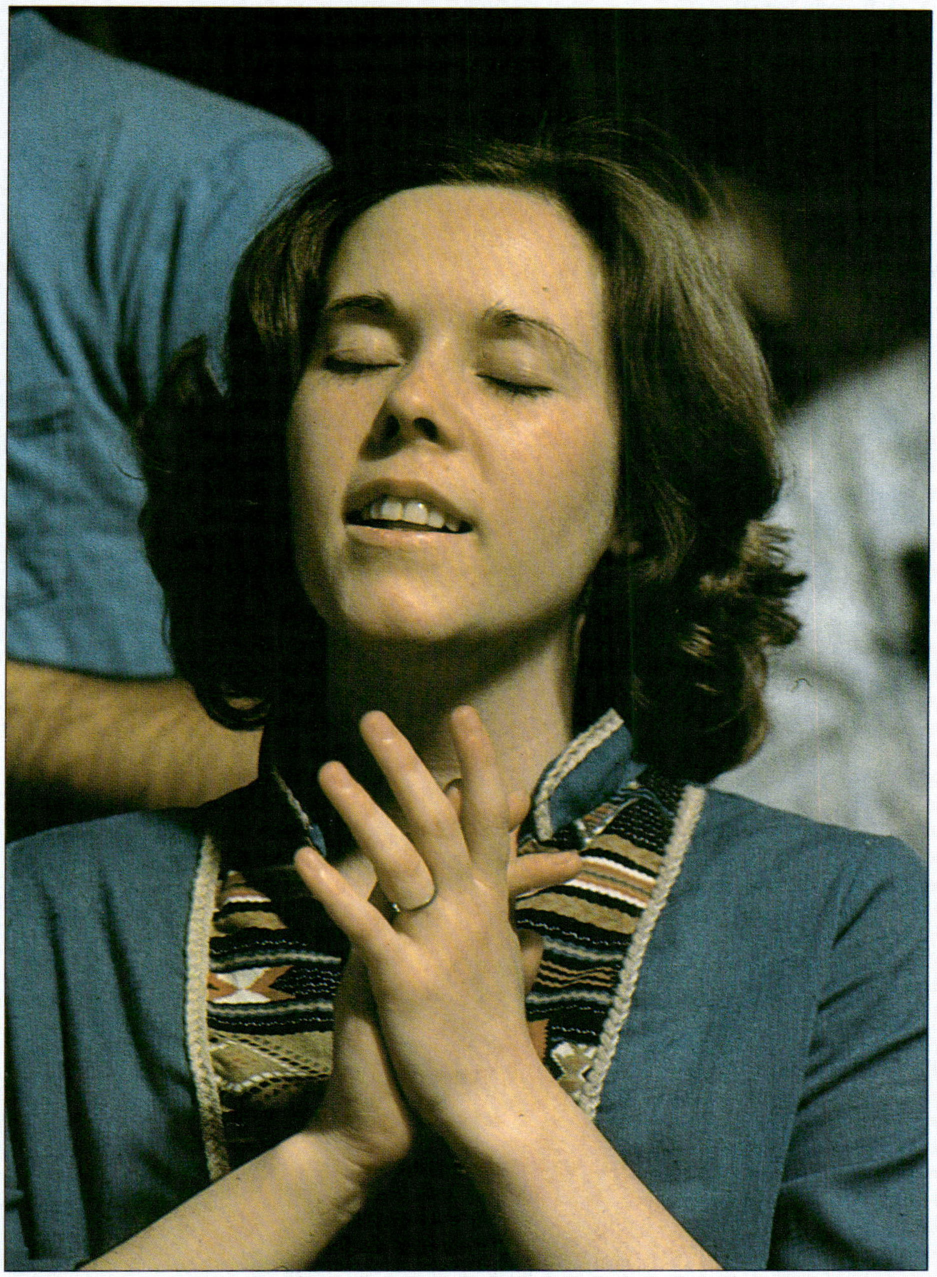

reaching a membership of around 25 000 half a century later.

New Thought. A product largely of the second half of the 19th century (though with some casting back to the earlier Transcendentalist movement), New Thought emphasizes the spiritual power immediately within one's grasp, a power that can bring health, wealth and happiness to its adherents here on earth. Best-known exemplars of this "harmonial religion" are Christian Science, founded by Mary Baker Eddy in 1879; the Unity School of Christianity, created a decade later by Charles and Myrtle Fillmore; and the Church of Religious Science, which attained formal status only in 1949 (Ernest S. Holmes, founder). None of these groups publishes membership figures; all stress the priority of spirit over matter, positive thoughts over negative values, and private well-being over social concerns. (Of course, much New Thought moves well beyond the confines of the Christian religion.)

Pentecostal. Phenomenally successful in the present time, Pentecostal churches in America emphasize healing, speaking in tongues, and the immediate influence of the Holy Spirit in all worship. Major groups include the Church of God in Christ which arose in the 1890s but has had dramatic growth to nearly four million less than a century later (its membership is largely black); the Assemblies of God, beginning in Arkansas in 1914, and spurting to a membership of around two million in little more than half a century; and the Church of God (Cleveland, TN), now about a century old and associated with the names of R. G. Spurling and A. J. Tomlinson, which also enjoys a membership of about two million.

Spiritualist. Perhaps more para-Christian than Christian, the Spiritualist movement swept much of the country in the second half of the 19th century. Associated in its beginnings with the Fox sisters in Rochester, New York, the movement quickly outgrew any single leader or restricted locale. Through a variety of means, Spiritualists sought to establish the reality of life after death, chiefly through seeking communication with the dead. Many Christians pursued Spiritualism while retaining membership in more traditional churches. Eventually, however, the movement created its own organizations, some more consciously Christian than others. The Universal Church of the Master, founded in Los Angeles in 1908, was largely a West Coast phenomenon for a generation or two; in the 1960s, however, it moved out across the nation, currently counting about 300 churches within its ranks. An older institutional structure, the National Spiritualist Association of Churches, debated its Christian status for many years, ultimately concluding that it was outside the fold. In the 1980s its membership was near 5000.

THE 18th-CENTURY CHURCH

The Church in society

Even the most casual observer of Europe early in the 18th century could hardly have escaped the impression that the Church was to be found almost everywhere. Despite its immense variety, from one region to another the similarities were striking. Those most outward and visible signs, the churches themselves, dominated skylines regardless of architectural styles; they sat at the heart of villages, and clustered profusely in most towns of any size. Their bells assaulted the ear; their services, processions and festivals not only helped mark the passage of time but provided entertainment as well as consolation. From Canterbury to Rome, and especially in towns little involved in commerce or industry, the church was also an important component of economic life, providing employment and requiring both goods and services. Ecclesiastical buildings needed both craftsmen for the work of maintenance and renewal, and others such as vergers or sextons; the clergy wanted food, clothing and frequently servants. Moreover, the churches were still, as they had long been, landlords and property owners, drawing income from tithes, rents or fees, and being drawn themselves into the negotiations or lawsuits inseparable from business transactions and the preservation of their wealth. In outline the position changed little during the century. In France in the 1780s, even after the growth of population and a decline in their own numbers, the clergy themselves, some 130 000, made up 0·5 percent of the people; their clients, creditors, tenants and suppliers were vastly more numerous. The Church owned as much as 10 percent of French land and property, and collected in tithes alone some 7 or 8 percent of the country's produce. Between 15 and 20 percent of the French grain supply, and in Spain or Italy an even higher proportion, was controlled by the Church.

Other functions of the churches were more directly expressions of religious concern and a specifically Christian ethic. The educational role of the clergy, for example, was everywhere very important. In Britain they dominated the universities of Oxford and Cambridge, played their part in the well-established "public" and grammar schools, and contributed to the activities of the Society for Promoting Christian Knowledge while continuing to oversee the work of parish schools. The Jesuits everywhere took responsibility for the education of the Roman Catholic upper classes, and other orders such as the Lazarists or Frères des Écoles Chrétiennes contributed to the schooling of a wider lay population. There was a role too for the churches in matters of philanthropy, often in the

Right: Religion in Europe at the end of the 17th century
Maps can easily create impressions of neat static uniformity: it is therefore important to remember the continual movement and change of religious life. This arose most immediately from the tensions created by superimposing one layer of authority on another—diocese over parish, metropolitan see on lesser bishops, and the Vatican's authority nominally over all Catholics. Like geological plates they ground inexorably against each other. Political structures too cut through and were interleaved with ecclesiastical organization, for secular authorities were as ever uneasy about religious allegiances which overrode national boundaries. As communications and travel became easier in the 18th century, the Pietists and Methodists for example were extending their geographical range, forming new international brotherhoods. Ancient ecclesiastical centers lost ground in wealth, status and influence. At different social levels, there were striking contrasts in the nature and components of belief and in the speed with which they changed.

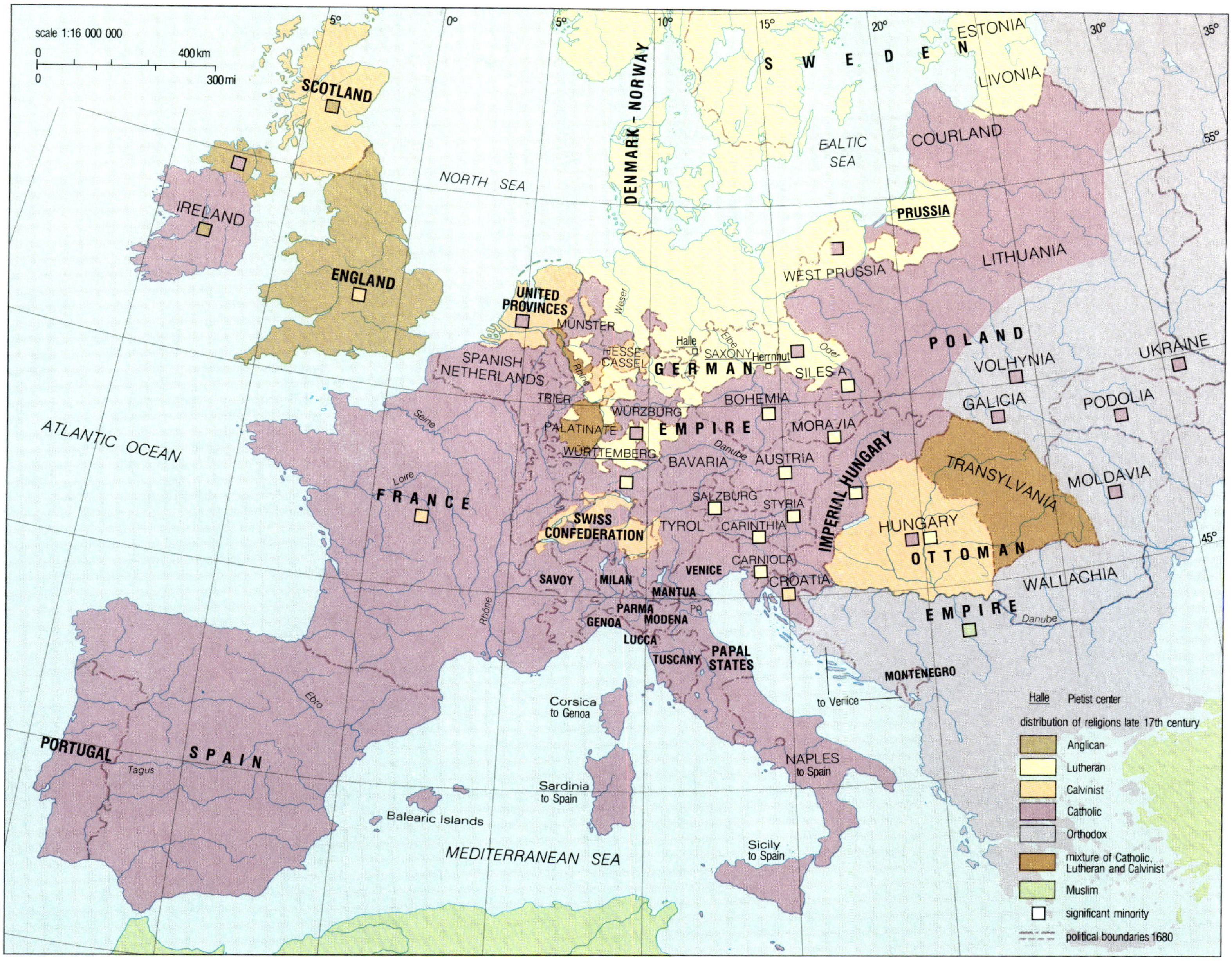

Left This festival was celebrated in revolutionary France on 8 June 1794, following steps aimed at abolishing Christianity. It was not, however, the break with the past which some radicals wanted and their critics feared. Dechristianization was never successful with the majority, and the cult of the Supreme Being, while superficially attuned to the rationalistic, deistical wavelengths of 18th-century thought, was also steeped in the imagery and phraseology of Catholicism. For Robespierre, its chief exponent, "My God is he who created all men for equality and for happiness, who protects the oppressed and exterminates tyrants; my worship is that of justice and humanity. I dislike priestly power . . . It is one of humanity's fetters but an invisible fetter of the spirit which reason alone can break." He believed in an afterlife, a personal God intervening in human affairs and the source of morality, and rejected atheism as corrupting.

direct provision characteristic of many Catholic orders of hospitals or orphanages, in the management of local charities and benevolent endowments, and in the everyday business of poor relief.

Church and state

It was at such points that the interpenetration of Church and society passed over into the mutual involvement and support characteristic of the relations between Church and state. Mutual support, however, did not necessarily entail equal standing: it usually went together with lay domination in both spheres. Religious establishments remained a fact of life despite the ending of Europe's religious wars and a measure of acceptance for the principle of toleration. In France the Roman Catholic Church was the only one officially recognized by the state and allowed to hold services: the clergy took precedence over the other estates of the realm, had their own courts and possessed extensive financial and administrative privileges. Significant appointments, however, were controlled by the Crown, and royal favors required recompense in the performance of secular duties. An archbishop like Brienne could move easily into the position of first minister, and the state played a large part in matters such as the reform or suppression of religious orders from the 1760s. In England the subordination of the Church was symbolized by the suppression of Convocation in 1717, and by the party-political nature of episcopal appointments. In Prussia rulers appointed church officials, attempted to unite the orthodox Lutheran with the Reformed Church and forbade discussion of theological disputes in the public pulpit, all in the interests of social and political control. Parish clergy, whether appointed by provincial notables and landowners as was usual in Protestant regions or by the Catholic diocesan bishop, were also in varying degrees local administrators. To their basic tasks of keeping parish registers of births, marriages and deaths were frequently added other secular responsibilities such as those of magistrate, overseer of road maintenance or supervisor of census and tax returns.

The deep involvement of the Church in the life of the *ancien régime* was thus universal. High ideals and enthusiastic commitment found their place in individuals, as did clerical resentment of abuses within their churches; but the atmosphere was overwhelmingly settled if not always comfortable, the ecclesiastical outlook at once profoundly utilitarian and frequently unselfcritical. Such conditions were reflected in or reinforced by much contemporary theology, notably that of the Latitudinarians or the aptly named Scottish Moderates. Writers like Bishop William Warburton stressed the fundamental rationality of religious belief. The existence of God was not only supported by the evidence of history and philosophical investigation but, together with his attributes of power and benevolence, was to be deduced from the facts of creation. The world was quite clearly organized, and man himself was the most obvious example of God's design. The Christian revelation with the biblical record provided the essential complement of the natural world, extending man's understanding of God's nature and confirming by its ethical teaching the identity of happiness and right behavior already evident in the conditions of life.

Intellectual challenges to Christian belief

This accommodation of established Christian leaders and thinkers to the social and intellectual pressures of the early 18th century rested on a developing religion of common sense and an ever more rational theology. To many people, however, it represented an unsatisfactory compromise. From one side, recurrent challenges were therefore mounted by those who felt that reason and logic should be pressed further and the remaining elements of superstition or irrationality in Christian belief ruthlessly exposed. During the first half of the century it was the Deists who were most active in this cause. In England Anthony Collins and Matthew Tindal were the chief representatives of those who attacked the traditional sources of Christian authority such as the Bible and the Church as highly unreliable. Beginning instead with the inconsistencies of early Christian accounts, the Deists argued the case against prophecy and miracles, and ended by rejecting matters central to Christianity itself such as the Resurrection. They appealed instead to a natural religion, rationally deducible from the evidence of the natural world and man's unchanging conscience, and requiring no additional revelation.

The English Deists were spurred on in part by popularity, partly by the fact that their opponents took their arguments seriously, and also by a mixture of anticlericalism, intellectual arrogance and naive self-confidence. Nevertheless their manner, when compared with that of their French counterparts, was often sober, and apparently scholarly. Traditional authority on the continent was far more robust and forthright in its self-assertion, inclined to resent provocation and turn to the law rather than meet critics on their own ground. In resorting ineffectively to censorship and denunciation, the French Church only encouraged its critics. Many of the *philosophes,* those brilliant propagandists and popularizers of 18th-century France such as d'Alembert, Diderot and above all Voltaire, gave extreme expression to the ideas of the Deists. They lent their wit and sarcasm to the portrayal of Christianity as gross superstition and the Church as the enemy of all virtues as well as independent or rational thought. There were limits to their onslaught: very few thought of themselves as atheists, and many were prepared to regard even Christianity as appropriate for the poor and ignorant. Yet the impact of their work was potentially very destructive of traditional institutions and forms of belief, less through its establishment of different values than for the cynicism and undiscriminating condemnation which its anticlericalism inspired.

The fireworks of the *philosophes* showed how reasoned criticism carried to extremes might produce an irrationalism similar to that which had been their original target. David Hume suggested a different line of attack, by carefully demonstrating the limits of reason and calling into question the

Right Count Nicholas von Zinzendorf (1700–60) established the evangelical settlement of Herrnhut in Saxony, from which there spread worldwide the missionary communities of the Moravian Brethren.

Overleaf John Wesley (1703–91) was the son of an Anglican rector. Briefly an S.P.G. missionary in Georgia, he was deeply influenced by the Moravians and from 1739 his life was given to evangelism. Traveling some 12 000 kilometers annually, he was the chief inspiration and mainstay of the Methodist movement.

Left The 18th century witnessed a rationalist reaction against religion and ecclesiastical establishments. This reached its climax with the elevation of "the Goddess Reason" in France during the 1790s.

Below The early "methodists" went to the people, feeling compelled to share their experience of a living religion and seeing the futility of waiting for others to come into the parish churches. This picture of George Whitefield, despite the stylized portrayal, captures the self-assurance and forwardness of these 18th-century enthusiasts as well as their opposition to the coarseness and triviality of many popular pastimes.

rational defenses of Christianity which 18th-century apologists were trying to construct. Knowledge, he argued, was limited by the possibilities of human experience and perception; the only ground for religious belief is the evidence of design, and thus of purpose or will, in the natural world; such evidence however does not entitle one to venture further and attribute particular qualities or purposes to God. Given also that the evidence for miracles and particular acts of revelation is always less convincing than the counter-arguments, real knowledge of the supernatural is thus impossible. Religious belief, he implied, had necessarily to be restricted to a vague theism. Hume thus elaborated a position as critical of the earlier optimistic Deism as it was of orthodox defenses.

Movements for Protestant revival: the Moravians, Methodists and Pietists

It is still unclear how widely the ideas of these 18th-century writers circulated; even less certain is the extent of their influence. However, discontent with all aspects of the status quo evidently ran very much wider than either. A counterpart to the rationalist challenge existed in the extensive growth of mysticism, religious zeal and popular enthusiasm, forces dreaded by many orthodox churchmen as equally subversive of scriptural authority, ecclesiastical order and moral discipline. The 18th century was marked by several great movements of religious revival, such as German Pietism or John Wesley's Methodism. These satisfied a popular desire for a personal religion, combining as they did emotional fulfillment with a sense of individual responsibility.

In the late 17th century it was already clear especially in Prussia that the Lutheran Church, controlled by the state and dominated by lay patrons, was failing to provide the inspiration people expected of it. Drawing on earlier strands in German religious life, P.J. Spener and more especially August Francke at the new university of Halle worked to refocus Lutheran thinking on the importance of personal experience of justification by faith. The key to a vigorous Christianity lay not in state enforcement or public theological debate, but in the inner development of individuals' lives assisted by careful attention to the Bible itself, the only real source of authority. It was a teaching which led in various directions, either to a quietist attitude, a preoccupation with the quality of one's own religious life and that of one's immediate circle, or to a personal transformation of which the natural expression was work for a much wider social regeneration through direct involvement in public life. Not surprisingly its appeal was wide, particularly in Prussia and Saxony; large numbers of commercial and professional people as well as nobles were deeply influenced by it, and in certain areas such as Württemberg there was a substantial popular following. The emphasis on good works as the natural expression of genuine faith very soon led in the direction of missionary activity. This was associated above all with the so-called Moravian Brethren from the community established in 1722 at Herrnhut by Count Nicholas von Zinzendorf. By the 1740s Moravian missionaries were to be found as far afield as South Africa, Greenland and the West Indies.

Movements of a related kind also emerged in Britain, first in the shape of Scottish dissent and then in the Anglican evangelical revival. One persistent question at the center of the 18th century's religious discontents was the role of the ordinary laity in the congregations and their relation to priest or minister. Scottish matters came to a head in the 1730s over the rapidly increasing power of patrons to force unwanted ministers onto unwilling congregations: the subsequent ecclesiastical history of 18th-century Scotland was in part one of recurrent secessions as successive congregations tried to preserve their preferred forms of Presbyterianism. In England the reticent or elitist nature of old forms of religious dissent and the continuing restrictions on dissenters' worship together left the way open for religious revival to begin within the Anglican Church. After earlier stirrings reflected in the voluntary religious societies, and influenced by the Moravians, John Wesley and his friend George Whitefield took the lead in the extensive movement of conversion and revival which marked the period 1740–90.

The key to Wesley's great success was that he made Christianity accessible. Theologically this meant a religion of hope based on personal experience of conversion and knowledge of salvation, enabling people to live with their own weaknesses and also making tolerable a measure of congregational discipline. More important still was Wesley's taking religion to the people, traveling about the country, preaching when and where listeners could be gathered, stressing the pastoral role of laymen regardless of their rank, and establishing a highly organized system of meeting houses as the basis for each itinerant minister's circuit. It was a message and organization which attracted those, like Wesley himself, who were impatient of the established Church's haphazard combination (especially at parish level) of compulsion and neglect, as well as many left cold by fashionable theology or casual liturgy. From the 1770s Congregationalists and Baptists began to experience the same voluntary enthusiasm and expanded in similar fashion among the lower classes.

The well-established churches were rarely able to develop their own ideas or reform their practices sufficiently to contain either skepticism or dissent. Some churchmen were ready with intellectual defenses of Christianity, perhaps nowhere more so than in England. There the latitudinarian tradition of tolerant rational debate was sustained, most notably by Bishop Butler whose book *The Analogy of Religion* did much to silence glib deistical argument. However, Butler's awareness of the limitations of man's reason ceased eventually to be a source of strength. It not only opened the way to Hume's skepticism; it also encouraged the bland assurances of Archdeacon William Paley's *Evidences of Christianity* (1785). The difficulties men found in perceiving God's grand design in the natural world, or the evidence of his power in the utility of existing social and ecclesiastical arrangements, were too readily attributed to the insufficiency of human reason. The need for adjustment was thus overtaken by a new conservatism which the subsequent upheavals of the French Revolution only reinforced. The drift of ideas was matched in the pattern of institutional change towards greater

interdependence of clerical and lay authority. Lay patronage remained very widespread, and many clergy, lacking any distinctive training, aspired to the life of the landed squire. Those who could afford to took up the fashions for country sports and agricultural improvement, and became magistrates; those who could not, whether for reasons of poverty or the difficulties of urban parishes where populations were beginning to grow rapidly, were ill-placed to make changes. Evidence of hardening and unimaginative attitudes became clear in the 1770s as more and more Anglicans turned against Wesley and his "methodists." Refused licenses, livings and ordination, Wesley began in 1784 to ordain his own presbyters, and Methodism moved out of the Church of England.

On the continent reform movements, although aiming at goals akin to those of the Methodists, either developed in ways which reinforced ties between Church and state to the detriment of a revitalized popular Christianity, or proved too feeble to overcome vested interest and inertia. At first the outlook for Pietist influence was favorable, for despite Lutheran opposition, Pietists were encouraged by Prussia's early 18th-century rulers. They were appreciated for their schools and influence in the universities; their concern with social improvement and their lack of interest in the institutionalized Church were turned to state purposes, with Pietists being welcomed into the army and bureaucracy. Established in public life, they ceased to appear as radical reformers and drew closer to orthodox Lutherans. Their popular appeal seems to have waned after 1750, and Frederick the Great clearly felt it unnecessary to encourage them above others. Although the example of Pietist individuals often remained strong, Pietism as a widespread expression of dissent was contained by the same institutionalization which had often caused the established churches to decline in popular esteem.

Movements for Catholic reform

The tendency evident in Prussia for religious reformers and secular authorities to look to each other was paralleled elsewhere. In desiring a reinvigorated parish life and a more educated priesthood, Roman Catholic reformers reemphasized objects of the Counter-Reformation; but they also added an emphasis on the Bible, on popular education and an end to superstition, and on the need for a purified liturgy people could understand. To promote these ends, they wanted religious foundations reformed and many of their endowments turned to pastoral uses. Here their objects coincided with those of secular reformers nurtured in the Enlightenment, who were intent on fostering economic growth and legal change only to find ecclesiastical privilege in the way, or were anxious to cut back clerical pretensions in the interest of more efficient government. Occasionally this was a powerful combination, as the Austrian empire's history illustrated. With Jansenist advice, Maria Theresa and her son Joseph II limited ecclesiastical jurisdiction, taxed the clergy, brought education under state control, established new dioceses, parishes and schools, and suppressed monasteries in order to endow them. Joseph would have gone further, with liturgical reform for example, but at this point reformers met their match in the extent of popular attachment to local saints and superstitions. Much Catholic reforming thought thus remained the private convictions of intellectuals; more than early Pietism or Methodism it generated popular hostility rather than enthusiasm.

In France, where the strongest of Europe's Catholic churches was already closely identified with established secular authority, changes were less effective. In contrast to Austria, there was no happy coincidence of interest between the state and those pressing for ecclesiastical reform. In the pursuit of religious unity, Louis XIV relentlessly opposed critics of prevailing orthodoxy, and welcomed the papal bull *Unigenitus* (1713) condemning works associated with the Jansenists. Far from promoting solidarity, this seriously divided the Church and involved ecclesiastics in the political and legal battles over the powers of the Crown. This was not an atmosphere conducive to adaptation or revival. The leaders of the French Church rarely demonstrated an intellectual willingness to defend their faith; many indeed saw no problems, and used their place in the state rather to safeguard privileges and rights. Monastic vocations declined, and the lower clergy lost in status and dignity, many of them alienated from a religious system increasingly ill-suited to the society it theoretically served. The feeling inevitably grew that laymen and secular authorities should take the matter of religious reform into their own hands.

The underlying direction of these European changes lay towards increasing the influence of the laity in Christian life, through continuing domination and control of the Church by the state, through the influence of secular ideas on religious thought, and through the development of dissenting or reforming movements alienated by clerical practice. The incidence of these changes was naturally haphazard like the popular anticlericalism which reinforced them; given the widespread susceptibility to religious enthusiasm and the rapid growth of an educated, commercial or professional middle class, they were changes to be expected. Sometimes they were strikingly sudden, for example in the suppression of the Jesuit order which began in Portugal in 1759 and was reluctantly confirmed by the pope in 1773. Less immediately obvious was the gently pervasive activity of lay men and women which gathered momentum. For example, by no means all those touched by the evangelical revival in England followed Wesley. Within the Anglican Church committed laymen, notably those nicknamed the Clapham Sect, began to use acquired powers of patronage to revive parochial life, and engaged themselves in good works as a vital element of their faith. Their charitable and educational activities blossomed in voluntary societies which attracted members of other denominations. The Sunday School movement for the children of the poor, and their commitment to the movement for abolishing the slave trade, were particularly outstanding. After 1790 energies also went into the formation of missionary societies. The non-denominational London Missionary Society (1795) and the Anglican Church Missionary Society (1799) were among indications that a revived Christianity was once more set to assert its claim to be a worldwide faith.

THE 19th-CENTURY CHURCH

The 19th century is too often seen as a period in which Christianity went into irreversible decline. Changes in the previous century have been interpreted as signs of incipient disintegration which were turned into progressive collapse under the dual impact of the Industrial and French Revolutions. The role of the Church shrank as other institutions such as the modern state assumed greater powers; the bases of belief and theological scholarship were further undermined by the development of scientific knowledge; the notion of the Christian community was finally exposed for the fiction many had long thought it to be, by evidence of the alienation from Christianity of much educated or working-class opinion in the countryside as well as the industrial cities. The reality, however, defies any such easy description: the undoubted "secularization of the European mind" cannot be equated with any simple process of "dechristianization."

Church and state: the balance adjusted

The association of Church and state, for example, came under fire more than ever before from reforming radicals and anticlericals, but the connection nevertheless survived. Although there were for long conservatives who believed that Church and state should be united, everywhere the relationship necessarily became a more pragmatic one. The privileges and material possessions of the churches were cut back, and governments often took over functions once largely ecclesiastical, like education and social welfare. Nevertheless, although the churches became less obviously powerful, they retained many channels of influence and were appreciated perhaps even more than before for their contribution to social and political stability, morality and order. Many churchmen, while disapproving much done by secular authorities, saw clearly that the needs of the state and the political necessities of governments could also be their own opportunities, offering means of defense against religious rivals and other critics.

These calculations were made throughout Europe, and were most graphically illustrated during the French Revolution. The years 1789–91 saw first the placing of church property at the disposal of the nation, followed by the dissolution of the monastic orders, and the establishment of the Church as an arm of the state under the Civil Constitution of the Clergy. This divided the French clergy between those willing to swear allegiance to the Constitution and those refusing, especially in the wake of its condemnation by the pope: here was a division of attitudes to secular power which was constantly to reassert itself. More immediately it was overtaken by the Terror and Jacobin attempts to suppress Christianity itself (1793–94). Both this and subsequent attempts to separate Church and state reflected powerful and continuing sentiments, but finally gave way to the Concordat of 1801 between Pope Pius VII and Napoleon Bonaparte. Against the background of a popular Catholic revival, this represented a recognition by the state that the religion of "the great majority of Frenchmen" was too important to be left to the Church; on the Church's part it signified a reluctant acceptance of the loss of ecclesiastical properties and substantial state powers of intervention, in return for protection from further excesses and hope of future influence. It represented a temporary balance of power which large numbers of Frenchmen were determined to tilt in their own direction. The ease with which the

Keep holy the Sabbath! This allegorical French landscape, designed to reinforce the lessons of the catechism, reflected widespread 19th-century worry that Sunday as a day of rest and religious preoccupation was seriously threatened. This was felt to result especially from the spread of industry, with its incessant demand for labor and remorseless search after profit, and the growth of cities with their numerous secular amusements. Regular churchgoing was thought essential to a sober, virtuous, essentially "respectable" life.

Nineteenth-century Christians were deeply preoccupied with questions of authority, notably that of bishops, particularly that of the pope. How far did their authority extend, not only in ecclesiastical or theological matters, but in politics, morals and intellectual life? In France the debate was fired by Félicité Robert de La Mennais (1782–1854) (*above*), noted editor of *L'Avenir* and author of *Paroles d'un croyant*, during a tempestuous career which ended with his complete rejection of Catholicism. In Germany, Johann Ignaz von Döllinger (1799–1890) (*top*), the distinguished professor of church history at Munich, was excommunicated for leading a reaction against, first, papal pretensions to political power and then the Vatican's attack on liberalism of all kinds. Outstanding in defense of papal authority was Pope Pius IX (pope 1846–78) (*right*) who, it seemed to many, wished to compensate for the progressive loss of papal territories in Italy by condemning most modern thought in the Syllabus of Errors (1864), and presiding over the definition of papal infallibility at the council of 1869–70.

Church recovered ground under the Restoration confirmed clerical expectations; however, the identification of Catholicism with that regime's reactionary political conservatism only intensified the anticlericalism of liberals determined to protect their position in matters such as education.

Outside France interest in religion as a conservative force was equally common before 1830. In Britain political radicals and religious dissenters were the targets of demonstrations in support of Church and king, and reform of the Anglican Church was postponed. In Prussia links with the state were reinforced by the notable role the Church played in stirring up resistance to French invasion: the result was Frederick William III's union in 1817 of the Lutheran and Reformed churches and the vesting of authority over them in a new ministry for religion and educational affairs. Clerical training was standardized, appointments centralized in Berlin, and the renewed pietism of an increasingly aristocratic clergy encouraged, all reminiscent of events a century earlier.

Anti-Erastian reactions

Inevitably anti-Erastian reactions followed. Sometimes new pressure for loosening Church–state ties came from governments, confident of their own strength or sensitive to the irritations generated by close cooperation with particular denominations. In 1828–29 the British government removed most of the civil and political restrictions on Protestant dissenters and Roman Catholics; Catholic emancipation in particular was partly a response to events in Ireland, where Daniel O'Connell's Catholic Association had shown how popular religious sentiment could be mobilized against a political regime tied to an alien (in this case Protestant) religious establishment. In Prussia, just as Frederick the Great had earlier opened the state door to Catholics after seizing Catholic Silesia, so further steps in the 1830s and 1840s advanced them to full religious and political parity at the same time as the liberalizing movement in the Lutheran Church was firmly suppressed.

More often the reaction came from churchmen angered at the loss of spiritual authority which civil government and secular controls encouraged. In Scotland the long-standing disputes over patronage and popular control of ministers came to a head in the disruption of 1843 when large numbers of Presbyterian clergymen and their congregations seceded from the established Church to found the Free Church. In England Anglican leaders in association with Whig governments produced in the 1830s a crop of reforming legislation, on tithes, civil registration of births and deaths, ecclesiastical law, and church property: this provided the essential background to the Oxford Movement. Led by John Keble and J. H. Newman, the movement combined a romantic nostalgia for an imaginary past with a fear of state interference being extended even to matters of doctrine; its promoters were anxious to reassert the position of bishops and priests as successors to the apostles and, therefore, the only source of authority in the Church. Reform and revival were to be led from within the Church. In a parallel reaction against the July Monarchy (1830–48), many French Catholics and especially clergy began to support the Ultramontanism first of La Mennais and later of Louis Veuillot: they wanted a Church free to control its own affairs and open once more to the revived power and authority of the papacy.

At first the papacy, still in possession of the papal states, was not anxious to abridge the rights of territorial governments; its weakness and past experience made it careful to preserve good relations with governments where possible. However, the reign of Pius IX saw the official line of the Church and Ultramontanist arguments become increasingly authoritarian and reactionary. Thus where opportunities were offered for attacking liberals and republicans, for example under Napoleon III, they were taken. Papal pretensions were also heightened by events in Italy, where political unification led by 1870 to the total loss of territory beyond the Vatican. Extensive powers were claimed against republican governments; the liberal Catholicism of men like Dr Döllinger and Bishop Dupanloup was rejected; and the uncompromising papal stand was expressed in the Syllabus of Errors (1864) which dismissed any possibility of "agreement with progress, liberalism and modern civilization." The damage caused by this strategy was immense: it alienated governments and ordinary people everywhere, encouraged the Church to turn in on itself, and severely restricted the activities of Roman Catholics of liberal vision and goodwill. Pius IX's successors slowly began to restore a balance, but did little which could avert conflicts such as that between Bismarck and the German Catholics in the *Kulturkampf* of the 1870s, or that culminating in the French Law of Separation (1905).

Protestant churches in the late century were also often militantly defensive; this led some, unlike the

Christians in 19th-Century Oxford

Despite its physical separation from growing centers of political and economic power like Manchester, Birmingham or London, Oxford exercised great cultural influence. Until the 1890s the university was dominated by ordained bachelor members of the Church of England, who between them helped to educate a high proportion of Britain's established clergy and governmental elites. Oxford's religious disputes, personalized and magnified by its intimate collegiate society, were rapidly transmitted to far wider audiences. This was especially true of debate generated by the "Oxford Movement," which flourished from 1833 to 1841. Its luminaries, Keble, Froude, Newman and Pusey, wished to recover for the Anglican Church the respect, authority and mystery which it seemed to be fast losing. Above all, lay political control, influenced by the religious hostility of Irish Catholics and radical dissenters or by secular indifference, needed to be offset by restoring episcopal discipline and control in church life and dogma. When Newman and other more extravagant Tractarians were converted to Rome, the movement lost momentum. Only after 1868, with Gladstone's episcopal appointments, did leading Tractarians reach the ecclesiastical heights.

Above right E.B.Pusey (1800–82) was professor of Hebrew from 1828 until his death. Drawn into leadership of the Oxford Movement, whose supporters were known as Puseyites or Tractarians, Pusey was a distinguished and controversial preacher. He embodied the movement's asceticism, living a hermit's life of pronounced self-denial. His advocacy of private confession, belief in the Real Presence and encouragement of religious celibate communities were repugnant to many in an age of widespread anti-Catholicism. The cartoonist's humor (*right*) came close to self-parody for Protestants seeing institutions like Oscott College as designed to ensnare—even kidnap—the gullible and unwary.

Altogether less combative was John Keble (1792–1866), famous for his religious poetry in *The Christian Year* (1827). Thirty years vicar of Hursley, he elevated to particular prominence the pastoral responsibilities of ordinary clergymen. Keble College (*top right*), built by William Butterfield 1868–82, was his memorial, intended to defend high Anglican values against the secularization partially embodied in Gladstone's 1871 university legislation.

Roman Catholic Church, into closer association with secular authority. The German Protestant Church, with much support from the propertied classes and conservative agrarian interests, emerged as a still stronger pillar of the nationalist state. The Anglican Church remained established, in large part because its privileges had been whittled away to a point where nonconformists no longer felt substantially aggrieved. Certainly denominational conflicts seemed at times to be waning; but this owed more to changing social composition and political preoccupations than to the growing signs of ecumenical enthusiasm. The influences of national sentiment proved far stronger than ties of Christian belief: in 1914 most churchmen readily identified the enemy with evil and supported the war efforts of their own states.

A new critical approach to religion

Christians not only had to come to terms with the development of the modern state, controlled often by men hostile to the institutionalized place of Christianity in public life or at best by others anxious to avoid taking sides in religious disputes. They were also faced with scientific and philosophical advances which necessitated theological developments if Christianity was not to be associated with intellectual obscurantism. The 18th century's emphasis on the evidences of Christianity had imparted considerable momentum to the scientific study of nature: before long it was plain that geological evidence in particular conflicted with received biblical accounts. The balance of scientific opinion moved away from belief in a single act of creation and a world only 4000 to 6000

Above John Henry Newman (1801–90), fellow of Oriel College and from 1828 vicar of the university church, St Mary the Virgin, was the intellectual leader of the Oxford Movement. Finally losing faith in the Anglican Church as embodying early Christian ideals, he became a Roman Catholic in 1845.

years old, to one in which the earth's surface had slowly changed and living things had appeared successively over vastly longer periods. Biologists struggled with explanations of new forms, couched in terms of development, adaptation and evolution. In 1859 Charles Darwin published *The Origin of Species* which seemed to offer an evolutionary mechanism by which higher forms of life had descended from lower ones independently of a divine creator. Simultaneous developments in historical scholarship raised further questions as to the authenticity of the biblical texts, the accuracy of their authors' memory and understanding, and the personality of actors on the biblical scene, notably that of Jesus Christ himself.

The way forward for Christian theologians involved a two-fold departure. They accepted the need for a new critical approach to the Bible. In so doing, they began to distance themselves from any literal understanding, and ceased to treat it as a basically historical record or as a work of divine inspiration. They preferred to consider it as a series of narratives designed to express religious ideas and understanding in comprehensible forms related to the writers' everyday experience. Christianity itself was to be understood through personal experience rather than by a trusting acceptance of certain established doctrines. German theologians paved the way, like Schleiermacher, Möhler, and subsequently Strauss whose *Life of Jesus* (1835) created a sensation by explaining away the divinity of Christ. At the same time it became accepted that Christianity had a history which, along with that especially of the Early Church, ought to be studied by the fullest possible examination of all the documentary sources, not just the Bible, relating to those societies in which it had developed. By this route biblical criticism and the dating of texts led in the direction of more scientific religious and ecclesiastical history. Again German scholars took an early lead, while Englishmen like Hort and Lightfoot acquired an international reputation towards the end of the century.

The development and diffusion of this theological work was a haphazard process. Even at the level of the universities, it proceeded rather slowly in Britain, as the outcry against Darwin and the authors of *Essays and Reviews* (1860) clearly indicated. In Scotland preoccupation with the effects of the disruption delayed its impact until the 1870s. In Roman Catholic circles adaptation was still more limited. Diplomatic concessions to advanced learning were made by Pope Leo XIII, but their limits were strikingly revealed in the papal condemnation of the modernizing theologians in 1907 and the excommunication of one of the leading figures, the Frenchman Alfred Loisy.

Evangelical and Catholic revivalism

Whether or not they understood them, many Christians in fact found the writings of their own theologians far more alarming than those of any critics of Christianity. Among both Catholics and Protestants the appeal of an uncomplicated literal faith, the importance of personal religious experience frequently in the form of conversion and the periodic renewal of both faith and experience through religious revivalism were all of great and continuing importance. Popular emotion and sentiment, not to say sentimentality, were quite as significant as theological learning in keeping Christianity alive. From the 1790s on, the "enthusiasm" of the Methodists not only lived on in the evangelical movement among Anglicans, but was transmitted to other denominations. The uncertainties of the French revolutionary period stimulated much popular religious excitement and speculation about the end of the world. This sometimes simply encouraged an intensified personal or congregational commitment, but it was also associated with movements much wider and occasionally more unorthodox in nature. Attempts to relate biblical prophecies to the modern world produced, for example, the bizarre but popular teachings of Robert Brothers and Joanna Southcott. Throughout the century millennialist ideas remained for many a periodic source of inspiration. Evangelical revivalism became an increasingly organized and professional activity, especially under the impact of Americans like Charles Finney or Moody and Sankey, and from the 1880s the regular evangelical conferences at, for example, Keswick brought together Protestants of all denominations from every part of Europe. In Catholic circles revivalism took rather different forms but was no less persistent or widespread. From the 1840s on, there was a marked revival of the religious orders, especially among women: in France alone, numbers grew from about 37 000 in 1851 to 162 000 50 years later. The practice of pilgrimage, the place of ritual in worship, cults of the Virgin Mary and other saints were all greatly enhanced, again with the hope that faith would be reinforced and rival secular ideologies kept at bay.

Ultimately the fortunes of the churches and of Christianity depended on the success with which institutions and beliefs seemed to meet the problems of everyday existence. The success of revivals of course suggested that Christianity could still appeal most powerfully to many people; equally clearly, the need for revivals with their aggressive missionary activity was evidence of waning enthusiasm within, and ignorance, indifference or hostility without, evidence of Christianity's irrelevance to still larger populations. These were hardly new circumstances; Christianity had always had to contend with the danger of ossification as well as the competition of magic and other beliefs. However, contemporaries during the 19th century had good reason to find certain problems particularly acute, if not peculiar to their age.

Europe experienced a massive rise in population after 1790 which was also associated with both the rapid growth of towns and the spread of capitalist industry. Nowhere were the churches able to provide the expanding numbers of priests and the financial resources necessary to keep pace with these changes. Even where the will existed, traditional methods of creating new parishes or shifting endowments to needy areas were wholly inadequate. At a time when economic change was also bringing insecurity, poverty and severe dislocation to long-established patterns of life, many churches suffered the further handicap of being closely associated with the secure or propertied classes of society; clergy and laity often lacked the necessary understanding, and the sympathy with the inequality and hardship around them, to be

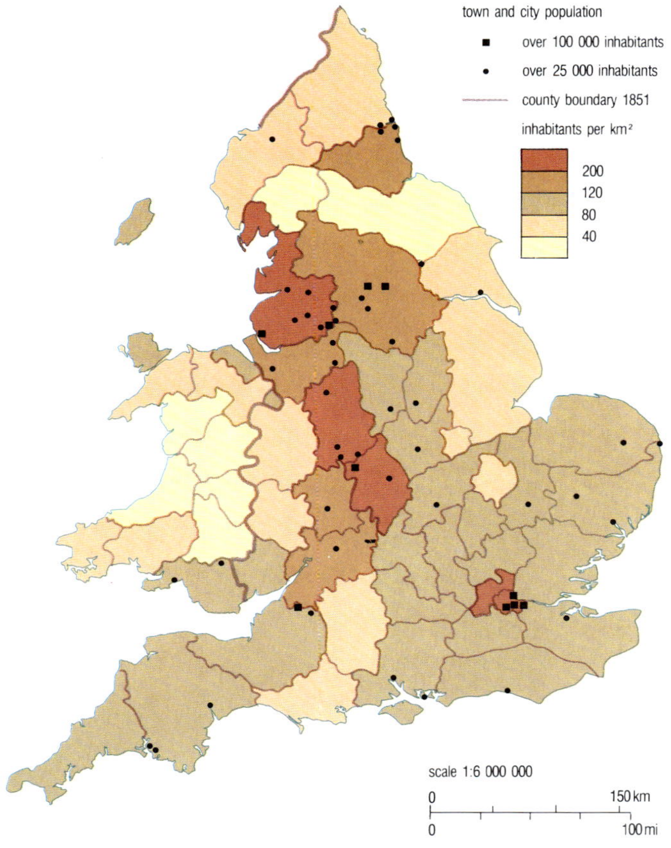

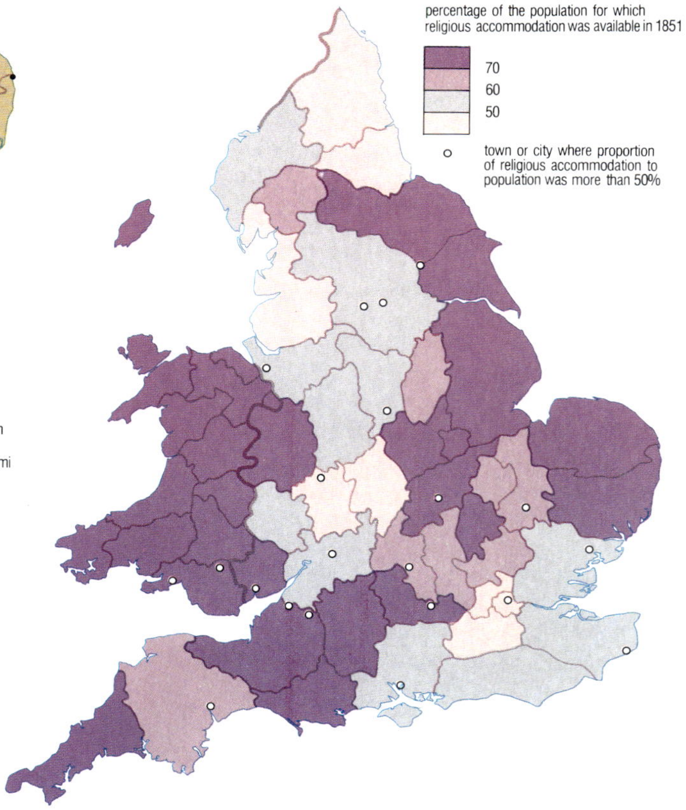

Religious worship in England and Wales in 1851
In 1851 the British government conducted a religious census. In some ways this seems unsurprising: the authorities were compiling statistics as never before and the state of the churches was hotly debated. However, the exercise was never repeated. Despite some serious weaknesses (Scottish figures were particularly unreliable), the census therefore remains an incomparable source of evidence. Unlike the simultaneous general census, it was not made compulsory for ministers to answer questions put to them. But most did so, if not always fully or accurately, giving the number of public places used for worship, the number of seats they provided, and the numbers of those present at each service on 30 March 1851. When the figures were published in 1854, attempts were made to estimate what percentage of the population could have attended church but did not; to consider how well provided different areas were with accommodation; to calculate the size of denominations and to judge whether they were declining or expanding in numbers. London was seen to be very poorly provided for; the Church of England was evidently strong in the east and southeast, dissent in the cities; dissenters appeared in total far stronger than had been generally thought.

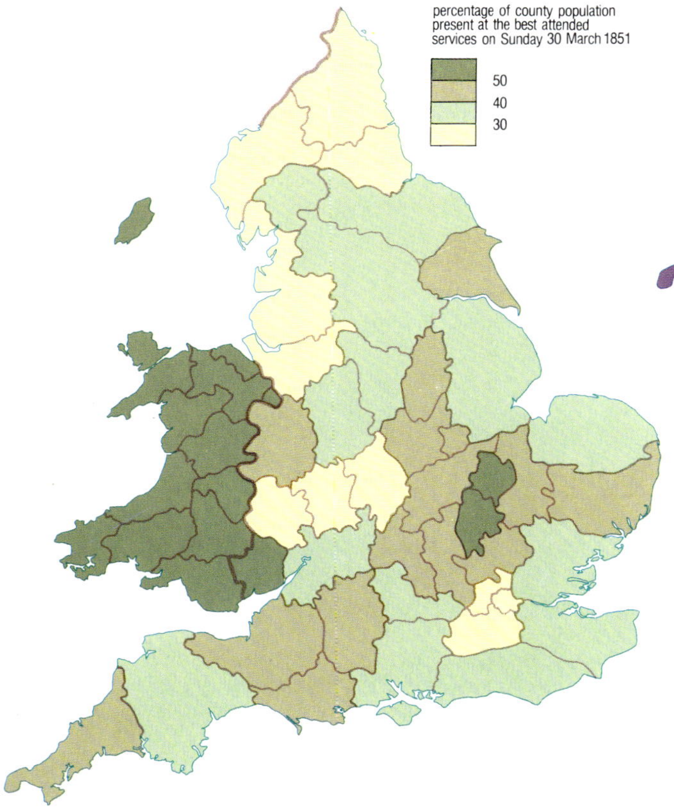

other than narrowly defensive. Thus to many, especially in urban areas and among the working classes, the churches became more and more remote; ignorance of or hostility to Christianity grew, and churchgoing continued to decline.

Positive responses by Christians, determined to maintain their faith in the face of social and economic change, were varied. In Protestant areas one answer lay in the multiplication of new sects or denominations. This was very evident in Britain, where the Baptists, Congregationalists and Methodists all expanded rapidly up to 1850 in areas ill-served by the Anglican Church. At the end of the century other sects like the Salvation Army appeared on the scene. The rapid expansion of chapels and meeting places illustrated the importance of establishing a physical presence in the towns. To many in Britain who might otherwise have rejected religion altogether, nonconformity and (for the immigrant Irish) Roman Catholicism for long provided the chance to belong to a community where criticism of the political and religious establishment was combined with companionship and vigorous Christian belief. Although militant secularism was not unknown, its

Below Joanna Southcott (1750–1814), seen here "excommunicating the bishops," was a Devonshire farmer's daughter, prophetess and religious pamphleteer who eventually led a nationwide body of "Southcottians."

Bottom As this German painting suggests, women and children everywhere made up the majority of practicing Christians. Church attendance, often boring and habitual, nevertheless gave opportunity for all manner of social activities.

appeal remained limited, and Britain's late 19th-century socialism had deep roots in working-class Christianity. Once the Anglican Church had overhauled its organization, it too joined the denominational race, and even recovered some of the ground lost in the century before 1840. Its impact was reinforced by clear evidence of a continuing social conscience; evangelical traditions of reform were developed further by laymen like Lord Shaftesbury, and were extended in new directions by the Christian Socialism of clerics like F. D. Maurice.

Elsewhere in Europe such adjustments as were made proved less successful. In Protestant Germany sectarianism was much less developed and the churches remained a conservative middle-class preserve; the working classes developed their own independent culture and a strong socialist movement, largely indifferent to organized religion. Some Protestants tried to develop in their churches a sense of social commitment. Johann Wichern's Inner Mission, and later Adolf Stocker's Christian Social Party, for example, echoed certain English developments but had a limited impact. In the mid-century at least, German Catholics were much more serious in tackling social problems. In France, too, many of the new orders like the Sisters of Charity or lay organizations like the Society of St Vincent de Paul occupied themselves in a similar way; in the 1840s and 1870s Buchez and la Tour du Pin called for a new Social Catholicism. Nevertheless, the Catholic hierarchy's conservatism, reinforced in the second half of the century by lay fears of socialism, seriously weakened attempts to carry Christianity further into the towns. In the absence of any parallel to Britain's nonconformity, large sections of French middle- and working-class opinion remained either republican or socialist, generally irreligious and often violently anticlerical.

A religion of individual choice

By 1914 formal churchgoing and religious observance had everywhere declined, and the status of clergymen was lower than ever despite many improvements in the quality of their training and commitment. There were more priests and churches than at any time since the 1790s, and devotional literature was more widely available than ever before. Yet the educated and ambitious rarely looked to the Church for a career; indeed, for most people there were few needs which the Church alone could satisfy. Births, marriages and above all deaths still brought families and friends to church; public holidays largely remained the feasts of the Christian calendar; Christian ideas and culture informed a great deal of popular education, even if education itself remained the central issue in dispute between churches and states. However, without enthusiasm and commitment such forms or habits were in danger of becoming little more than survivals.

Commitment had certainly not disappeared. It could be said that at the beginning of the 20th century, as the obligation to conform in religious matters had declined, so the faith of individuals and its practical expression had become linked more closely. Here in fact is the heart of the change which had occurred: Christianity was fast becoming, and in many places was already, a question of individual choice, a private matter. It survived as the basis of community most strongly in countries like Ireland or Poland, where popular religion and nationalist sentiment were inseparably interwoven; elsewhere it was being overtaken by the plurality of modern society. Political and social circumstances tended to weaken rather than underpin Christian associations, belief and ethics; other secular forms of association and codes of behavior competed vigorously with the churches for individuals' allegiance. If individual piety was more heartfelt, nevertheless Christianity as the religion of whole communities was disappearing.

THE AFRICAN EXPERIENCE

By 1790 missionary activity everywhere had reached a very low ebb. The lack of fervor characteristic of Europe's established churches and the suppression of the Jesuits had taken their toll, while those caught up in the evangelical revivals of the 18th century had as yet given little attention to foreign missions. With the exception of members of the historic Church in Ethiopia and the Copts of the Nile valley, Christians in Africa were few, being mostly expatriate white men—settlers, soldiers and traders. Even after the formation of the great Protestant societies in Europe and America between 1792 (the Baptist Missionary Society) and 1824 (the Berlin Society), limited geographical knowledge and the ravages of climate and disease, particularly in West Africa, held back missionary work until the 1840s.

Early missions to the Cape and West Africa

The first modern attempts to spread Christianity among Africans therefore began at the Cape of Good Hope where white settlement had been well established since the mid-17th century. In 1792 the Moravians revived their mission at Baviaanskloof (Genadendal). They were followed by the London Missionary Society, among whose many stations those at Bethelsdorp under the Dutchman Johan van der Kemp and Kuruman under Robert Moffat acquired particular fame. In West Africa the first sustained efforts were those by the German members of the Church Missionary Society from 1804 and the Wesleyans from 1811, operating in and around Freetown.

Early successes in converting Africans depended significantly on the association of missions with the humanitarian movement. In Sierra Leone, as the campaign for the suppression of the Atlantic slave trade gathered momentum, the Christian message was addressed primarily to former slaves who had returned to Africa and others liberated in increasing numbers from slave-trading vessels caught along the coast. At the Cape, mission stations offered to many a measure of protection from the harsh social and economic conditions of white-dominated society; missionaries' work for greater equality of civil and political rights, and their roles as teachers or advisers to native communities such as the Griquas, frequently alienated white settlers and colonial officials, but drew thousands of Africans to Christianity.

Right: Missions to Africa
Protestant evangelical revival gave birth to the modern missionary movement overseas in the 1790s, but with the exception of some stations established by the Church Missionary Society, the Wesleyans and the London Missionary Society, in Sierra Leone and at the Cape of Good Hope, few inroads were made by Europeans in Africa until after 1830. This map illustrates both the chronology of missionary expansion and its geographical distribution. Traces left by earlier Roman Catholic missions were few, and exerted little influence. The first great wave of activity occurred in the 1830s and 1840s, above all in West Africa. Following Livingstone's journeys, effort was concentrated in the 1860s and 1870s in East and Central Africa. The period of Africa's territorial partition among European powers after 1880 witnessed expansion everywhere, but chiefly south of the Sahara. In the north, where Islam was strong, the Christian presence was always very limited and its impact slight; the expansion of Islam into many parts of West and East Africa after 1860 seriously worried Christians of all denominations.

Left "Thy word is a light unto my feet, and a light unto my path. I love thy commandments above gold; yea above fine gold." This inscription from the frame of Barber's painting was widely felt to explain Britain's progress, prosperity and power. Nineteenth-century Britain flourished because it was a Christian, Protestant and free country: true religion and virtuous behavior were rewarded by Providence. Such good fortune, however, involved obligations to the unfortunate. The Christian missionary's task was also a national duty, symbolized here by Queen Victoria's gesture, and the conviction that Britain's expansion overseas helped diffuse Christian civilization was strong. While real enough, such idealism unquestionably ignored much in Britain's domestic life, and was often obscured by the brutality, corruption and arrogant selfishness also experienced by those caught up in the disruptive processes of European expansion and colonial rule.

Right George Grenfell (1849–1906), a skilled observer of African peoples and their customs, was also, like many other Baptists, an advocate of rapid peripatetic evangelism in areas such as the Congo Basin, still remote from European settlement and trade.

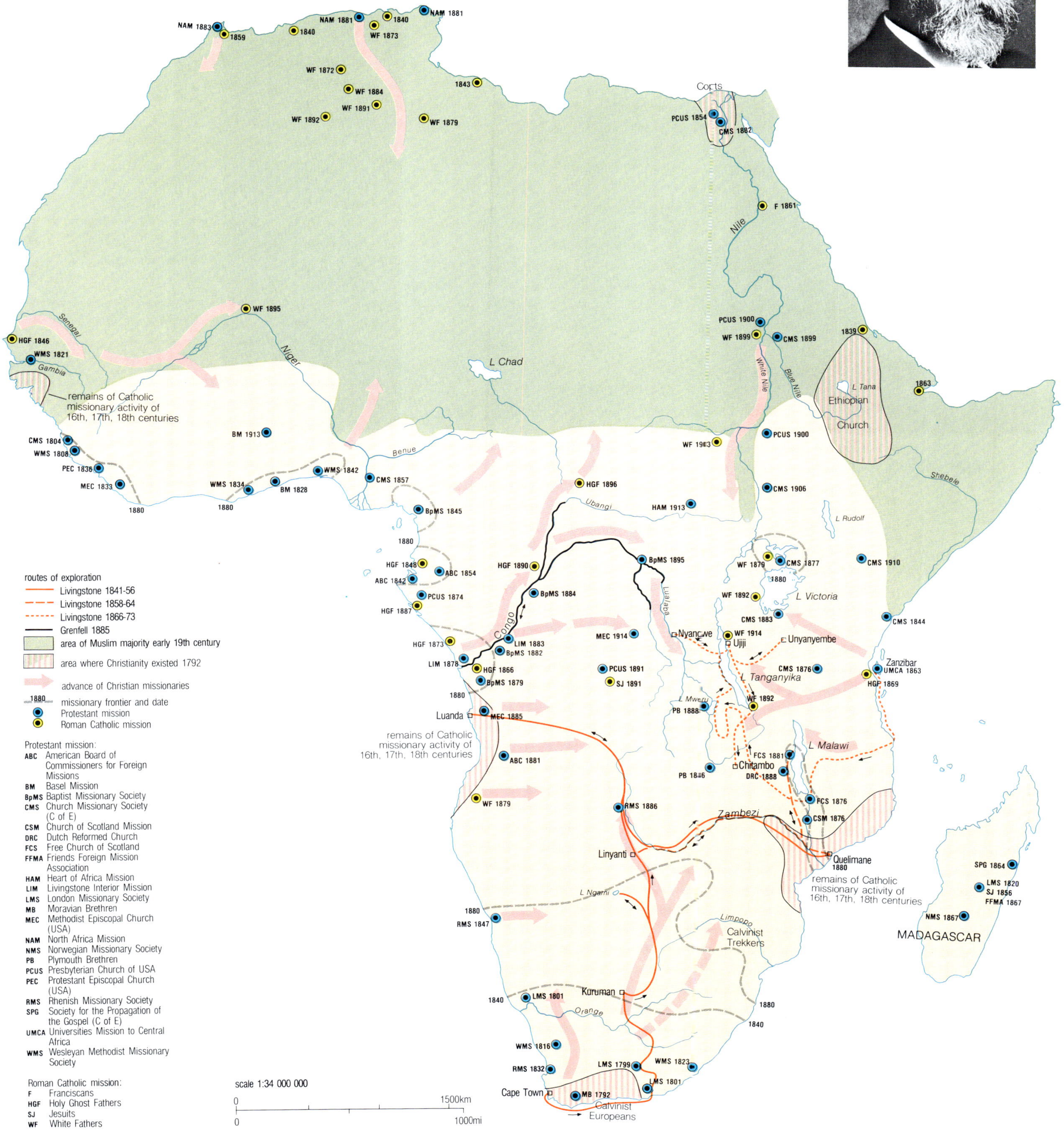

Dr David Livingstone (1813–73) was perhaps the most striking of Victorian missionary heroes. His epic journeys across Africa during 1853–56 and his acute geographical observation were highly regarded. His conviction that "legitimate" commerce and Christianity should expand together, erasing the slave trade and alleviating Africa's material and spiritual poverty, was widely shared. His disappearance, subsequent discovery by the American journalist Henry Morton Stanley, and death at Ujiji generated immense popular interest. Livingstone's heart was buried in Africa, his body in Westminster Abbey. The Universities' Mission to Central Africa and Scottish missionary enterprise in Nyasaland (now Malawi) were directly inspired by his work.

The spread of Christianity was thus always as closely related to the fortunes of individuals and the conditions of African society as to the efforts of foreign missions. Its attractions remained broadly two-fold. To the underprivileged, the insecure and the dispossessed it offered a new set of values and beliefs which might render their world more comprehensible and make them individually more confident, not only of communal support but of their own ability to control events. Others took a more directly utilitarian view: Christianity was frequently seen to go hand in hand with material or practical benefits—the prospect of a more just society, or the likelihood of an education and training bringing in turn personal status and advancement. Foreign missionaries themselves were also very dependent on African goodwill and assistance. They not only required permission from African rulers to settle and teach; evangelization itself could not have progressed without African sympathizers and catechists acting as interpreters, translators, mediators, laborers and companions.

Increased activity in the mid-19th century

These various forms of interaction and interdependence were well illustrated in the second phase of expansion from the 1840s to the 1870s. Following the work of the Swiss Basel and British Wesleyan missions on the Gold Coast, mission societies began to turn their thoughts increasingly to the evangelization of the interior. Three main developments encouraged this changing emphasis. Protestant missions, especially in Britain, were now far stronger, wealthier and more respectable: the Church Missionary Society, with the blessing of many bishops and an average annual income of £80 000 in the 1840s, was far advanced on the impoverished body of 1800. The rapid growth of the European palm-oil trade with West Africa held out the hope of developing lasting substitutes for the slave trade, and so too of social and economic conditions more conducive to missionary work. Finally, African converts from Sierra Leone began in the 1830s to return to their original homelands. Many were Yoruba from western Nigeria, and requests for missionaries to go there soon followed. The Protestant advance into Nigeria which now commenced coincided with the beginnings of missionary expansion in East Africa and work at Zanzibar.

Alongside this expanding activity there developed a freshly coherent interpretation of missionary strategy. Confident that the world was divinely ordered for the achievement of God's purposes, among which the conversion of its people to Christianity was preeminent, evangelicals came to regard trade as the chief mechanism for breaking down the isolation of heathen communities and opening the way for the Gospel. The progress of the Sierra Leoneans seemed to demonstrate that commerce and Christianity went together. Furthermore, rising numbers of educated African Christians pointed to the growth of indigenous churches, capable of financing, governing and ultimately propagating themselves. In this way the resources of foreign missions could be progressively freed for fresh evangelism and would eventually become superfluous: the transition from foreign mission to indigenous church would be accomplished without conflict. It was a European vision which chimed in well with African aspirations.

Perhaps the greatest propagandist for "commerce and Christianity" was David Livingstone. His epic journeys emphasized the extent of the task ahead, but provided knowledge and inspiration for the future. Churchmen of many kinds rose to his challenge, from the Universities' Mission to Central Africa to the Scots who made Nyasaland (Malawi) their sphere. The strategy seemed to bear early fruit in 1864 when Samuel Ajayi Crowther was consecrated as an Anglican bishop; not only was he the first African to be so, but he took for his diocese that great trading highway, the Niger. These years saw too the revival of Roman Catholic missions in Africa, the Holy Ghost Fathers (1848), the Society of African Missions (1856), and, especially in the east, the White Fathers, established by Cardinal Lavigerie in 1868.

Mid-century optimism did not last, because progress seemed slow and results imperfect. Even in West Africa it was clear that missionaries were welcomed more for the literate education and other practical benefits they brought than for their Christianity. In Central and East Africa social and economic organization frequently made the "trading" strategy irrelevant. For a long time, and regardless of denominational preference, mission stations there remained isolated from local African society. Converts and adherents were drawn often from great distances and were people cut off for various reasons from their own tribal society, people for whom the missions frequently provided employment or land. African rulers everywhere kept missionaries at arm's length, sometimes out of self-confidence or indifference, often from suspicion. The fortunes of missionaries and converts rose and fell not just with the fervor and income of metropolitan supporters, but also with the changing economic outlook and political balance both within and between African communities.

Other missionary strategies were called for. Influenced in part by American revivalism and a new millennialist theology, many rejected older ideas linked to westernization and steady conversion. Protestants above all called for a simpler, more individualistic, apostolic approach, abandoning schools, church building and administration in favor of a rapid "evangelization of the world in this generation." Alternatively, it was appreciated that Christianity spread most rapidly where indigenous societies were in crisis, where traditional beliefs were being undermined by ecological or other disasters. Foreign missions consequently allied themselves with those representatives of secular interests who saw the future of Africa in terms of European domination and control replacing indigenous organization.

The scramble for influence

Missionaries were thus caught up in the conflicts and tensions which precipitated the territorial partition of Africa among the European powers after 1880. As missionary numbers grew, so they too began to compete like merchants and governments for spheres of influence, Protestant against Roman Catholic, evangelical faith missions against those working by older, more settled methods. Colonial administrators well understood the value of missionary work in supporting European influence; even a self-confessed agnostic could assert that "each mission station is an essay in colonization" and welcome the financial savings to government. Missionary conflict, however, was deplored. In the interests of peace, stability and "prestige," governments increasingly allotted separate areas to different denominations, and favored some missionaries—especially their own countrymen—at others' expense where it strengthened administrative control. By 1914 the denominational divisions of western Christianity and Europe's national rivalries were entrenched in Africa alongside each other. In the Congo Free State, for example, British and American Baptists or Presbyterians were restricted in favor of Catholic missionaries, after an agreement between state and Vatican.

The blatant association of much missionary enterprise with both conquest and the progressive establishment of colonial administration was for many African Christians only the last stage in a general process of subordination. Criticisms of mid-19th-century missionaries and their methods, and the more stringent reviews of converts' religious and ethical standards, were frequently followed by steps to uphold or even restore white control of the churches, to restrict the role of the African laity, and to limit the advancement of Africans to posts of ecclesiastical or pastoral responsibility. For a time the prospect of creating new provinces of the Roman Church or new self-governing Protestant churches became more remote, and the development of an African clergy seemed to slow down. The Roman Catholic White Fathers only produced two ordained priests from their Nyanza seminary in 1914, 21 years after its foundation. Although this owed much to the traditionally austere demands of celibacy and a Roman Catholic education, the Protestant record was only slightly better.

However, while the growing identification of missions with the colonial state and the development of less tolerant or sympathetic European attitudes caused some friction within existing churches and Christian communities, it did not seriously inhibit the expansion of Christianity itself. From the first that expansion had often taken place in humble or informal ways. Missionaries had very early on learned local languages or dialects, reduced numbers of them to writing and provided vernacular translations of the Bible. Along with news of the white man, therefore, Christian ideas and literature had commonly advanced ahead of any formal evangelization; even once this had started, it was represented for most Africans by the small outstation, remote from the mission center and run by African catechists. Thus it was never possible to identify Christianity entirely with white missionaries, let alone with the colonial ruler: most of the time it was propagated by Africans to their own peoples and in their own way. This fact has contributed greatly to the increasingly rapid spread of Christianity since the early years of this century.

Of similar importance to this expansion were the inadequacies of indigenous beliefs in the face of the expanding colonial order. This was sometimes graphically demonstrated. Just as the Ijebu people of western Nigeria fought the British in 1892, so the tribes of southern Tanganyika (Tanzania) fought the Germans in 1905, both equally confi-

Left Mombasa c.1901. Such large gatherings of missionaries in the field were rare. As well as imported metropolitan habit, the hats betray contemporary medical wisdom which was coming to value felt, pith and the topee as protection against "solar rays." Note the African intruder!

Right Scottish Presbyterian missions were particularly renowned for their emphasis on western skills and practical training. Built with local materials and labor, this mission house makes few concessions to its Nyasaland setting. Such scale and comparative wealth, although arguably suited to mission headquarters in a colonial capital, risked isolating missions from the people and making them objects of envy or hostility.

Right Plural societies like Mauritius presented peculiar difficulties for Christians. Its people were sharply divided and rigidly stratified on economic and cultural lines. Long-established white planters, French-speaking and Roman Catholic, resented British rule and the intrusion of a rival white Protestant elite. African ex-slaves and their descendants, Indian immigrant laborers, and a middle class which included many of the local creoles also shared little in common. Religious and denominational variety was inescapable. Each Christian community's ambition or self-esteem required that it have its own priests, to interpret the biblical message not only in a familiar language but in an acceptable idiom.

dent of victory. In each case their serious defeat was rapidly followed by the abandonment of the spirits and magic which had failed to protect them, and by mass conversions to Christianity. Resentment of conquest did not prevent Africans seeking to share the religious sources of their conquerors' strength. Traditional religions were, however, also eroded in less dramatic ways. Colonial rule brought with it greater mobility and a growing sense of a wider world: it has been argued that Christianity, both in outlook and in ecclesiastical organization, was appropriate to this larger-scale society in ways which often highly localized indigenous beliefs were not. Medicine too was early recognized as a useful auxiliary to missionary efforts: in time this gave way to the medical missionary and still more professional missionary doctor, thereby encouraging more scientific or rational approaches to disease and death. Such attitudes, combined with Christian conceptions of an afterlife, slowly reduced the influence of the witch doctor or spirit medium, and set narrower bounds to beliefs in magic or sorcery.

Independent African churches

The growth of Christianity in Africa, however, cannot be understood in terms simply of the progressive incorporation of new members by foreign mission-linked churches and the inevitable triumph of an essentially superior modernizing religion. Africans, confronted with the inability or unwillingness of mission-dominated organizations to encourage their aspirations to leadership and communal advancement, often threw off such controls and established their own independent churches, such as the early Delta Pastorate in Nigeria or the Native Baptist Church. The African Episcopal Methodist Church (its American connections notwithstanding), spreading through southern and central Africa especially after 1918, along with many others fulfilled similar needs. In such white-controlled colonial societies independent churches have been particularly influential: today in South Africa, where the white Dutch Reformed Church is intimately linked to an increasingly totalitarian regime, they account for some 25 percent of black Christians. Other inadequacies in

Left Problems of encouraging and keeping in touch with isolated, widely dispersed congregations when few clergy were available were perennial. Traditional mule carts and a somewhat un-Anglican itinerancy could be, as here in the northern Transvaal, the only answer.

Below Christianity's diffusion was inseparable from spreading literacy. Missionaries, especially Protestants, emphasized the need for familiarity with the Bible, and Christian literature was often more easily available than either missionaries themselves or converts. Africans frequently welcomed missionary education even while lukewarm to its religious content. Black Africa's primary schools until well into the 20th century were the almost exclusive responsibility of missionary societies, and were largely run by African Christians.

western Christianity's institutions also prompted Africans to take the initiative. The perennial shortages of mission resources in men and money, always in one sense most serious checks to growth, could be simultaneously the Africans' opportunity. Such difficulties of provision were peculiarly acute during World War I: the impossibility of replacing mission staff and the internment or expulsion of enemy subjects by colonial governments often placed the whole burden of sustaining corporate Christian life on African Christians themselves. In many rural areas, and especially in the rapidly expanding towns of the 20th century, Africans supplied their own needs with the result that truly independent, as distinct from separatist, churches came into being, like the Union Church of the Copperbelt in the 1920s.

Traditions of separatism and independence have had a long history within western Protestant churches; it is from such roots, and still more from particular denominations such as the Methodists, that African independency has grown in its turn. In Africa, as in Europe, the spur to independency lay in theological and liturgical needs as well as in institutional dissatisfactions. For a long time most foreign missionaries were concerned to stress the cultural transformation which Christianity implied, and the gap which separated it from traditional African religion. Ignorance of African beliefs and contempt for pagan practice left little room in their minds for cross-fertilization, and made them insensitive to some destructive or demoralizing aspects of the colonial impact. Inevitably there remained large areas of African experience to which both missionaries and the formal religion of industrializing societies were ill-attuned. Independent churches were able to accommodate within a broadly Christian framework the traditional prophet, whose tasks involved alerting society to the causes of its present discontents, devising means of reform or regeneration and instilling a new spiritual unity or commitment. The careers of the prophets Garrick Braide and William Harris in West Africa between 1913 and 1917, and of Simon Kimbangu in the Congo, illustrate not only the immense following which such men could attract, but also the tendency for missionaries to ignore the parallels with revivalist preachers and movements in their own countries. Instead, the emotional enthusiasm, the apocalyptic visions and talk of miracles, put both Protestants and Roman Catholics in fear of a general abandonment of self-discipline and relapse into superstition. Similarly the independent churches offered a welcome emphasis on spiritual healing, found a liturgical place for customary singing and dancing, and established places of pilgrimage or retreat, elements only too commonly excluded from churches following western models.

In this, missionaries began to broaden their own comprehension of the Christian revelation and develop a greater sympathy and flexibility towards African preoccupations. Some signs of this were evident before 1914, for example in the debates which led up to the international Edinburgh Conference of 1910; the growing subordination of denominational differences to a recognition of a common purpose among western Christians evident there was an essential prelude to the greater toleration of variety in African Christianity. The 1930s witnessed a strengthening of attempts to promote a native clergy, the result of more than straitened resources and the growing number of African Christians. Increasingly attention was given by the metropolitan societies to the education of missionary recruits so that they understood something of African society and culture; on the spot churchmen were not only brought into the counsels of colonial governments as representatives of African interests, but in many cases emerged as critics of colonial policy. Occasionally this was open and vociferous, and involved metropolitan opinion: in Kenya the role of J. H. Oldham and others during the 1920s, and of the Reverend L. J. Beecher in the 1940s, stand out. More often, however, a policy of cooperation tempered by quiet influence behind the scenes was the missions' preferred approach. Such cooperation was also preferred by colonial rulers who, no less than precolonial African authorities, appreciated the practical benefits but also the revolutionary implications of Christianity for African societies

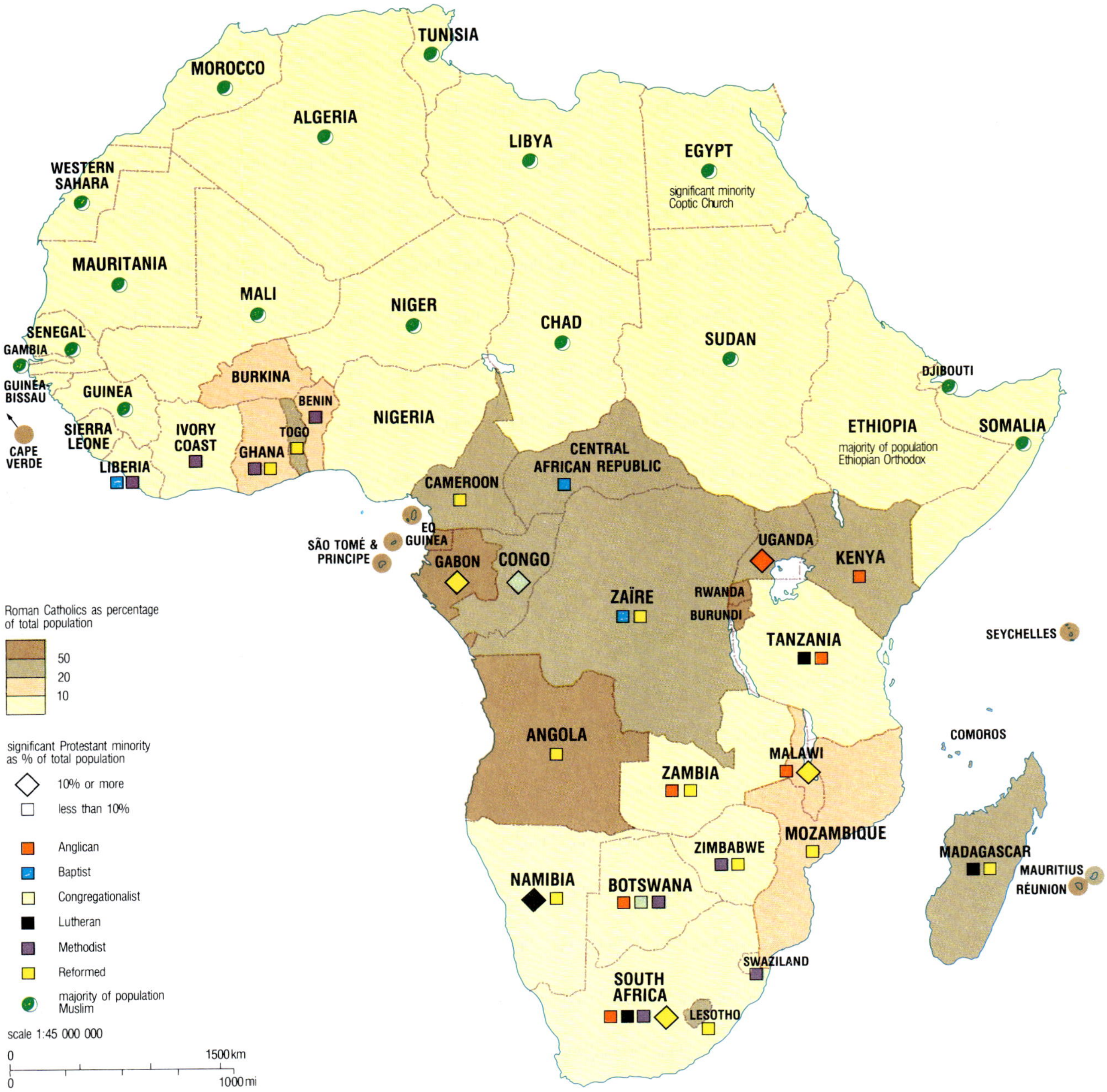

Left: The distribution of churches in Africa today
Today's distribution of churches still reflects patterns from the colonial past. Colonial powers preferred, despite their statements to the contrary, missions of their own nationality and predominant religious complexion. French territories such as Madagascar were essentially Roman Catholic in persuasion, and British territories Protestant, although there were notable British-based Catholic orders such as the Mill Hill Fathers in East Africa. Nationalistic exclusiveness was only slowly diluted after 1918, as German colonies were taken over under the League of Nations, demands for education grew, and American missionaries spread ever more widely. The distribution of Africa's own independent churches, while owing a great deal to the nature of individual African societies, has been similarly affected. Concentrations are to be found in "Protestant" rather than "Catholic" areas, or where white settlement was prominent. Christianity has also had to reckon with the presence of Islam which has expanded its influence considerably in this century.

and tried to control them. Stringent restrictions on preaching and teaching were imposed, especially in Islamic areas, for fear of local protest, much to the distress of Christians who since the 1870s had seen in Muhammad their greatest competitor.

Expansion of Christianity since independence
However, no governments, any more than mission societies, could control the process of expansion which has continually been linked to changes in Church, state and society. First the missions and then the churches were the great providers of education; educated African Christians, having first challenged missionary control of the churches, increasingly turned to demand a place in secular government. A mission education frequently lay behind the leaders of Africa's nationalist and independence movements, and the first generation of independent African politicians and administrators—such as Kaunda or Senghor—have had a Christian background. Decolonization notwithstanding, foreign missionaries have grown in number from about 12 000 in 1925 to some 40 000 in the mid-1970s. African Christians, already perhaps 12 million by 1939, are now estimated to exceed 90 millions, of whom some 44 percent are Roman Catholics. Such numbers alone have necessitated a rapid expansion of ecclesiastical organization and Africanization of the clergy; although this has proved most difficult in the Roman Church, even there change has been rapid since 1960. On this scale, Christian teaching about such subjects as marriage and the family, and the openings for women provided by the churches, have also had very significant social repercussions.

Christians still remain a minority of Africa's population. They are most unevenly distributed across the continent, and the provision of formal ecclesiastical organization as of trained personnel is extremely patchy. With a following above all among the poor and illiterate, and thousands of tiny, frequently ephemeral independent churches, Christianity sometimes appears institutionally ramshackle and ideologically confused. Ambiguity and

Left Cassocks and ruffs are universally regarded as appropriate for cathedral choirs, even if here a more austere color has been preferred to Europe's purples, reds and blues. The choristers' red ribbon of office is a sign of their affiliation to the British Royal School of Church Music. Uganda and its capital Kampala have been a major center of Christian activity since the 1880s. The foundation stone of Namirembe Cathedral was laid in 1901, and the church consecrated in 1919, its construction having been greatly helped by financial contributions from the Kabaka of Buganda and his leading chiefs. The history of relations between Christians and Ugandan rulers has, however, been far from smooth. The murder of Bishop Hannington and the burning of converts by Mwanga in 1885–86 have their recent parallels in the murder of Archbishop Luwum and other atrocities under the government of Idi Amin.

Above Originally "the Province of Freedom" established in the 1780s by evangelicals committed to eradicating the slave trade, Sierra Leone has always been associated with the expansion of Christianity in West Africa.

Left Churches outside Europe have frequently been sources of experimentation in liturgy or ecclesiastical organization. In Kenya the Kikuyu Conference (1913) provoked a storm by encouraging intercommunion.

conflict continue to characterize the relations of churches and governments, in "Marxist" Mozambique or Ethiopia, in Zaïre critical of the foreign connections of Christians, and in South Africa with its conflicting interpretations of Christian tradition and ethics. Yet simultaneously expansion continues to an extent unknown in the West. The larger independent churches, such as the West African Church of the Lord (Aladura), are following older models in developing more organized ministries and schools. The mission-connected churches are increasingly concerned with questions of inequality and social or economic development. The growth of tradition, whether in the development of African theology and church history, or shaped through events like the commemoration of the Uganda martyrs, is helping to crystallize and strengthen belief. Africa can thus also be seen as the greatest of the Christian continents.

Christians in South Africa Today

South Africa is a deeply divided society, committed to a system based on racial classification and segregation affecting many areas of life. It operates to maintain a white monopoly of political and economic power; this is achieved at great cost particularly to the vast black majority. Churches inevitably face immediate, fundamental questions about relationships with the state, and the application of a universal Gospel of love, freedom and equality. Many white Christians—especially in the Afrikaner-dominated Dutch Reformed Church—often combining intense conservatism with selectively literalistic approaches to the Bible, believe racial separation scripturally justified, not simply expedient. DRC leaders brushed aside theological qualms in 1857 and accepted racially separate congregations in principle. Intended as an exception, it became the norm in 1881 with the establishment of the DR Mission Church for Coloreds. Misgivings about apartheid have multiplied, notably since the Sharpeville massacre (1960). Church protests, however, have made little general headway. Mounting disquiet within the World Council of Churches gave way in 1970 to a decision to fund liberation movements like the African National Congress. The immense task of a new generation of black church leaders, such as Dr Boesak and Archbishop Tutu, is to sustain a credible Christian pressure on government for peaceful change.

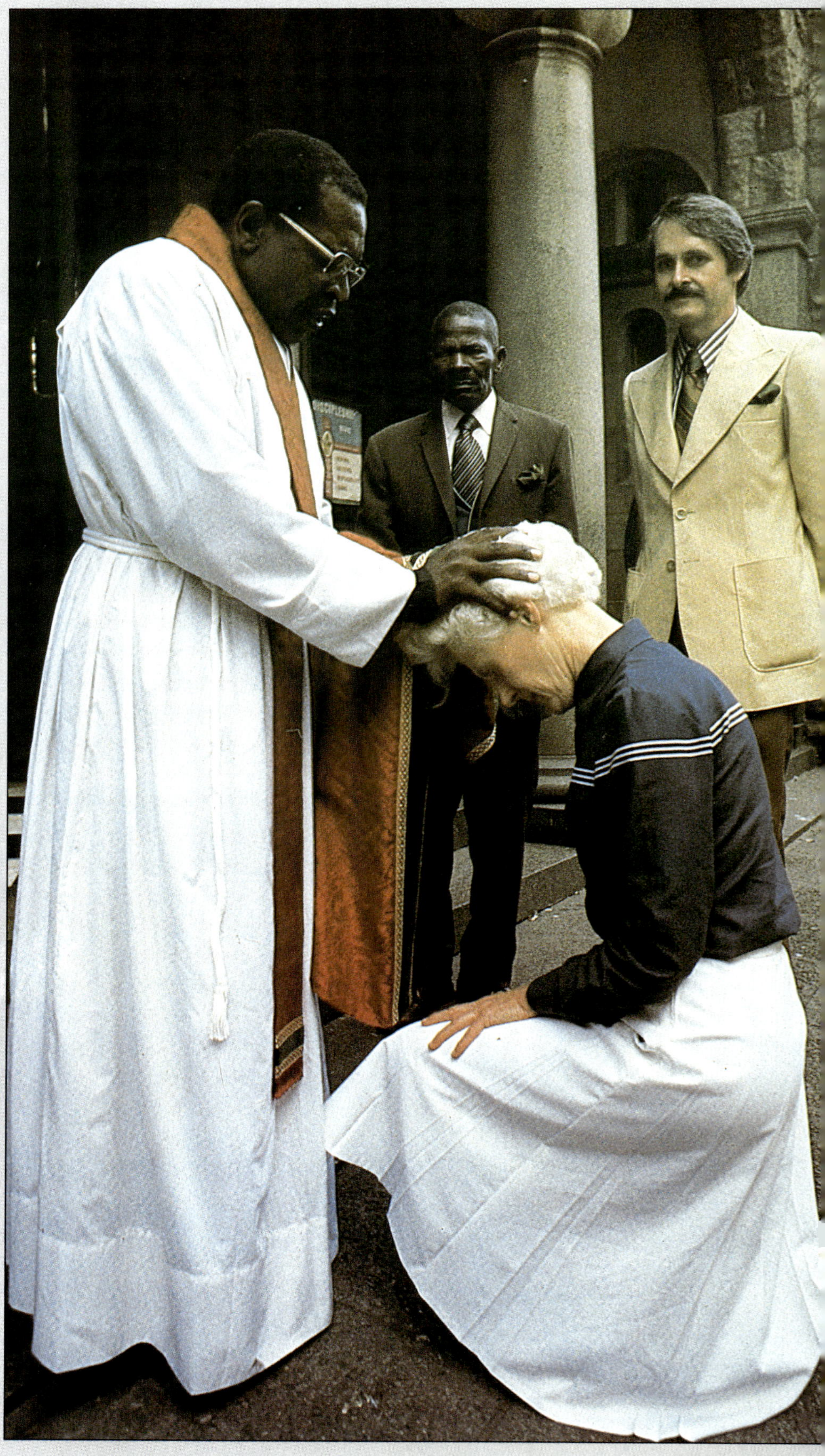

Anglican *(right)* and Roman Catholic *(above)* churches in particular have fought to preserve multi-racial worship, often with success. Of the cathedral in Johannesburg, Desmond Tutu wrote "I will always have a lump in my throat when I think of the children at St Mary's, pointers to what can be if our society would but become sane and normal. Here were children of all races playing, praying, learning and even fighting together, almost uniquely in South Africa. And . . . I have knelt in the Dean's stall at the superb 9.30 High Mass, with incense, bells and everything, watching a multi-racial crowd file up to the altar to be communicated, the one bread and the one cup given by a mixed team of clergy and lay ministers, with a multi-racial choir, servers and sidesmen—all this in apartheid-mad South Africa . . . That has been the tremendous witness of St Mary's over the past fifty years."

"The Christian's ultimate loyalty and obedience are to God, not to . . . a political system. If certain laws are not in line with the imperatives of the Gospel then the Christian must agitate for their repeal by all peaceful means. Christianity . . . has public consequences and we must make public choices. Many people think Christians should be neutral, or that the Church must be neutral. But in a situation of injustice and oppression such as we have in South Africa, not to choose to oppose, is in fact to have chosen to side with the powerful, with the exploiter, with the oppressor" (D.M. Tutu, 1978).

The Dutch Reformed Church has a total membership of roughly 1·4 million whites. Strongly entrenched at all levels of society, its role in providing a religious cement for the Afrikaans-speaking community was greatly enhanced by experience of British imperial rule. Members stepping out of line can be harshly treated. In 1963 Dr Beyers Naude, an eminent DRC leader, founded the Christian Institute to foster multi-racial, ecumenical debate on apartheid and Christian views of the just society. Ostracized by his church, he and the Institute were eventually banned after the 1976–77 wave of African unrest.

The United Rhenish Missionary Society, one among many, began operations in 1829 with Stellenbosch one of two stations. Its beautiful church (*above*) still stands on the town's common and was entirely restored in 1978, although the Society's work was taken over by the Dutch Reformed Church in 1943. African Christians number perhaps 12–13 million, of whom roughly one third belong to independent African-led churches (*left*). These vary immensely, above all in size, but are often divided into two main categories. "Ethiopian" churches are those which still retain many of the practices and ideas of their original parent body; "Zionist" churches blend Christian notions with African traditions, paying attention, for example, to the practice of spiritual healing, prophecy or interpretation of dreams. Individually their appeal is limited, and they are widely seen as marginal in the struggle for reform.

MISSIONS TO ASIA

Below The consecration of an indigenous bishop holds out the prospect that the role of the foreign missions in the churches of Papua New Guinea will now slowly decline. Among Roman Catholics, since their arrival in 1885, the Capuchins, Montfort Fathers and Sacred Heart Missionaries have been particularly important.

Left: Religious activity and European settlement in Asia
Given the evident size of their task, it is now perhaps difficult to take seriously those few European missionaries who embarked on the conversion of Asia in the 1790s. Contemporaries too, like the Reverend Sydney Smith, mocked those "little detachments of maniacs . . . benefiting us much more by their absence than the Hindoos by their advice." Their apparent foolhardiness is only explicable if one accepts that they held to a theology which made immaterial the facts of great distances, colossal populations, and deeply entrenched world religions. As William Carey put it in 1792, "this is an object we should be prompted to pursue, not only by the gospel of our Redeemer, but even by the feelings of humanity, so an inclination to conscientious activity therein would form one of the strongest proofs that we are the subjects of grace, and partakers of that spirit of universal benevolence and genuine philanthropy, which appear so eminent in the character of God himself."

Right Pilgrimage has always had both symbolic and practical importance for the world's major religions. Just as Benares on the Ganges draws Hindus, so for Indian Christians, largely concentrated in the south and frequently poor enough to value the support traditionally offered to pilgrims, sites of special significance include the shrine of St Thomas at Mylapore, near Madras.

An unreceptive mission field

To most of the Europeans scattered widely across Asia at the beginning of the 19th century, the support or propagation of Christianity was of little importance. This reflected in part a common set of priorities. During the Napoleonic wars to 1815 the security of their colonial possessions and the protection or expansion of their trade, preoccupations even in peaceful times, were frequently more pressing than ever. However, this lack of concern, even when reinforced by fashionable skepticism, was also a sign of prudence. Security and trade might be won by force, but were best maintained by cooperation and the avoidance of conflict. Although many informed Europeans were becoming highly critical of Asian states and cultures, the majority still saw little point in provoking "conservative" Hindus or "fanatical" Muslims by encouraging aggressive Christian proselytization.

This was most clearly the case in India. Although the British administered large areas of the subcontinent through the East India Company, missionaries before 1813 were not allowed to work in its territories. The Portuguese and French settlements in India and been seriously affected by the 18th-century setbacks to Catholic missionary work, and the four Portuguese dioceses were frequently without bishops even for existing congregations. Only in the Danish settlements of Tranquebar and Serampore was evangelization officially encouraged, and in the south at least, with the assistance of the English Society for Promoting Christian Knowledge, Lutheran missionaries gathered significant numbers of converts.

Elsewhere prospects for the establishment of Christianity depended more directly on the will of non-European rulers, and were generally more restricted still. Except for the tiny Dutch toehold permitted at Deshima near Nagasaki, Japan was totally closed to westerners. In China their presence was confined to commercial exchanges at Canton and the Portuguese colony of Macao. In both countries Christianity was outlawed, and vigorous persecutions had gone far towards eradicating traces of earlier Roman Catholic activity. Dutch Calvinist missions in Ceylon, Java and other parts of Indonesia, never very strong, had declined markedly by 1800; most of their efforts were devoted to undoing the work of the Catholics who had preceded them, an activity in which (except in Amboina) they were largely unsuccessful. In Ceylon, together with the Spanish-controlled Philippines, and parts of Vietnam, strong native Catholic communities continued to exist. In the remaining regions of south and east Asia, however, Christianity in any form was virtually if not completely nonexistent.

While this resulted from mounting strategic and commercial interests and declining missionary vigor, it also owed something to the limited scale of European evangelism, even at its peak early in the 18th century. However, it reflected far more the perennial imperviousness of societies which, like those of the European world, had their own long history of religious development. Islamic, Buddhist, Confucian, Hindu, Shinto and Taoist beliefs were deeply embedded and often mingled in a host of social relations, communal practices, institutions and literate traditions, difficult to overcome, especially through the individualistic approach to conversion favored by most Protestants. Ever since the adaptation of Catholic practices to those prevailing in Asian societies was effectively condemned, as a result of papal pronouncements during the 1740s on the Chinese and Malabar rites, the opportunities for Christianity to take hold had been still further restricted.

Nevertheless, the 19th and early 20th centuries in Asia as in Africa witnessed a massive expansion of Christian activity, beginning in the 1790s. The famous trio of Baptist missionaries, William Carey, Joshua Marshman and William Ward, established themselves in 1799 at Serampore not far from the English center at Calcutta, and their propaganda exerted an influence far outside the settlement. The East India Company itself could not remain untouched by the evangelical revival in Britain. Its officials began to turn a blind eye to missionary activity, and some of its chaplains even engaged in it. In Canton Robert Morison began his evangelism and worked on the first Chinese Bible while a translator for the Company. The revision of the Company's charter in 1813 allowed missionaries to operate under license in its territories; in 1833 they were allowed to range freely. The revival of Catholic missions from the 1840s produced marked effects throughout Asia, and by 1910 only Afghanistan, Nepal and Tibet remained closed to missionaries. To some extent these efforts were successful, both in reviving older communities of

Christians and in making new converts; yet massive indifference and very violent hostility remained characteristic Asian reactions to Christianity, with the result that Asian Christians have rarely acquired the status and proportionate significance or had a social and political impact comparable to that of African believers.

Steady progress in India

In India growing administrative concern with the reform of native institutions and society was paralleled by mounting evangelical condemnation of indigenous religions and ethics, and enthusiasm for conversion. Conflicts and mutual suspicion between churchmen and secular officials survived in India as everywhere else. Nevertheless, as government intervention deepened and Sind, the Punjab and Oudh came under British control, so the sphere of missionary operations grew and ecclesiastical hierarchies were established. Missions rapidly spread themselves in the south and west, moving rather later into central and northern India: the Anglican Church Missionary Society, for example, only reached Amritsar in 1852 and Peshawar in 1855. Anglican bishoprics were established at Calcutta in 1814 and Madras in 1835, and the Roman Catholics finally organized their hierarchy for India and Ceylon in 1886. Missionary strategies also broadened in the first half-century. The early emphasis lay on preaching and teaching in the vernacular languages through the medium of the mission schools in the villages. However, under the influence of the Scottish Presbyterian, Alexander Duff, much more attention was given after 1830 to the extension of higher education, intended to attract the Indian intellectual elites and so undermine native religions from the top.

It is important not to exaggerate the scale of these efforts. By 1851 there were 19 Protestant societies working in India, providing some 400 ordained missionaries for a population of perhaps 200 million. Results were scarcely more impressive: in the same year the number of Protestant converts was put at 91 000, most of them in the southern provinces. Far from winning members of the higher castes to Christianity, the missions' educational policy stimulated the reform and revival of both Hindu and Muslim belief. Christians were always a tiny minority of those receiving a western education, especially as the schools, with government financial assistance, grew rapidly from the 1850s. In the Bombay presidency they constituted only 1·9 percent of the college population, and 8·9 percent in high and middle schools, early in the 1880s.

The expansion of Christianity after 1870 was

Above James Hudson Taylor was the founder of the China Inland Mission (1865), the popular embodiment of a profound reaction against the denominationalism, bureaucracy and centralization of existing missionary societies. It was to be interdenominational and directed in China; its missionaries were to share the Chinese life-style as far as possible, and to promote rapid peripatetic evangelization, not build extravagant permanent stations.

Left: Missionary activity in China and Japan to 1920
A great expansion of Christian activity in the Far East took place in the 1880s and 1890s, inspired by the worldwide evangelical revivalism associated with the Keswick Conferences and the Student Volunteer Movement. One source of missionary confidence lay in the conviction that history and an interventionist God were on their side. William Cassels, one of the famous "Cambridge Seven" group who left for China in 1885, wrote shortly after his arrival "how my heart goes up to God at the sight of these crowds of Chinamen, that He would raise up His power and come among us, that He would speedily flood this place with a very tidal wave of blessing! And why not? If there are tidal waves in nature which completely flow over whole districts, why not a tidal wave in grace?" As bishop of western China on the eve of the revolution of 1911 he wrote again how "I am most anxious that it should be borne in mind that it is most probable that God is going to use this agitation for the extension of His Kingdom and the advancement of the Church. The Taiping rebellion and the Boxer outbreak played their part towards the breaking down of idolatry, the shaking of old foundations and in making the preparation for the setting up of God's Kingdom. This new agitation may carry the work a great deal further."

nevertheless more noticeable. Growing criticism of their strategy and lack of achievement prompted missions to concentrate their attention once more on those groups among which they had always had most impact, the depressed classes of Hindu society, and inhabitants of areas where Muslim and Hindu beliefs were weakest. Mass communal movements towards Christianity were not uncommon in this period. Lutherans, Scottish Presbyterians and Jesuits all had steady successes among the hill peoples of Bihar and Chota Nagpur. In the Telugu districts of the Madras presidency, and Sialkot in the Punjab, again conversion of whole communities occurred. Such transformations were aided both by renewed attempts to relate the Christian message more closely to conditions of Indian life, and by the critical problems of indebtedness, land shortages and more frequent famine. Directly related to both these developments was the extension of Christian welfare activity, not only providing education, but tackling debt, unemployment and disease. From 1881, when they were recorded at 417 372, the numbers of Indian Protestants rose to 1·6 million in 1911, a total very similar to that of the Roman Catholics.

The low-caste nature of most Indian Christianity has continued during the 20th century, and has had several important effects. There is little doubt that it has reinforced the dislike of other social groups for the faith. Lack of status and wealth also helped delay the development both of an Indian priesthood and of self-supporting churches. The Anglicans only appointed an Indian bishop in 1912, the Catholics in 1923, and attachment to western forms remained very strong. Their minority position also inclined Christians to play a very cautious role in Indian national politics, for they remained suspicious of the principal nationalist parties and concerned about their own future. In one area, however, that of church union, the Indian churches set an important example: with the creation in 1947 of the Church of South India from five Protestant denominations, episcopal and nonepiscopal churches joined together for the first time.

Success and reversals in China

Despite evangelical concern for the "perishing millions" of heathen in the Far East, the renewed expansion of Christianity in China and Japan was impossible until the mid-19th century. Britain's acquisition of Hong Kong and the Treaty of Nanking in 1842 concluded the first Opium War, and opened the way not only for traders but also for missionary work in the five so-called Treaty Ports. Despite constant missionary demands for further opportunities, western governments only secured these after another war. The Treaty of Tientsin (1858) and the Peking Convention (1860) increased the number of treaty ports, allowed missionaries into the interior and permitted purchase of property for religious purposes. These openings were rapidly seized. In 30 years the number of Protestant missionaries rose from 81 to 1269 and doubled again to 2818 by 1900. Roman Catholic priests were 639 in 1890 and 883 by 1900, along with many other religious, particularly women.

Although the arrival of missionaries in China in the wake of treaties extorted by force made them unpopular, their message had an early impact. The Taiping rebellion of 1850–64, which severely challenged imperial authority, claimed sufficient Christian inspiration for the new religion to pose a serious threat to the status quo. The traditional hostility of most Chinese towards foreigners was therefore increasingly concentrated on the missionary, who was for many the only foreigner they ever knew. The itinerant evangelism of, for example, the China Inland Mission (formed in 1865), whose members endeavored to live like the Chinese themselves and to forgo all contact with other western influences, did little to improve relations. Most missions were very assertive of their treaty rights, overtly contemptuous of Chinese customs such as ancestor worship, and overprotective of their converts, all in ways which angered local inhabitants and undermined the authority of Chinese officials and gentry. After 1860 antiforeign protests and literature grew: intellectuals took up criticisms of Christianity found in western thought, other writers portrayed Christian belief and ritual in ways repellent to Chinese, and popular violence erupted in events like the Tientsin massacre (1870). Protest culminated in the great Boxer Rebellion of 1900, but as with earlier incidents the outcome was repression, reprisals and payment of indemnities at the behest of the European powers.

Although hostility did not disappear, suppression of the Boxers, the final collapse of imperial authority, and the revolution of 1911 which heralded the republic marked a period of expansion and comparative success. Until the early 1920s Christian social work, teaching and numbers grew rapidly. Many Chinese saw in western education or Christianity a means to personal advancement and to the reestablishment of a stable, modernized China as a great power; correspondingly, more converts were drawn from groups other than the most marginal in Chinese society. This phase was short-lived: alongside the perennial difficulties of rendering biblical terms and theological concepts in ways comprehensible to Chinese, Christianity remained unrelated to China's fundamental problems. Two-thirds of missionaries and one-third of Chinese Christian evangelists lived in the largest cities; yet 94 percent of Chinese lived in the agricultural villages, and missions never really tackled the basic questions of rural improvement.

The understandable reluctance of missionaries in China's turbulent conditions to hand over control in the churches to the Chinese was resented as evidence of continuing foreign domination. Moreover neither Christianity nor foreign missions were of help to the nationalist leaders attempting to unify the country against the resistance of provincial military commanders or warlords. Nationalist leaders' attitudes to Christians, while occasionally friendly, could hardly be more than generally detached, especially against the background of extensive antiforeign riots in the cities from 1924 to 1927. Adjustments of missionary policy towards ecclesiastical and economic questions from the mid-1920s on were largely irrelevant to a country for two decades either ravaged by civil war between the Guomindang and Communists, or at war with Japan. The wars were immensely destructive of Christian enterprise as of China itself, and the years 1945–49 provided too short a time for recovery. When the Communists took over in 1949 there were at most some 4·7 million Christians; they rapidly found themselves deprived of their facilities and under great pressure to abandon their beliefs.

Restricted evangelism in Japan

In Japan access followed a similar pattern but more slowly and on a more limited scale. Western missionaries were admitted to Tokyo, Hakodate and Nagasaki in 1859, but Christianity remained proscribed. Although a tentative religious freedom was granted in 1873, not until the Meiji constitution of 1889 was it permanently guaranteed. By that time some 450 Protestant missionaries were at work, but travel in the interior remained restricted, and as late as 1899 their residence was confined to the foreign concessions. These continuing restrictions illustrate how the Japanese imperial government was far stronger than its Chinese counterpart, and also compelled western respect, especially after its victory in the Russo-Japanese war of 1905. It was thus always able to restrict Christian evangelism and schooling in the interests of respect for the position of the emperor and the strengthening of nationalist sentiment. This was particularly marked in the 1930s, and came to a head with the government's amalgamation of all Protestant bodies in 1940–41 to form the Church of Christ in Japan; those that resisted were dissolved.

Japanese Christianity, even more than Chinese, remained an urban religion, and in neither country were there the mass movements of conversion experienced in India. Both Protestants and Catholics devoted much of their evangelizing effort to the *samurai* class of warrior officials whose fortunes were seriously upset by the restoration of the emperor in 1867. Converts were made, but even to them western leadership, liturgy and denominationalism were always causes of discontent. Some members of the small "bands" of converts, originating in the 1870s at new institutions like the agricultural school at Sapporo, tried to formulate a distinctively Japanese theology and organization. Their work bred by 1900 the "churchless" Christianity of Uchimura, whose Mukyokai adherents combined an immediate personal experience of God with a puritan ethic, developed through membership of small, isolated Bible-study groups. This rejection of western institutional and doctrinal accretions was subsequently followed by other independent movements, such as the Spirit of Jesus Church in Tokyo, in the difficult years after Japan's defeat in 1945. At a more popular, less sophisticated level the Makuya Church has managed to mingle traditional folk religion and magic with Christian Pentecostalist practice.

The existence of these independent churches illustrates a certain vitality in Japanese Christianity, at least of the Protestant variety. However, the fundamentally secular temper of much Japanese culture and the closeness of family or communal ties have left Christianity little space for direct expansion, except occasionally at times of great personal crisis or social upheaval. Economic and political recovery since 1950 has inhibited further growth, and the total of professing Christians is estimated at barely 1 percent of the population.

Above Originally the largest Christian church in the Far East and one of some 60 parishes in Nagasaki, Urakami was destroyed by the atom bomb in 1945 but rebuilt by 1959. The Japanese constitution of 1946, allowing complete religious freedom, made it possible for the newly established National Catholic Committee to oversee a rapid revival of Roman Catholicism. Numbers rose from 108 000 in 1946 to 358 000 in 1973.

Religious voluntarism in Australia and New Zealand

In Australia and New Zealand Christianity was established not so much by missionary enterprise (although both Aboriginal and Maori populations attracted missionary attention) or by state imposition, as by the voluntary efforts of individual settlers and officials who carried their beliefs with them from Europe. Concerned primarily with setting up a penal colony at Botany Bay, the British government in 1785 barely considered a chaplain for its own officials, let alone a religious establishment and instruction or education for transported convicts. Its relative indifference lasted until the mid-1820s, when it created the Church and School Corporation endowed with one-seventh of the colony's land to support an Anglican establishment. By then, however, the addition of free immigrants to time-expired convicts had recreated Britain's own denominational variety. Scottish Presbyterians and Irish Catholics were particularly numerous, and resented any establishment of Anglicanism, not least when all denominations in this new setting lacked both clergy and endowments. The New South Wales solution of 1836, state grants-in-aid to major denominations, was copied for a time in other colonies, but by 1871 was generally abandoned in favor of religious voluntarism and state support only for secular education. In New Zealand, a British colony from 1840, the same principles were adopted in 1877, despite early attempts at founding denominational settlements in Christchurch (Anglican) and Otago (Presbyterian).

This early separation of Church and state reflected in part sectarian vigor, but far more the secular, liberal-democratic and materialistic temper of colonial society. Many colonists came from sections of British society hostile to organized religion of any kind; others became indifferent through lack of incentive or provision on the spot; liberal expenditure on religious causes was never an Australasian characteristic. Anglicans and Roman Catholics built up their hierarchies, and others consolidated their position, during the years of state grants, but thereafter had difficulty holding their own. Support for social welfare or foreign missions was varied and enthusiastic, but the fa-

Right: Australia and New Zealand
In these lands of recent white settlement churchmen like other emigrants looked forward to the creation of new model communities, appropriating the best of European life and leaving its blemishes behind. Australia's Cardinal Moran hoped he might see "Ireland born anew, pious and God-centred, but, this time, free." New Zealand's denominational settlements echoed the earlier ambitions of godly colonists in North America for well-ordered societies of the righteous. Such hopes were largely forlorn. Few New Zealanders seem ever to have developed the habit of regular church-going, and the stern morality of the Primitive Methodist or Presbyterian has no more pronounced legacy here than in other parts of the world. Commentators seem to regard Australia, ecclesiastical hierarchies notwithstanding, as decidedly more secular in tone than, for example, Canada. Its churches have been unable to keep pace with rapid urban expansion, and, as one historian recently observed, "There is no Sunday in the bush."

Below The baptism of non-European rulers was an important missionary goal. New Zealand's Maoris responded readily, not least in the vain hope that Christian influence might deflect demands for their land.

natical puritans often associated with these campaigns involving "moral improvement," known to Australians as "wowsers," were regarded with more levity than was common nearer the hub of empire.

Some of the most controversial aspects of Christian life were associated with the Roman Catholics, who always remained a large proportion of the population. Overwhelmingly Irish (until the influx of European refugees after 1940), largely working class and fiercely nationalistic, Australian Catholics had no time for the expatriate Englishmen first sent to organize them. From the 1860s to the 1930s clergy recruited from Ireland shaped the Church; defense of Catholic education drew them constantly into politics; and the needs of many Catholics aligned the Church with the emerging Labor Party from the 1890s. A departure from European patterns, this linking of sectarianism, class and nationality provoked much conservative and Protestant hostility, especially over Catholic opposition to conscription during World War I. The widening social composition of the Catholic community, and the social Catholicism encouraged by Pope Pius XI's program of Catholic Action, prompted a realignment in the 1940s. Members of the Catholic Social Studies Movement led a struggle against growing Communist influence in the trade unions, and ultimately split the Australian Labor Party in 1954. Many Catholics then turned away from the secular socialism of Labor, and in general Catholics' political activity became much less direct.

THE ORTHODOX CHURCHES

The year 1453 marked less the death of an empire than the end of an illusion. Some Orthodox, however, nurse the "Great Idea" of the recapture of Constantinople to this day. By the mid-15th century the overwhelming majority of the Orthodox were living under Turkish rule. In many ways the Turkish sultan's establishment of his capital at Constantinople saved the Byzantine Church from still further dislocation, dismemberment and impoverishment. The Constantinopolitan patriarchate might have gone the way of the other eastern patriarchates. As political and administrative institutions Jerusalem, Antioch and especially Alexandria were weak and only Jerusalem had some financial means, although considerable numbers of Orthodox Christians remained in Palestine and northern Syria, mostly Arabic-speaking and using an Arabic liturgy. Greek remained the official literary language of these patriarchates, and this acted as a high barrier between the Greek-speaking hierarchy and the villagers in the countryside. The Constantinopolitan patriarchate might, after a few generations, have become equally isolated even from those who remained Orthodox Christians, and the latter might have become Turkish-speaking. This did not happen because the Ottoman Sultan Mehmet II took the patriarchate under his wing, making it responsible for all the Orthodox *milet* ("nation"). The patriarchate of Constantinople was termed the "ethnarch" (*ethnos* = people, nation; *arche* = authority), and when in the 16th century the Ottomans conquered Syria, Palestine and Egypt, the Constantinopolitan patriarch's influence extended in practice, though not in theory, over the appointments to the patriarchates in Antioch, Jerusalem and Alexandria. For it was he who had the sultan's ear. As early as 1484 a council of all four eastern patriarchates met in Constantinople to denounce the Council of Florence and to provide for the reception into Orthodoxy of converts from the Roman Church (mainly Greeks living in Latin-ruled lands which had now been taken by the Turks).

The sultan and the patriarch

The Ottoman sultans were in many respects reminiscent of Byzantine "universal" emperors in their prime. Mehmet II, the conqueror of Constantinople, was keenly aware of the parallels when, on the day after the conquest, he went to St Sophia and prayed. He converted the church into a mosque, and proclaimed "Hereafter my capital is Istanbul!" His belief that Istanbul (from Greek *eis tēn polin,* "in the city") was the fitting center for a world empire was echoed by several contemporary Greek scholars. For example George Trapezuntios (1395–1484) wrote of Mehmet: "No one can doubt that he is emperor of the Romans. He who holds the seat of empire in his hand is emperor of right, and Constantinople is the center of the Roman empire." The prime concern of the conqueror was for order. Although desiring the ultimate prevalence of Islam, he, in conformity with Islamic tradition, regarded the Bible as a holy book, and Christians as "people of the book." They should therefore be spared, but relegated to second-class citizenship. This had already been the Ottomans' practice during their piecemeal conquest of Asia Minor and the Balkans.

Far from exploiting the fact that the patriarchal throne was vacant, Mehmet II filled the vacuum caused by the flight of Gregory III Mammas to Italy. He selected an experienced ecclesiastical administrator, Gennadios Scholarios, and ceremonially appointed him in January 1454, handing him the vestments, pastoral staff and pectoral cross appropriate to his office, and stating: "Be patriarch, with good fortune, and be assured of our friendship, keeping all the privileges that the patriarchs before you enjoyed!" The patriarch and his synod now with Mehmet's permission reasserted their supervision of episcopal appointments. Patriarchal law courts exercised jurisdiction over clergymen and the extensive jurisdiction which church courts or clerical "supreme judges" already wielded over Orthodox laymen in the 14th century was systematized. Civil cases involving morality or religion were to be held in church courts, for example matters of marriage, wills and inheritance. In return the Church's spiritual authority could be used to support the new order. For this reason the Armenian catholicos and the chief rabbi were brought by Mehmet II to reside in Istanbul. Each was to be the head of his *milet*.

The patriarchate as an institution benefited from the cessation of the anarchy preceding 1453, when it had been an island in a hostile Turkish sea. Already by 1400 at least eight metropolitan and episcopal sees had had to be abandoned in Thrace and Macedonia. For example Adrianople was long deprived of a resident metropolitan, and a 15th-century writer lamented that "the majority of our nation [in Adrianople] have slipped away, being creatures of a day, and taking thought only for human happiness." After 1454 there was a tightening of central authority over metropolitans, for the patriarchate was backed by the sultan. The patriarchate could also draw on a large pool of Orthodox personnel to fill the top administrative offices, for Mehmet brought to Istanbul many Christians, especially merchants, encouraging them to resume their commerce with tax exemptions and giving them houses to live in. They were transported from Adrianople and from other areas as they succumbed to the conqueror's armies—from Trebizond after 1461, from Argos in the Morea (Peloponnese) after 1463 and from Caffa after 1475. A contemporary westerner wrote that "within a short time these new arrivals had constructed remarkable houses and churches." Their numbers swelled during the 16th century, and far exceeded the meager population of Constantinople in the last centuries of the empire. Many of the richest fami-

A sacred strip cartoon. In the early 16th century Moldavian churchmen began covering the outside walls of their churches with scenes from the Bible and the recent past. These frescoes at Humor Monastery depict the siege of Constantinople in 1453, though wishful thinking and hatred of the Turks combine to persuade the artist to paint a Turkish defeat. Christianity had long had believers in the plains of Wallachia and the Moldavian hills, but only in the 14th century does an organized church appear there. The Byzantine patriarchate recognized two metropolitanates, and monasteries inspired by Mount Athos spread the latest ideas about prayer and mysticism across the land. Until the late 17th century services were in Church Slavonic, the literary language coined for the Slavs by 9th-century Byzantine missionaries. Since this was incomprehensible to the ordinary people, whose language derived from Latin, wall paintings such as Humor's spoke volumes. The Constantinopolitan patriarch exercised authority over Romania during the Turkish overlordship. Today, the Romanian Orthodox Church is run by its own patriarch, who resides in Bucharest.

lies lived in stately homes in the vicinity of the patriarchal headquarters, in the Fener (Phanar) district of Istanbul. These merchant princes were known as "Phanariots," after the district. They preened themselves on their often spurious claims to descent from noble Byzantine families, took pride in the Greek language and sought to dominate the senior offices of the Great Church. In the 17th century the Phanariots extended their interests to the principalities of Moldavia and Wallachia, and individual Phanariots became princes there, promoting Greeks to the Orthodox church hierarchy and encouraging Greek learning. Some Phanariots even harbored the "Great Idea" of a Greek-speaking empire, a revamp of Byzantium.

The relations between Patriarch Gennadios and Mehmet II were friendly and Mehmet even encouraged him to write a brief treatise on the Orthodox faith for translation into Turkish. But harmony between patriarch and sultan was short-lived. Mehmet's successors were generally less sympathetic towards Orthodoxy, and Selim I (1512–20), the conqueror of Syria, Egypt and Arabia, contemplated the forcible conversion of all Christians to Islam. The importance of the headship of the Orthodox *milet* caused Mehmet II himself to clip the patriarch's wings by enhancing the powers of the patriarchal synod, which already possessed the right to depose a patriarch by unanimous vote. It was now officially proclaimed that patriarchal decrees were only binding if they had the assent of the synod. Even a forceful patriarch could be hamstrung by this requirement, and the Turkish authorities could easily suborn enough of the metropolitans and top patriarchal officials who constituted the synod to swing its vote. Conversely churchmen sought to gain privileges for themselves, or even the office of patriarch, through lavish bribes.

Corruption and patronage at the Ottoman court

The Ottoman court was itself usually composed of factions competing for influence with the sultan or with intimates such as his grand vizier or his mother. The patriarchate, as a kind of department of state, thus became entwined in the networks and string pulling by which the Ottoman state operated. From the late 15th century aspirants to the patriarchal office paid money to the Sublime Porte, and the going rate for the job rose steadily. Money was not sovereign: respected churchmen in the synod could stymie the appointment of individuals of whom they disapproved; Mount Athos's continuing moral authority and landed wealth retained for it considerable influence with the patriarchate until the 17th century. Above all, the sultan's will could be capricious. A few sultans, such as Suleiman the Magnificent (1520–66), desired order and continuity in the top echelons of the patriarchate and during his reign lengthy tenures of the patriarchal office were permitted, for example, the 21 years of Jeremias I. But far more often the tenures were brief, as bribes for the office rolled in. Several patriarchs were deposed and reinstated repeatedly. But when "revolving doors" were propelled by bribes, and by incessant faction rivalries within the Church, they inevitably affected the quality of the whole structure. By the 17th century candidates for the patriarchate were likely to succeed only if they disposed of vast quantities of money. For these they usually had to turn to the Phanariot plutocrat families so conveniently near at hand. These, though they dominated the administration of the patriarchate, did not take holy orders themselves. They preferred to patronize those of humble origins who aspired to become metropolitans or higher. Sometimes they were moved by piety, more often by material considerations. Patriarchs and senior churchmen were in the 17th and 18th centuries in every sense indebted to them, and church resources were squandered on intrigues at the sultan's court and the repayment of Phanariots for loans and favors. Simony was virtually institutionalized and, from the 16th century onwards, most of the patriarchs were nonentities.

It must also be stressed that, for all its privileges, the Great Church headed a community of second-class citizens. Conversion from Islam to Christianity was punished by death. Theoretically, and in accordance with Islamic law, Christians were not to be forced to apostasize to Islam. But in practice forcible conversions were widespread, and martyrdoms not uncommon. The various sects of dervishes actively proselytized among the Orthodox country folk. Perhaps the most successful of them were the Bektashis, whose mystic trances, miracles and wild dances were combined with un-Islamic tolerance of wine drinking and free social intercourse between men and women. Their eclectic practices seemed acceptable and even attractive to many ordinary peasants, whose beliefs had probably always had room for magic and unauthorized rituals. The Turkish government tried to maintain surveillance on the Bektashis and occasionally persecuted them, but failed to stop the wanderings of their missionaries. In fact by the end of the 16th century the Bektashi order was closely associated with the Janissaries, the corps of guards directly under the sultan's command. The Janissaries themselves evince the official pressures on Orthodoxy. For they were mostly the children of Christian parents who had been seized at an early age, circumcised, brought up as Muslims and enrolled as slaves in the Janissary regiments.

There was a steady hemorrhage of Orthodox losses to Islam through the 16th and 17th centuries. Any non-Muslim suffered severe legal disadvantages. For all cases involving a Muslim had to be heard in Muslim courts, where Muslim *qadis* adjudicated. The testimony of Christians was invalid in these courts except when Christian wills were at issue. More ambitious or wealthy Christians were therefore tempted to "insure" their property or prospects by becoming Muslims. The decrees of sultans granting rights and privileges to Christians were supposed to be binding on their successors. But they could be pronounced invalid if they were shown to contravene Islamic laws, and in the 16th century churches were still being turned into mosques. The seepage away of church possessions, the lack of adequate legal safeguards and the high cost of running the patriarchal administration and buying Ottoman favor led to the Church being in a state of penury and debt in the 17th century. A late 17th-century English visitor to the Turkish lands, Sir Paul Ricaut, commented on the "tragical" state of the former Orthodox churches, "the oppression and contempt that good Christians are exposed to, and the ignorance in their churches occasioned through poverty in the clergy." The "miracle" was, he exclaimed, "that there is conserved still amongst so much opposition and in despite of all tyranny . . . an open and public profession of the Christian faith."

Serbia, Bulgaria and Albania

There were other Orthodox peoples in eastern Europe besides the Greek-speakers—notably the Serbs and Bulgarians. Their church organizations were brought under the hegemony of the "ecumenical" patriarch of Constantinople, apparently at the behest of Mehmet II. The Serbian and Bulgarian churches retained a degree of autonomy under, respectively, the metropolitans of Pec and Ternovo. Relations of these Slav churchmen with the Constantinopolitan patriarch were not good, and ferocious objections were raised when the patriarch appointed Greeks to the metropolitanate and to other high offices. In order to placate the Serbs, the Ottoman government permitted the reconstitution of the Serbian patriarchate at Pec in 1557, and it continued until 1766. The Bulgarians were accorded no such privileges. These Orthodox Slavs resented the collaboration and intrigues of the Greek-speaking hierarchs with the Ottoman authorities, both in their own countries and at Constantinople. Their resentment was eventually to lead them to a desire to be rid of the Ottomans and their Greek minions and a failure to join with the Greeks in their war of independence. But in fact the conditions of the Serbian and Bulgarian Orthodox at grass roots were not significantly worse than those of the Orthodox in the rural hinterlands of Greece. The pattern of Christian life was similar, with worship continuing to revolve around the holy liturgy and priests to minister the sacraments.

One difference between Greek-speaking lands and the rest of the Balkans was the fact that parts of the latter were key frontier zones, heavily populated with Turkish soldiers and their families. One such frontier region, facing Italy, was Albania. Large numbers of Turks were granted land in return for military service there and many of the native Albanians became Muslims and fought in the Turkish armies. The great strength of Islam in Albania affected neighboring districts inhabited by Orthodox Slav-speakers in the 16th and 17th centuries. Such districts as the plains of Kosovo were gradually Islamicized. Orthodoxy had still been prevalent there in about 1530 when a traveler recorded, "In almost every village there is a church and a priest who performs at times the rite as established by St Paul [the Orthodox], and for that service the whole community maintains him, his wife and children for life . . ." A century later a Roman Catholic churchman observed of various areas of Serbia that many Orthodox had become Muslims in order to escape the heavy burden of taxation imposed on the faithful. By the late 18th century Orthodoxy had become almost a matter for antiquarians in the area of Kosovo. A traveler recorded: "In almost all villages, Serb and Albanian, there are sites of churches, and in some villages there are sites of two or more churches." He observed numerous ruins of churches in

Above The Monastery of St John of Rila. John was a Bulgarian courtier who set aside the easy life and withdrew to wild mountains of the Rila range. He sought solitude and lived for many years in a hollow oak tree reminiscent of a coffin. But, as in the case of so many Orthodox holy men, his life-style attracted fame and followers and at the end of his life he founded a communal monastery for them. Monasticism flourished in Bulgaria from soon after its conversion and houses such as Rila became centers of plain living, learning and art. Bulgaria, while an independent country, had its own patriarch and owed only a nominal allegiance to the Constantinopolitan patriarch. However, it shared in the religious thought of the Orthodox world and Bulgarian monasteries played a key role in the 14th-century movement known as Hesychasm. Later, during the long centuries of the Turkish yoke, they helped to preserve Bulgarian literature and national pride.

villages which were then Muslim. Nonetheless sizable areas in the mountainous countryside remained Christian, although their beliefs and rituals were often wayward, and trained ecclesiastical supervision was lacking. Individuals eager to better their socioeconomic position tended to become Muslims.

The Russian Church under the Tatars and the tsars

Orthodoxy in Russia did not have to undergo this kind of pressure. Yet there are affinities between the Orthodox churches of the Ottoman lands and the Russian Church which have not fully been explored. For Russia had undergone a foreign (Tatar) occupation and overlordship at a somewhat earlier date, from the mid-13th century to the first half of the 15th century. The Church in Russia had been obliged to recognize the legitimacy of the infidel Tatar's rule, but in return its landholding and law courts had been sanctioned and in many ways the Russian Church benefited from having a powerful new protector. Its collaboration with the Tatars was even more blatant than that of the Greek patriarchate of Constantinople was to be: prayers were said in the churches for the well-being of the Tatar khan.

The Constantinopolitan patriarchate was deemed to have abandoned Orthodoxy by its assent to union with Rome (at the Council of Florence), and at a council of Russian bishops in 1448 a new metropolitan of all Russia was elected. Five years later the Byzantine emperor and patriarchate received, in Russian eyes, their just deserts at the hands of the Turk. The Russian Church did not immediately lay claim to be a separate patriarchate. It would only attain that status in 1589 and with the assent of the other Orthodox patriarchates. But

Right Onion domes triumphant. Although known worldwide as "St Basil's," this cathedral is properly called the Virgin of the Intercession. Ivan the Terrible commissioned it to commemorate his capture of Kazan, the Tatar city on the Volga, on 1 October 1552, the feast day of the Intercession. The church's popular name comes from Basil the Blessed, a holy fool who is buried in its wall. According to legend, Ivan the Terrible had the architect blinded to prevent him ever building another such masterpiece. Ivan certainly took a close interest in the design. At first sight a riot of Oriental fantasy, the church has a careful, symmetrical, groundplan and was originally red brick with white details. It is the variety of decoration (including ribbed domes) and bright colors that creates a sense of frozen chaos. Napoleon ordered that St Basil's be blown up before his retreat from Moscow in 1812, but his orders were not carried out.

some Russian churchmen had already prepared the way for such an elevation at the beginning of the 16th century, when they acclaimed the Muscovite ruler as "tsar" and hailed Moscow as "the third Rome," after old Rome and Byzantium. These churchmen were few in number, and the idea, with its implications, was only slowly appreciated by Muscovite statesmen.

Nonetheless the concept of Moscow as the "third Rome" is significant, especially for the circumstances in which it was propagated, and for the future direction in which the Russian Church developed. At the end of the 15th century a number of ascetic monks denounced the wealth, worldly involvements and vast estates of bishoprics and monasteries. These "non-possessors" maintained that the Church should not be subservient to earthly princes and that monks had no business with earthly possessions. Defenders of monastic landholding, like their leader Joseph of Volokolamsk, argued "If the monasteries are deprived of the villages they own, how will it be possible for an honorable and noble man to take orders? And if there are no honorable monks, where shall we find candidates for the metropolitanate, the archbishopric, the bishopric and other honorable offices? And if there are no honorable and noble monks, then faith itself will be undermined."

Basil III (1505–33) eventually decided to let the Church keep its possessions and its extensive jurisdiction over them. In return the Church endorsed his exercise of autocratic power and taught that the tsar was, in secular matters, the living law, and answerable only to God for his subjects' welfare: no man could justly oppose him. There was no "covenant" of the sort which the Greeks supposed to have been made between Mehmet II and Patriarch Gennadios, and in practice the Church could not impose restraints upon a ruler. When Metropolitan Philip I protested at the cruelties and lawless killings perpetrated by Ivan the Terrible, he was sent to a remote monastery and later put to death. In the mid-17th century Patriarch Nikon of Moscow tried to exploit his influence as former tutor to the young tsar Alexis, and proclaimed the supremacy of the ecclesiastical power over the secular. But once he antagonized Alexis he proved, for all his arrogant vigor, impotent, and eventually he was deposed.

The reforms of Nikon and Peter the Great

Earlier Nikon had tried to reform the Church, improving standards of education and morality among the clergy. He was particularly ruthless in eliminating irregular practices and incomprehensible or erroneous texts of religious books which had crept into the Russian Church over the centuries, and looked to the Greek Orthodox Church for a model of correct ritual and standards and for correct texts of service books and other religious works. Icons which deviated from the Byzantine pattern and showed western European influence were ripped off the walls of churches and private homes. Detailed regulations were prescribed on, for example, the number of genuflexions made during recitation of particular prayers, and the sign of the cross was to be made with three fingers rather than the customary two.

These reforms had the backing of state power. The tsar appreciated the need to bring order into worship and to clarify the Church's ritual. Furious opposition to any change in the time-honored traditions of Russian ritual came from the parish clergy, the monks and many laymen. These traditionalists were known as the "Old Believers" or "Old Ritualists." They feared eternal damnation from any such change as making the sign of the cross with three instead of two fingers. The dispute, known as the Schism, reminds us how important ritual and symbol were in the Orthodox Church, the overwhelming majority of whose congregations were simple peasants. For them salvation came through careful observance of sacred rites rather than from comprehending the texts of books. The Schism also shows that while Christian worship was well embedded in the grass roots of Russian society, its ritual had been considerably "russified" over the centuries, and at popular level there was little sense of membership of a wider ecumenical Orthodox Church. The state broke up the fanatical opposition to church reform of the Old Believers. Many of them preferred death as the surest means of saving their souls from the heresy which the changes in ritual were thought to constitute. Monks were in the forefront of the opposition to change, in a manner reminiscent of Byzantine monks in the controversies over Iconoclasm and union with Rome. Some Old Believers opted for suicide by burning. Many fled into the remote wilderness of the far north or to Siberia, and continued their practices there, a notable example of devotion to traditional worship prevailing over material considerations.

Nonetheless the tsar's will and power succeeded in imposing the new ritual on the overwhelming majority of the inhabitants of Russia. The council of 1666–67 had confirmed the tsar's domination of the Church in Russia. The senior clergy were deferential towards him, and the new patriarch, Joachim, said: "Whatever the sovereign orders, I am prepared to follow and obey in all respects." At the council Nikon's claim to superiority as patriarch was countered by this ringing declaration: "The lord tsar has the right to rule all subjects, including clergy and prelates, in all matters except doctrine." The ecclesiastical organization was thus amenable to the emperor's direction.

There was very little outcry when Peter the Great took various measures to reform and reorganize the Church in Russia and to deprive it of its tax exemptions and other privileges. The most radical of his moves was his decision in 1718 to abolish the patriarchate, whose throne had already been left vacant for 18 years. In 1721 Peter proclaimed the establishment of an Ecclesiastical College "which shall have, in accordance with the Regulation which follows, the authority to administer all ecclesiastical affairs in the All-Russian Church." The College, which was promptly rechristened "the most holy all-ruling synod," was a department of state, whose function was both to administer and to reform the Church. It would have been understood, though not wholly approved of, by Justinian.

While one of Peter's aims was to reduce the numbers of monks and nuns, another was to place

"Little Father" on the Eastern Front. Tsar Nicholas II displays an icon to troops. Peter the Great swept away church ritual from his court and introduced secular ideas and ceremonial from the west. Nonetheless, popular beliefs in the goodness of the tsar and in his special links with God remained strong. In the 19th century official credos such as "Orthodoxy, autocracy, nationality" reinforced the people's assumption that Church, tsar and Russianness were intertwined. When Alexander II was assassinated in 1881, the church of the Savior "On the Spilled Blood" was built over the spot, in St Petersburg, and a biography, *Tsar Liberator, Tsar Martyr,* appeared. "The tsar will give" was an old popular saying. In 1905 workers processed to the Winter Palace to petition Nicholas: "Raze the wall that separates thee from thy people and rule the country with them." They sang prayers and carried icons, but many were mown down by gunfire.

part of the Church's and the monasteries' colossal revenues at the disposal of the state. He also sought to improve the quality of the lesser clergy: as in Russia, so in the Balkans, the facts that priests married, and that their sons often succeeded them in the ministry, bonded them to their local communities, but gravely hindered the central supervision of their activities. Forty years after Peter's death, the church lands were secularized outright. The Church remained governed by the principles of Peter's ecclesiastical Regulation until 1918. Its watchword was utility to the state.

Belief and practice in the Orthodox world

The lack of significant controversies about or deviations from doctrine is in large part due to the uncerebral nature of church life during the Turkish centuries. Very little was thought, and less written, on matters of theology, and the lack of educational establishments perpetuated this state of affairs. Only in a few places, such as Thessalonica and Constantinople itself, were there solidly established and well-endowed academies for the further education of Greek Christians. Those exceptional Orthodox clergymen who showed interest in and talent for theological debate were, for the most part, educated on Italian-occupied islands, such as the Ionian islands or Chios, or in Venice or elsewhere in the west. Others drew on western writings. Relations were warmest with the Protestant churches, since the hostility of the Orthodox priesthood towards the papacy remained intense. Reflecting on his observations of the Polish Catholics' persecution of Orthodoxy in the Ukraine in the 1650s, Archdeacon Paul of Aleppo wrote: "God perpetuate the empire of the Turks! For they take their impost and enter into no account of religion, be their subjects Christians or Nazarenes, Jews or Samaritans." In turning to Protestant thinking for arguments against the Church of Rome, Orthodox theologians were prone to absorb and transmit Protestant ideas. Thus the patriarch Cyril Lukaris presented Calvinist ideas on predestination and justification by faith alone in his *Confession* (solemn statement of faith) which was printed in Geneva.

As in Russia, so in the Orthodox Balkans, there were strong bonds of affinity between the parish priest and his village community: often he was a local man speaking, in every sense, the same language as the villagers, and himself engaging in some degree of farming. The great human concerns of birth, death and fertility in both reproduction and the harvest continued to evoke practices which had their origins in pagan antiquity—the use of marriage crowns at weddings; the placing of money in a grave (an obol for Charon); the funeral meal. There was a profusion of local saints, who were regarded as personal protectors and even "friends" of the communities which celebrated their feast days and venerated their icons, rustic counterparts, so to speak, of St Demetrius of Thessalonica and the Mother of God of Blachernae, protector of Constantinople. Their numbers were augmented from time to time by "New Martyrs," Orthodox Christians who had fallen foul of the Turks. Saints were venerated by annual festivals (*panegyreis*), and these were one of the most vital expressions of popular Christianity in the Balkans. It is difficult to find much evidence that discipline was effectively imposed on the local congregations from above. Diocesan bishops varied greatly in personal qualities but were almost always handicapped by want of means. To a large extent, local parishes would seem to have been self-regulating, with all the abuses and irregularities which such a state of affairs invites. Perhaps the most significant binding thread running through the Orthodox lands are individuals whom we have encountered at many earlier stages of our survey: the monks, especially the monks of Athos.

Mount Athos

Mount Athos had early come to terms with the fact of Turkish overlordship and in return received decrees recognizing its status as a self-governing monastic federation. Even these Turkish decrees describe it as "the country in which night and day the name of God is revered" and "a refuge for the needy and for travelers." During the 15th and 16th centuries much building work was done and some of the finest wall paintings were executed, for example those of the great Cretan painter Theophanes in the principal church of the Great Lavra about 1535. In the mid-16th century there was even a new monastery founded, Stavronikita, on the site of a long-abandoned monastery bearing the same name. Funds for this were provided by the patriarch of Constantinople, Jeremias I, who periodically visited the Holy Mountain. Several other patriarchs of the 16th and 17th centuries had close ties with Athos, making gifts to it, sometimes retiring there, and drawing educated and principled monks from it for promotion to bishoprics. It is true that Athonite monks' journeyings increased in the 17th century because of their need to raise funds: such of their lands as were not confiscated by the Turks were subjected to heavy taxes and arbitrary impositions. But the fund-raising missions were also the occasion for the monks to display relics and to offer in their own persons examples of extreme piety to the Orthodox laity. In 1734 the prince of Wallachia granted an annual payment to the house of Philotheou, on condition that once a year one of its relics, the right hand of St John Chrysostom, be sent to his principality by way of a blessing.

Such regular exhibitions of relics and miraculous icons brought ordinary people as well as rulers into contact with monks of Athos and, as they believed, with manifestations of the divine. They kept alight a sense of unity among the Orthodox which patriarchal institutions could seldom offer. The monks of Athos, and other monastic centers such as Patmos, the Nea Mone of Chios and Meteora, performed a similar, if humbler, role among the Orthodox of the Balkans and Asia Minor. Individual wandering monks traversed the countryside offering up prayers for those who requested them, preaching and sometimes exhibiting an icon or relic. They enjoyed great popular esteem.

So monks continued to journey, even though many of Athos's monasteries fell into grave financial difficulties from the late 17th century onwards. On Athos itself the level of education declined and an attempt to remedy matters by establishing an academy there in the mid-18th century proved unsuccessful. The ignorance of monks and priests is a theme which becomes almost a cliché in 18th- and 19th-century travelogues. One of the most vivid accounts of the monks' indifference to books and learning was written by Robert Curzon, who toured Athos in quest of manuscripts in 1837. When he requested "a loose leaf of very ancient uncial Greek characters" which he found in one of the monasteries' libraries, the abbot obliged: "'Certainly . . . What do you want it for?' My servant suggested that perhaps it might be useful to cover some jam pots or vases of preserves which I had at home. 'Oh!' said the [abbot], 'take some more', and without more ado, he seized upon an unfortunate thick quarto manuscript of the Acts and Epistles and drawing out a knife cut out an inch thickness of leaves!" The monks' "ignorance" was in part deliberate: knowledge superfluous to the understanding of the essentials of the faith was considered idle and even dangerous. But some Athonite monks did continue to work on the "inner" learning relevant to spirituality, while leaving aside the "outer" learning of which Byzantine monasticism had always been distrustful.

The Greek war of independence and secession of the Greek Church

The close associations of the Constantinopolitan patriarchate with Ottoman rule inevitably incurred reproach from those trying to shake off "the Turkish yoke." A wide social and cultural gulf

Above Greek Orthodox celebration of the Annunciation, Cyprus. The celebration of saints' days and other religious festivals involves the whole local community. That the laity make up "the Church" jointly with their priest is a central feature of Greek Orthodoxy. In larger communities these events are carefully organized. Icons or saints' relics are ceremonially borne through the streets, sometimes with military guards of honor. Even in modern times such festivals were often also the occasion of commercial fairs, music and dancing.

Right Ouzo for two. The Greek Orthodox priest is also friend and neighbor to his parishioners, especially in country districts. He can relax and discuss the harvest with them perhaps after teaching their children in the school, or tending his own plot of land.

Above right Ever-Holy Russia. Processions bearing icons on festival days occur in Russia too. Nikita Khrushchev lamented: "People are set in their ways and continue to believe in God despite all the evidence to the contrary." During World War II the Russian Orthodox Church was permitted to reopen some of its churches. In return, churchmen urged on Russian patriotism against the invaders. In the 1950s Khrushchev reversed the policy of tolerance, but repression has now somewhat eased.

Below Armenian churchmen conducting their Christmas service in Bethlehem. In nearby Jerusalem there is an Armenian quarter. The Armenians became Christian c.300. They rejected the definition of the nature of Christ promulgated by the Council of Chalcedon (451) (see above, p.32), and so were "heretics" in the eyes of the Byzantine Orthodox Church. Their Church is headed by the catholicos, who has resided at Echmiadzin (now in Soviet Armenia) since the 14th century. The Armenians have maintained their doctrine, Church and alphabet through much oppression.

Bottom Monks in one of the four surviving Coptic monasteries of the Wadi al-Natrun. This has been a sacred area since the days of the pharaohs, and monks have lived here for over 1600 years. There are perhaps 5 or 6 million Copts in Egypt, including many government officials and professional men.

yawned between ordinary Orthodox laymen and their parish priests and the patriarch and his senior officials. Many of the latter were Phanariots, at once frequenters of the Sublime Porte, urbane sophisticates with a taste for western ("Latin") ideas, and determined champions of the Greek language. The Phanariots and the Constantinopolitan patriarchs had exploited their influence with the sultans to secure for Greek-speakers many of the top offices in the hierarchies of the other patriarchates and churches under Ottoman sway—in Alexandria, Jerusalem, Antioch and the Balkans. Many Phanariots hoped for the establishment of a Greek empire on the Bosphorus ("the Great Idea"), and Phanariots were instrumental in bringing about the revolt in the principalities of Moldavia and Wallachia in 1821. In the same year the Constantinopolitan patriarch Gregory V was put to death, together with several of the senior prelates of his synod. But these deaths did nothing for the prestige of the patriarchate, whose reaction to the revolt had been one of ambivalence and, indeed, of formal condemnation. It was provincial churchmen and monks who emerged as the heroes of the subsequent war of independence. The bishops of the Peloponnese played a prominent part in it, and Metropolitan Germanus of Old Patras took the initiative in proclaiming the revolt in the northern Peloponnese. Monks of the Nea Mone monastery on Chios were involved in the insurrection, and the mutilated skulls still kept in the monastery are reminders of the Turks' savage suppression of the revolt on the island in 1822. Some 25 000 persons were massacred there. Monks and parish clergy figured in later revolts too, often to the point of death. For example, during the Cretan rising in 1866, the monastery of Arkadi, near Rethymnon, became the last stand of the local peasants. Rather than give in to the Turks, the abbot Gabriel set fire to the powder kegs, blowing up attackers and gallant defenders alike.

It is therefore unsurprising that when an independent Greek state emerged after 1828, its leaders determined that their Church should not be subject to the patriarch still under Ottoman rule in Constantinople. In 1833 the Protestant regent of the young king Otto I declared the Greek Church to be autocephalous, a situation which the patriarchate begrudgingly acknowledged 17 years later. The Greek Church's constitution was modeled on German Protestant lines, being strictly supervised by the state, whose "procurator" attended meetings of the Church's synods. The archbishop of Athens and all Greece presided over these meetings. Fundamental change in the constitution occurred only in 1967, when, by decree of the military junta, the Church was conceded a greater measure of independence from the state. The Church in Greece long benefited from state support, gaining considerable control over the content of education in state schools, while such movements as the Brotherhood of Life (*Zoe*) created a network of schools and orchestrated the piety of the educated laity. At village level, priests continued to be married men rooted in their communities. To this day the figure of the *papas* (priest) officiating in the holy liturgy, pruning his olive trees or chewing tobacco outside the taverna poses no contradiction to the majority of his flock.

The patriarchate in decline

The new kingdom of Greece was at first very small, comprising merely the Peloponnese, Attica and the region north of the Gulf of Corinth. Thus the majority of Orthodox Greeks continued to live under Ottoman rule and the Greek congregation of the Constantinopolitan patriarch remained large, and even contented. Kinglake observed in the 1830s that "the people, by their frequent migrations from the limits of the constitutional kingdom to the territories of the Porte, seem to show that, on the whole, they prefer 'groaning under the Turkish yoke'." But the Ottoman government's supervision of the patriarchate tightened, so as to avert any repetition of the events of 1821, and the patriarchate's prestige sank lower still. Moreover there was a basic lack of sympathy between Greek-speakers and Slavs, which the antagonism between their monasteries on Mount Athos reflected.

As the Ottoman regime crumbled, the various emergent Balkan nations withdrew their allegiance from the detested Constantinopolitan patriarchate. In 1879 the Serbian Church became autocephalous, one year after Serbia attained independence as a state, and 113 years after the suppression of its earlier patriarchal status. In 1920–22 the five scattered groups of Serbian dioceses were reunited under one Serbian patriarch, residing in Belgrade. The Bulgarian Orthodox bitterly resented the Greek church authorities' attempts to discourage worship in Slavonic. In 1870 the sultan himself acceded to Bulgarian demands for a separate church organization. The patriarch's response was promptly to excommunicate the Bulgarians, and this schism persisted until 1945, long after the creation of an independent Bulgarian state. In Romania, too, national independence cost the patriarchate its authority, and in 1885 it was obliged to recognize the autocephalous status of the Orthodox Church of Romania, which the Romanians had themselves proclaimed 20 years earlier.

The patriarchate's long enjoyment of the Ottoman sultan's favor was now rebounding against it with a vengeance. After the Greeks' decisive defeat in the Greco-Turkish War nearly all the Greeks of Asia Minor were transplanted to Greece in 1922 and the Church in Greece for the first time comprised a clear majority of Greek Orthodox souls. The patriarchate's congregation was, in effect, reduced to the Orthodox citizens of Istanbul. The remarkable personality of Patriarch Athenagoras I (1948–72) did something to protect the rights of the surviving churches and Christians in the once "God-protected city." But the honorary primacy which Constantinople still holds among the Orthodox patriarchates is now a very hollow one. The heart of Orthodoxy has shifted to the land of Greece and further afield to North America and Australia. The complex relations between the many communities of Greek, Bulgarian, Romanian, Russian and Serbian Americans await resolution, and tensions over the status, affiliations and jurisdictions of these churches run high. That Greek Orthodox Christianity still has compelling appeal is suggested not only by its vitality in the New World but also by the success of Greek Orthodox missionaries in East Africa in the 1960s and 1970s.

PART FIVE

THE CHRISTIAN TRADITION

Membership of the Church

Baptism. Jesus was baptized by John the Baptist in the river Jordan, and the Gospels describe how the Holy Spirit was seen hovering upon him in the form of a dove and a voice said, "This is my Son, in whom I am well pleased." Jesus' disciples practiced baptism from the earliest days of the Church, always using water as the outward and visible sign of what was happening spiritually and invisibly within, and always baptizing in the name of Father, Son and Holy Spirit. Baptism is the sign and seal of belonging to Christ and becoming a member of his body, the Church; and of the washing away of sin and its consequences and the beginning of a new life.

Confirmation. In Christian communities where children are baptized as infants there is a service of confirmation when they are old enough to make a profession of faith and to promise to renounce evil for themselves. Before coming to confirmation children (or adults, for confirmation can take place at any age) are taught about the Christian faith. The bishop conducts the confirmation service as a token of the candidate's membership of the whole Christian community. He lays his hands on the candidate's head.

Eucharist. Members of Christ's Church met together from the beginning as he had taught them to do, to celebrate the memorial he himself had instituted. At the Last Supper he ate with his disciples, he took bread, and when he had given thanks he broke it and gave it to his disciples, saying, "Take, eat. This is my body which is given for you." In the same way after supper he took the cup of wine and said, "Drink this, all of you. This is my blood of the new Covenant, which is given for you and for many, for the remission of sins." He told them to "do this in remembrance." This Holy Communion or the Lord's Supper, or the eucharist or mass, as different Christian communities call it, is shared by Christians everywhere as the sacrament of their redemption.

Ordination. The apostles became natural leaders of the early Christian community. Judas Iscariot, the betrayer who had committed suicide, was replaced. The community prayed for the guidance of the Holy Spirit and made their choice with his help. The principles then established have continued ever since in the process of finding leaders for the community. The individual who is to accept this special responsibility is "called" by the people of God as well as by God himself. In practice this means today a process of selection and training culminating in a service of ordination which emphasizes the people's part as well as the role of the Holy Spirit. In early centuries it often meant literally snatching promising young men and ordaining them forcibly. The ordained minister is able to act as a focus for the thanksgiving and prayers of the

Top This font, used to hold the water for baptism, shows the baptism of Jesus with the Father and the Holy Spirit above, and John the Baptist with his hand on his head.

Above This "paten," or plate used to hold the communion bread, shows Jesus giving first the bread and then the wine to his disciples.

Right The penitent kneels in the "confessional." The priest to whom he is confessing cannot see him, so he can go ahead in confidence and without embarrassment.

Below These deacons, wearing stoles diagonally across their bodies, are being ordained to the priesthood. They have served for a year as ministers in parishes, but until they are priests they cannot preside at the Holy Communion or declare God's forgiveness to those who repent of grave sins.

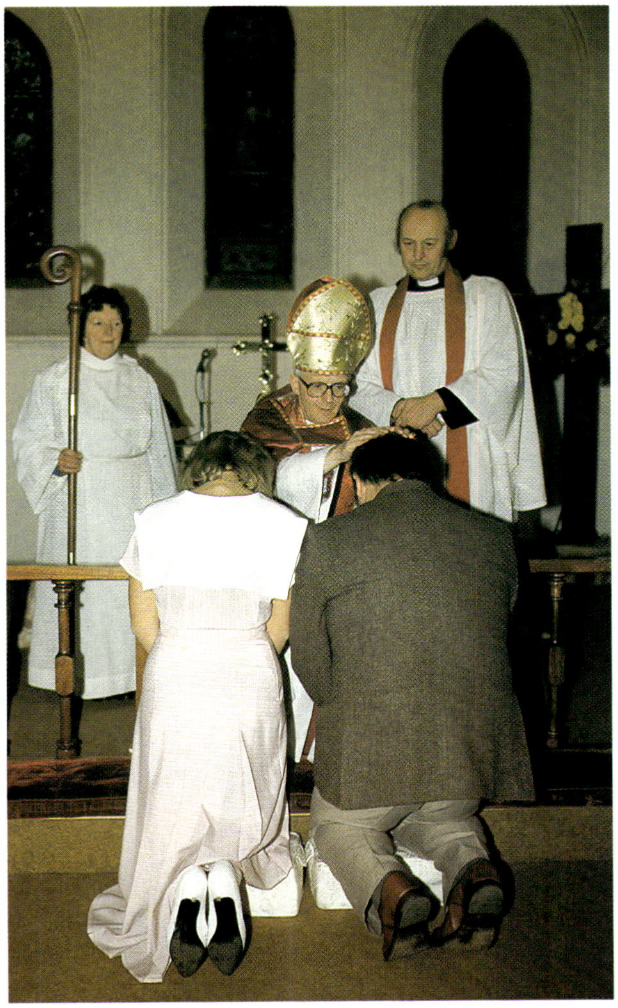

Left The bishop is seen here laying hands on a candidate during a service of confirmation.

Bottom left A marriage taking place in a Greek Orthodox church.

Bottom right A priest helping a dying soldier on the battlefield to die at peace with God.

community, to preside at Holy Communion and to declare God's forgiveness to those who repent.

Marriage. Marriage is celebrated by the Church as an institution ordained by God and as an image or reflection of the union of Christ and his people. (The Church is the Bride of Christ.) It is the beginning of a family in which the Church exists in miniature.

Confession. The Christian falls into sin again and again after he has been cleansed of sin by baptism. When that happens he breaks his relationship of trust with God and with the community. From Carolingian times in the west the practice of confessing one's sins regularly to a priest became established. In that way the penitent could show that he was sincerely sorry, and if he humbly accepted the penance the priest gave him to do, he would receive absolution, the reassurance that God had forgiven him. Roman Catholic practice continues in this way today, although in the USA and elsewhere it is less conscientiously adhered to than in southern Europe. Most Protestants follow the line taken by the 16th-century reformers, that all that is necessary is to confess one's sins to God.

Unction. When he is seriously ill, and especially when he is near to death, the Christian may be given the comfort of the Church's fellowship. He commends his spirit to God and repents of his sins and the priest gives him absolution and anoints him with consecrated oil. This practice, ancient in the Roman Catholic Church, is not always adhered to formally in Protestant communions; but many have found comfort in having an ordained minister to talk to.

The Church Interior

The church furnishings on these pages are typical of western church buildings in the Roman Catholic communion, and of some Anglican churches. Many Anglican and most of the Protestant churches in the west have much simpler furnishings, but the important things are always there: a font for baptisms, a table or altar for Holy Communion, a pulpit or platform for preaching, and usually a lectern. These represent the most important actions of worship, the ministry of the sacraments and the ministry of the Word.

In Orthodox churches the *iconostasis* or icon-stand is a very important feature. The members of the congregation say prayers there and kiss the pictures in veneration. Today western churches usually have seats, although in the past it was usual for the congregation to stand and even to walk about while the service was going on.

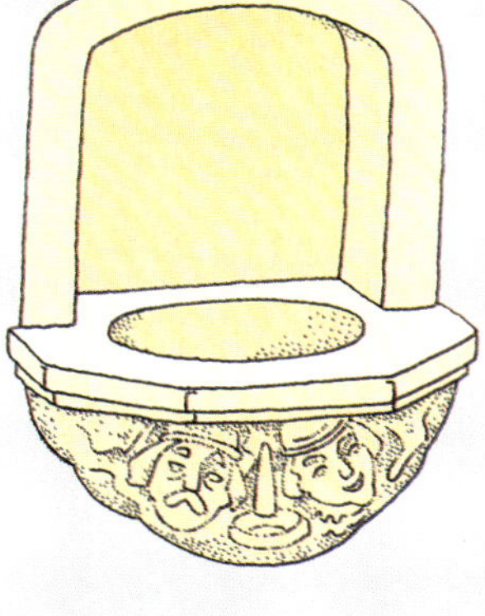

Above The stoup is a small basin near the door of the church containing holy water. Those who enter sprinkle themselves, perhaps as a continuation of the tradition of ancient Rome. There a fountain was placed in the entrance hall or *atrium* of the basilica so that those who came in could wash. The action symbolizes washing away the world and coming afresh to God.

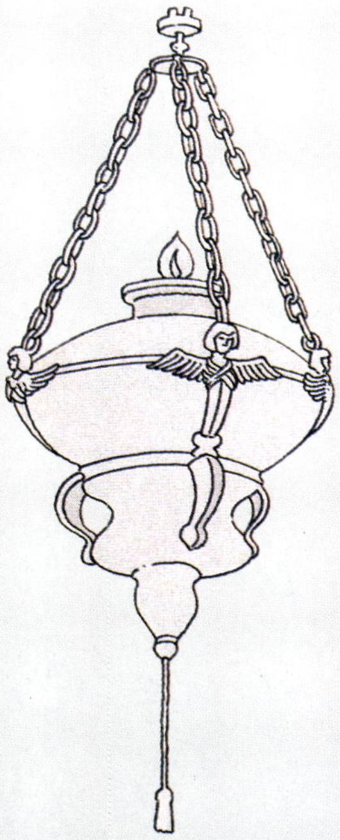

Left The ambry cupboard is built into the wall of the church and houses the vessels used in Holy Communion, or is used for relics or books. In some Anglican churches the bread and wine which have been consecrated are kept or "reserved" there ready to take to the sick who cannot come to the Holy Communion service. The ambry lamp is lit to show the sign of divine presence there.

Above The pulpit is a structure raised above the floor of the church on which the preacher stands to deliver his sermon. In early Christian times preaching by the bishop was usually done from his bishop's seat or *cathedra*. The pulpit began to be used in the Middle Ages.

Above The piscina, a niche in the wall beside the altar, is of medieval origin. It is used to hold water for the washing of the priest's hands when he celebrates Holy Communion, and for the washing of the vessels used to hold the bread and the wine.

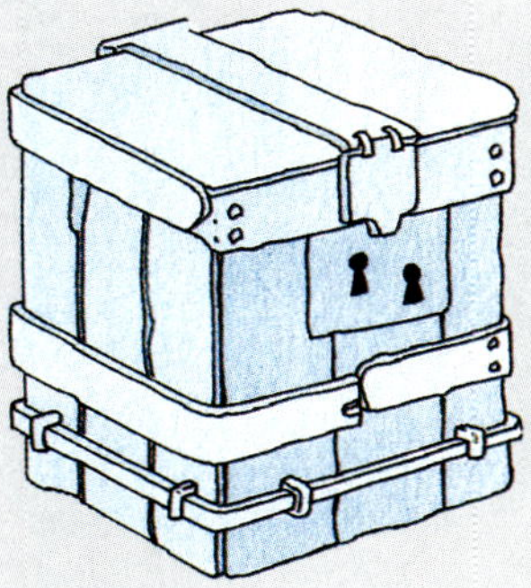

Above The alms box is for contributions for the poor, or (often today) for the upkeep of the church building. It is for free gifts given out of piety.

Right This altar has behind it a screen or reredos. Such backgrounds to an altar may have pictures or Christian symbols or make take the form of a rich hanging or a plain curtain. There are especially rich examples at Burgos in Spain and (of metalwork and jewels) in St Mark's in Venice. In front of the altar are the rails where the congregation comes to kneel to receive communion.

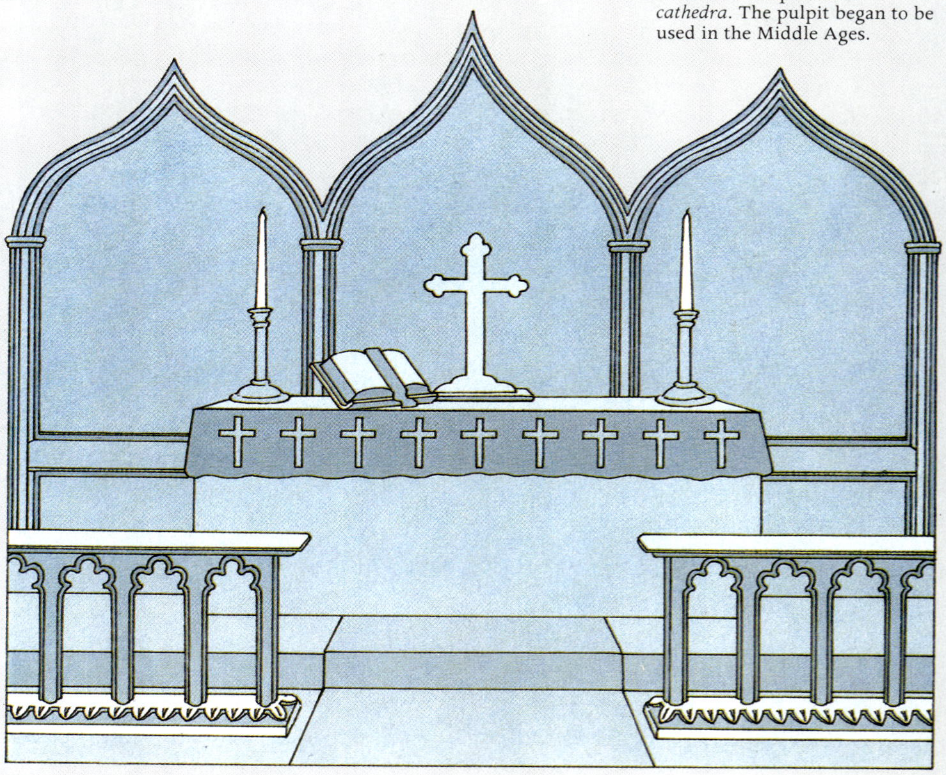

Below A cathedral is a church where a diocesan bishop has his "seat" or *cathedra*. It is usually larger and grander than a local parish church. The ground plan of this western cathedral takes the basic shape of a cross. The nave runs the length of the building (probably from *navis*, a "ship" in Latin, symbolizing the church seen as the vessel in which souls float safe from the seas of the world). Across run the transepts. Other parts have often been added on over the centuries—a cloister for monks or clergy to walk in, a Lady Chapel, or chapel dedicated to the Virgin Mary.

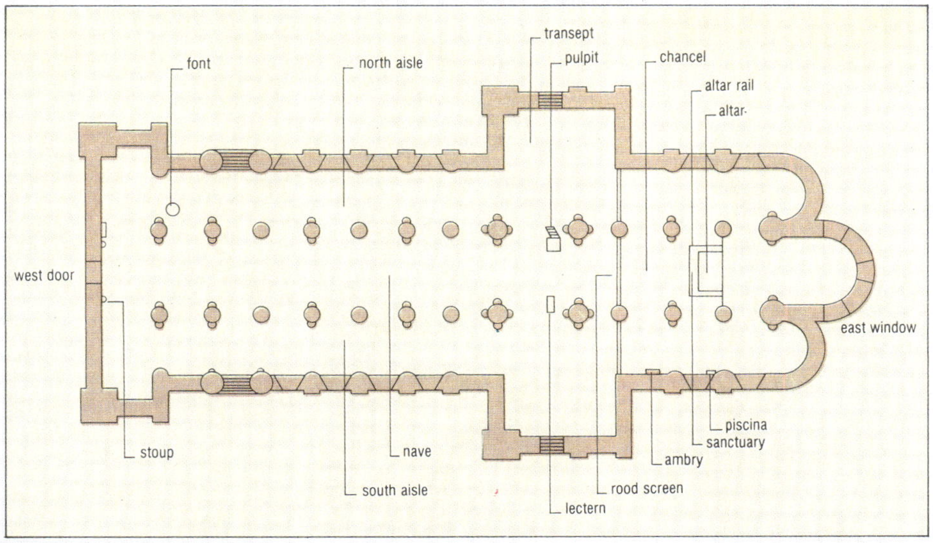

Below The lectern, often supported by an eagle, the symbol of St John the Evangelist, is used to rest the Bible on when readings are given during worship. Traditionally, at Matins and Evensong there are lessons from the Old and New Testaments. At Holy Communion lessons are read from an Epistle and a Gospel.

Right The font holds the water used in baptism, and is sometimes covered so that the water is kept pure. In the Early Church baptism was usually done by total immersion and the font was a large basin in which the candidate could stand. The beginning of infant baptism as the general pattern in the west from the 4th century made it convenient to have a smaller font raised above the ground.

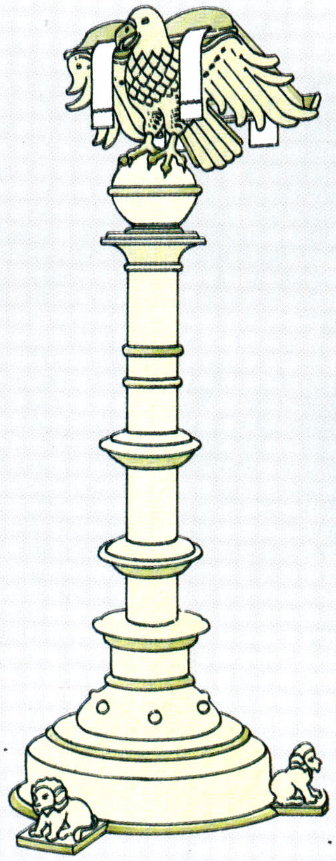

Above The rood screen stands in front of the area where the choir sits, and separates it from the main body of the church where the congregation assembles. It is named after the "rood" or cross which it supports.

The Church Exterior

The architecture of Christian churches has taken diverse forms. The earliest churches were simply people's homes. When larger buildings were needed the pagan temples were sometimes taken over, and the style even of some newly built churches of the Roman empire reflects this architectural heritage. In the east there has always been a tendency to concentrate decoration on the inside of the church. In the west the nave has been the central feature of the plan, with cross-pieces or "transepts" forming the sign of a cross on the ground, and with decoration inside and out. In old churches there is often architectural diversity within a single building, medieval and 18th-century monuments side by side. This diversity, although sometimes aesthetically incongruous, is nevertheless a witness to the continuity of faith in the community, the desire of succeeding generations to make their contribution to God's house. Church architecture has always striven to give God glory, and to that end it has sometimes gone to extremes of design or fantasy, and in periods when most people lived in poverty and small spaces churches have been vast and extravagant edifices. But—as here—they are also small and unpretentiously simple houses of God.

Below Here an Eskimo church in northwest Canada follows the "igloo" shape of local tradition. The building proclaims its function by the cross at the apex and the statue of the Virgin over the door but otherwise adapts its exterior to a form suited to the rigors of the prevailing climatic conditions. Roman Catholic missions have been active in the area since the mid-19th century.

Right A tiny church in the Dolomites, southern Austria. Similar small churches or chapels were established in remote and mountainous areas along the major pilgrimage routes in several parts of Europe. Far removed from the great pilgrim centers with their grand churches and hospices, such simple buildings were founded by charitable laymen or clerics as refuges for weary travelers.

Left The great cathedral at Siena with its dome and striped decoration reflects the extravagance and urge to stretch technical possibilities to the limit which characterize high medieval church building. Begun on romanesque lines in 1196, the structure was soon modified to accord with the new Gothic style. In the 14th century plans were made to build a vast new cathedral south of the dome, turning the existing nave into a transept, but the plague of 1348, economic decline and political instability forced the Sienese to abandon the scheme and to complete instead the present, more modest church. The roof in the right foreground covers the abandoned cathedral's surviving arches.

Above right This American "glass" church in Los Angeles tries to capture in a modern medium the medieval concept of soaring architecture going up to heaven.

Right This Russian Orthodox cathedral at Kiev has the "onion" domes characteristic of the area.

Far right This modern pilgrim church in Germany caters for huge numbers as pilgrim centers did in the Middle Ages. Its design reflects its function.

Church Music

Above Instruments were forbidden in the early Christian services, but by the Middle Ages the organ had been accepted and was used in those churches that could afford it. The 13th-century Rutland Psalter shows it being played by David, while a servant works the bellows with his feet. Above the organ is a set of chimebells for special occasions, and to the left another minstrel plays the symphony, which may have been used in churches that did not have an organ.

Right In a 15th-century copy of *The Mirror of the Life of Christ* we see a Corpus Christi procession outside a small church. A priest carries the Blessed Sacrament, while other clerics walk in front and the congregation behind. Perhaps they are singing the hymn *Pange lingua*, which was specially composed for the feast by St Thomas Aquinas.

Above In contrast to the small village procession (*above left*), here we see an event in the city of Venice, Gentile Bellini's *Procession of the Cross in the Piazza San Marco*. The reliquary of the Cross is carried in the foreground, preceded by singers from St Mark's Cathedral, together with musicians playing a harp, rebec and lute. To the right of the picture can be seen a group of trumpets, sackbuts and shawms, all loud instruments which would hold the congregation's singing together, in contrast to the softer group playing with the special choir.

The earliest music of the Church was for hymns and psalms, with the gradual addition of settings for parts of the mass and the office as they evolved. These were in the plainsong style named Gregorian Chant for Pope Gregory I, to whose reign (590–604) their organization is attributed. Meanwhile other rites such as that of Byzantium continued to preserve their own musical traditions.

From the 9th century onwards we can trace the growth of polyphony, in which two or more parts are sung together. This was enriched by the appearance of the bass voice around 1450, and it eventually became so intricate that, at the Reformation, Martin Luther characterized his church music by simple tunes known as chorales, which could be sung by the whole congregation.

The multiplicity of communions since that time allows us to single out only a few musical landmarks, such as the treatment of Lutheran chorales by Praetorius, Schütz, Bach, Brahms and Reger; the Church of England anthems by Purcell, Handel, Parry and Stanford; and the Catholic masses of Palestrina, Monteverdi, Haydn, Mozart and Beethoven.

The situation today is very complex, with a marked tendency towards music of a popular style. However, many churches of different denominations use music of all periods relevant to their liturgy, and still encourage the composition of magnificent new works to the glory of God.

Left A method of performance much used at St Mark's, namely polychoral singing and playing in which different groups performed in separate galleries. The style spread to Germany, and is shown here on the title page of *Theatrum Instrumentorm* by Praetorius, although he had already used it in his *Musarum Sioniarum* of 1606/7. There are three "choirs," each directed by a conductor, and the one on the left is clearly singing at the same time. Each group contains an organ, that on the left being accompanied by instruments of the violin family, that on the right by cornetts, and that below by sackbuts, while a man near them holds a very large reed instrument.

Left A typical 19th-century English church band is represented in this painting of *A Village Choir* by Thomas Webster, who was himself a chorister at the Chapel Royal. He shows us singers of most age groups, with the choirmaster in the center, and, in the absence of an organ, musicians playing a clarinet, bassoon and cello. Such instruments can still be found in country churches today, as mementos of the past, and they bring to mind the scenes evoked in Thomas Hardy's *Under the Greenwood Tree*. It is a pity, however, that Webster did not include in this band the serpent, which features in Hardy's book and was used in churches for the best part of three centuries.

Above In contrast to Webster's painting is the photograph of two girls singing near the altar in the Catholic church at Stapleton, Nebraska. They are accompanying themselves on guitars, and their music is clearly devotional. When played in this way, the guitar does add its own enrichment to the liturgy, but when it is performed in a manner too reminiscent of the secular world, its use can cause friction within a parish.

The Christian Calendar

This calendar for the year 2000 shows the major feasts and seasons of the Christian year as generally celebrated. Its structure is best explained by its origins. In the apparently chaotic successiveness of daily experience, human beings find order and meaning for their lives by giving particular significance to certain times (as also to certain places). The recurrence of the seasons, the solar year of $365\frac{1}{4}$ days, the lunar month of $29\frac{1}{2}$ days, provide a natural framework. The old Roman calendar was based on the solar year with 1 January as New Year's Day. The Old Testament calendar was lunar, the first month (Nisan) in the spring. As 12 lunar months fall short of the solar 365 days by almost 11 days, a thirteenth month had to be added every two or three years. The Roman solar year also had to add a day to February every fourth or "leap" year.

The Christian calendar combined the solar year, giving "fixed" dates, with the lunar (movable) feasts. It starts from the Gospel narrative: Jesus was crucified on Friday (the "preparation"), and raised from the sepulcher on Sunday (called in the New Testament "the first day of the week" or "the Lord's day"). The weekly eucharistic celebration is first a memorial of the Resurrection as key to interpreting the divine redemption of the Passion. The Christian insistence on Sunday, which by the 4th century was coming to inherit some of the rest-day aspects of the Jewish Sabbath on Saturday, made the week, a unit of time unknown to Greco-Roman society, a standard period in the Mediterranean world. This was reinforced by astrologers' calculations that each day was controlled by the planets in the order Sun, Moon, Mars, Mercury, Jupiter, Venus, Saturn. The Church fought an only partly successful battle against planetary names, to which northern barbarians like the English and Germans remained attached.

Day	January	February	March	April	May	June
1						*Ascension*
2		Purification of BVM				
3					Invention of the Cross	
4						
5						
6	EPIPHANY					
7						
8			*Ash Wednesday*			
9				*Passion Sunday*		
10						
11						*WHIT SUN* *(Pentecost)*
12						
13						
14						
15						
16				*Palm Sunday*		
17						
18						
19						
20		*Septuagesima Sunday*		*Maundy Thursday*		
21				*Good Friday*		
22				*Holy Saturday*		*Corpus Chr*
23				EASTER SUNDAY		
24						St John Baptist
25	Conversion of St Paul		Annunciation (Lady Day)			
26						
27				St Mark		
28						
29						SS Peter and Paul
30				*Orthodox Easter*		
31						

Jesus died on, or the day after, the Passover. "Christ our passover is sacrificed for us," said St Paul. So the Passion has a memorial annually as well as weekly. After long controversy, the celebration was put not on the Jewish Passover but on a Sunday at or up to a week after full moon after the vernal equinox (21 March). This broad principle called for astronomical expertise to reconcile solar and lunar years; many Christian computists produced tables based on different cycles. Few bishops ever understood the principles governing the calculation; but at times the differing calculations were used as controversial weapons in disagreements on other topics, such as jurisdiction or divergences between Greek east and Latin west. The Easter table of a monk from the Danube delta living in Rome, Dionysius Exiguus (525 AD), first reckoned dates from Christ's birth, and so created our "Christian era." Other chronographers soon

Left A medieval calendar for the month of June from the Hours of Nicolas von Firmian, probably made in Flanders c.1500. The red-letter days designate the celebrations of local saints.

Right A procession of palms en route to St Peter's Square, Rome, on Palm Sunday.

Day	July	August	September	October	November	December
1					All Saints	
2	itation BVM				All Souls	
3						*First Sunday in Advent*
4				St Francis of Assisi		
5						
6		Transfiguration				
7						
8			Nativity of BVM			Conception of BVM
9						
10						
11						
12						
13						
14			Holy Cross			
15		Assumption of BVM				
16						
17						
18				St Luke		
19						
20						
21			St Matthew			
22						
23						
24		St Bartholomew				
25	James					CHRISTMAS
26						St Stephen, protomartyr
27						St John the Evangelist
28						
29			Michaelmas			
30						
31						

The Christian Year 2000 AD

Movable seasons and feasts:
- Advent
- Lent
- Easter

EASTER SUNDAY

Palm Sunday

Fixed seasons and feasts:
- Christmas

EPIPHANY

St Luke

doubted if he had correctly reckoned the date of the Incarnation (a dispute that still continues), but the defense by Bede insured Dionysius' success. Bede was anxious to bring all the British churches to keep Easter on the Roman date.

On the date of Easter depended other movable feasts – Pentecost 50 days later; Ascension 10 days before that; the preparatory fast before Easter, at first the seven days of "Holy Week" beginning on Palm Sunday, but then 40 days, during which the bishop catechized candidates for baptism and penitents prepared for restoration to communion on Maundy Thursday. Baptism was given in the Early Church at the vigil of Easter or Pentecost. Characteristically, the biblical notion of a day lasting from evening (6 p.m.) to evening (Genesis 1:5) was continued from synagogue practice.

Devout Jews fasted twice a week (Monday, Thursday: Luke 18:12), Christians on Wednesday and Friday, the days of Christ's betrayal and Crucifixion, but the Wednesday fast dropped out; the two days remained in western custom occasions for litanies often chanted in procession. Abstinence and prayer also became normal not only before Easter but in Advent before Christmas.

The Nativity of Christ was being celebrated in the west by about 300 on 25 December, the winter solstice. In the east 6 January was celebrated as a feast of Christ's baptism but also of his Incarnation. During the 4th century the west accepted the feast of 6 January, retaining its Greek name "Epiphany" or manifestation; it became associated with the Magi coming to Bethlehem. Christ's birth placed on 25 December led to a memorial of the Annunciation on 25 March (from the 5th century), and John the Baptist's birth (Luke 1:35) on 24 June to rival pagan celebrations of the solstice.

Other feasts developed on 6 August for the Transfiguration, on 14 September for the Cross, and, for the Virgin Mary, on 15 August ("Falling asleep" or "Assumption," celebrating her place in the communion of saints), 8 September (birth), 8 December (conception). So also the honor of the apostles (e.g. Peter and Paul, 29 June, etc.), and of martyrs (Stephen, 26 December), including many with regional honor such as Stanislaus in 11th-century Poland, Thomas Becket of Canterbury in 12th-century England, Ursula of Cologne, Brigitta of Sweden, and others. Sometimes saints have become so popular that authority has had to check the festivals and cut down the calendar, as occurred in the Roman Catholic Church in 1570 and 1969. Of churches influenced by the Reformation, only those of England and Sweden retained saints' days; 25 December was long not observed by Puritans for being originally pagan.

Apart from Patrick among the Irish, and Anne in French Canada, Mary is honored in Catholicism, Orthodoxy and much Anglicanism as no other exemplary figure, except her Son. She is honored not for herself but for the child she bore.

The Bishops of Rome

Traditionally, the first bishop of Rome was the apostle Peter, the "rock" on whom Christ said that he would found his Church (John 1: 35–42). The Roman bishopric always had a special place for this reason and because as mistress of the Roman empire the city of Rome made a natural center for the Christian community in the west. Rome did not hold an unchallenged supremacy everywhere in Christendom. Its claim to primacy was disputed in the east throughout the Middle Ages and is not now recognized by Orthodox Christians. The bishops of Rome were forced by political circumstances into finding a *modus vivendi* with the Roman emperors. Constantine and Sylvester I brought a Christian empire together for the first time. Charlemagne tried to revive the Constantinian pattern as he understood it by setting up a special relationship with Pope Hadrian. Sylvester II (999–1003) chose his papal name in order that he and the Emperor Otto III might meet the year 1000 as a second Constantine and Sylvester at the end of the world. The world did not end, however, and not long after Sylvester's death the balance of power shifted. Gregory VII (1073–85) pressed for reform which would make the pope the supreme power in the world and secular rulers his subordinates. The papal claim to plenitude of power led to serious corruptions in the course of the later Middle Ages and contributed to the resentments which brought about the Reformation.

until c.64	St Peter	514–23	Hormisdas	827–44	Gregory IV
	Linus	523–26	John I	844–47	Sergius II
	Anacletus	526–30	Felix IV (III)	847–55	Leo IV
fl. c. 96	Clement I	530–32	Boniface II	855–58	Benedict III
	Evaristus	533–35	John II	858–67	Nicholas I
	Alexander I	535–36	Agapetus I	867–72	Hadrian II
c.117–27	Sixtus I	536–37	Silverius	872–82	John VIII
c.127–37	Telesphorus	537–55	Vigilius	882–84	Marinus I
c.137–40	Hyginus	556–61	Pelagius I	884–85	Hadrian III
c.140–54	Pius I	561–74	John III	885–91	Stephen V (VI)
c.154–66	Anicetus	575–79	Benedict I	891–96	Formosus
c.166–75	Soter	579–90	Pelagius II	896	Boniface VI
175–89	Eleutherius	590–604	Gregory I	896–97	Stephen VI (VII)
189–98	Victor I	604–06	Sabinianus	897	Romanus
198–217	Zephyrinus	607	Boniface III	897	Theodore II
217–22	Callistus I	608–15	Boniface IV	898–900	John IX
222–30	Urban I	615–18	Deusdedit or	900–03	Benedict IV
230–35	Pontian		Adeodatus I	903	Leo V
235–36	Anterus	619–25	Boniface V	904–11	Sergius III
236–50	Fabian	625–38	Honorius I	911–13	Anastasius III
251–53	Cornelius	640	Severinus	913–14	Lando
253–54	Lucius I	640–42	John IV	914–28	John X
254–57	Stephen I	642–49	Theodore I	928	Leo VI
257–58	Sixtus II	649–55	Martin I	928–31	Stephen VII (VIII)
259–68	Dionysius	654–57	Eugenius I	931–35	John XI
269–74	Felix I	657–72	Vitalian	936–39	Leo VII
275–83	Eutychianus	672–76	Adeodatus II	939–42	Stephen VIII (IX)
283–96	Caius	676–78	Donus	942–46	Marinus II
296–304	Marcellinus	678–81	Agatho	946–55	Agapetus II
308–09	Marcellus I	682–83	Leo II	955–64	John XII
310	Eusebius	684–85	Benedict II	963–65	Leo VIII
311–14	Miltiades	685–86	John V	964–66	Benedict V
314–35	Sylvester I	686–87	Cono	965–72	John XIII
336	Mark	687–701	Sergius I	973–74	Benedict VI
337–52	Julius I	701–05	John VI	974–83	Benedict VII
352–66	Liberius	705–07	John VII	983–84	John XIV
366–84	Damasus I	708	Sisinnius	985–96	John XV
384–99	Siricius	708–15	Constantine	996–99	Gregory V
399–401	Anastasius I	715–31	Gregory II	999–1003	Sylvester II
402–17	Innocent I	731–41	Gregory III	1003	John XVII
417–18	Zosimus	741–52	Zacharias	1004–09	John XVIII
418–22	Boniface I	752	Stephen II	1009–12	Sergius IV
422–32	Celestine I	752–57	Stephen II (III)	1012–24	Benedict VIII
432–40	Sixtus III	757–67	Paul I	1024–32	John XIX
440–61	Leo I	768–72	Stephen III (IV)	1032–44	Benedict IX
461–68	Hilarus	772–95	Hadrian I	1045	Sylvester III
468–83	Simplicius	795–816	Leo III	1045	Benedict IX
483–92	Felix III (II)	816–17	Stephen IV (V)	1045–46	Gregory VI
492–96	Gelasius I	817–24	Paschal I	1046–47	Clement II
496–98	Anastasius II	824–27	Eugenius II	1047–48	Benedict IX
498–514	Symmachus	827	Valentine	1048	Damasus II

1048–54	Leo IX	1389–1404	Boniface IX	1831–46	Gregory XVI
1055–57	Victor II	1404–06	Innocent VII	1846–78	Pius IX
1057–58	Stephen X	1406–15	Gregory XII	1878–1903	Leo XIII
1059–61	Nicholas II	1417–31	Martin V	1903–14	Pius X
1061–73	Alexander II	1431–47	Eugenius IV	1914–22	Benedict XV
1073–85	Gregory VII	1447–55	Nicholas V	1922–39	Pius XI
1086–87	Victor III	1455–58	Callistus III	1939–58	Pius XII
1088–99	Urban II	1458–64	Pius II	1958–63	John XXIII
1099–1118	Paschal II	1464–71	Paul II	1963–78	Paul VI
1118–19	Gelasius II	1471–84	Sixtus IV	1978	John Paul I
1119–24	Callistus II	1484–92	Innocent VIII	1978–	John Paul II
1124–30	Honorius II	1492–1503	Alexander VI		
1130–43	Innocent II	1503	Pius III	*Antipopes*	
1143–44	Celestine II	1503–13	Julius II	217–c.235	Hippolytus
1144–45	Lucius II	1513–21	Leo X	251	Novatian
1145–53	Eugenius III	1522–23	Hadrian VI	355–65	Felix II
1153–54	Anastasius IV	1523–34	Clement VII	366–67	Ursinus
1154–59	Hadrian IV	1534–49	Paul III	418–19	Eulalius
1159–81	Alexander III	1550–55	Julius III	498, 501–05	Laurentius
1181–85	Lucius III	1555	Marcellus II	530	Dioscorus
1185–87	Urban III	1555–59	Paul IV	687	Theodore
1187	Gregory VIII	1559–65	Pius IV	687	Paschal
1187–91	Clement III	1566–72	Pius V	767–69	Constantine
1191–98	Celestine III	1572–85	Gregory XIII	768	Philip
1198–1216	Innocent III	1585–90	Sixtus V	844	John
1216–27	Honorius III	1590	Urban VII	855	Anastasius
1227–41	Gregory IX	1590–91	Gregory XIV	903–04	Christopher
1241	Celestine IV	1591	Innocent IX	974, 984–85	Boniface VII
1243–54	Innocent IV	1592–1605	Clement VIII	997–98	John XVI
1254–61	Alexander IV	1605	Leo XI	1012	Gregory
1261–64	Urban IV	1605–21	Paul V	1058–59	Benedict X
1265–68	Clement IV	1621–23	Gregory XV	1061–72	Honorius II
1271–76	Gregory X	1623–44	Urban VIII	1080, 1084–1100	Clement III
1276	Innocent V	1644–55	Innocent X	1100–02	Theodoric
1276	Hadrian V	1655–67	Alexander VII	1102	Albert
1276–77	John XXI	1667–69	Clement IX	1105–11	Sylvester IV
1277–80	Nicholas III	1670–76	Clement X	1118–21	Gregory VIII
1281–85	Martin IV	1676–89	Innocent XI	1124	Celestine II
1285–87	Honorius IV	1689–91	Alexander VIII	1130–38	Anacletus II
1288–92	Nicholas IV	1691–1700	Innocent XII	1138, 1159–64	Victor IV
1294	Celestine V	1700–21	Clement XI	1164–68	Paschal III
1294–1303	Boniface VIII	1721–24	Innocent XIII	1168–78	Callistus III
1303–04	Benedict XI	1724–30	Benedict XIII	1179–80	Innocent III
1305–14	Clement V	1730–40	Clement XII	1328–30	Nicholas V
1316–34	John XXII	1740–58	Benedict XIV	1378–94	Clement VII
1334–42	Benedict XII	1758–69	Clement XIII	1394–1423	Benedict XIII
1342–52	Clement VI	1769–74	Clement XIV	1409–10	Alexander V
1352–62	Innocent VI	1775–99	Pius VI	1410–15	John XXIII
1362–70	Urban V	1800–23	Pius VII	1423–29	Clement VIII
1370–78	Gregory XI	1823–29	Leo XII	1425–30	Benedict XIV
1378–89	Urban VI	1829–30	Pius VIII	1439–49	Felix V

Bottom Julius II (1503–13) was a nephew of Sixtus IV who elevated him to the cardinalate and sent him on diplomatic missions. He was much involved in the politicking over the election of Innocent VIII and fled when his enemy Rodrigo Borgia was elected Alexander VI. After his return to Rome in 1503 he himself became pope. He was primarily a military and political leader at a time of corruption at Rome, but he was also an important patron of Renaissance art.

Below John XXIII (1958–63) was a pope of great holiness of life.

Far left St Peter, traditionally first bishop of Rome, a 6th- or 7th-century representation in the Vatican Museum in Rome.

Left Innocent III (1198–1216) from the "Holy Cave" at Subiaco, traditionally the place of Benedict of Nursia's hermitage. Innocent, lawyer and reformer, caused a monastery to be built around this cave.

Right Pius VII (1800–23) was a politician pope, who had the responsibility of the papacy during the period of the Napoleonic wars. He found time to be a patron of art and learning.

The Church and War

The Church has never been able quite to decide where to stand on the question of war. The image of the "soldier of Christ," fighting for the faith, is to be found from very early times. It should be remembered that most societies until the 20th century (and many still) have been of necessity military societies, in which the soldier's profession was respected and he was felt to do a valuable job for the state. Nevertheless, the shedding of blood has never seemed a Christian activity. St Augustine of Hippo tried to establish a difference between the "just" war, to repair damage done by invasion, and the war for gain or mastery. At the time of the crusades the idea of a holy war, a war backed by God and undertaken in his service, was widely accepted in the west, though never in the east. Although anti-Muslim crusades were preached with great vehemence, the preachers' arguments were often weak, and the enthusiasm with which westerners followed the call to arms may often have had more to do with local political considerations than with religious zeal. Renaissance debates on international law again raised the question of the "just" war which had preoccupied Augustine of Hippo. The morality of the colonial war, as waged by the Spanish *conquistadores* in the New World, exercised scholars like the 16th-century Salamancan theologian Fray Francisco de Vitoria, who saw that military subjugation of indigenous peoples could not be simplistically justified in terms of Christian rectitude vanquishing pagan error. Today the armed forces have chaplains, whose main function is to look after the spiritual welfare of soldiers. Many modern Christians in the developed countries of the west are pacifists, campaigning against war and arguing for nuclear disarmament. But elsewhere – in Northern Ireland for example—war goes on between Christian communities and Protestants and Catholics honestly believe themselves to be fighting somehow for God as well as for Ireland.

Above St George of Lydda, recently removed from the canon of saints in the Roman Catholic Church, stood for many centuries for the soldier of Christ fighting the dragon of sin (Satan). Here he is shown in an Ethiopian painting. The prototype of all such Christian warriors is St Michael, whose war in heaven against the "great dragon" is described in the Book of Revelation. By his appeal to chivalric values, St George became patron of England, Portugal and Aragon.

Below A celebration of the eucharist in the bombed and roofless church of St John, Waterloo, in London during World War II. Speedily restored at the end of hostilities, St John's served in 1951 as the church for the Festival of Britain, held to symbolize the country's recovery from the ravages of war. Elsewhere bomb-damaged churches have been deliberately left in their ruinous condition as a witness for later generations to the destruction caused by war. At Coventry the shattered walls of the ancient cathedral stand next to the postwar building.

Below This cartoon by Gillray in the late 18th century shows the archbishop of York leading an army of prelates who want to extend episcopal jurisdiction to the colonies—in order, the cartoonist implies, to add to their own wealth and power.

Below right Christian groups in the west in the 20th century have led pacifist movements; here a march through Oxfordshire in support of the Campaign for Nuclear Disarmament carries banners announcing the marchers' Christian commitment.

Below Soldiers in San Salvador resting on either side of a portrait of Christ while they wait to go on patrol duty. The icon exemplifies the widespread popular cult of the sacred heart of Jesus in the Roman Catholic Church. Ironically, in view of the soldiers' battle-readiness, its liturgical celebration focuses on the desire to make amends for man's injuries to divine love. A further unconscious irony in the military context is that the picture of Christ's revealed heart echoes the placing of a card as a target over the heart of a person about to be executed by firing squad.

The Church in the Town

In the urban society of the Roman empire where Christianity began, it flourished among slaves and—in time—among the richer and more influential. The "church in each place" needed to be where there was a center of population. We hear of society preachers in the Roman world, among them the British Pelagius, whom St Augustine attacked for his argument that people need only try hard in order to overcome sin in themselves. From the end of the Roman empire until the later Middle Ages towns were a subordinate feature of economic and social life in northern Europe. Only in Italy did something like the old pattern continue. The focus shifted to village communities and great landed estates, served often by a local monastery. As towns began to become important in northern Europe from the 12th century, articulate laymen could be heard, questioning the need for so many clergy and for so much ecclesiastical pomp. These dissidents appear all over Europe, with much the same complaints. An attempt was made to answer them, by the mendicant orders, the Franciscans and Dominicans. From the early 13th century they concentrated their preaching ministry in the towns and cities. The rise of the universities, also in towns and cities, reinforced the concentration of preaching and teaching there, and often the country districts were left very inadequately staffed by clergy, and subjected to misleading teaching by ill-educated curates. The dissolution of the monasteries in the England of Henry VIII marked a change which was to occur elsewhere later. The traditional responsibility of the Church to look after the poor and needy had long fallen principally to the monasteries, which were now no longer able to give help as they had done. Slowly experiments were tried in giving relief or welfare help. The Church became, and has remained, a caring and practical force in relieving the urban poor throughout the world. Missionaries have nursed and healed bodies as well as souls.

Below The two "military" religious orders, the Hospitallers and the Knights Templar, served in the Holy Land from the time of the crusades, living a monastic life while being active soldiers. They said their office while resting or preparing for battle, and saw themselves as literally soldiers of Christ.

Bottom The Church has run schools since the 6th century. Here is a school for young children in Italy where the teachers are nuns. Similar examples can be found today in Roman Catholic communities everywhere. The emphasis is upon a balance of moral and intellectual training, and worship plays a regular part in community life.

Left The town guilds were an early form of trade union or professional association, fiercely protective of both membership (a "closed-shop" policy was more or less universal) and standards. The masters of the guild judged the work of the young aspirant who had completed his seven years' apprenticeship and become a journeyman. Prosperous merchants and tradesmen and craftsmen liked to show off their wealth and success by building richly furnished churches, such as this one in Florence.

Below The church is shown here as the center of the life of the community. Market trading, housework, children's games, are going on around it and nuns and clergy mingle with the townspeople. Going in and out of the church is as natural as going in and out of one's home. The painting by Brueghel from which this detail comes is a portrayal of the tension this mingling produces between carnival and Lent.

Left Here a preacher is speaking to a large crowd in the open air in medieval Oxford. The artist has been careful to show that the mixed audience contains laity, monks and clergy. Such preaching could only be effective in the large centers of population that towns and cities provided. It was highly popular as entertainment as well as being edifying in intention.

Above The Salvation Army was the first Protestant movement to concentrate systematically upon the social and spiritual needs of the urban poor. Rousing hymn-singing to band music, military-style uniforms and a clear, simple message have always been its hallmarks, and it has the respect and trust of society's outcasts.

The Religious Life

Monasticism in its broadest sense encompasses a number of different ways of setting oneself apart from the world for God. The first monks got as far from the world as they could by going to live in the desert, either singly (as hermits) or in loosely knit communities which met from time to time for meals or worship. The first major figure to give order and system to these "desert saints" was Pachomius. The eremitical tradition continued strong in the east. In the west it was more usual for monks to live in communities. Here the strongest influence was the Rule of the 6th-century St Benedict of Nursia. From his Italian monastery his Rule spread and was taken as a basis for monastic life all over Europe until the 12th century. He provided practical rules, a balanced pattern of life and above all a system of government within the community which made it possible for the abbot to run it effectively. In the Benedictine communities the monks or nuns took vows of poverty, chastity and obedience and practiced "stability." The ideal (not always realized) was that they should remain for the rest of their lives in the community where they had taken their vows. The next major development came in the 12th and 13th centuries, when contemplative life was placed alongside active work in the community by the regular canons (priests living under a rule) and then the friars. The missionary work they were able to do developed in more recent times into medical, nursing and educational work in a vast number of "active" orders. Beside them the contemplatives have continued their life of prayer for the world.

Below The monastery of Mar Saba in Israel. Eastern, or Orthodox, monasticism has had a different pattern from monasticism in the west. The hermit life of the early Egyptian desert fathers has remained more central than hermit life in western monasticism. Many Orthodox monasteries allow all individuals to live according to their own pattern in separate cells, meeting for worship or for meals at intervals.

Above The monasteries of both east and west in the Middle Ages were responsible for much of the book production of the day. Here we see copying going on.

Right Bernard of Clairvaux had rare powers of oratory as a preacher. He attracted huge numbers of recruits to the Cistercian order from the moment he entered it in the early 12th century. The Cistercians lived lives of austere simplicity and great strictness, and strove to avoid the traps of gifts of wealth and lands into which the Benedictines had sometimes fallen.

Above The abbey of Cluny led a reform of Benedictine monasticism before the year 1000. Its success led to the spread of "Cluniac" houses, where the liturgy was lengthy and elaborate. In the early 12th century it seemed to many that Cluny itself was in need of reform and the Cistercians began to attract young men away from Cluny. The picture shows the

Below St Francis of Assisi founded an order of wandering preachers in the early 13th century. He was drawn by the simplicity of an "apostolic life," following Christ in poverty and humility. This representation of him not long after the beginning of the order emphasizes his deep spirituality.

Below right Benedict of Nursia was a leading monastic figure of a key period in the development of monasticism in the west. His Rule resembles others by contemporaries or near-contemporaries (particularly the anonymous one known as The Rule of the Master), but it proved widely acceptable as a balanced guide to the daily details of religious life. It became the Rule for almost all communities in the west for several centuries.

consecration of the abbey of Cluny by Pope Urban II in 1095.

Below There is a long tradition of women in the religious life; St Jerome wrote letters of guidance to Roman ladies living in their own homes under an ascetic rule in the 4th and 5th centuries. Abbesses in Carolingian times were often women of considerable learning. These young nuns taking their vows as brides of Christ have gone through a period as postulants and then as novices.

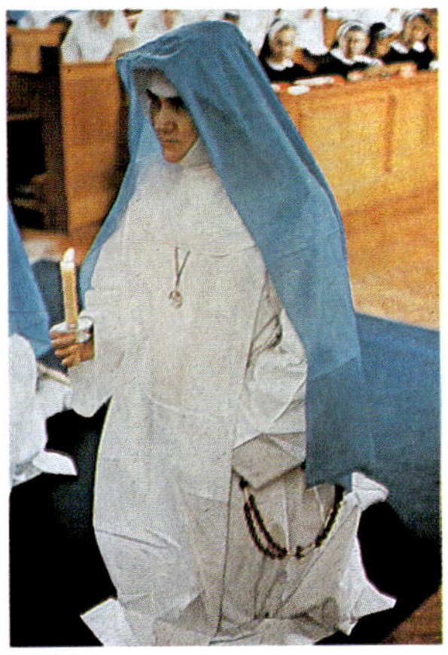

In the history of monasticism there have been periods of enthusiastic reform and experiment, when new orders have proliferated. The common theme of these movements towards a better quality of monastic life has been the urge to return to a *Vita Apostolica*, an "apostolic" way of life such as the disciples lived, simple and holy. The late 11th to 13th centuries, the 16th and the 19th centuries have been the most fruitful of these periods of multiplication of monstic orders. The major new division to arise has been between "contemplative" and "active" models of the religious life. The difference is one of emphasis and reflects different solutions to a dilemma discussed by monastic authors from at least the time of Cassian (c.360–435). The religious who retires from the world to dwell in the presence of God in silent concentration finds the practical necessities of daily life a distraction. Others see their dedication to God as issuing naturally in the work for the practical good of the world for which they are freed in this way. The monastic ideal has appealed to Christians in many communions. The following notes describe selected western religious orders.

Augustinian Hermits. This order was formed by Pope Alexander IV in 1256, in order to bring together a number of Italian congregations. They followed the Rule of St Augustine and began to work increasingly in towns. Luther belonged to one of the houses of this order.

Benedictines. Benedict of Nursia became the leader of a community at Monte Cassino in the late 6th century. His Rule proved to be the one almost universally used in the west until the 12th century. He placed an emphasis on a balance of labor, reading, prayer and worship in the monastic life, upon stability and on poverty, chastity and obedience.

Canons Regular. The Canons who served the cathedrals of the early Middle Ages were encouraged to submit themselves to a Rule, not one as restrictive of movement as the Benedictine Rule, but one which would give them orderliness of life. In the 12th century other orders of Canons, Premonstratensian and Victorine, served local communities as priests.

Capuchins. The Capuchins were an early 16th-century offshoot of the Franciscans, who sought to return to the primitive simplicity of the Franciscan ideal. Their arrival was resented by other Franciscans, but they proved immensely useful to the Church as missionaries.

Carmelites. The Carmelites began in the 12th century in Palestine, where they claimed to be continuing a tradition of hermit life on Mount Carmel going back to Elijah. After the crusading

period they moved into Europe and became widespread there.

Conventuals. Conventuals were Franciscans who opposed the view that poverty was essential during the long controversy of the 13th century and after on the question of poverty.

Dominicans. The Dominicans were founded in southern France and Spain in the early 13th century as an order of preachers to work against the heretics.

Franciscans. The Franciscans were founded in the same period as the Dominicans, also as an order of preachers, but with the ideal of living a simple, poor, wandering life as the apostles did, bringing people to the kingdom of God.

Jesuits. The Jesuits, or Society of Jesus, founded by Ignatius Loyola in the 1530s, had a military structure, with great emphasis on obedience. They became important as scholars and missionaries.

Marianists. The Marianists, or Society of Mary of Bordeaux, were founded in 1817, to stir up lukewarm faith by educational efforts. Members include laymen as well as priests.

Marists. The Marists, or Society of Mary, were founded in 1824 to do missionary and educational work. They have a special devotion to the Blessed Virgin and follow a Rule based on the Jesuits'.

Minims The Minims, or Friars Minor, are a 15th-century order, with some debt to the Franciscan ideal, and a tradition of extreme austerity.

Salesians. The Salesians, or Society of St Francis de Sales, were founded in 1859 to foster the vocations of young men for the priesthood and to act as educators.

Sisters of Charity. The Sisters of Charity, founded in the early 17th century by St Vincent de Paul, were the first order of women to work in the community for the care of the poor.

Trappists. Trappists are a reformed Cistercian order of strict observance who observe perpetual silence and unremitting austerity of life. They take their name from the house of La Trappe, where their Rule of life began in 1664.

Ursulines. The Ursulines, founded in 1535, are the oldest teaching order of women in the Roman Catholic Church.

The Image of Christ

The portrayal of Christ in Christian art is intended to convey what he means as Redeemer to believers. Ancient sarcophagi represent him as a sitting teacher with standing disciples around him, on the model of contemporary portrayals of philosophers with their pupils. In the art of the Greek east he is characteristically portrayed as the Pantocrator, the almighty who holds everything in his hand. He is frontally represented with a beard and rather long hair, often seated on the throne of majesty with the gospel book in one hand and holding up the other hand in benediction. In short, he is the lover of humanity and Savior. Other representations, as in the sarcophagus of Junius Bassus (359 AD) in the treasury at St Peter's, Rome, portray Christ as a young beardless figure. In the west the Crucifixion became the most usual scene from Christ's life on earth, together with the Nativity showing him as an infant with his mother.

The artist's object was not necessarily to portray a man in any naturalistic way, but somehow through the human form to convey the mystery of divine presence and indwelling, in short incarnation as God-Man.

Deep respect was accorded to the cloth held to be the towel offered to Christ on the way to Calvary by "Veronica," as also to the shroud of Turin with its exquisitely beautiful features.

Below This wooden 17th-century head of Christ from a sculpture of a Crucifixion in Quito, Ecuador, shows the crown of thorns and a face shadowed with pain and sorrow.

Bottom Christ carrying his Cross from a Spanish church at a convent in Cordoba. No attempt is made to clothe the figure appropriately, but the head expresses the suffering and weakness recorded in Scripture in contrast to the fine robe and gleaming halo.

Below This Byzantine Christ in majesty from Constantinople shows a somber and dignified figure blessing his people. The austere aloofness characteristic of portrayals of Christ in the eastern Church has a theological basis in the Orthodox stress upon the divine aspect of Christ's nature—as opposed to the tendency in western Christian art to stress Christ's identity with suffering mankind. Mosaics in a Byzantine church were generally arranged according to a rigid hierarchical scheme, with Christ as the Pantocrator in the central vault, overseeing all creation and transcending scenes of his earthly life depicted on the lower walls.

Below This taxi in Port-au-Prince, Haiti, shows a colorful West Indian rendering of Jesus riding into Jerusalem on a donkey. The festival procession follows the details of the biblical account with the laying of the palm fronds and garments in the street, but the artist has enlivened the scene with a touch of humor in the barking dog. Christ gazes directly out of the picture at the onlookers, challenging them with the question of whether they are ready to receive him.

Above A crude but powerful 7th-century German portrayal of Christ as a Frankish warrior from the Rhineland emphasizes the need of newly converted peoples to identify Christianity with the preoccupations of their own way of life. Similarly, Old English poetry very often speaks of Christ as a warrior chieftain, his disciples as his war troop and the Crucifixion as a battle.

Left A romanesque Christ in majesty from the cathedral at Toulouse carries a book with the legend "Peace be with you" and gives a blessing with the same gesture as the Byzantine Christ in majesty from Constantinople (*opposite*). Around the central seated figure are ranged the symbols of the four evangelists, the eagle of St John, the man of St Matthew, the lion of St Mark and the ox of St Luke.

Above A small, simple 11th-century ivory Crucifixion in romanesque style gives prominence to the head and the hands and feet. The expression has an inwardness which it owes to the rendering of the eyes.

Overleaf Della Robbia's sensitive face of Christ (c.1500) reflects the new consciousness of the fullness of his humanity which was developing in the later Middle Ages.

PART SIX

THE CHRISTIAN WORLD TODAY

CHRISTIANITY AND THE OTHER WORLD RELIGIONS

Christians believe in one God, the almighty and good creator of all things visible and invisible. This monotheistic faith, shared with Judaism and Islam but not the other world religions, creates a double reaction. On the one hand, monotheism stands in strong antithesis to folk and tribal religion, to regional and local cults, to "natural religion," through which the worshiper seeks earthly success, a fertile spouse and crops, mercantile prosperity and filial loyalty in children. On this side monotheism is or can be fiercely intolerant of compromises with polytheism. The three great monotheistic religions are all felt by their adherents to impose unqualified demands, so that their ethic is dominated by the concept of willing obedience. On the other hand, monotheism immediately reduces to merely relative status whatever is merely regional or transitory, and therefore puts a large Halt sign against identifications of Christendom with, say, Europe or "Western values." In criticism of the closed particularity of ancient Judaism, the apostle Paul asks: Is not God the God of all the earth? Therefore there is "that which may be known of God" (Romans 1: 19), accessible to all men by the light of creation, a universal capacity to respond to God which Christians believe the New Testament Gospel brings to realization. It follows that the religious aspiration of those who are not Christians is not negatively judged.

Early contacts with Judaism and Islam

From the start the Church was in debate with the Synagogue, where conservative minds resented the universalist missionary call of those fellow Jews who were convinced that in Jesus of Nazareth the expected Messiah of ancient prophecy had come. Once the Christians had decided that Gentile adherents of the people of God were not required to observe circumcision, Sabbath and the feasts of Jewish tradition, relations between Christianity and Judaism (as distinct from relations between Christians and Jews, though they tended to be confused) were made difficult and sensitive. In the Greek and Roman world the Christians were at once in touch with polytheism and idolatrous worship, which raised delicate questions of conscience. Step by step the Church captured ancient society, especially after the conversion of Constantine the Great (312), and by the end of the 4th century the government was closing pagan temples and forbidding polytheistic cult, to the anger of the many surviving pagan adherents who could concede that their local gods were inferior powers but thought that they needed to be propitiated if earthly prosperity was to be experienced.

Of the ancient religions with which Christianity contended, only Judaism effectively continues today. Contact between the Mediterranean world and the Indian subcontinent was limited to a few adventurous merchants. The Christian teacher Clement of Alexandria had heard of the Buddha. In the 8th century a biography of Buddha was adapted for Christian purposes to make the romance of Barlaam and Ioasaph, but there was little exchange of ideas in antiquity and early medieval times. There were early Christian missions to India, especially on the Malabar coast, soon associated with the name of the apostle Thomas, but we do not learn of theological or philosophical discussions. In the 14th century Greek monks on Mount Athos used techniques of prayer astonishingly like Yoga, but there is no evidence of Indian influence.

In the 7th century the impact of Muhammad's new religion of "surrender" to the will of God (Islam) imparted a fierce military zeal to the tribes of the Arabian peninsula. They had already discovered the weakness of the east Roman empire, which normally expected its eastern enemy to be in Persia. The Arabs or Saracens swept into Palestine, capturing Jerusalem (638) and Alexandria, betrayed to them by the patriarch (641). They moved relentlessly across the rich Roman provinces of North Africa, and finally across the straits of Gibraltar into Spain. Only the power of the Franks halted them at Poitiers in 732.

The loss of major provinces in which Christianity had long been dominant made believers ask agonizing questions about divine providence in human history. Islam incorporated a heretical form of Christianity, denying for example the reality of the Crucifixion of Jesus, but affirmed Jesus to be a prophet of God preparing the way for Muhammad. The Arab armies posed a huge military threat to Europe; Muslim scholars posed an ideological threat. Like the Christians, they had in the Koran a sacred book. They were monotheists. They set high value on Jesus, his mother Mary, the Old Testament prophets, the apostles. But Muhammad was sent as divine plenipotentiary: "There is no god but God and Muhammad is his prophet." The religion of Islam spread far beyond Arabia, into black Africa, Turkey, Persia, Pakistan; the Turkish Ottoman empire left enclaves of Muslims in Europe, still present in the Balkan peninsula. But Arabia was and remained the Muslim heartland, with pilgrimage to Mecca as the dream and obligation of every devout Muslim. Islam has represented both a claim to universality and a kind of Arab imperialism.

Contacts with the Muslims were initially military and commercial, but then passed into a cool coexistence and mutual attempts at conversion. The military threat helped to provoke the crusades, in which Europe sought to repel the Muslim Arabs with the religious objective of recovering the holy places of Christianity.

The Arabs read ancient Greek books on mathematics and science and, through Latin translations of Arabic adaptations of these books, Greek science passed to the medieval west, especially at Toledo

Above: Christianity and the other world religions
The spread of Christianity through the world reflects the political and economic successes of the nations which carried it abroad. The Roman empire carried Christianity to its furthest bounds; Spanish and Portuguese conquerors took it to the New World in the 16th century; British traders brought it to the Far East. But it also bears the marks of missionary endeavor: 19th-century Africa, for example. Christianity has been assimilated into many cultures but it has never been blurred in its identity with any other religion. Christians live in many parts of the world side by side with believers in the other great world religions, as the map shows. Numbers of believers can be only approximate, but the map indicates the broad distribution of the major religions in today's world.

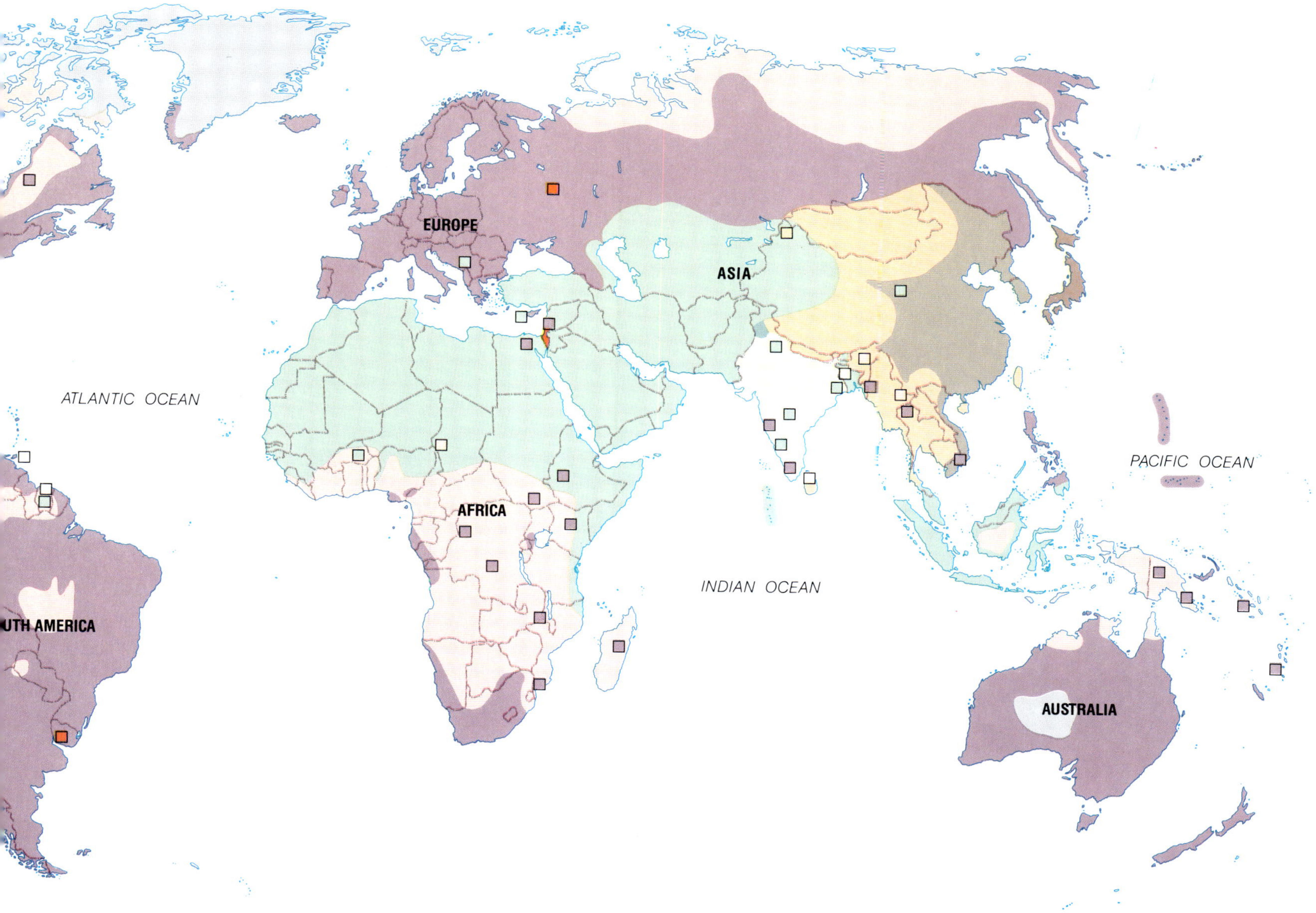

Right In this building in Los Angeles Christian and Jewish congregations both worship. They share the use of the building without joining in worship together, but they do so in amity and mutual respect.

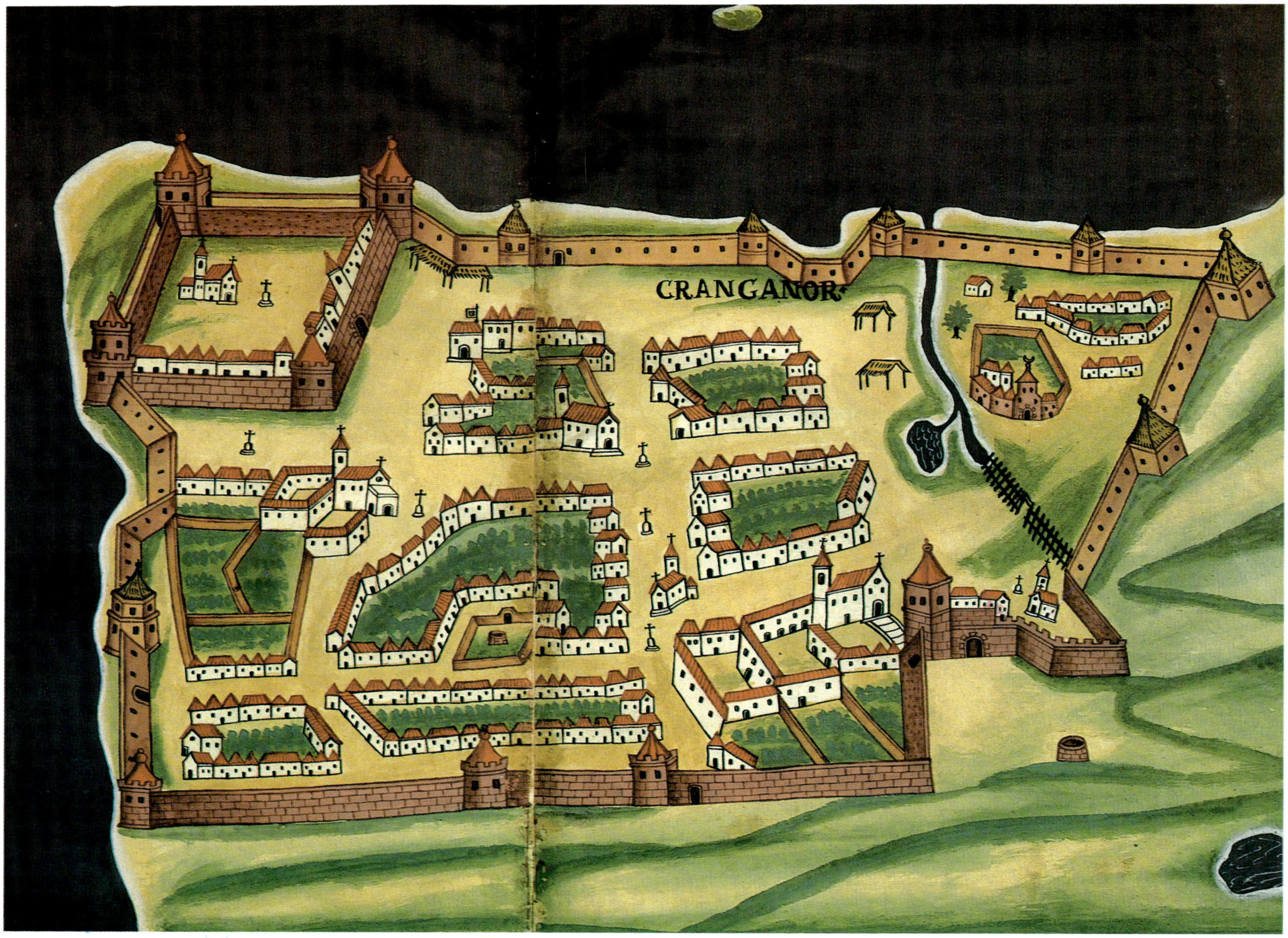

and Cordoba. The massive intellect of the 12th-century scholar Averroes deeply influenced Christian theology (but was little appreciated by his fellow Arabs).

Today there are about 400 million Muslims in the world. Islam has almost from the start been split into different sects and schools of interpretation. The simplicity of the basic creed has enabled Islam to overcome barriers of race and color, often with more success than Christianity. Yet Arab unity has never been easy. The secular spirit of the modern West has profoundly infiltrated Turkey and the Arab states, so that the preservation of Islamic principles and values has become a sharp anti-Western reaction, seeing the West as both political enemy and diabolical underminer of Muslim devotion. Nevertheless there are today many very thoughtful and well-educated Muslims who do want the traditional face of Islam changed, and in fact would like it to have a greater resemblance to Christianity.

Christianity in India and Japan

The great European explorers of the Renaissance not only opened trade routes but made way for the great Catholic missions of St Francis Xavier and the Jesuits, reaching to Goa in India and to the Far East. In India the Christian missionaries were faced by a religious situation strikingly parallel to that of the Roman empire. Indian religion makes room within its capacious embrace for sacred cows and fetishes, polytheistic and phallic fertility cults and temple prostitution, side by side with a profound personal piety in the language of loving surrender to the God Krishna-Vishnu (Bhakti). Asceticism is juxtaposed with erotic license. In short, there are aspects of Hinduism that come close to Christian aspirations, other aspects that a monotheist must reject.

The Christian reaction to Japanese Shintoism is similar: Shinto is the vehicle of family and state religion and deifies natural forces, especially the sun and to a lesser extent the moon. Shinto religion is also highly tolerant of the erotic to an extent that surprises the westerner who notices how restrained the Japanese are in giving any outward expression to passion. As the expression of Japanese nationalism, Shinto placed the veneration of the emperor at the center. The secularization of 1945 ended the emperor cult, but has not changed the way in which the people think. Japan has been a difficult soil for the seed of the Christian Gospel.

The Christian response to other cultures and religions

The Christian relation to these world religions is

formed by the approach of, say, the apostle Paul in Acts 17 or Romans 1–2: highly positive towards the aspiration, negative towards the deification of anything merely creaturely, to superstition, folk religion and (for example) animal cults. The combination of positive and negative is illustrated by the difference between different types of theological approach to the subject. The positive estimate of other religions has been encouraged by the facility of modern communications (though the efficiency of the modern travel agent is often judged by his skill in protecting the tourist from any real contact with the people of the country he is visiting). It has above all been stimulated by the psychological and sociological study of religion. Early in the 19th century Schleiermacher defined religion as the sense of absolute dependence, awe and reverence, prior to any mental or verbal formulation of doctrinal belief. Rudolf Otto in this century wrote of the idea of the holy or numinous as a universal experience of humanity, to which different religions give a variety of ritual forms in different cultural settings. The primary data of religious experience were also greatly emphasized by William James (1901), but on the assumption that feeling is prior to thought. The non-rational approach to religion was taken much further by Carl Jung. In 1901 Ernst Troeltsch urged that Christians should cease speaking of the finality or absoluteness of their faith, and proposed to see the religious values of the various world religions calibrated on a scale, allowing Christianity to be the highest point hitherto reached in the ascent of man. Twentieth-century Protestants found themselves dissatisfied with 19th-century ways of speaking of the "failure" of other religions, and wished rather to speak of their "contribution."

Left This 16th-century map shows the Portuguese settlement at Cranganor where several churches stand side by side with a mosque, Christianity and Islam flourishing in a single community.

Below In Sri Lanka, a Buddhist dagoba and a Dutch Reformed church behind it. Here Buddhism survives side by side with Christianity in the east.

Large missionary conferences were held in Edinburgh in 1910, Jerusalem in 1928 and Tambaram in 1938. At Edinburgh the predominant note was still one of Christian confidence in the face of the other religions, a confidence which perhaps subconsciously reflected the general technological and cultural confidence of a Europe before August 1914. The main problem in 1910 was seen in the divided state of the Christian churches: how could one invite an Indian to believe and be baptized when he was confronted with 13 competing versions of Christianity? Edinburgh 1910 therefore gave impetus to the ecumenical movement.

At Jerusalem (1928) there was talk of the religions of the world making common cause against secularism, and of the ways in which Christianity brought answers to questions asked by Buddhists and Hindus. On the other hand, the relativism of Troeltsch was vigorously attacked by Karl Barth, the Swiss theologian then teaching in Germany. For Barth authentic faith is a gift of revelation and grace, not something man finds by searching: that is, we come to God through Christ, not vice versa. The Dutch theologian H. Kraemer similarly insisted that unless Christians affirm revelation through Christ, they surrender any claim to speak the truth of God to all mankind. Either the Gospel "is true for all or it is not true at all."

By 1938 the third International Missionary Conference was concerned about rising threats to world peace, and about the increasing opposition to Christianity in some parts of the world. Held in India, the conference was sensitive to the precariousness of western power in the east, and of the British Raj in India. The Christian Gospel would be weakened in its approach to Indians if it were identified with an alien occupying power. Therefore there must be no social pressure or veiled coercion.

The implicit question has therefore been whether Christianity, which assimilated for its own purposes the cultural heritage of Greece and Rome and formed the mind of Europe over nearly two millennia, can be sufficiently detached from this classical heritage and metaphysical framework so as to enable it to assimilate other cultures. Recent years have seen in India the establishment of "Asrams" that seek to bring together common elements of Christianity and Hinduism. Pentecostalists have unhesitatingly made their own African music and rhythm. Obviously there is a danger of confusing the kernel and the husk. In Africa the churches have made a place in worship for dancing, an expression of human vitality of which European Christianity has been curiously afraid. But throughout history Christians have tended to be indifferent to the external form and to care primarily for the substance of the Christian faith and life.

Christians in Beirut Today

Since the outbreak of civil war in 1975 Beirut has been a mirror to the political and religious divisions of the Middle East. From being the commercial and tourist center of the region, it has been transformed into a war zone still inhabited by civilians who have become accustomed to the sounds of shelling, car bombs, sniping and the sirens of ambulances madly racing through the streets.

The deserted heart of the city lies like a fatal wound between its two populations—the largely Muslim inhabitants of what used to be the thriving western area of the capital, and the Christian inhabitants of the eastern sector. The killings and kidnappings of recent years have made west Beirut more exclusively Muslim, and east Beirut more solidly Christian than ever before. While the revival of militant Shi'ite Islam and the influx of refugees from the south have transformed the face of west Beirut, violent divisions within the ranks of the Christian militia have brought a new threat to inhabitants in the east of the city. For long they have been used to barricading themselves against snipers, upending containers from the port to give cover along streets near the so-called "green line." Now there is the threat of insurgency by dissidents from within their own community.

Left A cross proclaims a Christian area near the wasteland of the Beirut battles. A fashionable street has been shattered and littered with the debris of war: here, the cross has become a symbol of the intransigence of the Christians and their determination to stay in their homes. These people look for protection to the Phalangist militia built up by Pierre Gemayel and his son Beshir (assassinated shortly after his election as president in 1982). The Gemayels are Maronites in faith, as are the majority of Lebanon's Christians. The Maronites are eastern-rite Christians in their worship and traditions, but have been in communion with the see of Rome since the 12th century. Some Maronites among the militiamen see themselves as crusaders of modern times, defending an outpost of Christianity against Muslim incursions.

Above A Latin-rite mass is celebrated by the Franciscans; many historic ties exist between Lebanese Christians and western Catholicism. Among the Maronites, French is still the language of polite society, and in east Beirut the Jesuit Université S. Joseph provides instruction in French for degree courses. Naturally enough, many Lebanese Christians have sought refuge in France in recent years.

Left A Maronite priest stands with Phalangist militiamen at a memorial mass for Beshir Gemayel. Not all Maronites are equally with the militia; in particular, their patriarch Nasrallah Sfeir has tried to calm the hotheads among his community. Lebanon's Christians include significant numbers of Greek Orthodox, Greek Catholics, Armenians (Orthodox and Catholic), Syrian Orthodox, Syrian Catholics, and Protestants. These Christian communities have differing political stances on Lebanon's conflict: the Greek Orthodox have traditionally been pro-leftist, while the Armenian Orthodox have developed a policy of "positive neutrality."

Far left This Maronite bride is celebrating her wedding in typical Lebanese style; amid the sunshine and the rejoicing, the smart cars and the ribbons, it is possible for a moment to put the agony of the recent years aside. In Lebanon all weddings are according to the law of church or of mosque; there is no civil marriage, and no marriage can be contracted between Christian and Muslim. If a Christian and a Muslim wish to marry, they must travel abroad to arrange the legalities.

CHRISTIANITY, COMMUNISM AND NATIONAL IDENTITY

The survival of Christianity in Russia since 1917
From the outset the Russian Revolution of 1917 was hostile to Christianity. It had inherited from Karl Marx the theory that religion was merely an opiate, an illusion, that would vanish as socialism advanced. In Russia the tsars and the Orthodox Church had been partners in oppression for many centuries. The Romanovs were swept away, and it was expected that the Church would soon follow the royal family into extinction. This was a "law of history."

Lenin, however, was not opposed to helping along an "inevitable" process, and in a series of draconian decrees he enforced the "separation of Church and state," which in practice meant that the Church lost all its property and most of its rights. He launched a vigorous campaign to free peasants and workers from the remains of "superstition." "Scientific atheism" became the state ideology, and was taught from the nursery to the university. Those who got in the way were dealt with harshly: between 1917 and 1923 over 1200 Orthodox priests and 28 bishops met their deaths.

Lenin's successor, Stalin, had once studied in a Georgian seminary. In 1928 he introduced a law on "religious associations" which substantially remains in force today; it provided the model for other Communist countries after 1945. A church may continue to exist provided all its members are registered, all its appointments are supervised, its activities are confined to the church building (leased from the state), and it indulges in no "propaganda." In every Communist country there is a "ministry of cults" or its equivalent: its task is to keep the Church subservient and docile.

In the 1920s and 1930s Stalin's law was a matter of controversy within the Orthodox Church. Some said that there should be no compromise with the powers of evil, and that Russia was simply reliving the Passion of Christ; one day it would merit its Resurrection. Others argued that the Orthodox Church should share in the destiny of the fatherland, and that it was now being duly punished for its past arrogance. But it was never easy to know just how sincere such protestations of loyalty to the Soviet state were. Fear and drugs were already being used to extort all manner of statements. The atmosphere was unhealthy with mistrust and anxiety.

What Russians call "the Great Patriotic War" of 1941–45 radically changed the situation of the Orthodox Church. Stalin needed help to bolster

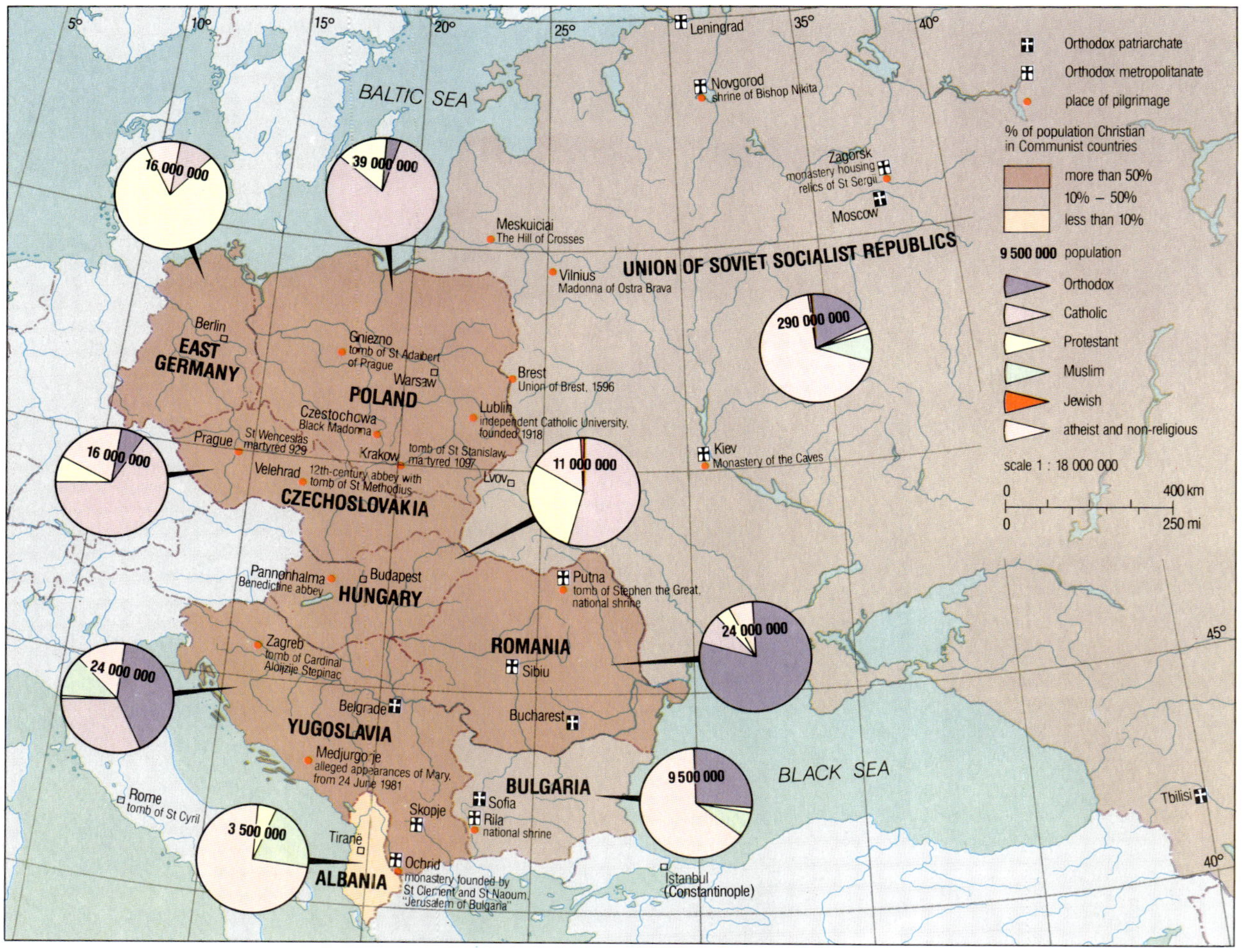

Left: Christianity and Communism
The map reflects traces of the two waves of evangelization which converted eastern Europe just over a thousand years ago. From the west went Latin-speaking Benedictine monks. Prague was their staging post on the way eastwards. From Constantinople missionaries moved northwards through Bulgaria and Romania. The two waves met in southern Poland and Yugoslavia.

Saints Cyril and Methodius in the 9th century were unique in that they were Greek monks who set off with the blessing of the pope of Rome (Cyril is credited with devising the "Cyrillic" script). East and west, Orthodoxy and Catholicism, were in full communion with each other until 1054. Pope John Paul dreams of recreating "the spiritual unity of Europe" about which he spoke at Gniezno in 1979.

Above The monastery of St Sergii on his feast day. It houses his relics. Zagorsk is also a theological college, the headquarters of the Moscow patriarchate and a great showplace for ecumenical visitors. But appearances are deceptive: in 1914 there were 1025 monasteries in Russia; now there are only 16.

morale and stiffen the will to resist the Nazi invasion. The Church was now exploited as thoroughly as it had been persecuted. In 1943, after a meeting with Stalin, Metropolitan Sergii was elected patriarch of Moscow, leader of the Russian Orthodox Church. His predecessors had all perished. The patriarchate was transferred from a log cabin on an unpaved street to the impressive setting of the former German Embassy.

This was because Stalin had work for the Moscow patriarchate in the postwar world. Countries with a high proportion of Orthodox believers—notably Romania and Bulgaria— had now fallen within the Russian orbit. The Moscow patriarchate demonstrated that "religious liberty" existed in the Soviet Union, and taught them the art of survival by compliance. In the Ukraine sterner measures were needed: the four million "Uniates" (Christians of Oriental rite but in communion with the pope) were forcibly converted to Orthodoxy. On the international front, the Moscow patriarchate took part in the work of the World Council of Churches in Geneva, where it could be counted upon to support the government's party line on peace, disarmament and national liberation movements.

But it got no thanks for this subservience. In the 1960s there was another wave of religious persecution under Khrushchev. Antireligious propaganda was stepped up. The remaining 63 monasteries (there had been over a thousand before the Revolution) were reduced by half. Alexander Solzhenitsyn, novelist and Nobel prize-winner, protested in an "open letter" to Patriarch Pimen in 1972: "The Russian Church expresses its concern about any evil in distant Asia or Africa, while it never has anything to say about injustices here at home . . . The Church is ruled dictatorially by atheists—a sight never seen before in two millennia."

Under the brief presidency of Yuri Andropov, former head of the KGB, there was another attempt to "intensify the ideological campaign" against Christians. Article 142 of the Soviet Penal Code, banning offenses against "the separation of Church and state," was used to suppress prayer or Bible-study meetings in private apartments, and to stop religion being taught to children by anyone other than parents. These measures were a response to the religious revival that has taken place in Russia. Underground and unregistered, small groups of Christians have continued to meet privately. Besides Orthodox Christians, they include Baptists, Pentecostalists and Mennonites, as well as Roman Catholics in the Ukraine and Lithuania.

Polish Catholicism and a Polish pope

In the "Peoples' Democracies" established after 1945 the Soviet pattern of legislation and control was swiftly imposed. But historical and sociological factors made for variations.

The most striking instance of successful resistance to Communism is Poland. Polish Catholics make up 93 percent of the population—proportionately higher than before the war when there were sizable Jewish and Orthodox minorities. From 1946 onwards a handful of Moscow-trained men attempted to impose on the Poles an alien and

Christians in Poland Today

For over a thousand years the Roman Catholic Church in Poland has seen itself as a beleaguered outpost of the Christian west. It embodied the soul of the nation throughout the 19th century, when Poland was carved up between its powerful neighbors Russia, Austria and Germany. After a brief two decades of independence in the interwar years, the Church once again stiffened the national will to resist during the Nazi occupation. In Communist Poland, the Church, at first persecuted, has gradually moved into a position of uneasy coexistence and occasional cooperation. It deals with Polish Communists lest it might have to deal with Russian Communists. It still acts as the conscience of the nation, and saw the birth of Solidarity as an expression of Christian values (cooperativeness, the dignity of work) that are deeply rooted in the Polish people. The regime's antireligious propaganda, despite total control of education and the mass media, has been a complete failure. On the contrary, there has been a religious revival. It is not unconnected with the fact that Pope John Paul II has made everyone aware of the link between Poland and faith.

Above The funeral of Father Jerzy Popieluszko, 3 November 1984. Popieluszko preached fiery patriotic and pro-Solidarity sermons, which is why the security forces thought they could get away with his abduction and brutal murder. But the nation was shocked, his murderers were brought to trial, and his funeral became a Solidarity demonstration.

Left Pope John Paul II during his second journey to Poland in 1983 when martial law was still in force. A third journey was planned for 1987. He believes that his election as pope was some divine compensation for the many sufferings of Poland. Many Poles agree with him.

Above right In St Brigitta's, the shipyard workers' church in Gdansk, on hearing of the arrest of Lech Walesa in 1983. Though the pugnacious Walesa was not in prison for long, Solidarity was officially declared illegal. In September 1986 the remaining political prisoners were amnestied, and Walesa and his friends began to work for "pluralism" in trades union activity.

Right A striker locks the gate at the Lenin shipyards in Gdansk. The picture is a copy of the Black Madonna of Czestochowa, an icon that arrived mysteriously from the east. It was slashed by Swedish Protestant troops in 1655. In times of peril, the whole nation has been "consecrated" to the Black Madonna of Jasna Gora (the Bright Mountain).

unpopular creed. No wedge could be driven between clergy and people; over 2000 priests had been shot by the Nazis or died in concentration camps. In 1966 Poland celebrated its millennium, and this dramatized the way the Church and the nation had been born together through the baptism of the king. So the Church embodied national consciousness, tradition and resistance to foreign oppression. Against this the party's claim to represent the vanguard of socialism never had much of a chance.

Its hollowness was laid bare by the unexpected election of a Polish pope in October 1978. He promptly went on a triumphant tour of his homeland for a visit that was in effect a plebiscite on the question: "Who really rules in Poland?" Solidarity, the free trades union, was a product of the self-confidence created by the papal visit. But it was a dangerous novelty; its contagious power began to be felt throughout eastern Europe; so it had to be suppressed. Pope John Paul's second visit to Poland in June 1983, under martial law conditions, was more restrained and sober. He prepared Polish Catholics for a long and difficult haul, confident however that the "moral victory" had already been won.

Czechoslovakia and Hungary

Czechoslovakia never had the religious unity of its neighbor Poland. Roman Catholics dominated, especially in Slovakia, but the Czechoslovak Hussite Church and the Evangelical Church of the Czech Brethren had a better claim to embody the national tradition. The burning of Jan Hus for heresy in 1415 had never been forgotten. In the Stalinist period the Catholic Church was repressed with great harshness, partly because its leader, Pope Pius XII, was regarded as "the pope of the Atlantic Alliance." And he was foreign.

Protestants found that they could come to terms with the regime. The great theologian Jan Hromadka believed that Communism was not necessarily antireligious, and that it could be seen as part of man's struggle for freedom and justice. A Communist version of the international ecumenical movement known as the Christian Peace Conference was set up in Prague in 1958. It was in Czechoslovakia that the first "Christian–Marxist dialogues" took place: each side believed that it had something to learn from the other. These meetings helped to prepare the intellectual ground for the Dubcek "spring" of 1968. But the hope was soon cut down. After 1968 neo-Stalinist methods were revived in dealing with all the churches.

Roman Catholics make up just over 70 percent (6·5 million) of Hungary's population, and there were two million in the Reformed Church (Calvinist) and another half-million Lutherans. The Catholic Church was statistically strong but sociologically weak. It had collaborated with Austrian repression in the Counter-Reformation period; in the interwar years, a great landowner itself, it had supported the Fascist Horthy regime. This made it a vulnerable target after the war for the Communists.

The show trial of Cardinal Jozsef Mindszenty in 1949 placed the conflict before the eyes of the whole world. Evidently confused and drugged, the cardinal was found guilty of currency offenses, espionage and planning to overthrow the government. He was given a life sentence. But during the 1956 uprising he emerged from prison, and spent the next 16 years as a voluntary prisoner in the US Embassy in Budapest. It took skillful diplomacy to persuade Mindszenty to go into permanent exile in 1971. His removal made possible an improvement in Church–state relations, and his successor, Cardinal Laszlo Lekai, has been accommodating where Mindszenty was combative. Figures for church attendance are unreliable, but the best estimate is that it is no higher than 15 percent in the country and sinks as low as 3 percent in big cities. "Secularization" and "consumerism" in Hungary have wrought greater havoc than persecution ever did.

Romania and Bulgaria

Romania and Bulgaria resemble each other in that during the four centuries of Turkish rule it was the Orthodox Church that kept alive the spirit of the nation. They owed their belated independence—Romania in 1859, Bulgaria in 1878—to Russian help. But under Communism their fates and fortunes have been very different.

In Romania the Church bowed to the inevitable and conceded that atheism would replace religious instruction in the schools. But there were compensations: the clergy were to be paid in part by the state, they were exempt from military service, and church law was recognized as part of civil law. This arrangement, unique in eastern Europe, was largely the work of Petru Groza, president from 1952 to his death in 1958. He combined being a Communist with being a devout Christian.

The death of Groza happened to coincide with Khrushchev's revived antireligious campaign in the Soviet Union. That may explain why the Romanian Orthodox Church now began to be persecuted. There was an attack on monastic life: nuns under 40 and monks under 50 were released from their vows and given "more socially useful work." Under President Nicolae Ceausescu the need to assert national independence and solidarity *vis-à-vis* the Soviet Union brought Church and state closer together again.

Bulgaria offers a gloomier picture. In the 1950s the government skillfully exploited the Church's resentment against the ecumenical patriarch of Constantinople. The patriarch, nominal head of the Orthodox Churches, had refused to concede the title of "patriarch" to the Bulgarian church leader. So regaining the patriarchate as an expression of national sentiment became one of the objects of Communist foreign policy. It was achieved in 1953 and recognized by Orthodoxy as a whole in 1961. But the price paid for this largely symbolic achievement was high: young people ignorant of Christian faith, church attendance down, monasteries regarded as curious instances of folklore. According to one sociologist, with the exception of Albania, Bulgaria is the most completely secularized country in the world.

East Germany

East Germany—more correctly, the German Democratic Republic—differs from all the other countries here considered in that the majority of its population were Lutherans. Most of the places associated with Luther are found within its terri-

Above Openair liturgy at Ieud, Romania. The association of the Church with folklore is not discouraged by the regime. But Romania still has 122 Orthodox monastic foundations.

Left The monastery of Bačkovo, Bulgaria, maintained largely for the benefit of tourists. Yet monks played a crucial part in maintaining the life of the nation through the four centuries of Turkish rule, and it was a monk, Paissi of Hilander, who made possible the 19th-century revival of Bulgaria, culminating in independence in 1878.

tory, and in 1983 the government joined with the Church in celebrating the four hundredth anniversary of his birth. The Evangelical (or Lutheran) Church is well integrated into society and runs over 2000 hospitals, clinics, nursing homes and hostels for handicapped children. In exchange for this privilege of service, the Church is expected to give unquestioned support to government policies. This it does in a spirit of what is called "critical solidarity." From time to time prophets arise who denounce the church leaders as compromised and supine. Roman Catholics number 1 300 000 (about 8 percent of the population) and tend to keep themselves to themselves. All the churches are put under strain by the *Jugendweihe,* a vow to be loyal to the state, which is intended to replace the sacrament of confirmation. It leads to much double-think.

From 1917 to the present is not a long time in the perspective of history. But it is long enough to suggest that religion has deep roots in the human spirit and that it is unlikely to vanish as Marx predicted. This has been recognized in the more "pragmatic" regime of Mikhail Gorbachov. It is not "more liberal" but it is "more sophisticated" in its approach. Though pressure has continued to be put on "religious dissidents" and there have been some enforced television "recantations," there are also hints of new (and so far secret) legislation giving greater legal recognition to churches and more freedom to preachers to move about. But this may be designed to keep them quiet in the run up to the millennium celebrations of Christianity in Russia in 1988. The emphasis falls on the cultural role of the Church in the distant past. Every effort is made to avoid the "contagion" spreading from Poland to nearby Lithuania, Slovakia and the Ukraine. Far from withering away, religion in the Soviet Union and Eastern Europe is in some respects healthier than in the secularized West. The 2nd-century maxim has been rediscovered: "The blood of martyrs is the seed of the Church."

Christians in Italy Today

For the country folk of Italy Catholicism can be strongly regional, and often fused with old peasant customs and ceremonies, which it is then the task of the clergy to stamp with a Christian character. The people of that land have suffered, and somehow survived, many calamities, including war, tyranny, drought, earthquake. They naturally feel themselves to be close to God, and are strongly conscious of their solidarity with the best friends they have, namely, the saints and especially Mary. Their immemorial traditions and colorful ceremonies are felt as a link to the Rock of Ages, giving a stability beyond the innumerable hazards and uncertainties of life.

Popular Italian religion is mainly organized around not only the feasts of local patron saints and shrines but also high festivals of the Christian calendar: Christmas, the three wise men of the Epiphany, Lent, Palm Sunday and Holy Week, Good Friday and Easter, Ascension, Pentecost, Corpus Christi (the thanksgiving for the gift of the eucharist instituted in the 13th century, originally on the Thursday after Trinity Sunday, now commonly celebrated on the following Sunday). Painted statues of Christ or the saints are carried in procession representing, for example, the triumphal entry of Christ to Jerusalem, or the Via Dolorosa. The people often wear white or colorful clothing. Bonfires and fireworks may add to the celebration's delights and hazards.

Right and opposite below At Monte Autore by Vallepietra, on the borders of the Abruzzi and Latium, for at least five centuries past pilgrims have made their hard way in procession to a shrine of the Holy Trinity 1200 meters up in the hills, there to venerate God and to honor an old fresco, especially on Trinity Sunday and on St Anne's feast of 26 July. The shrine is in a narrow grotto about 15 meters long, subdivided with different sections. Outside stands a neoclassical church built about 1860. The pilgrims chant hymns and brush the walls of the shrine with the palms of their right hands, which is not good for the preservation of the paintings. On ordinary days the circuit of the walls is made seven times reciting the Creed, but only once on the two high festivals, when many hundreds come and special measures of crowd control are necessary.

Below In a funeral on the beautiful but sad waters of the lagoon at Venice the hearse is a motor launch. At the cemetery on the island of San Michele the simple and the great, including Igor Stravinsky, have gone to man's long home.

Below At Gubbio the patron saint is St Ubaldo. On his feast of 15 May a statue of the saint, with St George and St Antony, preceded by vast candles, is carried in solemn procession through the streets and around the city. The elevation of the statues to a vertical position is strenuous and accompanied by a complex ritual. The ceremony goes back to a victory won by Gubbio over rival towns in the 12th century.

Overleaf The thanksgiving for the eucharist (Corpus Christi) may be marked by colorful processions, with crowds lining the route, and a solemn benediction at the end. At Gandino near Bergamo lay confraternities have their own distinctive silk robes and insignia, the houses are hung with decorated cloth and flowers, and the people gather for a major popular festival.

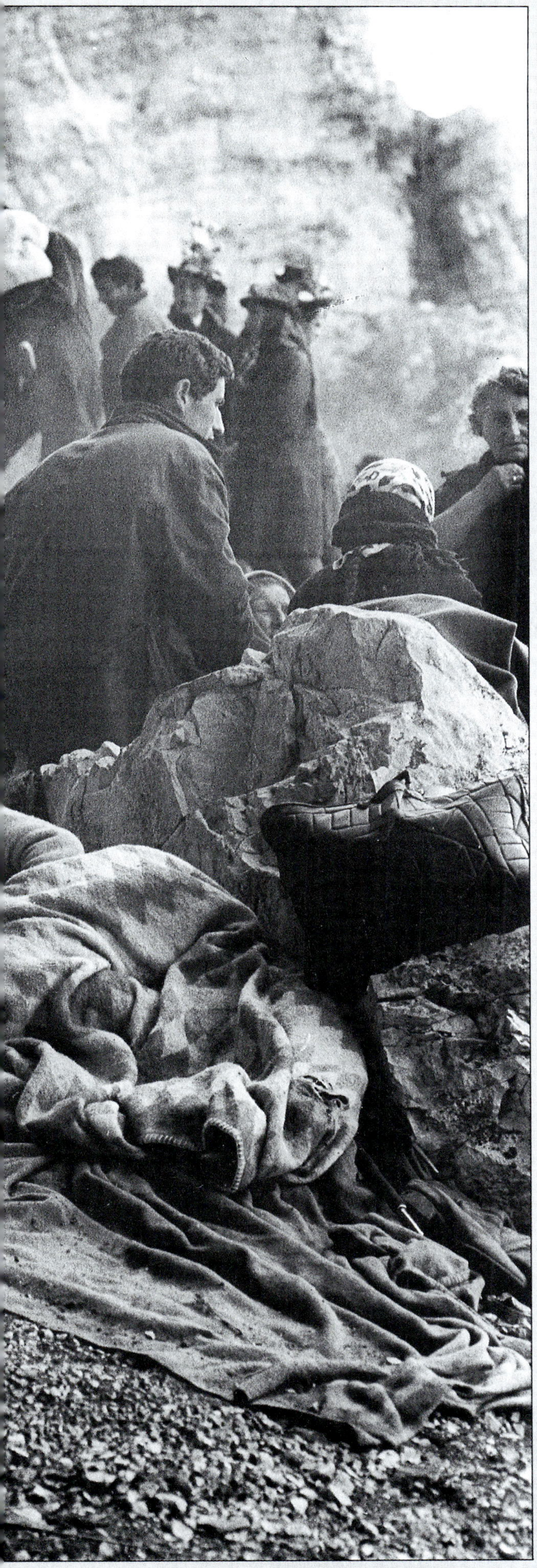

CHRISTIANITY AND SECULAR MODERNITY

Institutional strength and weakness

Just after World War II the churches mainly experienced a period of consolidation, at least outside Eastern Europe. So it is useful to begin with a profile of strength and weakness in the mid-20th century.

Roman Catholic strength radiated out from a hub in south central Europe: Catholic Switzerland, mountain Austria and France (including the Massif Central), southern Germany, the Veneto, Croatia and Slovenia. There were three outer bastions: in the northeast Slovakia, Poland and Lithuania; in the northwest the Pas de Calais, Flanders, southern Holland, the Palatinate; in the southwest the northern Iberian peninsula, especially northern Portugal and the Basque region. And there were outer pockets in Brittany and Eire. Areas of weakness or of a disorganized superstitious semi-Catholicism ran through southern Portugal and Spain, and southern Italy. In the Orthodox world strength was concentrated in Greece and Romania, and such relative strength as remained in the USSR was to be found in the westernmost areas and the Ukraine. Orthodoxy was weak, or being systematically weakened, in southern Yugoslavia and Bulgaria. As for north European Protestantism, religion was already institutionally enfeebled, though this was not necessarily incompatible with a diffuse religiosity. The only partial exceptions were certain bastions of neo-Calvinist rigor in Holland, and peripheries like Ulster, Wales, Scotland and western Norway. Throughout the whole of Christian Europe the capitals of secularity were London, Birmingham, Amsterdam, Stockholm, Copenhagen, Hamburg, Berlin, the Paris basin, "red" Emilio-Tuscany, Prague, Titograd and Sofia.

So far as North America was concerned, Protestantism was institutionally much more vigorous; indeed it was expanding. A gross characterization would indicate relative weakness for all churches in the Appalachians, the Rocky Mountains and the Pacific regions. American Catholicism was predominantly urban and concentrated in the mid-Atlantic and east central regions, while evangelicalism was strongest in the rural and small-town South. Folk Catholicism began at Mexico and was universal throughout Central and South America. Some countries, for example, Brazil, approximated the disorganized or superstitious religion of southern Europe.

Ethnicity and religion

Such patterns of strength and weakness are not arbitrary, and generalizations have been established which apply generally throughout the whole period of modern industrialism. Religious practice decreases with the size of urban concentration and the extent to which an area is homogeneously working-class. It also decreases with the size of industrial operation: "heavy" industry is inimical to the vitality of religious institutions. Indeed, because religious institutions are based on personal and communal association, they are adversely affected by size in general: by large-scale farming, without personal attachments to the land, by vast bureaucratic systems, by megalopolitan concentrations. Social and geographical mobility and rapid change also erode attachment to institutional religion.

Other things being equal, religious attachments are fostered where life is relatively stable, where relationships are personalized, where dependencies are paternalistic and where people have a stake in the community, through owning houses (as in the suburbs) or having their own farms. Religious attachments are also strengthened where a suppressed or threatened nationalism (or an ethnic enclave) can be defined by religion. Sometimes this ethnic solidarity is more clearly defined by language, as in parts of Catalonia; but quite often cultural defense is organized simultaneously around language and religion. There are many examples: Quebec, Flanders, Croatia, Slovakia, Lithuania, Poland, Eire, the Basque region, Brittany, Romania, "Welsh" Wales. A weaker version of this relationship between religion, language and ethnicity is found in certain provinces, often but not always relatively undeveloped, which cherish

Above Reaching the top of Croagh Patrick in County Mayo. The feast of St Patrick—17 March—occurs in Lent, and some pilgrims climb the mountain on their knees, taking three to four days over this penitential exercise. Irish Christianity was austere and rigorous, and shaped by monks. It was renewed in more Roman fashion after the potato famine of the 1840s.

Right In the folk memory of French Protestants the "Massacre of St Bartholomew's Day," 25 August 1572, remains vivid. A defeated minority, their right to exist (and hold 100 fortified towns) was asserted by the Edict of Nantes in 1598. The edict was revoked by Louis XIV in 1685. It meant that the Huguenots had to go into exile or meet clandestinely (as here).

a distinctive character and dialect against the threat of a secularized cultural center, for example western Norway, north Jutland, western England, parts of Languedoc. Indeed, even the American South can be seen as an example of this provincial religiosity.

Ethnicity and religion also reinforce each other where a nation is displaced, as in the case of Armenians and Jews, or where mass migration to another country involves a threat of total absorption in the receiving culture. Examples are legion: the Irish in Preston, Liverpool and Glasgow, or in New York and Boston; the Poles and Greeks in Chicago; the Muslims and Sikhs in the English north and Midlands. Sometimes this results in a recovery of cohesion, even in religious conservatism since lost in the original homeland, like the Lutheranism of the Missouri Synod.

Obviously the way religion is carried, or reinforced, by migrants depends partly on the way political power, class and religion were related to each other in the homeland. "Hispanics" in the USA will often be unchurched when they come from cultures where the Church is aligned with privilege. Irish and Germans in late 19th-century New York had very different attitudes to religion, the former patriotically papist, the latter often indifferent. So we are led now to consider these crucial configurations of power, class and religion as they affect the religious attitude of particular status groups, the intelligentsia and the state apparatus.

Varying political and social patterns

Here it is necessary to begin by distinguishing cultures still affected by the English revolutions of the 17th century, by the French Revolution and by the Russian Revolution. Each successive revolution has been more intolerant of conservative religion, more ideologically all-embracing and atheistic. In the English case revolution remained within a religious frame with overtones of millenarianism; in the French and Russian cases religion was translated into secular utopianism.

The social consequences of all three revolutions remain with us today. The English Revolution informs the whole Anglo-Saxon world, especially the "white" Commonwealth. That revolution received definitive form in America in 1776, intermixed with elements derived from the Enlightenment. Its dynamic became individualism and "the Protestant Ethic." The French Revolution infiltrated the whole Latin world as well as affecting the German-speaking intelligentsia. Characteristically it led to patterns of massive confrontation between the Church and anticlericals, especially those concentrated in the intelligentsia and (sometimes) the liberal professions. Counterrevolution succeeded revolution and vice versa, with social warfare concentrated in particular on education and the monastic orders. The Russian Revolution, which was essentially energized from the secular intelligentsia born of the French Revolution, took the process one stage further. It was armed with a militant middle-class ideology, hiding behind a utopian myth of the "proletariat." Not only did it deepen the confrontation with the institutional Church, but it set up a secular "religious" monopoly, aided by all those agencies of conformity and state pressure previously associated with the Roman Catholic Church. These agencies were also transferred to the whole of Eastern Europe after World War II.

However, less global subpatterns can also be discerned. At least four exist in the Protestant world and can be briefly described: (1) the American, (2) the English, (3) the German and Scandinavian, (4) the Dutch (and in a sense the South African). Each of these patterns shows a different relationship between the two basic forms of Protestantism: the established "folk" church and the voluntary association. The advent of the voluntary association, divorced from an explicit connection with the state and nationality, is a crucial aspect of the process of social differentiation or "separating out" of functions which will be the concern of the final section.

In the USA all direct links between state and Church had decomposed by 1830. On the one hand were religious bodies, originally organized as voluntary associations, above all the Baptist and Methodist churches. On the other were sometime established or majority churches, Presbyterian, Anglican, Roman etc., which had either evolved towards the status of voluntary associations or had suddenly acquired it on arrival in an America which was already ethnically and religiously plural. The ex-majoritarian churches still largely tended their ethnic constituencies (Irish, Greek, Polish etc.), while the voluntary associations proliferated in size and number, creating innumerable styles according to the pressures of this or that social milieu. This broke the kind of identification between religion and state which might encourage promoters of social change to adopt a militant secular ideology, and disrupted those direct links between privileged social class and the practice of (say) Anglican or Roman or Lutheran religion which might lead newly mobilizing social groups to dissociate themselves from religious practice.

Left Pope Paul VI, shortly after his election in July 1963, greets President John F. Kennedy, the first Roman Catholic to be president of the United States. The audience was to have been with Pope John XXIII, but he died; and Kennedy was to be assassinated on 22 November that same year. This picture captures the illusion of a new era in which "the most powerful man in the world" and "the parish priest of the world" might have worked together. Ironically, the double-chinned figure on the right is the formidable Cardinal Alfredo Ottaviani, who believed that the separation of Church and state was immoral. Subsequent events have shown that it was easier for a non-Catholic president, Ronald Reagan, to establish diplomatic relations with the Vatican.

Below The alliance of Church and state, of throne and altar, is clearly on view at a coronation. Since the time of Elizabeth I the monarch has claimed the title of "Supreme Governor of the Church of England." But since she is also queen of her non-Anglican and unbelieving subjects, Her Majesty does not stress this role. It is only on the great occasions, like the coronation and royal weddings, that the full panoply of establishment is brought into play, and the archbishop of Canterbury presides as though there were "one church in one nation." But even that is changing, and ecumenical participation was taken for granted in recent royal weddings.

The state retained a link, not with a fallible and socially compromised church, but with a form of utopian Americanism partly embodied in the rituals, aspirations and rhetoric of a "civil religion."

Two further aspects are noteworthy. Secularization expressed itself within the religious framework, initially by decomposing dogma into transcendentalism, or ethical and humanitarian sentiment, as in New England, and then in the 20th century through the liberalization of the control points in most of the mainstream Protestant bodies. This left religious conservatism in two main forms, both associated, though in very different ways, with the Democratic Party. One was Roman Catholic, the other evangelical and (principally) Baptist. Roman Catholics, by beginning low in the status system, and by adopting Democratic politics, broke the connection between religious and political conservatism, religion and privilege. This, indeed, was a consequence of the low status of Catholics in the whole Anglo-Saxon ambit: Canada, Australia, South Africa, New Zealand and England.

Evangelicals moved to some extent in a reverse direction to Roman Catholics. Having been socially powerful in 19th-century America, as well as in England and the white Commonwealth, they went into crisis and then recession between 1880 and 1920. They found themselves despised by liberalized or mildly secular metropolitan elites, and became disproportionately concentrated in small towns, rural areas and lower-status groups. However, as will be indicated below, they managed to rebuild an infrastructure which in the 1960s enabled them to reemerge with new power, once a triumphant liberalism started to corrode its own ecclesiastical base.

The English pattern is a variant of the American. The fabric of the established Church remained, with direct links between throne and altar, landed power and Anglican religion. The voluntary associations could not expand as freely as in America. They became associated with the social self-consciousness of certain areas of the developing countryside, miners and fishermen, shopkeepers, those in small-scale industry and the "respectable working class." Since this self-consciousness was initially associated with the Liberal Party, the result was that yet another force assisted in disconnecting political conservatism from religion as such. (The very strong links between religion and party, especially Nonconformity and the Liberal Party between 1880 and World War I, retreated before alignments based partly on class from the 1920s onward.)

Thus, in the whole Anglo-Saxon world, liberalism and "progress" could advance in some partial alliance with religion and without the massive anticlerical thrust necessary in most traditionally Roman Catholic countries. However, the maintenance of the established connection in England meant that religious practice declined with each move down the social scale, a decline most marked at the point dividing lower middle from working class. The white Commonwealth is poised between the American and English patterns. Compared with England, there is a greater expansion of the principle of the voluntary association, a diminished Anglican dominance, a larger Roman Catholic minority, and somewhat higher levels of practice.

The Scandinavian (and north German) pattern accentuates the principle of the folk church and diminishes the role of the voluntary association. The result is a dissociation of each newly self-conscious group from the religious practice of the privileged, leaving only parts of the "old" middle class and landed classes in direct contact with the

Church. However, since Lutheran churches have lacked the theocratic and international claims of the Roman Church, this has led either to a diffuse identification with "personal" religion or to a participation restricted to the rites of passage. The new social democratic elites who controlled the state were religiously indifferent. Anticlericalism was relatively muted, however, though the late 19th and early 20th centuries saw clashes between religious conservatives and social democracy. In Germany, indeed, hostility was considerable, and the decay of the various state churches was accelerated by an alliance of throne, aristocracy and altar which alienated middle as well as working classes. In this way the great plain of northern Germany became and remains an area of very low institutional vitality. In Sweden a prohibition of religious dissent, and persecution of dissidence in general, alienated new political elites and led to very low working-class practice. The 1930s were the period of maximum tension.

The Dutch pattern is worth noting because it illustrates the principle of the religious ghetto, assisted by the fact that different religious confessions are, to some extent, locally concentrated. Different religious subcultures, and especially the Roman Catholics, have defended themselves in comprehensive ghettos which are—or were—mirrored by socialist "ghettos." The result was that these religious subcultures succeeded in organizing life comprehensively and thus arresting social differentiation. They also competed among themselves and engaged in various shifting alliances against (and occasionally with) the liberal metropolitan elites. No system of predominant social power was established, and liberal elites were always confronted by the powerful force of a partially excluded Catholic minority as it mobilized itself for cultural defense and social advancement. Echoes of this situation are found in Germany where the Catholicism of south and western Germany established a network of cultural and political defense based on local Catholic elites counterpoised to the "state-bearing" Protestant elites. Even in America local Catholic elites and Catholic populations established in the major cities created a similar system of cultural and political defense.

In South Africa the cultural defense of the ghetto was utilized by the displaced Afrikaner elite against the English elites. The result has been a specialization of religious groups, with a conservative Afrikaner Calvinism eventually gaining control of the state, and the voluntary associations like the Methodists, the separatist African bodies and the Roman Catholic Church disproportionately concentrated among the black outgroups. The Calvinist sector of the elite in Ulster (like the Maronite sector of the Christian elites in Lebanon) has acted similarly, supported and even outbid by more militant popular elements in their associated ethnic enclaves. Wherever the ghetto principle is adopted, religious identification is strong. Both in South Africa and in Ulster the institutional vitality of Roman Catholic and Calvinist groups is high, and even the practice of groups poised in between like Anglicans and Methodists is higher than normal. Political debate retains elements of religious rhetoric and confrontation.

The Roman Catholic patterns exhibit the same principles, but affected by the confrontation between *'intégriste''* elements in alliance with the ecclesiastical elite against militantly secular liberal elites. The theocratic ambitions of international Catholicism continually deepened this confrontation until it became a pitched battle in France between 1870 and 1905 when state and Church were separated. In Spain the battle proceeded through a century of revolution and counter-revolution up to a climax with the civil war of the 1930s. A parallel confrontation ran through the Mexican revolution. In Italy itself, papal power confronted liberal and national forces from the 1860s on It is noteworthy that these Latin countries have been characterized not only by secular liberalism and militant secular masonic influence in the middle classes, but also by extensive eruptions of militantly secular anarchism, anarcho-syndicalism and Communism.

These tight spirals of antagonism have partially unwound since the mid-20th century. In any case, there are certain exceptions where antagonism has been less acute or less long-lasting, for example in Belgium, Austria and Portugal. Poland and Eire, as already indicated, are exceptional in that Catholicism mobilized a whole people against alien political domination.

South and Central America nowadays also offer partial exceptions to the classic picture of confrontation between militant secular elites—liberal or socialist, and "*integrista*" elements, especially the military and great proprietors, in alliance with ecclesiastic elites. The modern development of South America mostly occurred after the heat of the war between "fortress Catholicism," centered in the Vatican, and secular elites had abated. Moreover, Catholicism had already experienced some dissociation from the relatively new Creole elites by having supported Spanish domination. Certainly in some countries a conservative alliance of a sort remains, as in Argentina. But particularly in Brazil and Chile, and in Nicaragua, the Philippines and El Salvador, a large section of the ecclesiastical hierarchy has sided with radical middle-class groups and genuinely popular elements of the dispossessed against right-wing dictatorships, though should power be achieved, these alliances will probably disintegrate; signs of tension already exist in Nicaragua. In one country, Cuba, the Church was simply ejected from social and political power, a task made easier by its prior association with Spanish domination, alien clergy and social privilege. In Venezuela and Uruguay the Church has emerged in a settled but weak position, following on historic clashes with the radical middle class and the effects of extensive urbanization.

The consolidation of total power by secular elites in Eastern Europe is more or less effective, depending on the previous historical-political configuration. If the Church was closely tied in with privileged and landed groups as in Hungary, or associated with a form of monarcho-fascism as in Bulgaria, then the attack on ecclesiastical power and influence is relatively easy. In Hungary and Bulgaria the combination of industrialization and state hostility has led to a substantial decomposition of institutional religion. In East Germany and

Christians in Latin America Today

By the year 2000 more than half of the world's Catholics will be in Latin America. Hence its strategic importance and the repeated papal visits. But the folk religion of Latin America is changing. Since the Latin American bishops' conference at Medellín, Colombia, in 1968, a "theology of liberation" has spread to many of the 27 countries of the continent. Though treated with some suspicion by the Vatican, its exponents claim that it goes back to the beginnings of faith in Latin America, when the bishop was the only defender of the poor against the rapacious soldiery. The Jesuit "Reductions" of Paraguay (seen on film in *The Mission*) illustrate another way in which the Church defended the oppressed. Devotion to Mary the Mother of Jesus is yet another traditional aspect of liberation, for in her Magnificat she sings that "the powerful will be cast down from their thrones, and the poor exalted." In her Latin American "appearances" Mary talked in the Indian languages. So what appears most traditional may be most revolutionary.

Below Easter in Guatemala. A figure hangs from a tree: very picturesque. But the persecution of the Church has led some to say that "Christ is not yet risen here." Indians comprise 57 percent of the population, the rest are of mixed descent; 63 percent are illiterate; 34 percent of the labor force are unemployed. Genocide is part of counterinsurgency policy.

Right Another idyll: the Yanqui priest celebrates mass for the simple-minded Indians. By now he will have been expelled from Guatemala, and the lay catechists assassinated (the fate of over 10 000 of them). Why? The government is happier with American-financed evangelical "sects" which bring the comfort of individual salvation without any political challenge.

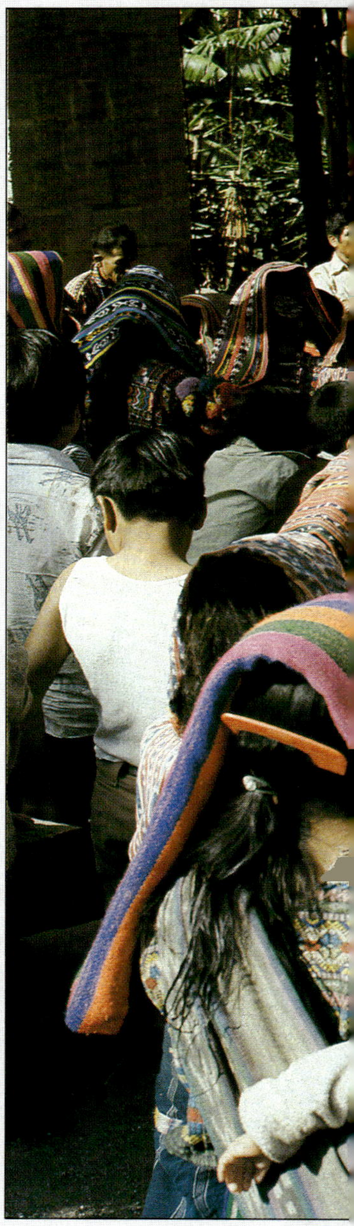

Above Ex-votos, offered in thanksgiving for cures, in a church at Juaneiro in northeast Brazil. With 50 million blacks of African origin, Brazilian Catholicism has had to struggle with syncretism, remnants of tribal religion and voodoo.

Right Two million Aymara Indians live in the Altiplano of Peru, scorched in the summer, frozen in the winter. Praying for the souls of departed relatives is a way of expressing the communion of saints.

Far right The Sunday morning procession to the parish church of Santo Tomás in Chichicastenango, Guatemala. Christianity in Latin America is not felt as an imposition: it is popular and fulfills human as well as religious aspirations.

Estonia Lutheranism was already weak and religion is now mostly found in lively minorities of Lutheran activists and sectarian enthusiasts. In Czech lands the long tradition of liberal and Hussite hostility to the Church, combined with a sense of the alien character of the Roman Church since the enforced conversion after 1625, made the task of the Communist elite easier. On the other hand, a nationalistic Communist elite, as in Romania, may find it politic to ally with the ecclesiastical hierarchy against ethnic and religious outgroups, and as a way of expressing national solidarity and historic identity against external Russian threat. Within Russia itself a partially successful attempt has been made to expropriate and control the national churches of the Ukraine, Georgia and Armenia. In this way national churches can be systematically decomposed from the inside, and folklore elements dressed up to stand in for national identity. Nevertheless, an association between distinctive national culture and historic religion remains. For that matter it remains powerful among Great Russians themselves, though most influential in those areas of farming and industrial production, least integrated under the aegis of large-scale state enterprise. Religion has been pushed out towards marginal groups and enormously reduced in the technological and administrative echelons, while its social functions have been partly taken over by a huge network of secular rituals.

Long-term differentiation and the decompositions of the 1960s

Throughout all these complicated interlocking processes involving contests between secular centers and religious peripheries, and/or between ecclesiastical elites allied to *intégriste* elites and elites armed with secular ideologies, together with the relationships between religion and class, religion and ethnicity, there are long-term processes of differentiation at work. These had dramatic consequences as they reached an advanced state in the 1960s. As society separates out into complex functions, religion loses its place as the center of the solidary social network and shifts to a more specialized role. In Protestant societies the emergence of the voluntary religious association, separating Church and state, is one element in this process. Similarly, the economic, welfare and educational networks associated with these bodies are progressively taken over by secular agencies. The same processes, involving separation of Church from state, and partial loss of welfare, economic and educational functions, occur in Roman Catholic societies, though, as has been suggested, with greater degrees of violence, greater ideological coherence on every side and the explicit involvement of the Church in politics and trade unions.

The process will tend to be peaceful if societal problems, like civil rights or economic injustice or the mobilization of subordinate ethnic subcultures, can be handled sequentially, as, for example, in England, Denmark and Switzerland. The process will be violent and likely to involve periods of totalitarian rule if these problems occur in too rapid a sequence, or are suddenly exacerbated by defeat in war as in Germany and Russia. As has been suggested, the process of differentiation is arrested in different ways according to the patterns delineated above. In Scandinavian and English cultures differentiation has worked itself out so as to leave the Church-state symbolism still in place, while slowly eroding a great deal of the social substance and reducing church functions quite drastically. In Holland, Ulster, South Africa and Lebanon differentiation has been held back by varying forms of organization in tight-knit ghettos.

The most recent manifestations of differentiation are best dealt with at three levels: the developed Protestant world, the developed Catholic world, the underdeveloped Catholic world. However, with the increasing emergence of a world system, processes which would have been very distinctive at these different levels have become more similar and play into each other.

If we take first the developed Catholic world, the advent of the Second Vatican Council had fed into it many unresolved tensions and, in turn, set off chain reactions, which played into the various economic and social changes of the 1960s and 1970s. These changes included, for example, an accelerating "open" pluralism, an expanding freedom and affluence, especially in a distinctive youth culture (or cultures), which corroded personal discipline, and an undermining of those remaining ties of community and mutual assistance in which many religious bodies were rooted.

One index of change was a sharp fall in Roman Catholic institutional participation, particularly in those areas of the North American/Anglo-Saxon world—England, the USA, Australia, Canada (i.e. Quebec)—where it had been notably high. In other areas, where the ghetto walls existed to some extent, above all in Holland, but also in Flanders and Germany, gaps appeared in the defenses. Institutional participation dropped sharply, and with it, quite often, support for Catholic unions and parties. Moreover, institutional prestige and respect fell, even in loyal bastions like Flanders. Attempts to recover positions by conservative appointments, as in Holland, generated intense resistance and alienation.

The fall in Catholic participation and in explicit party or union activity occurred all over Europe, and the power of "Christian Democracy," so prominent since 1945, was visibly weakened. The governments of Spain and Italy, once tender to Catholic moral teaching, adopted a more neutral stance, assuming more and more a plurality of moral options and personal styles. In France, the eldest daughter of secularity, participation began to approximate Protestant levels, and in Switzerland, for example in Geneva, the levels of participation and moral styles of Catholics and Protestants became barely distinguishable. Throughout Catholic Europe the withdrawal from the old political styles was matched by the adoption of socialist or progressive "existential" styles by large sectors of the clergy.

In the underdeveloped Catholic societies a phase of Christian Democracy was succeeded by a phase of liberation theology, often counterposed to the "national security" states. The resulting conflict meant that the state counterattacked by profaning sacred spaces, rites and personnel, thus weakening the religious supports of its own legitimacy. Latin American Catholicism had always ranged from local cults of saints and deities, some of them outside priestly control, to more coherent theologies of which liberationism was only the latest manifestation. But various developments exemplified the decomposition of institutional solidarities and all-embracing communal ties. In Venezuela and Uruguay, for example, sectors of indifferent secularity appeared. In other countries, particularly Brazil, there was a notable resurgence of spiritistic, diabolistic and healing cults, which affected even the middle class. Perhaps most significant of all was a massive expansion of Protestant sectarianism, above all Pentecostalism, but also Jehovah's Witnesses, Mormons and a hundred and one fissionable groups, offering warmth, fellowship and

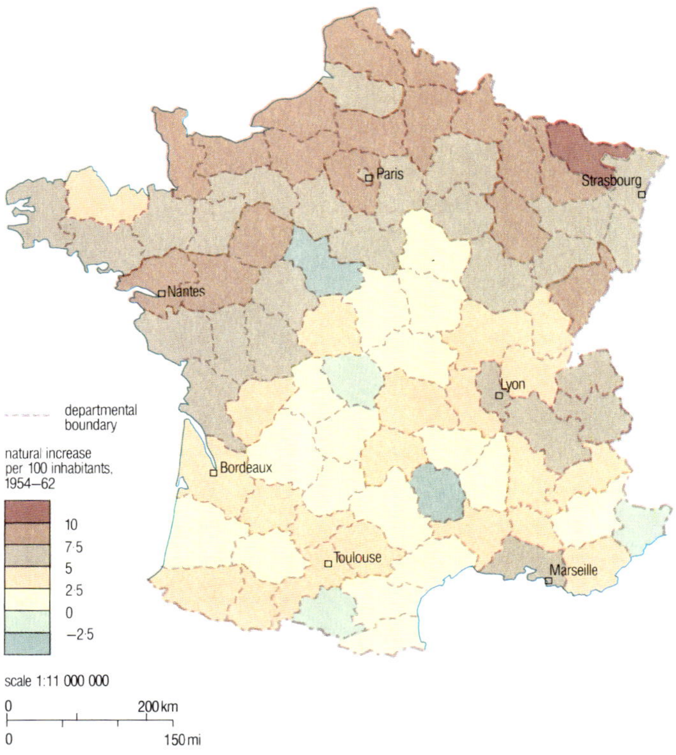

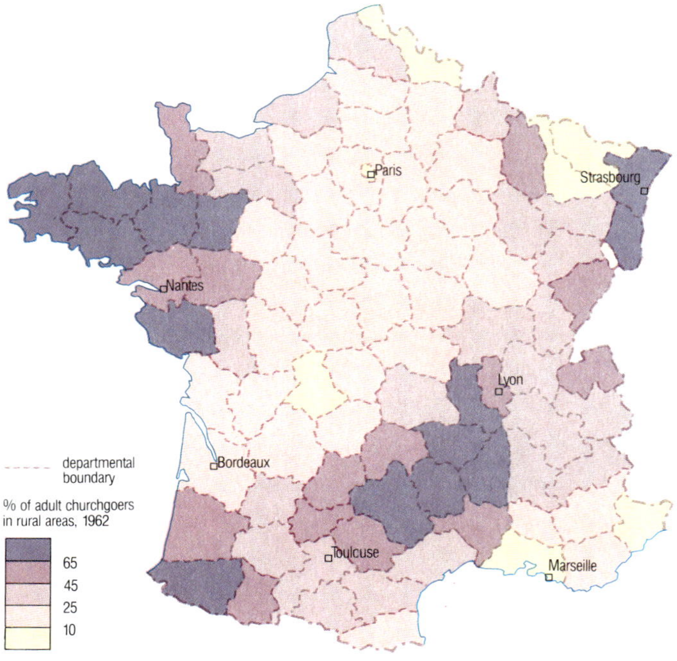

Right Bob Geldof, an Irish pop star, was shocked by reports of famine in Ethiopia in October 1984. He made it his mission to awaken the social conscience of the pop world. Immensely successful Live Aid concerts at Wembley Stadium and in Philadelphia in July 1985 raised vast sums for the famine victims. Geldof lectured African politicians on corruption and the European Parliament on the scandal of its food surpluses. In 1986 he was nominated for the Nobel Peace prize. The whole Geldof phenomenon was sometimes taken to show that there existed reserves of compassion and solidarity among young people that had not so far been tapped.

Left: Sunday attendance in France
The figures for churchgoing tell us a number of different things. In Roman Catholic countries they refer to attendances at mass, and give a reliable figure for what may be called "practicing" Christians. In earlier centuries the figure would be almost 100 percent of those able-bodied and capable of getting to church in person. In other parts of the world many Christians go to Holy Communion perhaps only a few times a year, although they may attend a service of worship regularly on Sunday. In the secularized west others, even among those who are committed Christians, may not go every Sunday, but sometimes spend the day with their families in some leisure activity. Figures for Sunday attendance can then be misleading indicators of Christian numbers. A comparison of the maps of natural increase and church attendance in France suggests that in areas where the population is growing fastest churchgoing is most in decline and vice versa. After Isambert and Terrenoire.

"power" for life's exigencies. In Brazil and Chile Protestant sectarian groups multiplied to include perhaps one in ten of the population; in Nicaragua and El Salvador the proportions were perhaps similar, and in Guatemala even higher. Hardly any Roman Catholic country in the underdeveloped world from the Philippines to Mexico is without this expansion of the Protestant principle of the voluntary association, that is, differentiation.

In the developed Protestant world there was less ecclesiastical cohesion to lose, though bodies which had been fairly stable, like the Anglican Church in the USA and England, experienced quite sharp declines. But more significant perhaps was the adoption by many young people of a post-Protestant personalist anarchism, the face of which was equally recognizable from Amsterdam to Los Angeles and Melbourne. At the same time the hostility between the expressive professions and the commercial middle classes increased notably. The suburban, and to some extent church-going, mentality came under increasing attack, especially from those who now populated the electronic media. Educational institutions more and more dropped any attachment to a specific religious belief or any support for moral prescription, and opted for a multi-faith or multi-ideology approach. They espoused the goals of personal fulfillment and were hostile to all forms of institution or involvement in organizations promoting esprit de corps. In this

Drive-in Sanctuary of the Garden Grove Community, Los Angeles, where "the future has already arrived." But it is arguable that "the electronic Church," with its fund-raising and pretensions to healing, is now more decisive in American religion. Jerry Falwell, leader of the "Moral Majority," has given way to more extreme right-wing TV evangelists, one of whom is a presidential candidate.

state of moral confusion many churchmen emerged as champions of personal liberation or, at least, loosed themselves further from their old conservative moorings.

A reaction was inevitable, and it came in various forms. Rome restored discipline where it could. Evangelicalism began to edge out of a disintegrating liberal religiosity. Powerful pressure groups emerged, espousing traditional morality, such as the "Moral Majority" in America, the National Viewers and Listeners Association and the Festival of Light in England. Parties expressing Christian values made their voices heard in Scandinavia. And the disintegrated flotsam and jetsam of the 1960s experienced small rigorist reformations in various sects operating from California to Finland, but also increasingly penetrating Catholic Europe.

If we conclude with certain general characteristics, it is possible to point to very widespread institutional decomposition commencing in the 1960s, though the declines to some extent bottomed out in the late 1970s. Nevertheless, the style of the communal religious group, often outside traditional ecclesiastical control, remained very popular. In England it might take the form of charismatic groups and house churches, in El Salvador of expanding Protestant enthusiasm, in southern Europe of "base communities," in East Germany and Hungary of unofficial activist cells.

The traditional churches themselves tried to borrow many motifs from this alternative religious culture, and from "alternative" styles in general. More often they adopted a muted pseudo-communitarianism in liturgy, while the specialized agencies of the Church engaged in a muted version of political criticism. These tendencies were often at variance with the natural preferences of their remaining constituencies, thus increasing the distance between ecclesiastical bureaucracy and the ordinary Christian. Above all, the churches tried to withdraw from all particularistic attachments to their respective nations and respective historic church identities. Ecumenism is part of this, with its new access of charity and drawing together for mutual support.

The World Council of Churches was a notable solvent of all such specific loyalties and traditions, and created a forum for a critical political style which more often reflected third-world attitudes than the preoccupations of the ordinary Christian in the sometime Christian heartlands of Europe.

If all these tendencies persist, then the term of the differentiation process could be almost in sight—the separation of religion from state, nation and natural local community, and from the networks of mutual economic support, personal welfare and education, even from the creation of "character" and distinctive moral profiles.

Christians in the Philippines Today

Below The Filipinos took over Spanish Counter-Reformation and baroque forms of piety, particularly their gaudy street processions. Here a Madonna and saints are being trundled through the streets of Lucban.

The Spanish explorer Ferdinand Magellan planted a cross in Cebu City in 1521. Thus the Philippines became the cradle of Catholicism in the Far East and the gateway to China and Japan. Over 80 percent of its 53 million people are Roman Catholic. No other Asian country has such a strong Christian presence.

The Church has recognized the strategic importance of the Philippines for Asia, especially after Vietnam—the only other comparable country—fell into the hands of the Communists. The Catholic Radio Veritas broadcasts regularly to China, where it has many listeners. Pope Paul VI visited the Philippines in 1970 (where a crazed Brazilian painter tried to assassinate him). Pope John Paul II went there in 1981 and urged President Ferdinand Marcos to reform—or else. The Church, led by Cardinal Jaime Sin, archbishop of Manila, had at first an attitude of "critical solidarity" towards Marcos and moved into outright "denunciation" towards the end of 1985. The display of "people power" that led to the overthrow of Marcos was supported, indeed inspired, by the Church.

The Philippines raises a crucial question for Asia and its neighbors across the Pacific in Latin America. Can a society be transformed in the direction of greater justice and fraternity without violence and without recourse to Marxism? Can reconciliation with guerrillas and the Muslim minority be the basis of the state?

Below Filipino religion is public, emotional, literal and inclined to excess. Here in Paombong, Bulacan province, is a scene from a Passion play with a woman playing the part of Christ. Filipinos took over Spanish religion, but they do not have Spanish machismo.

Below right Another scene from the Paombong play in which Christians are scourged on Good Friday, believing that in this way they can have a share in Christ's Passion—and so in his glory.

THE ECUMENICAL MOVEMENT

The historical divisions

Believers share one Lord, one faith, one baptism, but have found it uncommonly hard to stay together, and their dissensions have profoundly weakened Christian witness to the world. Of the splits four types emerge.

(1) The "pre-Chalcedonian" or "Monophysite" churches: Armenians, Syrian Orthodox ("Jacobite"), Copts, Ethiopians, who accept the authority of Scripture and the first three general councils, but not the Christological definition of Chalcedon (451). In modern times there has been good fraternal contact between them and other traditional churches (Rome, Orthodoxy, Anglicanism).

(2) The division between Roman Catholicism and Greek Orthodoxy, the nerve center of which lies in the Latin claim that the bishop of Rome as Peter's successor possesses a right and duty to exercise sovereign jurisdiction and teaching authority over all churches in the one universal Church, and that all local bishops derive their jurisdiction from him. The Orthodox east, conscious of being mother of all, rejects that claim as commonly formulated, and thinks it undermined by the unauthorized western addition of the *filioque* to the clause about the procession of the Spirit in the ecumenical Creed of the Council of Constantinople (381). In medieval times tensions reached breaking point on this and minor matters of discipline, for example clerical celibacy. Mutual excommunications exchanged in 1054 were lifted in 1965 by Pope Paul VI and the Ecumenical Patriarch Athenagoras, but problems remain. The Orthodox model of the universal Church is a eucharistic communion of local churches led by their bishops in the historic ancient patriarchates (Rome, Constantinople, Alexandria, Antioch, Jerusalem), having equal jurisdiction in their own spheres, but granting Rome first place among equals. In Roman Catholic eyes, the Orthodox model leaves regional churches vulnerable to nationalism that obscures universality. The two great bodies have imperfect communion with one another, each recognizing the validity of the other's sacraments and orders, yet remaining in practice independent.

(3) The traditionalist churches separated from Rome at the Reformation, but in varying degrees preserving much of the "classical" shape of church life: Anglicans, Lutherans, Presbyterians ("Reformed"), Congregationalists, Methodists.

(4) The tradition-rejecting wing of the Reformation, especially the Baptists, regarding baptism as a public sign and seal of inward faith rather than a sacrament through which the believer receives grace and is incorporated into Christ, and the Pentecostalists ("Assemblies of God" etc.) who feel the historic churches, with their restrained and ordered ways of worship, reasoned theology and formal liturgical pattern, to be suffocating the spontaneity and ecstasy of the Spirit.

Three hundred years of strenuous endeavor failed to reconcile the Monophysite churches to Chalcedon. Medieval ecumenism between Greek east and Latin west achieved short-lived paper reconciliations (Lyon 1274, Florence 1439) which had no effect because Greek memories of Latin rule in the east, after the Fourth Crusade had sacked Constantinople (1204), left the people alienated. Christians in Orthodox countries in full communion with Rome, called Uniates, still have a delicate relation with Orthodox national churches. At the Reformation the breach in the west was so bitter and bloody that it is only in the 20th century that official encouragement has been given to attempts to heal the wound.

The World Council of Churches

The modern ecumenical movement emerged out of the realization by Protestant missionaries from the west that the old European schisms caused bewilderment when exported to Asia and Africa. An international Protestant missionary conference at Edinburgh (1910) began a process of convergence, ably led by the American John R. Mott and the English J. H. Oldham. A series of conferences developed in two areas, "Life and Work," and "Faith and Order" (Stockholm 1925, Lausanne 1927, Edinburgh and Oxford 1937, and subsequently). These meetings were attended by numerous delegates from Asia and Africa. In 1937 the proposal was made for a central bureau to provide a forum for ecumenical studies and to avert unintended duplications and rivalries. By an inspired choice the Dutch theologian W. A. Visser 't Hooft was appointed secretary. The vision became reality at Amsterdam (1948) when the World Council of Churches (WCC) was formally constituted with its office in Geneva. The confession of faith of member churches is the

The unity of the Church was first broken after the Council of Chalcedon (451), and again in 1054 when the eastern and western churches divided. In the 16th century reforming movements led to further divisions, and the process of fragmentation went on until the beginning of the movement for reunion at the end of the 19th century.

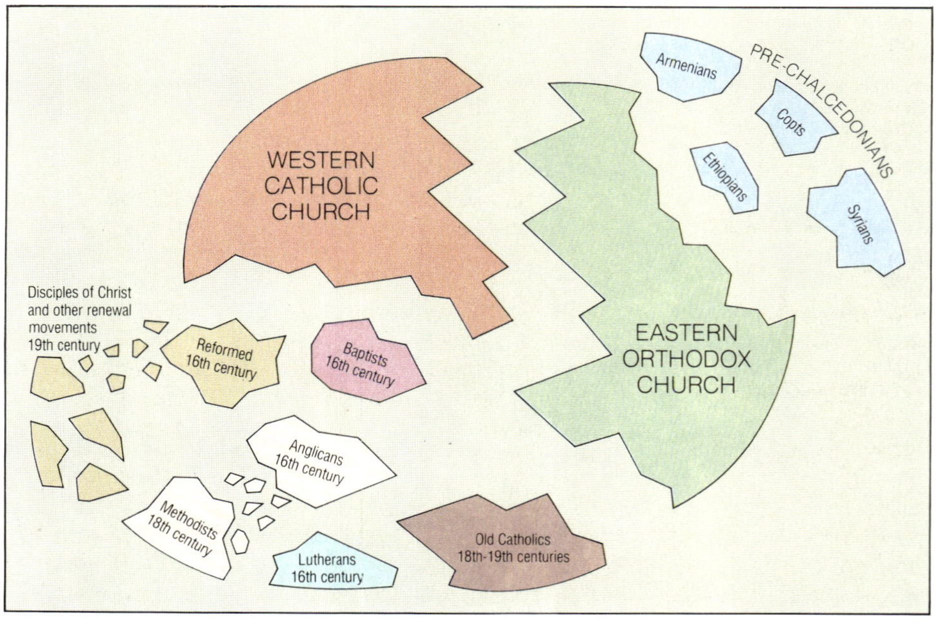

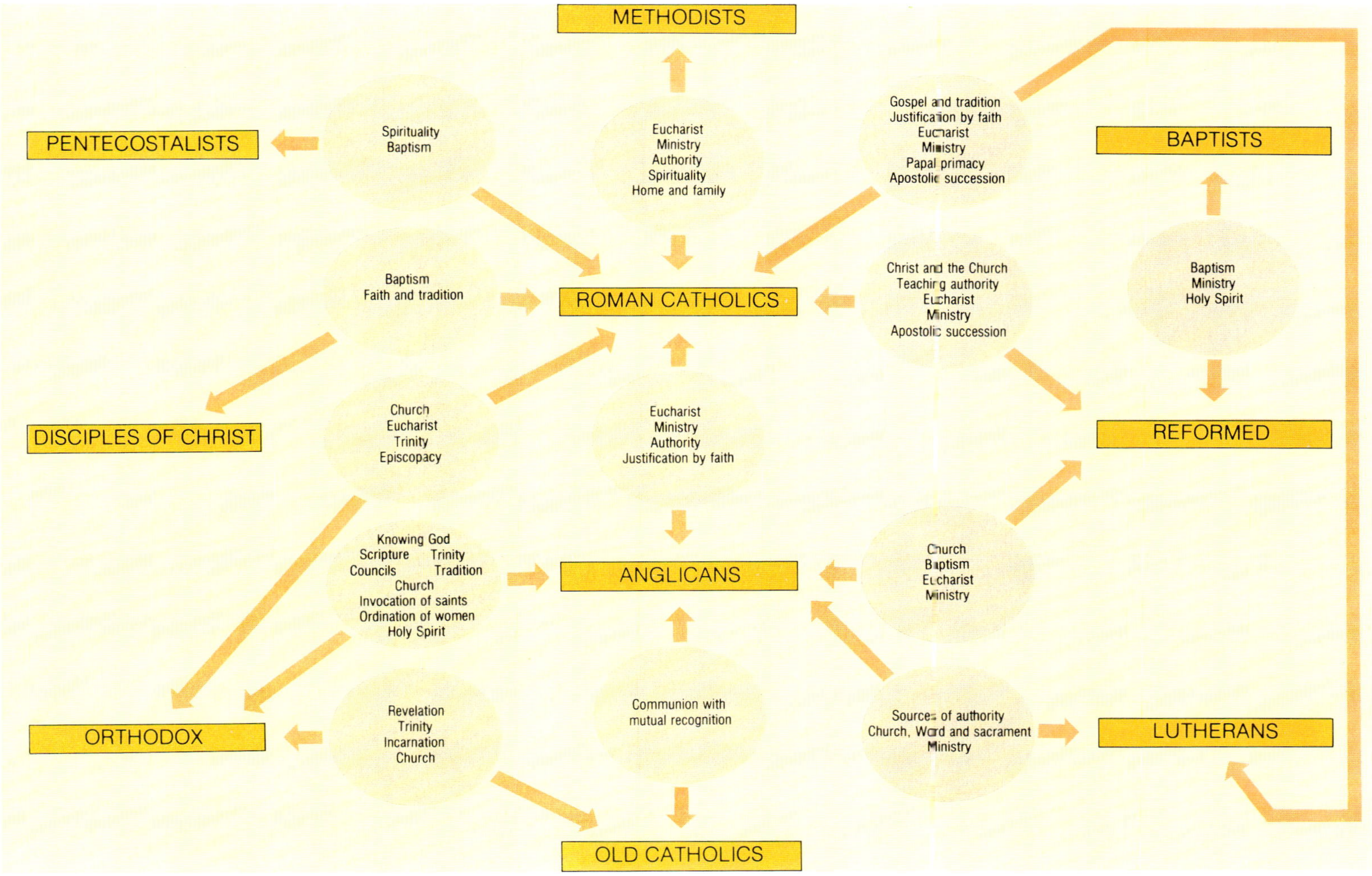

Above The diagram shows how different denominations have been meeting in recent decades to discuss and try to resolve their ancient differences. The topics they have considered together have been decided by the areas of traditional disagreement between them and, more positively, by the deep concerns of each for what has historically been most precious to them as a communion.

Below The Greek word OIKOUMENE crowns the outline of a cross and ship in this symbol which is used by the World Council of Churches. *Oikoumene* ("the world") gives us the word "ecumenism" in English.

divinity of Christ and the Holy Trinity.

Throughout its history the WCC has been concerned not only with promoting theological understanding, but also with social and political issues—peace and control of armaments; race (the 1937 conference spoke out against Nazi anti-semitism); religious liberty; aid to refugees and those oppressed by injustice. It has also fostered the study of lay ministry, and helped churches to adopt a constructive approach to the revolt of Western women against domesticity.

Born in a Protestant milieu, the movement that produced the WCC initially presupposed a conception of the Church in which minor importance was attached to continuous and ordered ministry in apostolic succession; but the difficulty of a shared eucharist for both episcopal and non-episcopal churches was felt in 1910. From 1925 Orthodox participation was weighty, and thereafter it became difficult for the WCC to propose solutions to the ecumenical problem on the basis of a liberal Protestant understanding of the Church.

Although from early in the century groups of Roman Catholics had observed a week of prayer for unity, 18–25 January, the official attitude of Roman authority to the WCC was aloof. The encyclical *Mortalium Animos* (1928), reacting against the unofficial Anglican/Roman Catholic talks at Malines (1925–26), forbade ecumenical discussion and any common prayer as likely to imply indifferentism. But in 1937 new direction was given to Roman Catholic thinking by the Dominican Yves Congar, author of *Chrétiens désunis*. The atmosphere changed only slowly. In 1948 the Curia warned all Roman Catholic theologians against attending the WCC meeting in Amsterdam; this did not prevent a number from taking their holidays in the Netherlands at the time. In 1950 the Holy Office relented, giving permission for meetings and for common worship only to the limit of the Lord's Prayer. In France the ecumenical spirit was strong. Pioneering work was done by the Abbé Couturier of Lyon, gathering a group of Catholics and Protestants at the Trappist abbey of Dombes, and then by Dominicans at the Istina center in Paris. In 1960 the Vatican Secretariat for Unity was set up under Cardinal Bea, then Cardinal Willebrands. In 1961 five Roman Catholic observers were sent to the WCC assembly in New Delhi.

The Second Vatican Council and its aftermath

On 21 November 1964 the Second Vatican Council promulgated a decree on ecumenism, *Unitatis Redintegratio*. Nothing could have been less like the aloof stance of the 1928 encyclical. The momentous decree, together with the shift in emphasis in other constitutions of the Council, left the Roman Catholic Church gasping with astonishment at its own moderation. The decree recognizes in the Orthodox a sister church with valid sacraments, and in members of the Reformation churches "brothers in the Lord" in communions used by the Spirit as means of salvation, yet because of a defect of ministerial order lacking the full substance of

the eucharistic mystery. Protestants' devotion to the Bible is warmly praised. It is noted that they have a different view on the relation of the Bible to the Church and on moral questions (presumably the reference is to birth control, perhaps to gambling), and have no conception of an authoritative teaching office. At one point the Anglican communion is recognized to have a "special place among the communions in which some Catholic traditions and institutions continue." A warning against dialogue in which the dogmatic position of the Roman Catholic Church is less than fully presented is amply balanced by a concession that not all dogmas are equally central: there is a "hierarchy of truths." Likewise "unity in essentials" in no sense excludes "legitimate diversity" in liturgy or in the theological elaboration of revealed truth. Above all, the decree asks for a change of heart, setting aside rivalry, seeking to listen and never to hurt or misrepresent other parties in the dialogue.

Since Vatican II, bilateral dialogues have been officially established, notably with Anglicans, Orthodox, Lutherans and Methodists. The first Anglican/Roman Catholic International Commission (ARCIC) presented its report in 1982, a document whose publication was accompanied by a predominantly negative critique (but expressly not a negative *verdict*) from the Holy Office or Congregation for the Doctrine of the Faith, under the prefecture of Cardinal Ratzinger. Nevertheless, a

Above In 1962 the Second Vatican Council met, attended by 2600 Roman Catholic bishops, from all over the world. Pope John XXIII is shown here opening the council. This, the first ecumenical council for 92 years, launched a new era in the life of the Church, and a series of changes in patterns of worship. One of its most important results was the new commitment to ecumenical endeavor.

second ARCIC was set up after a joint declaration by Pope John Paul II and Archbishop Runcie of Canterbury when the pope attended service at Canterbury (Pentecost 1982). Also in 1982 the Faith and Order commission of the WCC met at Lima to agree a major statement on Baptism, Eucharist and Ministry, the general pattern of which has much in common with the ARCIC report. Lutheran/Roman Catholic conversations in the USA and Germany have also revealed an unexpected rapprochement in highly sensitive areas.

The ecumenical movement has not enjoyed unimpeded progress without critical opposition. Roman claims to universal jurisdiction continue to evoke fears in Orthodox and Anglican minds. The decision of some provinces of the Anglican communion to admit women to the presbyterate has cooled Roman and Orthodox enthusiasm for progress in dialogue. On the Protestant side, the movement has met vehement negative criticism from two opposed camps: (a) ultra-conservative groups, especially but not only in America, wherever absolute biblical inerrancy is a touchstone of recognition; (b) ultra-liberal or Unitarian circles, to whom ecumenism represents an unwelcome reconfessionalization, above all a return to the essentially unliberal idea that in the Bible and the living tradition of the Church there is an authoritative or classical form of Christianity by which the present Church is to be evaluated.

Despite the zigzag of setbacks, the advances, especially since Roman Catholic participation and Vatican II, have acquired great momentum. The movement certainly marks an irreversible recognition on the Protestant side that the nationalism which emerged prominently in the Reformation era can obscure and obstruct a fundamental task of Christ's universal Church. On the Roman Catholic side, Vatican II's decree irreversibly marks an acknowledgment of the truly Christian character of the Reformation churches; it not only expressly denies that those who belong to them are thereby in a state of sin but further accepts some Roman Catholic responsibility for the fact that division ever came about. The legacy of the past includes formularies and confessions of faith, some of which were worded to be exclusive; and these easily create the impression that ecumenism is an exercise in ecclesiastical diplomacy where elite theologians join a private club and produce reports that unscrupulously surrender principles for which men and women once went to the stake. Agreement is possible in principle if those engaged in dialogue are allowed to go behind the polemical and divisive formulas and to ask what positive affirmation they seek to protect.

Right Pope Paul VI offers his ring to the archbishop of Canterbury, Dr Michael Ramsey, during the archbishop's visit to Rome in 1966. The two leaders joined in a service of prayer and pledged their churches to "serious dialogue" in the search for Christian unity.

LIST OF CONTRIBUTORS

Alan Amos, Vice-Principal of Westcott House, Cambridge, contributed the feature on Beirut.

Henry Chadwick, some time Dean of Christ Church, Oxford, Emeritus Regius Professor of Divinity in the University of Cambridge, and now Master of Peterhouse, Cambridge, wrote on the Early Church, the Ecumenical Movement and Italy Today.

Priscilla Chadwick, Head of Bishop Ramsey Church of England Comprehensive School, Hillingdon, London, wrote on Christianity and the Other World Religions.

Eamon Duffy, University Lecturer in Divinity and Fellow of Magdalene College, Cambridge, wrote the chapters on the Late Middle Ages, Reformation, Counter-Reformation and War, Settlement and Disunity.

Gillian Evans, University Lecturer in History and Fellow of Fitzwilliam College, Cambridge, wrote on the Medieval Church in the West.

Edwin Gaustad, Professor of History, University of California, Riverside, wrote on the Church in North America.

Peter Hebblethwaite, author of many books including *Christian-Marxist Dialogue and Beyond* (1977) and *John XXIII, Pope of the Council* (1984), wrote on Christianity, Communism and National Identity in addition to the features on Poland, Latin America and the Philippines.

David Martin, Professor of Sociology, London School of Economics and Political Science, wrote the chapter on Christianity and Secular Modernity.

Andrew Porter, Reader in History at King's College London, wrote the chapters on the 18th-Century Church, the 19th-Century Church, the African Experience and Missions to Asia.

Mary Remnant, Lecturer at the Royal College of Music, London, contributed the feature on Church Music.

Jonathan Shepard, University Lecturer in History, Cambridge, wrote on the Medieval Church in the East and the Orthodox Churches.

LIST OF ILLUSTRATIONS

Abbreviations: t = top, tl = top left, tr = top right, c = center, b = bottom etc.
BBC HPL = BBC Hulton Picture Library; RH = Robert Harding Picture Library; SH = Sonia Halliday, Weston Turville, Bucks.
The location of picture sources is London unless otherwise stated.

Endpapers. Carte des chemins de S.Jacques de Compostelle: Camino Frances de Santiago de Compostela, 1648.

page
2–6. Details from the Communion of the Apostles, Church of the Holy Cross, Platanistasa, Cyprus: SH.
8–9. Drawings: John Fuller, Cambridge.
13. St Paul: Leonard von Matt, Buochs, Switzerland.
14–15b. Sheep and bread: André Held, Ecublens, Switzerland.
15t. Malta: Ann Bolt.
15b. Christ teaching: André Held.
18t. Reconstructions: Dick Barnard, Milverton, Somerset.
18–19. Papal chamber, catacomb of Callistus, Rome: Zefa/Konrad Helbig.
20t. Plan: John Brennan, Oxford.
201. Adam and Eve, ivory: Scala, Florence.
20–21. Christ the shepherd, sarcophagus: Scala.
20bc. Santa Costanza mausoleum, Rome: Scala.
20br. Vintage scene mosaic Santa Costanza, Rome: Scala.
21c. Christ between St Peter and St Paul, Crypt of St Peter and St Marcellinus, Rome, 4th century: SH.
21b. Portrait of Christian family: Scala.
22t. Three women at the tomb, ivory: SH (National Museum, Munich).
22b Good shepherd, Lucina Crypt, catacomb of Callistus, Rome, 3rd century: SH.
23t. Samson routing Philistines, catacomb of the Via Latina, Rome, 4th century: SH.
23b. Junius Bassus sarcophagus, Vatican: RH.
24. Orant figure from Tarragona, Spain: Foto MAS, Barcelona.
27. Third ecumenical council held at Ephesus, mural by Symeon Axenti, 1513, church of St Sozomenos, Galata, Cyprus: SH.
29. S. Apollinare in Classe, Ravenna: Scala.
30t. St Augustine by Pacino di Buonaguida, Accademia, Florence, 14th century: Art and Architecture Library.
30b. Water Newton silver bowl: British Museum.
31. Statue from Chartres cathedral: Equinox Archive.
32. Justinian coin: SH (Bibliothèque Nationale, Paris).
33. St Catherine's Monastery, Sinai: Werner Braun, Jerusalem.
34t. Qalaat Seman Monastery, Syria: SH.
34c. Coptic monk, 6th–7th century: Courtesy of the Byzantine Photograph Collection © 1986 Dumbarton Oaks, Trustees of Harvard University, Washington DC 20007.
36. Basilica of St Demetrius, Thessalonica: Nikos Kontos, Athens.
37. The judgment of Photius: SH (National Library, Madrid).
381. Virgin and child, St Catherine's, Sinai: Jerusalem Publishing House.
38r. Icon of Christ, St Catherine's, Sinai: Jerusalem Publishing House.
39b. Forty martyrs, ivory: Staatliche Museen Preussischer Kulturbesitz, Berlin.
39t. Iconoclastic debate: British Library, Add. MS. 19352, f.27v.
41t. Church of the Dormition, Orchomenos: Graham Speake, Oxford.
41b. Syrian monastery at Qalb Louzeh: Jason Wood, Lancaster.
42. Dionysiou Monastery, Mount Athos: Zefa/Konrad Helbig.
47. Two Frankish noblemen accepting Christianity, c. 1040: Hirmer Verlag, Munich.
48t. St Augustine, St Mary's, Stowting, 15th century: SH.
48b. Gregory I, 7th century: Museo Civico, Brescia.
49. Lindisfarne Gospels, f.93b, St Mark; Phaidon Archive (British Library).
51. The psalmist David enters the house of the Lord, ivory cover from prayer book of Charles the Bald, c. 870, Schweizer Landesmuseum, Zürich: Equinox Archive.
52–53. Patmos: Zefa.
54. St Luke: British Library, Add. MS. 28815.
55. Mosaic of Christ, Constantine and Zoe, St Sophia, Constantinople, 12th century: SH.
57tr. Sts Sergius and Bacchus, Constantinople; Agenzia Titus, Turin.
57b. Monastery of Christ Pantocrator, Constantinople: By courtesy of Electa Editrice, Milan.
57cl. St Sophia narthex, Constantinople: By courtesy of Electa Editrice, Milan.
60t. Constantinople: British Library, Add. MS. 42130, f.164.
60bl. Pope Urban II preaching the First Crusade, Livres des Passages d'Outremer, 15th century: SH.
60–61. Krak des Chevaliers: Aerofilms.
61tl. Richard and Saladin: British Library, Add. MS. 42130, f. 82.
61tr. Crusader crosses, Holy Sepulcher, Jerusalem: SH.
61cr. Ship of war: British Library, Add. MS. 42130, f.161v.
61br. Siege of Jerusalem, 15th-century MS., British Library: Michael Holford.
62. The genealogy of Christ, cupola, south dome of Kariye Cami, Constantinople: SH.
64–65. Monastery of the Pantanassa, Mistra: Graham Speake.
66. Donation of Constantine, SS Quattro Coronati, Rome, 13th century: Scala.
68. Coronation of Emperor Frederick III by Pope Nicholas V, 1452, Flemish Master: Germanisches Nationalmuseum, Nuremberg.
70. Dante's *Divine Comedy,* 15th century, Sienese: British Library YT/36, f. 131.
721. King's court, Séance de la cour des pairs, procès de Robert d'Artois, Bibliothèque Nationale, Paris: Equinox Archive.
72t. Relief from south porch of the cathedral of Notre Dame, Paris, showing a lecture at Paris University, 13th century: Alinari S.p.A., Florence.
72tr. Plan: Inkwell, Bicester, Oxford.
73t. Hussite caricature of pope: Knihovna Narodniho Muzea, Prague.
72–73. The pope judging heretics: Staatliche Museen der Stiftung Preussicher Kulturbesitz, Berlin, Min. 4215.
74. Coronation of emperor of Constantinople, St Sophia: Magnum, Paris/Erich Lessing © 1986.
75. Pilgrim: Bodleian Library, Oxford, MS. Laud. Misc. 93, f.89.
76t. Pilgrim medallion from St John's basilica, Ephesus: SH.
76–77. Allegory of the Pilgrims by Domenico Ghirlandaio, San Martino dei Buonomini, Florence: SH.
77t. Pilgrim window, Trinity Chapel, Canterbury Cathedral: SH.
78–79. Easter pilgrimage, Kalwaria Zebrzydowska, Poland: Magnum.
80–81. St Peter's Square, Rome, Holy Year 1975: RH.
81t. Lourdes: Magnum/Bruno Barbey.
81b. Palm Sunday procession, Jerusalem: SH (Jane Taylor).
82t. Outdoor service at Souzdel: Magnum/Fred Mayer.
82b. Procession to Notre Dame de Copacabana, Argentina: Magnum/Rene Burri.
83. Pilgrims at Fatima, Portugal: Magnum/Bruno Barbey.
84. Piazza, Loreto: Pepi Meriso, Bergamo.
85. Emperor and Antipope: Vatican Library, Vat. Reg. Lat. 580.
87b. Sixtus IV and Platina by Melozzo da Forli, Vatican Art Gallery: Scala.
87tl. Alexander Borgia by Pinturicchio, App. Borgia, Sala dei misteri della Fede, Vatican: Scala.
87tr. Leo X with Cardinals Giulio de Medici and Luigi de Rossi by Raphael, Uffizi, Florence: Phaidon Archive.
88–89 Reliquary by the Master of Montefallo, 14th century, Umbrian: Michael Holford (Victoria and Albert Museum).
90–91. Procession: Fotomas Index (British Library).
90b. From *In Praise of Folly,* marginal drawing by Holbein: Kupferstichkabinett, Öffentliche Kunstsammlung, Basel.
91. Erasmus by Dürer: Phaidon Archive.
92. Seven Deadly Sins by Bosch: Foto MAS (Prado).
93tl. Luther as a monk by Lucas Cranach, 1520: Phaidon Archive.
93tr. Luther preaching by Lucas Cranach: Kupferstichkabinett, Staatliche Museen Preussischer Kulturbesitz, Berlin.
95. Luther's German Catechism, 1529: Equinox Archive.
95br. *Limoges* by Pierre Viret, Louvre: Service de documentation photographique, Réunion des musées nationaux.
95c. Anabaptists: Fotomas Index (British Library).
95bl. Dies Dominica: Eamon Duffy, Cambridge.
95–97. *Fishing for Souls* by A. van der Venne: Rijksmuseum, Amsterdam.
97b. Altar frontal from Torslunde Church: National Museum, Copenhagen.
98–99 Calvinist congregation, attributed to Jean Ferrissin, Temple de Lyon, nommé paradis: Bibliothèque Publique et Universitaire, Geneva.
101. Henry VIII triumphing over the pope; National Portrait Gallery, London.
102tl. *Four Horsemen of the Apocalypse* by Dürer: Phaidon Archive (British Museum).
102r. Cranmer's *Book of Common Prayer,* 1549: Equinox Archive.
104. *Auto de fé celebrado por la inquisicion francesa en Albi durante la cruzada contra los catars,* by Pedro Berruguete: Foto MAS (Prado, Madrid).
104–05. Council of Trent: Fotomas Index (British Museum).
106t. Risen Christ by Michelangelo, Santa Maria sopra Minerva, Rome: Phaidon Archive.
106–07b. *The Allegory of the Holy League* by El Greco: Phaidon Archive (National Gallery, London).
109t. Ignatius Loyola: Foto MAS.
109b. *The Triumph of the Catholic Church* by Rubens: Phaidon Archive (Prado, Madrid).
110. *Le Sette Chiese* by A. Lafrery: Kunstbibliothek mit Museum für Architektur, Modebild und Grafik Design, Staatliche Museen Preussischer Kulturbesitz, West Berlin.
113t. St Bartholomew's Day Massacre: André Held (Musée Cantonal des Beaux Arts, Lausanne).
113b. Fortifications at La Rochelle: Zefa/Kerth Klaus.
115t. *St Odolophus's Church* by Saenredam: Rijksmuseum.
114–15b. *St John the Baptist Preaching* by Pieter Brueghel the Elder: Museum of Fine Arts, Budapest.
117t. Old woman reading lectionary by Gerard Dou: Rijksmuseum.
116–17. Mère Agnes Arnauld and Catherine de Ste Suzanne by Champaigne: Giraudon, Paris.
120tl. Oaxaca, Mexico: Zefa/G. Heil.
120tr. Crucifix, Institut des Beaux Arts, Mexico: Giraudon, Paris.
121b. Baptism of Indians, from Codex Azcatitla: SH (Bibliothèque Nationale, Paris).
122t. Portuguese priest, Goa: British Library, Sloane MS. 197, f.56v.
122–23. Arrival of St Francis Xavier at Goa by Doningos de Gunha: Michael Holford (Museu Nacional de Arte Antiga, Lisbon).
123b. Matteo Ricci: BBC HPL.
125t. Landing at Jamestown: BBC HPL/Bettman.
126t. Pilgrim Fathers by G. H. Boughton: BBC HPL.
127b. Methodist camp meeting, 1819, aquatint: Library of Congress, Washington.
128–29. Paintings by Lewis Miller: Historical Society of York County, Pennsylvania.
130t. Mission San Luis Rey: Mirielle Vautier, Paris.
130b. Shakers, Lebanon, New York: BBC HPL.
132t. Baptist preacher: Richard and Sally Greenhill.
132b. Haitian community: Magnum/Abbas.
133t. Jesus People: Frank Spooner Pictures.
133b. Baptism: Frank Spooner Pictures.
134b. *Feast of the Supreme Being* by De Machy: Jean-Loup Charmet (Musée Carnavelet, Paris).
136t. A procession of the Goddess Reason: SH (Bibliothèque Nationale, Paris).
136c. Whitefield preaching in Moorfields: BBC HPL.
137. Count Nicholas von Zinzendorf: Mansell Collection.
138–39. Wesley preaching in Old Cripplegate Church: Fotomas Index.
140. *Sunday,* French lithograph: Jean-Loup Charmet, Paris.

141bl. Félicité Robert de La Mennais: Bibliothèque Nationale, Paris.
141tl. Johann Ignaz von Döllinger: Mary Evans Picture Library.
141tr. Pope Pius IX: Scala (Museo del Risorgimento, Milan).
142tl. E. B. Pusey: BBC HPL.
142tr Keble College, Oxford: Linda Proud, Oxford.
142bl. Boys netting converts: Oscott College, Sutton Coldfield.
142br. John Henry Newman: By permission of the Warden and Fellows of Keble College, Oxford.
145b. *Drei Frauen in der Kirche* by Liebl: Hamburger Kunsthalle, Germany.
145t. Joanna Southcott: Mary Evans Picture Library.
146. Queen Victoria presenting Bible: National Portrait Gallery, London.
147. George Grenfell: Bodleian Library, Oxford.
148. David Livingstone: Council for World Mission (School of Oriental and African Studies).
150t. Group of missionaries, Mombasa, c.1901; 150c. African, Mauritian, Creole and Indian Priests; 151t. Scotch Mission Station, Blantyre; 151c. African deacon on trek; 151b. Primary reading class, G.E.A.: All photographs by courtesy of The Royal Commonwealth Society, London.
152–53. Cathedral choir, Uganda; Magnum/Chris Steele Perkins.
153b. Roman Catholic bishops at Kisumu, Kenya: RH/David Lomax.
153r. Sierra Leone: Magnum/Jean Gaumy.
1541. Sunday morning mass near Pretoria; Magnum/A. Venzango.
154r. Black priest blessing white woman, Johannesburg: Abbas Magnum.
155tl. Enthronement of Archbishop Tutu, Cape Town Cathedral: Frank Spooner Pictures.
155tr. Dutch Reformed Church, Worcester, Cape Province: Magnum/Berry.
155bl. Baptism in Lake: Magnum/Berry.
155br. Rhenish Mission church, Stellenbosch: Graham Speake.
156. Village church, Papua New Guinea; Zega/Dr D. Holdsworth.
157. Christian pilgrim, India: Magnum/Ian Berry.
159. J. Hudson Taylor: Overseas Missionary Fellowship, Sevenoaks, Kent.
160. Urakami Catholic Church, Nagasaki: AGE Fotostock, Barcelona.
160–61. Baptism of the Maori chief, Te Puni, Otaki Church, New Zealand, by Charles Decimus Barraud, 1853: Rex Nan Kivell Collection (NK 1103), National Library of Australia, Canberra.
163. Painted church of Moldavia: Romanian National Tourist Office.
164. Rila Monastery, Bulgaria: Zefa.
165. St Basil's Cathedral, Moscow: Zefa/L. Hrdlicka.
166–67. Tsar Nicholas II holding icon before soldiers: Popperfoto.
168t. Cypriot church: SH.
168b. Greek priest: Magnum/Rene Burri.
169tl. Russian Orthodox church: Magnum/Fred Mayer.
169tr. Armenian church, Israel, Christmas: Magnum/Micha Bar.
169b. Coptic church in Egypt; Magnum/Alex Webb.
171. Christ in Majesty from the Athelstan Psalter: British Library, MS. Cott.Galba A VIII, f.21.
172t. Bronze font showing baptism: Foto Marburg.
172c. Riha Paten, Constantinople, 565–78 AD: Courtesy of the Byzantine Photograph Collection © Dumbarton Oaks, Trustees of Harvard University, Washington DC 20007.
172b. Confession: David Richardson, Coventry.
172–73. Ordination, Vatican: Magnum/Eve Arnold.
172–73b. Russian Orthodox wedding: Magnum/Fred Mayer.
173tr. Confirmation: David Richardson, Coventry.
173br. Last rites: Magnum/Robert Capa.
174–75 Illustrations of interior of church: Dick Barnard, Milverton, Somerset.
175tl. Plan of church: Inkwell, Bicester, Oxford.
176t. Canadian church: Magnum/Taconis.
176b. Siena Cathedral: Zefa.
176–77. Dolomite church: Zefa.
177tr. Crystal Cathedral: Mirielle Vautier.
177bl. St Sophia, Kiev: Zefa.
177br. Pilgrim church, Neviges, Germany: Zefa.
178tl. David and church instruments: British Library, Add. MS.62925, f.97v.
178tr. Singers in procession: National Library of Scotland, MS. 18.1.7, f.149v (Collection Mary Remnant).
178br. Title-page of *Theatrum Instrumentorum* by Michael Praetorius: Collection Mary Remnant.
178–79t. *Procession of the Cross in St Mark's Square* by Gentile Bellini: Scala (Accademia, Venice).
179b. *A Village Choir* by Thomas Webster: Bridgeman Art Library (Forbes Magazine Collection, New York).
179cr. Modern music in Catholic church, USA: Sally and Richard Greenhill.
180. Medieval calendar, from the Hours of Nicolas von Firmian, Flanders, c. 1500: Sotheby's 10 Sept. 1980.
181. Palm Sunday procession, Rome: Impact/Mark Cator.
182bl. St Peter: Leonard von Matt.
182br. Innocent III: Scala (Subiaco).
183bl. Pius VII by Davide: Giraudon (Louvre).
183br. Julius II by Raphael, Uffizi, Florence: Phaidon Archive.
183tr. Bust of John XXIII by Giacomo Manzu, Vatican City, modern religious art collection: Scala.
184t. St George, Ethiopian painting: RH (British Library).
184tr. Bombed church: Magnum.
184bl. Church militant cartoon: Equinox Archive.
184br. Christian CND: Andes Press Agency.
185. Salvadorian soldiers and icon: Magnum.
186tr. Tabernacle by Orcagna, Orsanmichele, Florence: Scala.
186c. Hospitallers prepare to defend Rhodes against Turks, 15th-century MS.: SH (Bibliothèque Nationale, Paris).
186b. *At the Nun's School* by G. Pennasilco: Galleria d'Arte Moderna, Milan.
187t. The fight between Carnival and Lent by Pieter Brueghel the Elder, Kunsthistorisches Museum, Vienna: Phaidon Archive.
187c. Salvation Army in 19th century: Salvation Army.
187bl. Lecture at New College, Oxford: Fotomas Index (British Library).
188–89t. Mar Saba: SH.
188cb. St Bernard, St Peter's, Rome: RH.
188bl. Monk at desk: Fotomas Index (British Library).
189b. Consecration of Abbey of Cluny by Pope Urban II, 1095: SH (Bibliothèque Nationale, Paris, MS. Lat. 17716, f. 91).
1891. St Francis by Cimabue, Assisi: SH.
189tr. St Benedict, Subiaco: Scala.
189br. Young nuns taking their vows: Magnum/Eve Arnold.
190–91 All pictures: Frank Monaco/Rex Features.
192c. Head of Christ, 17th century: Mirielle Vautier (Collection Olga Fisch).
192bl. Cristo de los Toreros, Convento de San Cayetano, Cordoba: AGE Fotostock *4-RMT-32015-0*.
192–93 Mosaic from St Sophia, Constantinople: Zefa *544.9-5*.
193tl. Taxi, Port-au-Prince; Mirielle Vautier.
193tr. German stele from Niederdollendorf: Rheinisches Landesmuseum, Bonn.
193r. Christ crucified, 1063, Monasterio de Carrizo, Leon: AGE Fotostock *4-JBZ-51487-0*.
1931. Christ in Majesty, St Sernin, Toulouse, c. 1090: Leonard von Matt.
194. Terracotta bust of Christ by Giovanni della Robbia, c. 1500: Victoria and Albert Museum.
195. Ronchamp, church by Le Corbusier: Zefa.
197. Church and synagogue, USA: Zefa.
198. Mosque in Christian settlement: British Library, Sloane MS. 197.
199. Buddhist dagoba and Dutch Reformed church, Sri Lanka: AGE Fotostock, Barcelona.
200b. Wedding: Magnum/Raymond Depardon.
200–01t. Cross in street: Magnum/Abbas.
201t. Inside church: Magnum/Raymond Depardon.
201b. Priest with phalanx of soldiers at Gemayel's funeral: Magnum/Abbas.
202–03. Zagorsk monastery and shrine, Russia: RH.
204t. Funeral of Father Popieluszko: Frank Spooner Pictures.
204b. John Paul II and crowd: Photo Source.
205t. Poles praying: Frank Spooner Pictures.
205b. Picket and icon: Photo Source.
206–07. Backovo Monastery, Bulgaria: Zefa/Dr Hans Kramarz.
207t. Mass in Ieud, Romania: Magnum/Mark Riboud.
208bl. Venetian funeral: Pepi Meriso, Bergamo.
208–09, 209b Pilgrims at Monte Autore: Pepi Meriso.
209t. Raising of the candles, St Ubaldo's Day, Gubbio: Pepi Meriso.
210–11. Procession of Carmines at Corpus Domini, Gandino: Pepi Meriso.
212–13t. Pilgrimage to Croagh Patrick, Ireland: RH.
213b. Huguenots: RH.
214t. J.F. Kennedy and Pope Paul VI: Popperfoto.
214b. Coronation of Elizabeth II: Popperfoto.
216c. Judas, Passion play, Guatemala: Magnum/Gilles Peress.
216l. Ex-votos, Brazil: Mirielle Vautier.
216b. Prayer for the dead, Peru: Magnum/Sebastio Salgado.
216–17t. US missionary celebrating mass, Guatemala: AGE Fotostock.
217b. Procession, Chichicastenango: P. Chadwick.
219. Live Aid concert, London: Frank Spooner Pictures.
220. Drive-in church, Los Angeles: Magnum/Paul Fusco.
221tr. Saints carried through the streets of Lucban, Philippines: Magnum/Philip Jones Griffiths.
221bl/r. Crucifixion and Good Friday flagellants, Paombong, Bulacan Province, Philippines: RH.
222–23. Illustrations: Inkwell, Bicester, Oxford.
224. Vatican Council II: Popperfoto.
225. Archbishop Ramsey and Pope Paul VI in Rome, 1966: Popperfoto.

BIBLIOGRAPHY

The Early Church

J. Beckwith, *Early Christian and Byzantine Art*. Harmondsworth 1970.
L. Bieler, *The Life and Legend of St Patrick*. Dublin 1949.
G. Bonner, *St Augustine of Hippo, Life and Controversies*. 2nd ed. Norwich 1986.
P. Brown, *Augustine of Hippo*. London 1967.
—— *The Cult of the Saints*. London 1981.
H. Chadwick, *The Early Church*. 2nd ed. Harmondsworth 1986.
—— *Early Christian Thought and the Classical Tradition*. Oxford 1966.
—— *Origen contra Celsum*. 3rd. ed. Cambridge 1980.
—— *Augustine*. Oxford 1986.
O. Chadwick, *John Cassian*. 2nd ed. Cambridge 1968.
D.J. Chitty, *The Desert a City*. Oxford 1966.
L. Duchesne, *The Early History of the Church*, 3 vols. London 1924 (French original 1907).
W.H.C. Frend, *The Donatist Church*. 2nd ed. Oxford 1985.
A. Grabar, *The Beginnings of Christian Art*, London 1967.
—— *Christian Iconography. A Study of its Origins*. London 1969.
R.M.Grant, *Augustine to Constantine*. London 1971.
—— *Eusebius as Historian*, Oxford 1980.
—— *Early Christianity and Society*. New York 1977.
A. Grillmeier, *Christ in Christian Tradition*. 2nd ed. London 1975.
L. Hertling and E. Kirschbaum, *The Roman Catacombs and their Martyrs*. London 1960 (German original, Vienna 1950).
E.D. Hunt, *Holy Land Pilgrimage in the Later Roman Empire*. Oxford 1982.
J.A. Jungmann, *The Early Liturgy to the Time of Gregory the Great*. London and Notre Dame, Ind. 1962.
J.N.D. Kelly, *Early Christian Creeds*. London 1972.
—— *Early Christian Doctrines*. 5th ed. London 1977.
——*Jerome*. London 1975.
R. Krautheimer, *Early Christian and Byzantine Architecture*. 3rd ed. Harmondsworth 1979.
R. Lane Fox, *Pagans and Christians*. London 1986.
H. Lietzmann, *The Beginnings of Christianity; The Founding of the Church Universal; From Constantine to Julian; The Era of the Church Fathers*. English tr. reissued London 1986 (German original 1932–42).
R.A. Markus, *Saeculum, History and Society in the Theology of St Augustine*. Cambridge 1970.
K.S. Painter, *The Water Newton Early Christian Silver*. London 1977.
J. Pelikan, *The Emergence of the Catholic Tradition*. Chicago, Ill. and London 1971.
P. Rousseau, *Authority and the Church in the Age of Jerome and Cassian*. Oxford 1978.
—— *Pachomius*. Berkeley, Ca. 1985.
K. Rudolph, *Gnosis*. London 1983.
M. Simon, *Verus Israel*. English tr. Oxford 1985 (French original 1948).
J.M.C. Toynbee and J. Ward-Perkins, *The Shrine of St Peter and the Vatican Excavations*. London 1957.
F. van der Meer, *Early Christian Art*. London 1967.
F. van der Meer and C. Mohrmann, *Atlas of the Early Christian World*. London 1972.
H. von Campenhausen, *The Origin of the Christian Bible*. London 1970.
—— *Ecclesiastical Power and Spiritual Authority*. London 1965.
—— *Fathers of the Greek Church*. London 1964.
—— *Fathers of the Latin Church*. London 1964.

The Church in the East

P. Brown, *The World of Late Antiquity*. London 1971.
R. Browning, *Justinian and Theodora*. 2nd ed. London 1987.
A. Bryer and J. Herrin (eds.), *Iconoclasm*. Birmingham 1977.
A. Cameron, *Continuity and Change in 6th-Century Byzantium*. London 1982.
R. Cormack, *Writing in Gold. Byzantine Society and its Icons*. London 1985.
J.V.A. Fine, *The Early Medieval Balkans*. Ann Arbor, Mich. 1983.
J. Galey, *Sinai and the Monastery of St Catherine*. Cairo 1985.
J.M. Hussey, *The Orthodox Church in the Byzantine Empire*. Oxford 1986.
D. Obolensky, *The Byzantine Commonwealth*. London 1974.
L. Rodley, *Cave Monasteries of Byzantine Cappadocia*. Cambridge 1985.
S. Runciman, *The Byzantine Theocracy*. Cambridge 1977.
P. Whitting (ed.), *Byzantium. An Introduction*. 2nd ed. London 1981.

The Church in the West

D. Ayerst and A.S.T. Fisher (eds.), *Records of Christianity*. Vol. 2. Oxford 1977.
T. Burns, *The Ostrogoths: Kingship and Society*. Wiesbaden 1980.
T. Hodgkin, *Italy and her Invaders 376–814*. Rept. New York 1967.
D. Knowles, *Christian Monasticism*. London 1969.
P Llewellyn, *Rome in the Dark Ages*. London 1971.
P. Riché, *Education and Culture in the Barbarian West*. Columbia, Ohio 1976.
R.W. Southern, *The Making of the Middle Ages*. London 1953.
—— *Western Society and the Church in the Middle Ages*. London 1970.
J. Pelikan, *The Christian Tradition*. Vol. 3. Chicago, Ill. 1978.
W. Ullmann, *The Growth of Papal Government in the Middle Ages*. London 1955.
J.M. Wallace-Hadrill, *The Barbarian West*. Rev. ed. New York 1962
G. Wickham, *Early Mediaeval Italy*. London 1981.

East and West Drift Apart

M. Angold, *The Byzantine Empire, 1025–1204*. London 1984.
C.M. Brand, *Byzantium Confronts the West, 1180–1204*. Cambridge, Mass. 1968.
G. Every, *The Byzantine Patriarchate, 451–1204*. 2nd ed. London 1962.
J. Godfrey, *1204: The Unholy Crusade*. Oxford 1980.
J. Meyendorff, *Orthodoxy and Catholicity*. New York 1965.
S. Runciman, *A History of the Crusades*. 3 vols. Cambridge 1951–54.
—— *The Eastern Schism*. Oxford 1955.
K.M. Setton (ed.), *A History of the Crusades*. Vol. 1. Madison, Wis. 1955.
P. Sherrard, *The Greek East and the Latin West*. Oxford 1959.

Schism and Union

G.P. Fedotov, *The Russian Religious Mind*. 2 vols. Cambridge, Mass. 1946–66.
—— *A Treasury of Russian Spirituality*. London 1950.
D.J. Geanokoplos, *Emperor Michael Palaeologus and the West: A Study in Byzantine–Latin Relations*. Cambridge, Mass. 1959.
J. Meyendorff, *A Study of Gregory Palamas*. London 1964.
—— *Byzantium and the Rise of Russia; A Study of Byzantine–Russian Relations in the Fourteenth Century*. Cambridge 1981.
—— *Byzantine Theology*. 2nd ed. London 1983.
D.M. Nicol, *Church and Society in the Last Centuries of Byzantium*. Cambridge 1979
—— *The End of the Byzantine Empire*. London 1979.
P. Sherrard, *Athos. The Mountain of Silence*. London 1960.
S. Runciman, *The Fall of Constantinople*. Cambridge 1965.
—— *Mistra: Byzantine Capital of the Peloponnese*. London 1980.
D. Talbot Rice, *Byzantine Art*. London 1968.
P.A. Underwood (ed.), *The Kariye Djami*. 4 vols. London 1967–75.
C. Walter, *Art and Ritual of the Byzantine Church*. London 1982.

Church and State

G. Barraclough, *The Mediaeval Papacy*. London 1968.
R.L. Benson and G. Constable, *Renaissance and Renewal in the Twelfth Century*. Cambridge, Mass. 1982.
M.D. Chenu, *Nature, Man and Society in the Twelfth Century*. Chicago, Ill. 1968.
S.C. Ferruolo, *The Origins of the University*. Stanford, Ca. 1985.
E. Kantorowicz, *The King's Two Bodies*. Princeton, N.J. 1957.
J. Leclercq, *The Love of Learning and the Desire for God*. Fordham 1974.
G. Leff, *The Dissolution of the Mediaeval Outlook*. New York 1976.
B. Smalley, *The Study of the Bible in the Middle Ages*. 3rd ed. Oxford 1983.
J. Sumption, *Pilgrimage*. London 1974.
(and see also Knowles, Southern and Ullmann, above)

The Late Middle Ages

R. Bainton, *Erasmus of Christendom*. New York 1969.
J. Bossy, *Christianity in the West 1400–1700*. Oxford 1985.
R. Finucane, *Miracles and Pilgrims*. London 1977.
D. Hay, *The Church in Italy in the Fifteenth Century*. Cambridge 1977.
J. Huizinga, *The Waning of the Middle Ages*. Harmondsworth 1955.
R. Kieckhefer, *European Witch Trials 1300–1500*. London 1976.
I. Origo, *The World of San Bernardino*. London 1963.
S. Ozment (ed.), *The Reformation in Medieval Perspective*. Chicago, Ill. 1971.
P. Partner, *Renaissance Rome*. Berkeley, Ca. 1976.
T.F. Tentler, *Sin and Confession on the Eve of the Reformation*. Princeton, N.J. 1977.
K. Thomas, *Religion and the Decline of Magic*. London 1971.
C. Trinkaus and H. Oberman (eds.), *The Pursuit of Holiness in Late Medieval and Renaissance Religion*. Leiden 1974.
D. Weinstein and R.M. Bell, *Saints and Society*. Chicago, Ill. 1982.

Reformation

R.M. Bainton, *Here I Stand. A Life of Martin Luther*. New York 1950.
O. Chadwick, *The Reformation*. London 1964.
A.G. Dickens, *Reformation and Society in 16th Century Europe*. London 1966.
—— *The German Nation and Martin Luther*. London 1974.
—— *The English Reformation*. London 1964.
H.J. Grimm, *The Reformation Era 1500–1650*. London 1973.
W. Monter, *Calvin's Geneva*. New York 1967.
S. Ozment, *The Reformation in the Cities*. New Haven, Conn. 1975.
T.H.L. Parker, *John Calvin*. London 1975.
G.R. Potter, *Zwingli*. Cambridge 1976.
E.G. Rupp, *Luther's Progress to the Diet of Worms*. London 1951.
——*Patterns of Reformation*. London 1969.
R. Scribner, *For the Sake of Simple Folk: Popular Propaganda for the German Reformation*. Cambridge 1981.
—— *The German Reformation*. London 1986.
G.H. Williams, *The Radical Reformation*. London 1962.

The Counter-Reformation

J. Brodrick, *The Origin of the Jesuits*. London 1940.
—— *The Progress of the Jesuits*. London 1946.
W. Christian, *Local Religion in Sixteenth Century Spain*. Princeton, N.J. 1981.
J. Delumeau, *Catholicism between Luther and Voltaire*. London 1977.
A.G. Dickens, *The Counter Reformation*. London 1968.
D. Evennett, *The Spirit of the Counter Reformation*. Cambridge 1968.
D. Fenlon, *Heresy and Obedience in Tridentine Italy*. Cambridge 1972.
F. Haskell, *Patrons and Painters*. New Haven, Conn. 1980.
H. Jedin, *Crisis and Closure of the Council of Trent*. London 1967.
M. Mullett, *The Counter Reformation*. London 1985.
A.D. Wright, *The Counter Reformation*. London 1982.

War, Settlement and Disunity

P. Benedict, *Rouen during the Wars of Religion.* Cambridge 1981.

W.J. Bouwsma, *Venice and the Defence of Republican Liberty: Renaissance Values in the Age of the Counter Reformation.* Berkeley, Ca. 1968.

P. Collinson, *The Religion of Protestants.* Oxford 1982.

P.M. Crew, *Calvinist Preaching and Iconoclasm in the Netherlands.* Cambridge 1978.

N.Z. Davis, *Society and Culture in Early Modern France.* London 1975.

R.J.W. Evans, *The Making of the Habsburg Monarchy.* Oxford 1979.

H. Kamen, *The Rise of Toleration.* London 1967.

W. Monter, *Ritual, Myth and Magic in Early Modern Europe.* Brighton 1983.

M. Prestwich, *International Calvinism.* Oxford 1986.

(and see also Delumeau and Wright, above)

To East and West

C. Boxer, *The Christian Century in Japan.* London 1951.

—— *The Portuguese Sea-Borne Empire.* London 1969.

—— *The Church Militant and Iberian Expansion.* Baltimore, Md. 1978.

V. Cronin, *The Wise Man from the West.* London 1955.

—— *A Pearl to India.* London 1959.

G.H. Dunne, *Generation of Giants, the Jesuits in China.* London 1969.

J.H. Elliott, *Imperial Spain.* London 1963.

J. Gernet, *China and the Christian Impact.* Cambridge 1984.

S. Neill, *A History of Christianity in India.* 2 vols. Cambridge 1984–85.

R. Ricard, *The Spiritual Conquest of Mexico.* Berkeley, Ca. 1966.

The Church in North America.

S.E. Ahlstrom, *A Religious History of the American People.* New Haven, Conn. 1972.

C.L. Albanese, *America: Religion and Religions.* Belmont, Ca. 1981.

J.W. Carroll *et al., Religion in America: 1950 to the Present.* San Francisco, Ca. 1979.

M. Douglas and S.M. Tipton, *Religion and America: Spirituality in a Secular Age.* Boston, Ma. 1983.

Gallup Report, *Religion in America, Fifty Years: 1935–85.* Princeton, N.J. 1985.

E.S. Gaustad, *Historical Atlas of Religion in America.* Rev. ed. New York 1976.

R.T. Handy, *A History of the Churches in the United States and Canada.* New York 1977.

W.S. Hudson, *Religion in America.* 3rd ed. New York 1981.

M.E. Marty, *Pilgrims in Their Own Land: 500 Years of Religion in America.* Boston, Ma. 1984.

J.G. Melton, *The Encyclopedia of American Religions.* Wilmington, N.C. 1978.

J.M. Mulder and J.F. Wilson (eds.), *Religion in American History: Interpretive Essays.* Englewood Cliffs, N.J. 1978.

M.A. Noll *et al.* (eds.), *Eerdsman's Handbook to Christianity in America.* Grand Rapids, Mich. 1983.

I.I. Zaretsky and M.P. Leone, *Religious Movements in Contemporary America.* Princeton, N.J. 1974.

The 18th-Century Church

W.J. Callahan and D. Higgs (eds.), *Church and Society in Catholic Europe of the Eighteenth Century.* Cambridge 1979.

O. Chadwick, *The Popes and the European Revolution.* Oxford 1981.

G. Cragg, *The Church and the Age of Reason 1648–1789.* The Pelican History of the Church. Vol. 4. Harmondsworth 1960.

A.D. Gilbert, *Religion and Society in Industrial England. Church, Chapel and Social Change, 1740–1914.* London 1976.

N. Hampson, *The Enlightenment.* The Pelican History of European Thought. Vol. 4. Harmondsworth 1968.

J. McManners, *French Ecclesiastical Society under the Ancien Regime.* Manchester 1960.

—— *Death and the Enlightenment. Changing Attitudes to Death in Eighteenth-Century France.* Oxford 1981.

K.S. Pinson, *Pietism as a Factor in the Rise of German Nationalism.* New York 1967.

R. Porter and M. Teich (eds.), *The Enlightenment in National Context.* Cambridge 1981.

N. Sykes, *Church and State in England in the 18th Century.* Cambridge 1934.

M.R. Watts, *The Dissenters.* Vol. 1. *From the Reformation to the French Revolution.* Oxford 1978.

The 19th-Century Church

O. Chadwick, *The Victorian Church,* 2 vols. Vol. 1. 3rd ed. London 1971. Vol. 2. 2nd ed. London 1972.

—— *The Secularization of the European Mind in the Nineteenth Century.* Cambridge 1975.

G. Faber, *Oxford Apostles. A Character Study of the Oxford Movement.* 2nd ed. London 1974.

E.E.Y. Hales, *Pio Nono. A Study in European Politics and Religion in the Nineteenth Century.* London 1954.

J.F.C. Harrison, *The Second Coming. Popular Millenarianism 1780–1850.* London 1979.

H. McLeod, *Religion and the People of Western Europe 1789–1970.* Oxford 1981.

—— *Religion and the Working Class in Nineteenth-Century Britain.* London 1984.

J. McManners, *Church and State in France 1870–1914.* London 1972.

E. Norman, *The English Catholic Church in the Nineteenth Century.* Oxford 1984.

A.R. Vidler, *The Church in an Age of Revolution.* The Pelican History of the Church. Vol. 5. Harmondsworth 1961.

—— *A Century of Social Catholicism 1820–1920.* London 1964.

The African Experience

J.F.A. Ajayi, *Christian Missions in Nigeria 1841–1891: The Making of a New Elite.* London 1965.

C.P. Groves, *The Planting of Christianity in Africa.* 4 vols. London 1948, 1954, 1955, 1958. Repr. 1964.

J. Guy, *The Heretic. A Study of the Life of John William Colenso 1814–1883.* Pietermaritzburg and Johannesburg 1983.

A. Hastings, *African Christianity: An Essay in Interpretation.* London 1976.

—— *A History of African Christianity 1950–1975.* Cambridge 1979.

M. Hope and J. Young, *The South African Churches in a Revolutionary Situation.* Maryknoll, N.Y. 1979.

T. Jeal, *Livingstone.* London 1973.

M.D. Markowitz, *Cross and Sword: The Political Role of Christian Missions in the Belgian Congo.* Stanford, Ca. 1973.

S. Neill, *A History of Christian Missions.* The Pelican History of the Church. Vol. 6. Rev. ed. Harmondsworth 1986.

R. Oliver, *The Missionary Factor in East Africa.* 2nd ed. London 1965.

A. Ross, *John Philip (1775–1851). Missions, Race and Politics in South Africa.* Aberdeen 1986.

F.B. Welbourn, *East African Rebels: A Study of some Independent Churches.* London 1961.

Missions to Asia

C. Caldorola, *Christianity: The Japanese Way.* Leiden 1979.

J. Ch'en, *China and the West. Society and Culture 1815–1937.* London 1979.

P.A. Cohen, "Christian Missions and their Impact to 1900," in J.K. Fairbank (ed.), *The Cambridge History of China.* Vol. 10. Cambridge 1978.

R.H. Drummond, *A History of Christianity in Japan.* Grand Rapids, Mich. 1971.

N. Gunson, *Messengers of Grace. Evangelical Missionaries in the South Seas 1797–1860.* Melbourne 1978.

K.S. Latourette, *A History of Christian Missions in China.* New York 1929.

—— *Christianity in a Revolutionary Age.* Vols. 3 and 5. London 1961, 1963.

W.P. Morrell, *The Anglican Church in New Zealand: A History.* Dunedin 1973.

S. Neill, *A History of Christianity in India 1707–1858.* Cambridge 1985.

P.J. O'Farrell, *The Catholic Church in Australia: A Short History 1788–1967.* Melbourne 1968.

D. Potts, *British Baptist Missionaries in India 1793–1837.* Cambridge 1967.

B. Sundkler, *Church of South India. The Movement towards Union 1900–1947.* Rev. ed. London 1965.

The Orthodox Churches

G. Dédéyan (ed.), *Histoire des Arméniens.* Toulouse 1982.

P. Evdokimov, *L'Orthodoxie.* Paris 1959.

D.M. Lang, *The Armenians: A People in Exile.* London 1981.

Mother Mary and Kallistos (= T.) Ware (trans.), *Liturgy and Ritual: The Festal Menaion.* London 1977.

O.F.A. Meinardus, *Christian Egypt: Faith and Life.* Cairo 1970.

—— *Christian Egypt: Ancient and Modern.* 2nd ed. Cairo 1977.

J. Meyendorff, *The Orthodox Church.* New York 1981.

L. Ouspensky and V. Lossky, *The Meaning of Icons.* Olten 1952.

M. Rinvolucri, *Anatomy of a Church. Greek Orthodoxy Today.* London 1966.

S. Runciman, *The Great Church in Captivity.* Cambridge 1968.

A. Salaville, *An Introduction to the Study of Eastern Liturgies.* London 1938.

N. Struve, *Christians in Contemporary Russia.* London 1967.

B.H. Sumner, *Survey of Russian History.* 2nd ed. London 1947.

T. Ware, *The Orthodox Church.* London 1963.

—— *Eustratios Argenti: A Study of the Greek Church under Turkish Rule.* Oxford 1964.

—— *The Orthodox Way.* London 1981.

Christianity and the Other World Religions

S.G.F. Brandon (ed.), *A Dictionary of Comparative Religion.* London 1970.

M. Eliade, *Patterns in Comparative Religion.* London 1958.

H.H. Farmer, *Revelation and Religion.* London 1954.

J. Finegan, *The Archaeology of World Religions.* Princeton, N.J. 1952.

J. Hastings (ed.), *Encyclopaedia of Religion and Ethics.* 13 vols. Edinburgh 1908–26.

E.O. James, *Christianity and Other Religions.* London 1968.

S.C. Neill, *Christian Faith and Other Faiths.* London 1961.

G. Parrinder, *Comparative Religion.* London 1962.

R.C. Zaehner, *At Sundry Times.* London 1958.

—— *Concordant Discord.* Oxford 1970.

Christianity, Communism and National Identity

S. Alexander, *Church and State in Yugoslavia since 1945.* Cambridge 1979.

T. Beeson, *Discretion and Valour, Religious Conditions in Russia and Eastern Europe.* Rev. ed. London 1982.

B.R. Bociurkiw and J.W. Strong (eds.), *Religion and Atheism in the USSR and Eastern Europe.* London 1975.

M. Bourdeaux, *Faith on Trial in Russia.* London and New York 1971.

—— *Land of Crosses (Lithuania).* Keston 1979.

—— *Be Our Voice.* Keston 1984.

R. Boyes and J. Moody, *The Priest who had to Die. The Tragedy of Father Jerzy Popieluszko.* London 1986.

I. Ratushinskaya, *No I'm not Afraid.* Newcastle-upon-Tyne 1986.

M. Scammell, *Solzhenitsyn.* London 1984.

Cardinal S. Wyszynski, *A Freedom Within.* London 1985.

See also the journals *Religion in Communist-Dominated Areas* and *Religion in Communist Lands.*

Christianity and Secular Modernity

P. Berger, *The Heretical Imperative.* New York 1979.

J. Billiet and K. Dobbelaere, *Godsdienst in Vlaanderen.* Leuven 1976.

K. Dobbelaere. "Secularization: A Multi-Dimensional Concept" in *Current Sociology.* Vol. 29. No. 2. Summer 1981.

M. Douglas and S. Tipton (eds.), *Religion and America.* Boston, Ma. 1983.

J. Hunter, *American Evangelicalism*. New Brunswick, N.J. 1983.
C. Lane, *Christian Religion in the Soviet Union*. London 1978.
H. McLeod, *Religion and the People of Western Europe 1789–1970*. Oxford 1981.
—— "Protestantism and the Working Class in Imperial Germany" in *European Studies Review*. Vol. 12. 1982.
W. McSweeney, *Roman Catholicism*. Oxford 1980.
G. Marsden, *Fundamentalism and American Culture*. New York 1980.
D. Martin, *A General Theory of Secularization*. Oxford 1978.
J. Whyte, *Catholics in Western Democracies: A Study of Political Behaviour*. Dublin 1981.
B. Wilson, *Magic and the Millennium*. London 1973.
—— *Religion in Sociological Perspective*. Oxford 1982.
W. Zdancewicz, *Religion and Social Life*. Poznan-Warsaw 1983.

The Ecumenical Movement
Y.M.J. Congar, *Chrétiens désunis*. Paris 1937. (= *Divided Christendom*. London 1939.)
—— *Je crois en l'Esprit Saint*. Paris 1979–80. (Eng. tr. London 1983.)
—— *Essais oecumeniques*. Paris 1984.
U. Duchrow, *Konflikt um die Oekumene*. Munich 1980. (= *Conflict over the Ecumenical Movement*. Geneva 1981.)
A. Dulles, *The Catholicity of the Church*. Oxford 1985.
N. Goodall, *The Ecumenical Movement*. 2nd ed. Oxford 1964.
B. Leeming, *The Church and the Churches. A Study of Ecumenism*. 2nd ed. London 1963.
H. Meyer and L. Vischer, *Growth in Agreement*. New York and Geneva 1984.
J. Ratzinger, *Theologische Prinzipienlehre*. Munich 1982.
R. Rouse and S.C. Neill, *A History of the Ecumenical Movement*. 2 vols. London 1954, 1970.
W.G. Rusch, *Ecumenism, a Movement towards Church Unity*. Philadelphia, Pa. 1985.
B.G.M. Sundkler, *Church of South India*. London 1965.
J.D. Zizioulas, *Being as Communion*. New York 1985.
Annual surveys in the journals *Istina, Irenikon, Ecumenical Review, One in Christ, Midstream*.

GAZETTEER

An entry followed by an asterisk indicates a small territorial unit (e.g. a county, duchy, province, subkingdom or region).

INDEX

Page numbers in italics refer to illustrations or their captions. Saints are listed under their Christian names, followed by epithets or family names.